THE LAND WAS OURS

THE
LAND
—— WAS ——
OURS

How Black Beaches Became
White Wealth in the Coastal South

ANDREW W. KAHRL

THE UNIVERSITY OF NORTH CAROLINA PRESS
Chapel Hill

The University of North Carolina Press has been a member
of the Green Press Initiative since 2003.

Cover illustration: Jennie Brown and Vinnie Drake lounging on
Bay Shore Beach, outside Hampton, Virginia. (Rare Book, Manuscript, and
Special Collections Library, Duke University)

ISBN 978-1-4696-2872-1 (pbk.:)
ISBN 978-1-4696-2873-8 (ebook)
Library of Congress has cataloged the original edition of this book as follows:
Kahrl, Andrew W., 1978–
The land was ours: African American beaches from Jim Crow to the Sunbelt South /
Andrew W. Kahrl.
p. cm.
Includes bibliographical references and index.
ISBN 978-0-674-05047-1
1. African Americans—Land tenure—Southern States—History. 2. Land tenure—
Social Aspects—Southern States—History. 3. Coasts—Southern States—History.
4. Coasts—Social Aspects—Southern States. 5. Coasts—Economic
Aspects—Southern States. 6. Real estate development—Southern States—History.
7. Real estate development—Social Aspects—Southern States. I. Title.
E185.8.K215 2012
333.3089'96073075—dc23   2011029761

For Aileen

CONTENTS

Introduction: "Bring Back My Yesterday"   1

1 Corporate Ventures   20

2 A Sanctuary by the Sea   52

3 Building Black Privatopias   86

4 Surviving the Summer   115

5 Family Ties   155

6 Spinning Sand into Gold   178

7 The Price We Pay for Progress   210

Epilogue   250

Notes   261
Primary Sources   325
Acknowledgments   329
Index   333

A section of photographs follows page 154

MAPS

1. Atlantic seaboard   5

2. Gulf of Mexico   6

3. Potomac River basin, ca. 1900   35

4. Gulfside Assembly and surroundings, ca. 1923   55

5. Land acquired by Gulfside Association, 1923   63

6. Highland Beach and surrounding communities   98

7. New Orleans before and after the Lakefront Reclamation Project   120

8. The Potomac River waterfront in Washington, D.C., 1920s   124

9. African American neighborhoods of New Orleans in relation to canals and beaches   142

10. Norfolk, Virginia, 1920s   144

11. Coastline of New Hanover County, North Carolina   160

12. Annapolis Neck Peninsula, Anne Arundel County, Maryland, ca. 1945   184

13. Bay Shore Beach, Hampton, Virginia   194

14. Annapolis Neck Peninsula, Anne Arundel County, Maryland, ca. 2010   236

And so, walking the beach, we become aware of a most fascinating problem—the colonization of the shore, and especially of those "islands" of rock (or the semblance of rock) that occur in the midst of a sea of sand. For whenever a seawall is built, or a jetty, or pilings are sunk for a pier of a bridge, or rock, long hidden from sun and buried even beneath the sea, emerges again on the ocean floor, these hard surfaces immediately become peopled with typical animals of the rocks. But how did the colonizing rock fauna happen to be at hand—here in the midst of a sandy coast that stretches for hundreds of miles to north and south?

Pondering the answer, we become aware of that ceaseless migration, for the most part doomed to futility, yet ensuring that always, when opportunity arises, Life shall be waiting, ready to take advantage.

RACHEL CARSON, *The Edge of the Sea* (1955)

THE LAND WAS OURS

INTRODUCTION:
"BRING BACK MY YESTERDAY"

On Sunday June 28, 2009, they came back for one last dance on the beach. Except now it was the parking lot of Sam's on the Waterfront. Some might have looked in vain for the cavernous, open-air pavilion where James Brown, Lloyd Price, Dinah Washington, Etta James, and others performed before sweat-drenched crowds. Instead they found tennis courts, boat slips, and clusters of luxurious, air-conditioned, waterfront condominiums. For the persons who passed the security gate leading to the Villages of Chesapeake Harbour that afternoon for the First Annual Carr's Beach Historic Music Festival, there was little visual evidence to remind them of the past they had come to commemorate. Only a country road recently rededicated as "Carr's Beach Road" bore testament to an earlier stage of coastal capitalism on the Annapolis Neck Peninsula.[1]

But came they did, to, as George Phelps put it, "bring back my yesterday." On this day, the persons old enough to remember Carr's Beach shared their memories with the enthusiastic, mostly white residents of the private, gated community that emerged following the beach's demise in the early 1970s. As they danced in the parking lot, they evoked a bygone era when, as a homeowner's blog read, "people would pack into the pavilion to listen and dance to the music of Major R&B stars of the day, who's [sic] voices and music could be heard throughout the area for miles."[2]

By the first decade of the twenty-first century, this and similar attempts to commemorate the world African Americans made under segregation proliferated and became woven into public history narratives, public policy debates over the persistence of racial inequality, and real estate redevelopment strategies both in the city and along once-rural, now-exurban shorelines. And they came to hold a mirror on an America striving to become postracial and color-blind. Magnified is the heroism and creativity that emerged from black spaces and institutions on the "colored" side of

1

the "color line"; obscured are the larger forces that made—and ultimately unmade—both the color line and places behind it. Here on this summer afternoon in Anne Arundel County, Maryland, few seemed to note (or want to note) the irony of a corporately owned condominium developer paying tribute to a black cultural institution whose demise proved so essential to their own rise, and to a place that, while it still lived, proved more a nuisance to neighbors and an obstacle to waterfront real estate developers. Back when those voices could be heard for miles, they were more likely to inspire a call to the county sheriff's office reporting loud noise and suspicious activity rather than a written tribute. The property's history of black ownership was more likely to be mentioned by those seeking to direct development elsewhere than touted by real estate agents as a marketable "piece" of history. Back then, one African American Chesapeake property owner remembered, "if you had flown over the Chesapeake and pointed down [there], whites would have said, 'that's nigger land.'"[3] Back then, the sandy shores of Annapolis Neck Peninsula suffered from what real estate insiders euphemistically referred to as a "stigma." Today, that stigma has become a selling point. "The Villages of Chesapeake Harbour," a local real estate agency website reads, "have a unique identity not found anywhere else in the Annapolis area. . . . In addition to Carr's Beach, Sparrows Beach and Bembe Beach are adjacent to the property. All were popular in their day."[4] And all were, at one time, part of the approximately 246 acres owned by African Americans on the peninsula; today, only 6 of those acres remain in blacks' possession.

Though he came to the Carr's Beach Music Festival, and accepted an award for his lifetime of community service, George Phelps seemed in no mood to celebrate. "That was a very important piece of land [and] African Americans owned just about all of it," he later told me. Indeed, properties on the peninsula are some of the most expensive in the mid-Atlantic region, with homes routinely sold at the height of the housing bubble between 2003 and 2006 for over $1 million.[5] "[But] the children s[old] the damn land for nothing, and now they're bawling that they ain't got this and they ain't got that and the other. They *had* the land. . . . Goddamn, they gave it away. . . . I don't know, I get so frustrated."[6]

Most conversations with African Americans old enough to remember this and other separate black beaches and resorts that once dotted the shores of the Chesapeake and the Atlantic and Gulf coasts similarly veer from nostalgia to frustration, from before to after "integration." "It was just like being in heaven," Juanita Doris Franklin said of the black Methodist resort, Gulfside Assembly, on the Mississippi Gulf Coast. "When you got on Gulfside's grounds, your whole everything changed. . . . If you went down and stayed a week, it was just like medicine. . . . It was truly a spiritually uplifting place." Asked to describe the resort's three-decade-plus struggle to survive in the face of dwindling finances, malignant neglect from public officials bent on coastal redevelopment, and, finally, the destructive winds of Hurricane Katrina, Franklin added: "It hurts me to my heart to even think about going down there."[7] On those dwindling finances, fellow Gulf Coast resident Pat Harvey explained, "[After integration] we got caught up in the magic of 'we can go to the beach down here,' and we've been going to this same beach all our lives."[8]

Others shared similar stories. "When I moved to [the African American summer community] Arundel-on-the-Bay in 1971," John Moses remembered, "the houses were very, very inexpensive . . . because white people wouldn't live here because black people lived here and black people wouldn't live here because black people lived here." "After integration," Ray Langston said of the neighboring African American summer village, Highland Beach, "this was the last place in the world [young African Americans] wanted to go. They'd been coming here since they were children. . . . It was very dead, very few people here on the weekends. And then sometime shortly after that came an awakening period where people came to realize what they had and how valuable this property is and . . . that, of course, was around the same time white people wanted to buy back waterfront property."[9] "Now [that] all those rich folks bought up all that property over there and built those million dollar homes" on the land where the former black-owned Bay Shore Beach in Hampton, Virginia, once stood, Bill Carson commented, "you would never know it was here, [that] they used to have dance halls, bars, a hotel, everything. . . . This place has changed since then, I'll tell you. This place has changed."[10]

Indeed, it has. Fifty years ago, a wooden groin topped with a metal fence extended into the waters off Hampton's shore, dividing "white" from "colored" sand and water and, perhaps fittingly, accelerating rates of erosion on both sides. Fifty years ago, the presence of a black man or woman on or near white sands in anything but a waiter's jacket or pushing a white baby's stroller would have, at the least, elicited hostile stares, and more likely, catcalls, threats of violence, and summoning of local authorities. Today, those visible signs of American apartheid are a thing of the past. In their place you will often find vacation resorts facing well-groomed sand beaches forcibly stabilized by beach nourishment projects aimed at halting natural and human-caused processes of erosion and beach movement. Along beaches where signs that read "No niggers or dogs allowed" once stood, you will instead find "no trespassing" signs erected by private homeowners and beach associations, or, as often, you will find the beach no longer there, washed away by the effects of decades of coastal real estate development and the endless, and hopeless, struggle to fortify and preserve coastal property. Also washed away in Americans' rush to the sea are the mom-and-pop restaurants, do-drop inns, nightclubs, and seaside amusement parks that sustained black social life, nourished cultural traditions, and gave rise to forms of black business activity and struggles for economic empowerment throughout much of the twentieth century.

How did we go from a time when it was unremarkable for African Americans to own comparatively large amounts of property in coastal and waterfront areas but unthinkable for them to be seen among whites on public beaches except in a service capacity, to a time when racial but not class diversity at commercial resorts and beachfront communities is increasingly common and unremarkable, while black coastal landowners have become, as one African American native of the South Carolina Sea Islands described in 1982, an "endangered species"?[11] How did we go from a time when living by the beach meant living day to day, far from the main channels of commerce and power, to a time when sand itself is a valuable commodity, and living by the sand the pinnacle of success? How did we go from rural and sparsely populated to segregated shores, and from segregated to gated, overdeveloped shores? And how is the disintegration of black landholdings and small business ownership tied to the pursuit of reckless and unsustainable environmental policies?

Through a series of thematic case studies set along the coasts of the Atlantic and the Gulf of Mexico and their related estuaries (see Maps 1 and 2), this book excavates the histories of African American beaches and traces the evolution of what I label "coastal capitalism"—characterized by the commodification of the beach as a commercial asset, exploitation of natural resources and environmental engineering of coastal zones and bodies of water for aesthetic and recreational purposes, and the transfer of public lands to private entities.[12] In this story, the shore itself—that liminal, mercurial, and volatile space dividing land from water, where the boundaries separating public resources from private property become indistinct

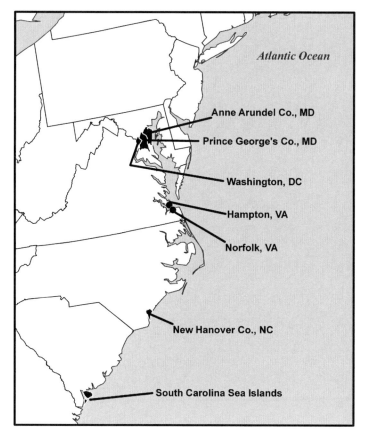

Map 1. Atlantic seaboard

and highly contested, and where the limits and consequences of humans' historic quest to tame unruly environments are laid bare—earns its rightful place as a dynamic historic actor in its own right. The shores that persons of color owned and frequented during the first half of the twentieth century highlight the pivotal role of landownership and development strategies in shaping and giving spatial definition to African Americans' performance of class, pursuit of pleasure, and struggle for economic empowerment. Conversely, the shores that African Americans steadily lost over the course of the second half of the twentieth century (and continue to lose at alarming rates today) demonstrate the inextricability of environmental and human exploitation—power over lands and power over persons—and force us to reassess the familiar story of America's triumph over

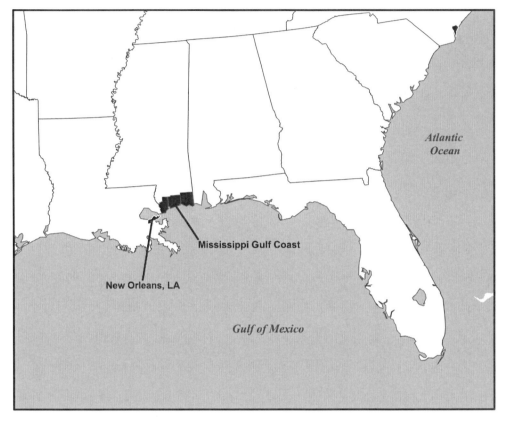

Map 2. Gulf of Mexico

segregration, its achievement of civil rights, and its slow, painful, but nevertheless inexorable progress toward a more just and equitable future.

The history of African American coastal landownership begins in the decades following emancipation. By the time General William Tecumseh Sherman completed his march to the sea in 1864 and his victorious campaign northward in early 1865, the South's Atlantic coastal region, once home to some of the largest and most profitable plantations in North America and richest cash crops on the global market, lay in ruins. Sherman administered the coup de grâce, but the region's economic ruin was also a casualty of, to various degrees, unsustainable farming techniques, unmanageable labor regimes, and the inherent environmental limitations and vulnerabilities that, quite literally, came with the territory.[13]

In the decades following the war, coastal regions that once constituted the heart of slave power in the United States witnessed a profound transformation. As railroad lines linked farms to factories, and the agricultural Black Belt to the industrial cities of the North and the textile mills of the Piedmont, the region's political and economic power shifted to the interior. Coastal lands that once generated considerable wealth for the South's slavocracy and sold for upwards of $5,000 per acre before the war could, by the 1870s, be fetched for $50 an acre or less. Other stretches of southern coastlines remained, as they were before war and emancipation, forsaken and forgotten—the land of mosquitoes, predatory animals, dense forests, and sandy, nonarable soil. As a result, coastal zones became ripe for black landownership during an era when, as the historian Manning Marable notes, "the development of a strong black land base became an ideological imperative of black thought."[14] For many freedmen and women, living by the sea promised an opportunity to realize propertied independence and a deliverance from the coercive labor arrangements that emerged in the wake of slavery's demise. By 1910, African Americans owned over 15 million acres in the South, with coastal counties exhibiting some of the highest rates of black landownership.[15]

It was here where a different South took shape during an era that historians and the public alike referred to by way of the racist minstrel character Jim Crow. To venture into many of the small towns and villages situated on barrier islands or peninsulas was to venture outside of what was—and remains—the archetypal "Jim Crow South" and into places characterized by high rates of religious and ethnic diversity, social practices and cultural sensibilities that shocked, horrified, and piqued the curiosity of visitors, and more fluid relations of power. Recounting a visit to Plymouth, North Carolina, a remote river town near the Albemarle Sound, in 1921, Bruce Cotten, a tobacco planter's son, speculated that the inhabitants had "partaken too heavily of the Lotus Plant[s]" that lined the waterways leading into town. "A motley crowd of whites and blacks [crowded] the sidewalks and . . . streets . . . [giving] the impression of an Oriental Market Place. . . . There was plentiful signs of bootleg whiskey, as well as intimacies between black girls and white boys, which were openly going on and jested about. . . . My first impulse was to inquire my way to the American Con-

sulate."[16] The black landowning families who carved out remote com-
pounds along shorelines proved no less curious to African American outsiders. Black Carolinian Evelyn Williams described the striking contrast
between the black families who lived in the town of Wilmington, North
Carolina—and who labored in whites' homes, worked as schoolteachers
and in other professions, and preached habits of frugality, sobriety, and
respectability—and her ancestors, the extended Freeman family, who shared
in common several hundred acres of land along the Atlantic coast and Myrtle Grove Sound and were "notorious for their clannishness, hard drinking,
and economic independence derived from fishing, farming, and operating
illegal moonshine stills . . . [and who] reciprocat[ed] the disdain in which
they were held by Blacks in the city."[17] Like the land itself, the people who
lived by the sea lived in what the marine geologist Orrin H. Pilkey describes
as a state of "dynamic equilibrium" resistant to legal definition and political
categorization.[18]

As blacks came to the coast seeking refuge from the South's unique brand
of "racial capitalism," a broader economic and cultural revolution began to
transform the political economy and ecology of the coastal South.[19]
Throughout the second half of the nineteenth century, small pockets
along the Atlantic and Gulf coasts emerged as summer playgrounds and
winter havens for the nation's monied elite. Following completion of a
railroad line connecting the port city of New Orleans to the bucolic, undeveloped shores of neighboring Mississippi in 1869, a steady stream of
planters and merchants fled from the humid city, frequently host to yellow fever epidemics during the summer months, to newly built second
homes by the sea. Offshore, large yachts owned by deep-pocketed pleasure seekers floated past flatboats and skiffs manned by black, Italian, and
Eastern European fishermen. Places of labor became places of pleasure.
On the Georgia coast, the collapse of long-staple cotton and the rise of
black subsistence fishing and farming were soon followed by the development of exclusive winter resorts owned by prominent families of the nation's Gilded Age aristocracy, where, as one writer later described, "Rice
fields became duck ponds for hunters [and] field hands became guides
and caretakers."[20]

By the 1920s, this trickle of pleasure seekers and second-home owners
already showed signs of becoming a flood. The emergence of the field of
coastal engineering, the mass production of the automobile, investment in
roads and infrastructure development on the state and federal level, and the

rise of a white-collar workforce with weekends off, paid vacations, and disposable incomes led to an infusion of capital investment in coastal real estate and the rise of leisure-based economies, fed the notion that coastlines could be stabilized and made habitable on a mass scale, and increasingly made protection of coastal property a matter of state and federal concern.[21]

As witnessed most spectacularly in South Florida (and repeated elsewhere on a smaller scale), a speculative fever descended onto America's shores in the 1920s, and a culture of coastal capitalism took shape and spread. There were fortunes to be made from these unproductive sands and volatile shores, and it required little effort—just lots of guile. America's coasts gave birth to some of the most outrageously corrupt and fraudulent investment schemes imaginable, and witnessed some of the most epic collapses.[22] Privatization of formerly common-use lands accelerated, as did the conversion of environmental "amenities" into capital. As early as 1918, rural sociologist Charles J. Galpin observed, "The rural picnic spot has been turned into a commercial amusement park; the sylvan retreat into the private estate; the swimming place on the lake into the bathing beach; the fishing grounds into the private game reserve; the quiet lake with its rowing parties into the center for the private launch parties or public regattas. It is either 'no trespass here' or 'pay as you enter' there."[23] In early 1920s South Florida, John Kenneth Galbraith commented, "an inordinate desire to get rich quickly with a minimum of physical effort"[24] drew in trainloads of speculators and led to a remarkable period of environmentally reckless development and unfathomable appreciation of waterfront real estate—followed by a storm that temporarily washed those dreams of quick and easy profits out to sea. Surveying the wreckage of a busted speculative real estate market in South Florida in 1928, Henry S. Villard reported, "Dead subdivisions line the highway, their pompous names half obliterated on crumbling stucco gates. . . . Gaping structures, tragically uncompleted, are mute reminders of ambitious schemes for apartments, casinos, [and] country clubs. . . . All the extravaganza of picture cities, all the fantastic hokum of lot-selling and lot-buying, all the hypnotism of get-rich-quick—which used to transform the most unsuspecting tourist into a frenzied financier—has vanished like a soap-bubble."[25]

Reports of coastal capitalism's demise were, to say the least, greatly exaggerated. Nature's devastating assaults on coastal zones and burgeoning vacationlands did not hasten a flight of capital, but instead brought it under the protection and subsidization of the state. In 1926 the American

Shore and Beach Preservation Association, a group dedicated to further-
ing state and federal governmental involvement in the "economical development and preservation" of beachfront property, was formed. Its efforts
to draw legislators' attention to the growing importance of these coastal
natural resources in a more mobile, consumer-driven economy quickly
became apparent with the passage, in 1930, of the Rivers and Harbors Act,
which led to the creation of the Beach Erosion Board (BEB) within the
Army Corps of Engineers. Prior to the formation of the BEB, the Army
Corps of Engineers' involvement in the fortification of coastal zones had
remained strictly limited to federally owned lands and in the interests of
national security. Beginning in the 1930s and accelerating in the decades
following World War II, the Corps' interests in shoreline protection veered
from protection from invasion to protection of coastal leisure economies
and real estate markets. In 1936, Congress passed the Act for the Protection
and Improvement of Beaches along the Shores of the United States, which
(albeit vaguely) made the protection of all shorelines against erosion a
federal responsibility and elevated the role of the BEB from that of adviser
to administrator. That same year, Congress also passed the Flood Control
Act of 1936, which established protection of property from flooding as a
federal responsibility and led local administrators of New Deal agencies in burgeoning coastal zones to use the threat of coastal erosion to
justify embarking on massive, and often ecologically disastrous, measures
of fortification.[26]

Along with making beaches seemingly more stable, New Deal–era programs helped to make the beach more desirable to an increasingly mobile
American public through funding of research and development of pest
control chemicals and local efforts at mosquito control. In burgeoning
"vacationlands" federal grants and work programs allowed cities to construct ditch drainage systems and establish mosquito control districts.[27] At
the tiny resort town of Virginia Beach, Virginia, workers in Civilian Conservation Corps camps, and later, German prisoners of war, drained wetlands that bred mosquitoes (and sustained marine life and migratory populations) as part of a broader effort to stimulate the region's severely depressed
economy by enhancing its recreational appeal.[28]

The rise of coastal capitalism played a vital role in the broader transformation of the South from what President Franklin D. Roosevelt labeled in
1938 "the Nation's number one economic problem" into the nation's fastest-
growing region by the turn of the twenty-first century. On the beach, the

ethos of growth liberalism that grew out of the New Deal and came to characterize post–World War II federal economic policies succeeded beyond its wildest imagination. By 1954 the National Park Service called the "spectacular acceleration" of "private and commercial development" of seashores "nothing short of a business phenomenon." In 1936 a thirty-mile stretch of undeveloped seashore recommended (unsuccessfully) for designation as a national seashore was worth roughly $9,000 a mile; two decades later, the nine remaining undeveloped miles of that shore could be fetched for no less than $110,000 a mile, a 1,100 percent appreciation in value.[29]

As southern shores steadily moved from the periphery to the center of the region's economy from the 1930s to the 1950s, the difference that race made on the beach, in planning and zoning board meetings, and at real estate offices, changed. On the shores of Biloxi, Mississippi, for instance, racial segregation remained indistinct and negotiable prior to the completion of a massive flood control and coastal property stabilization project in the early 1950s. As black Biloxian Lee Owens described:

> And we'd go out there and take our baths in there. Women used to go out there and take baths out there with towels on them and everything else. And later in the evening, that beach would be full. . . . Anybody could go down there and sit on the beach all night long, because I used to sit down on that beach, water used to slap all over my feet down there. Fish down there. White and black used to sit down there together.

But after the Army Corps of Engineers dumped over 7 million cubic yards of sand on the coast, giving Mississippians "the longest manmade beach in the world," "those white folks went stone crazy. 'That's our beach. This ain't no nigger beach.' . . . We got along good, until that beach come in down there."[30] On miserably hot summer days in the years that followed, Gulf Coast resident Eva Gates remembers, black children "wanted to go on that beach so bad and get in that water, but we knew if we went on the beach, white people didn't care whether or not you were a child or not, they would kill you, beat you, or do anything that came to their mind."[31]

Instead, many took their chances in dangerous, polluted waters. In Charleston, South Carolina, black children often resorted to swimming in "Horse Hole," a ditch filled with water from street runoff. Mamie Garvin Fields recalled that, when she was a child, her parents warned her to stay away from the place. But, as she put it, the law said no, you children mustn't swim in the Cooper River, and no, you mustn't swim in the Ashley River or in Colonial Lake. If you do, the cop will arrest you, and you never know where the cop will carry you off to. But the summertime gets very hot, and very humid, so the bolder ones would disobey their parents and cool off in one of the rivers, or they would go on into the dirty water of the Horse Hole.

And, nearly every summer, Fields recalled, several children drowned there. Public officials ignored black parents' pleas to cover "Horse Hole," and instead blamed them for allowing their children to "run wild." And Fields, just like her parents a generation earlier, was forced to instruct her children to also avoid Horse Hole.[32]

It was no coincidence that the policing of blacks' physical mobility during the summer months became a matter of constant vigilance as states and municipalities devoted greater attention and resources to enhancing the aesthetic value of urban shorelines, and as Americans' growing thirst for the beach promised to breathe life into stagnant coastal economies. Though less examined than federal intervention into the housing market, federal, state, and local public recreational works and coastal engineering projects proved no less influential in shaping the spatiality and political economy of race in twentieth-century America. Because of the potential profits to be wrested from these fragile and migratory shores, combined with glaring liabilities (among others, a legal status as public versus private property that quite literally changed with the tides and the whims of judicial interpretation),[33] public and private agents of coastal capitalism engaged in some of the most determined efforts to inscribe clear racial categories onto the land, employed some of the most innovative, cynical, and revealing uses of race as a tool of profit and market control, and, not unrelated, embarked on some of the most daring, innovative, and often reckless feats of civil engineering ever witnessed. As cities engineered sections of shorelines for public recreation and real estate development, black populations were not merely excluded from the benefits that accompanied efforts to engineer coasts and waterfronts in the interests of recreation, commerce, and real estate, but invariably bore the brunt of its hazards.[34]

Long before it was labeled as such, urban and rural black working poor experienced a seasonal form of environmental injustice, as rates of death and disease soared with rising temperatures, punctuated by the familiar screams of a mother forced to watch her child's lifeless body pulled from a dangerous and polluted stream or a rock pit filled with runoff. Blacks mobilized against these more pernicious forms of environmental racism by writing to or speaking before local public officials who refused to clean or cover over the dangerous waters that lurked on the edges of black residential districts, or worse yet, designated them as "colored" bathing beaches. And blacks worked to overcome the deadly and humiliating dangers of summer through utilizing the means (and the land) at their disposal. Well aware that an afternoon of rest and play provided a tonic for the toxic environments that enveloped their daily lives, groups and individuals worked to force unresponsive public officials to provide black citizens safe, accessible, and equitable beaches and outdoor leisure spaces of their own. They then worked to turn the grossly inferior public beaches set aside for "colored" persons into vibrant community gathering places.

The same decades that witnessed the rise of coastal development and simultaneous descent of Jim Crow onto previously remote and undeveloped shores also witnessed the rise of independent and collaborative efforts to create and maintain separate black social spaces—and give spatial definition to a black public sphere—through coastal land acquisition and private development. Seeking to alleviate (and capitalize on) what W. E. B. Du Bois called "the color problem of summer,"[35] white and black investment groups and individuals sought, throughout the first half of the twentieth century, to acquire and turn existing waterfront properties into social institutions and entrepreneurial ventures for African Americans. Small, exclusive cliques of "cultured" and educated blacks collaborated to acquire beachfront property for the building of summer cottage communities. Existing black beachfront landowners, once on the margins, moved to the center of an emergent black leisure industry. A few "passed" as white to purchase property and circumvent the sand curtains that wealthy coastal landowners erected following the "discovery" of an enviable stretch of shore. Many converted their family properties into beachfront resorts and summer getaways that catered to and sought to profit from an increasingly mobile black middle class.[36] Other white and black capitalists worked (sometimes in competition, other times in collaboration) to acquire waterfront property and build wealth from the pennies of working blacks in search of moments of pleasure and relief. Others embarked on spiritual missions to uplift and transform "the race" through acquiring and developing coastal property.

Along African American–owned beaches and rural getaways, young and old came in search of what sociologists St. Clair Drake and Horace R. Cayton, writing on Bronzeville in Chicago, called "rest from white folks as well as from labor."[37] While hard to quantify, it is not difficult to discern the significance of these places of retreat in the lives of the persons who came there. As the bus carrying impoverished black children from the darkest corners of rural Mississippi to the Gulf of Mexico rounded the bend and passengers caught their first glimpse of the Gulf, mother and Gulf-side volunteer Juanita Doris Franklin recalled, children leapt from their seats, tugging on fellow passengers' shirts and shouting, " 'Ohhhh, ohhhh, look at that water!' . . . They could not believe [what they saw]." When kids came to Gulfside for the first time, Pat Harvey added, "they were in a sheer panic. They had never seen the vastness [before]."[38]

As these places grew in popularity and notoriety, so too did the numbers of monetary and cultural transactions. The search for rest from labor and rest from white people became, in turn, a form of work and an increasingly significant component of black urban and rural economies. During the summer, a truck owner became a shuttle driver, a mother and wife became a caterer or restaurateur; vice peddlers found a customer base and place to launder their earnings, and aspiring musicians and promoters acquired a venue from which to grow entertainment industries. Much like the leisure- and entertainment-oriented mass-consumer marketplaces of the black metropolis, for a few months each summer black beaches nourished cultural practices and cultural industries whose impact on black social, economic, and intellectual life resonated long after the crowds dispersed and the waters chilled.

The types of African American beaches that dotted the shores of rivers, lakes, and oceans reflected and gave expression to the diversity of black America and to the evolving spatial structure of Jim Crow. Some black beaches were places for high-toned, exclusive retreats where entry was restricted to a chosen few. Others were religious campgrounds where spiritual uplift took precedence over "careless" amusements. Bawdy, raucous beaches were where the sound of jazz and R&B drifted out onto the waters, where flasks of moonshine passed from coat pockets to hands, and where pairs of dice bounced off hard surfaces. As African Americans stepped up demands for access to whites-only public beaches or, at the very least, decent and equitable public places of outdoor leisure, public officials, working in concert with private developers and white landowners, designated remote, polluted, dangerous, and wholly inferior stretches of shore as suitable for "colored" people. So, in this respect, the places where African Americans were allowed to picnic, bathe, and fish along urban shorelines also served as mechanisms of social and environmental inequality that, in addition to endangering their lives, became another in a litany of "self-perpetuating stigma[s]" that served to justify blacks' second-class citizenship and that wove notions of race into the land itself.[39]

W. E. B. Du Bois captured the primacy of race as a legal category when, in 1940, he wrote that a black person was, quite simply, "a person who must ride 'Jim Crow' in Georgia."[40] Similarly, the persons who owned, acquired, or fought to claim or maintain control over beachfront lands in the pages that follow were united only in their shared exposure to legal and extralegal forms of humiliation, exploitation, and expropriation that came with their lacking equal access to credit or protection from the state, and by the power of the state to determine the places black persons could occupy and who could profit from them. The legal history of race and real estate, though, cannot be understood without a close consideration of place. Macro trends in twentieth-century American law, such as the ascendance of a market-based valuation of real property in which the pressure to develop land and maximize individual and corporate wealth increasingly trumped considerations of land tenure and ecology, had a specific set of implications for coastal zones and the fortunes of the people who lived there.[41]

The Land Was Ours is also a chapter in the larger story of real estate in America—told through the experiences and perspectives of African American holders, investors, speculators, and developers of property in areas experiencing dramatic social and environmental change—that seeks to change how we understand that history as a whole. It is a story of hope, ambition, and initiative, often followed by devastation and disillusion. Working within discriminatory real estate markets and denied equal access to credit, African Americans with ambitions to own land and start businesses were often led to enter into dubious investment schemes, take out large loans on usurious terms, or engage in other necessary risks in order to achieve the American dream of landed and economic independence. Their struggles demonstrate one of the central ironies of black life in Jim Crow America: in pursuing the very markers and adhering to the basic principles that connoted success and equality, African Americans were not only more likely to be the targets of various forms of brutality and retaliation, but also—and more subtly—to be exposed to the most pernicious and exploitative extremes of American capitalism.[42] As a result, possession of valuable property—and fear of losing it—accentuated and hardened class divisions among black Americans and gave rise to a defensive property politics that until now historians have almost exclusively examined through the lens of white suburbia.[43] Like the real estate markets they were excluded from, African Americans' land-use patterns and practices reflected the possessors' judgment of others, aimed to satisfy and protect their sense of status, and betrayed their own fears and anxieties.

Indeed, the exclusion of African Americans from public places of leisure under Jim Crow, and the exclusion of poor and minorities by income and residency on our modern, privatized landscape—a matter of urgent concern and, in recent decades, a subject of growing interest among scholars—demand an equally close consideration of the dynamic spaces that emerged out of these conditions, and how they came to shape (and frustrate) the long, unfinished struggle for freedom.[44]

The Land Was Ours treats Jim Crow and the Sunbelt not as geographic descriptors but rather as representing a social and public policy "ethos," or, as another historian aptly describes it, as "stage[s] of capitalism" that were not bound to any region but which took on certain characteristics within given environments.[45] To date, scholarship on the rise of the Sunbelt has remained tethered to the metropolis and focused primarily on the political culture that emerged in Sunbelt suburbs and the role of the federal government in channeling economic growth to the South and Southwest in the post–World War II era.[46] These works have identified a shared set of features of the Sunbelt political economy—among others, a capital-intensive and growth-oriented understanding of land and its "best use," promoted and accomplished through a symbiotic relationship between law, public policy, and private, corporate interests; and, not unrelated, the construction and enforcement of racial and class privilege and segregation through space and the built environment rather than through Jim Crow laws and customs. In practice, the emergence of forms of race management and real estate development characteristic of the coastal Sunbelt—and coastal capitalism—led inexorably toward African American loss of land

and, moreover, the unraveling of forms of community formation and familial ties through the land.[47]

On southern coastlines, both Jim Crow and the Sunbelt assumed distinct spatial forms that reflected changes in the geography and political economy of work and leisure and bore distinct implications for human societies and coastal ecosystems. In tracing the manifestation of the Sunbelt ethos on southern shores, and its constitution through leisure-based economies, I show how the Sunbelt was not simply a political and economic phenomenon, but also an environmental one, and how the changing landscape of opportunity and inequality that accompanied the collapse of Jim Crow and the rise of the Sunbelt was inseparable from "changes in the land" itself.[48]

Second, this book complicates and enriches our understanding of what Jacquelyn Dowd Hall labeled the "long" civil rights movement.[49] Fundamentally, it reasserts the primacy of land ownership, and the right to the land for pleasure, amusement, community life, and commerce, in shaping and informing the twin struggles for civil and environmental rights. In coastal zones and along urban shorelines, the right to the land was synonymous with the right to enjoy one's leisure without fear of harassment or humiliation, and the right to summers free of the specter of epidemic, injury, or death. Indeed, the struggle to integrate beaches, parks, and swimming pools in the 1960s emerged as one of many tactics in a broader assault on an unequal and hazardous landscape that annually subjected the urban poor to health crises and claimed countless numbers of black youth each summer.

For others, the right to the land meant the right to profit and build wealth from lands that were rapidly appreciating in value, and the ability to become co-partners in the making of Sunbelt shores. Just as some African Americans and their allies worked to dismantle a Jim Crow economy that other black Americans had learned to navigate with precision and gain a sense of power and influence within, efforts to make public shorelines truly public, and to chip away at the foundations of a privatizing nation, were counterbalanced by African Americans who sought to become partners in the corporate development of coastal and waterfront property, and who used their personal and familial ties to the land as a means of personal enrichment, often with devastating consequences for those fellow African Americans who found themselves torn from the land. The feelings of frustration and ambivalence, outrage and injustice, toward the decline of black landownership from the 1960s to the present (a crisis felt most acutely in coastal zones) do not merely underscore the unfinished work of the black freedom struggle, but call for greater attention to the diverse and at times oppositional visions of freedom that united and divided black Americans—then and now—and, especially in the wake of the subprime housing crisis, for greater awareness of forms of race-based economic exploitation masquerading as tools of empowerment.

Finally, this book builds on the works of those who have called attention to the ways that racism, as George Lipsitz put it, "takes place"—both in a figurative and literal sense. But in examining race and place-making from the shores that black persons owned, fought to acquire, or sought to protect, this book also calls into question the segregation-as-congregation paradigm that has so deeply informed studies of black life in Jim Crow America.[50] Despite its appeal, the notion that the experience of segregation necessarily gave rise to congregation among black Americans has become an overused—and under-analyzed—cliché whose reassessment is long overdue. Likewise, efforts to draw hard distinctions between a white and black "spatial imaginary"—the former associated with "hostile privatism and defensive localism," the latter, "privileging use value over exchange value, sociality over selfishness, and inclusion over exclusion"—lead inevitably toward romanticizing black life behind the so-called "color line" and concretizing African Americans' "place" in the American experience, while downplaying the dynamism and divisiveness that accompanied African Americans' efforts to claim space in a capitalist society. In casting victims of oppression as exemplars of communalism, mutuality, and sustainability, we fail to fully appreciate what Lipsitz himself calls the "pernicious power of the white spatial imaginary" and tend to underestimate the role of land-based capitalism in shaping and giving texture to black struggles for freedom.[51]

Segregation at times produced congregation, but it also produced, among some, an even more pronounced dedication to harnessing the exploitative capacities of a capitalist order that had, for centuries, trapped them in an endless cycle of deprivation and ostracism. This book sheds light on some of the undemocratic, ruthlessly exploitative, and capital-driven features of African American life as witnessed in areas experiencing sudden and profound changes in their political economy and ecology—not in order to de-emphasize the devastating effects of antiblack racism, but to magnify them. For some of the persons in the pages that follow, radical visions of a beloved community took place on the beach, while for others, the sands beneath their feet inspired dreams of abundance and personal liberation from the burden of race. Only by telling these stories side by side, grounded in a distinct type of place on the American landscape, can we begin to untangle the ties that bind race, power, and pleasure to the land.[52]

1

CORPORATE VENTURES

He "made personal sacrifices to accommodate his people." He stood "as a beacon light to his race," a "man whose words [were] household aphorisms." "His reputation is known by the entire community to be a man who gives the people of this city enjoyment when all others fail." Following his incorporation, in 1902, of the Freedman's Transportation, Land, and Improvement Company in Washington, D.C., and the opening of the city's only "colored" riverside resort, the name Lewis Jefferson became, for some black Washingtonians, synonymous with "race enterprise," a man whose sagacity and empathy saved fellow black Washingtonians from humiliation and indignation in their summertime pursuit of pleasure, and whose personal success exemplified a race on the rise. To others in a city where, as the writer and poet Paul Laurence Dunbar put it, "the big men of little towns come to be disillusioned," Jefferson was another swindler masquerading as a leader, who promised riches to his investors but delivered only debt, and who preached race loyalty and race pride but only to the dollar remained true.[1] Still to others, he was a black competitor in the lucrative, white-controlled "colored excursion" trade, whose message of race loyalty in consumer spending demanded and gave rise to new measures to enlist black class chauvinism and white racism as tools of profit and market control.

As a young black capitalist seeking to build wealth through real estate and turn fellow blacks' thirst for modern amusements into profit, Jefferson was, if anything, a man of his times. His incorporation of a transportation company, acquisition of Potomac waterfront real estate along with an outdated and mechanically unsound steamboat, and development of the city's first black-owned amusement park resort exemplified the structure and culture of black investment strategies and entrepreneurial activity from the late nineteenth through the early twentieth centuries, as did his appeals to potential investors, grounded in the often-incongruous promise

of personal riches and economic empowerment of "the race." To his supporters and detractors, it was no surprise that Jefferson channeled his energies toward real estate acquisitions and leisure and transportation industries, nor that he built his fortune through exploiting while skillfully
appealing to the black masses. In his 1936 study, *The Negro As Capitalist*,
Abram Harris wrote: "From the [18]80s on, the Negro masses, urged by their
leaders, were led to place increasing faith in business and property as a
means of escaping poverty and achieving economic independence. Although ostensibly sponsored as a means of self-help or racial cooperation . . .
Negro business enterprise was motivated primarily by the desire for private
profit and looked toward the establishment of a Negro capitalist employer
class." Lacking the capital, connections, or market to sustain large-scale
commercial and industrial development, turn-of-the-century black capitalists, Harris found, turned to real estate speculation and amusement
enterprises as two of the primary means through which to secure an economic foundation in urban settings.[2] Perceiving possibilities arising from
the segregation of public outdoor space and privately run amusements,
Jefferson and others adhered to Booker T. Washington's maxim "Every
condition which creates a new want offers at the same time a new business
opportunity."[3]

   It was no coincidence that black Washingtonians loaded the hopes and
dreams of a rising race onto aging steamboats and unloaded them on the
shores of the Potomac. Since man first secured sail to mast, fortunes have
been squandered on the mythical allure of boat ownership, that most notorious of risky investments. The high risks involved, in turn, made water
transportation vessels one of the few industries and commercial pursuits
open to black investors, as sellers sought to unload often-frail and dilapidated vessels or excess or unprofitable real estate onto those desperate to
secure a tangible investment in future success, or used the promise of
riches from the amusement trade to lure black investors into fraudulent
schemes. As urban waterfronts and nearby seashores connected by rail
grew in popularity and profitability in the first decades of the twentieth
century, African American corporate investments in pleasure resorts increasingly fell victim to arson and other forms of racial terrorism by those
who saw in such visible symbols of black economic initiative an affront
to relations of power being inscribed onto these new land and waterscapes.
By the turn of the twentieth century, countless numbers of ambitious
young men and women had staked their future in volatile industries and

21

notoriously unprofitable assets, their rare instances of success-against-all-odds overshadowed by equally epic (and far more common) failures. For many, their savings and investments sank, quite literally, to the bottom of the river or sea, along with their faith in the power of the marketplace to deliver freedom from racial oppression and exploitation.

✦

In an 1886 editorial in the *New York Globe*, T. Thomas Fortune told his readers that, rather than spend precious dollars at white-owned resorts and picnic grounds, they should build and support a black-owned public resort.[4] A glimpse of leisure and enterprise on Washington's Potomac River seemed to testify to the wisdom and urgency of Fortune's advice. In the preceding decades, the city's African American population had grown exponentially.[5] Many arrived at the wharves of the city's Southwest district aboard one of the steamboats that plied the Potomac and Chesapeake, after a voyage spent confined to the lower decks, forced to withstand the heat and breathe in the soot from the engine, while white passengers danced and dined on the decks above.[6] By the late nineteenth century, steamboats had long ceased to be the quickest and most reliable form of transportation for persons or freight in the mid-Atlantic region, but remained popular as a form of leisurely transportation. With each passing season, steamboat owners and operators refitted freight boats as excursion steamers offering day and overnight trips.[7] Among burgeoning communities of freedpeople in Washington and other cities, summertime steamboat excursions emerged as both a popular activity and a fund-raising source for churches, social clubs, secret orders, lodges, and other mutual aid societies.[8] By the 1880s, African American organizations routinely rented out excursion steamboats for private events and ventured to riverside resorts, often taking advantage of lower rates on weekdays or during the off-season months of April and September. The riverside landings where excursion parties disembarked remained, into the 1880s, little more than a cleared field suitable for picnics, hiking, and flower picking, and offered travelers a chance to "get away from the heat of the city and enjoy the fresh air of the river . . . [and] a few pleasant hours in the woods."[9]

Like other bodies of water located in or near urban centers, the Potomac had, throughout the nineteenth century, attracted a wide and varied assemblage of persons and activities. Alongside stately and decorated steamboats floated gambling and prostitution dens, known as arks; on the shore, sporting crowds gathered for illicit boxing matches within earshot of Mount Vernon, the home of the "father of the nation." Prostitution flourished in coves and shoal waters that were inaccessible to harbor patrol boats. Located on the border of Prince George's and Charles counties in Maryland and surrounded by steep hills, dense forest, and thick under-brush, Bull Town Cove housed a floating village of gambling, drinking, and prostitution dens and became a favorite rendezvous for sailing crews headed to and from the capital city. In the city, prizefight promoters sold tickets and accepted wagers at the wharfs in Washington or Alexandria, loaded interested parties onto steamboats, and traveled down the river in search of an open landing or a sheriff or night watchman they could bribe to allow them to come ashore and commence the affair. Along the city's waterfront, small-business owners set up shops, with legitimate services up front disguising faro rooms in back.

It was no coincidence that illegal activities flourished along the water. Maryland's boundary extended to the Virginia shoreline, thus giving it nominal authority over the Potomac's waters south of the District. Follow-ing the retrocession of Arlington and Alexandria to Virginia in 1848, the waters north of the District's southern boundary became a subject of legal debate, with neither the District nor the state of Virginia willing to claim jurisdiction. Thus, at the convergence of Maryland, Virginia, and the District, illicit pleasures flourished with virtual impunity, as offenders could easily move into another jurisdiction at the sight of an approaching patrol boat. Gambling proprietors such as Alexandria's Jack Heath anchored river-boat casinos at the intersection of these boundaries of authority, "flirt[ing] around the law with the dexterity of a swallow." Heath's Ark, one reporter noted, "is always cunningly anchored within close proximity to the chan-nel and boundary intersection."[10]

While Heath floated in the river, growing numbers of riverboat owners sought out the shore. Excursion boats marketed to city dwellers the chance to travel down the river, breathe fresh air, and watch the rolling country-side of Maryland and Virginia as they passed by. But ultimately, an excur-sion needs a destination, and its passengers expected to reach a place along the sandy shores of the Potomac where they could disembark and picnic. As they became increasingly engaged in the business of pleasure, riverboat owners acquired riverfront properties with the intent of devel-oping pleasure resorts. Picnic groves that previously consisted of little more than cut grass were transformed into modern amusement parks, while formerly common lands were landscaped, fenced, and privatized. Excursion steamboat companies bought up waterfront property and streamlined operations by running a set, daily schedule of trips open to the public to a single location, in place of a series of trips for different groups to various locations. In 1895, L. L. Blake and Joseph C. McKibben, owners and operators of the *Charles Macalester* and the *River Queen,* purchased the grounds of the venerable Marshall Hall, a colonial mansion and the former home of one of Maryland's oldest and wealthiest families, located across the river from Mount Vernon. They equipped the 412-acre tract with rides, lights, and concessions and began running a daily schedule of excursions from Washington to Mount Vernon and Marshall Hall. In the shadow of the old plantation house, excursion parties enjoyed "planked shad, hot from the fire and washed down with foamy extract of malt or fragrant mint juleps, and afterward the various amusements of bowling alleys, rifle ranges, merry-go-rounds, strolling under the trees or loafing quietly in the shade." The composition of and atmosphere aboard riverboat excursions and at new modern pleasure resorts both reflected and shaped a broader redefinition of "respectability" in the age of public amusements, one set in contrast to the mixed, sporting crowds that characterized past summers on the Potomac. At places like Marshall Hall, guests were expected to adhere to standards of conduct. "Positively no improper characters," one excursion boat publicized, "will be allowed aboard."[11]

In this and other public places of amusement, persons of color were, without exception, defined as improper. Part and parcel of becoming a "respectable" riverboat or riverside resort was the drawing of the color line.[12] If blacks were lucky, they could enjoy these new facilities on certain days of the week, or during the off-season. More often, though, owners simply barred blacks from entry altogether. In July 1887, the Excelsiors, a social club composed of "aristocrats of color," enjoyed another annual excursion aboard the *Mary Washington* to River View, a small resort on the Virginia side of the river. There they marveled at the resort's "spacious and elegant booths, its young tress and its roller coaster." The following summer, however, the resort's managers, having established the park as a "public" resort, "swor[e] against colored organizations of every description." In June 1891, "three colored men called at one of [the riverboat] ticket offices . . . to inquire what boat they could take to some point down the river, when an insignificant jack commenced braying. He told them to get away from the window; that colored people were not allowed at Marshall Hall, and he refused to sell them tickets."[13]

Many of these same ticket offices would soon come to welcome black excursionists' money, but only aboard one of their Negro excursion boats. L. T. Woolen, a young white captain and owner of the steamer *Pilot Boy*, was among the first to perceive the profits to be drawn from black Washingtonians' yearning for an afternoon or evening on the Potomac. In 1888 he designated the *Pilot Boy* as a "colored excursion boat" and began accepting reservations from the city's black churches, social clubs, and mutual aid societies. He leased the Virginia resort Collingwood Beach to host "colored" excursion parties throughout the summer (see Map 3, p. 35). Woolen outfitted Collingwood Beach with ample attractions, including "a splendid Pavilion, a Gravity Railroad, Flying Horses, Swings, Boats, Bath Houses, etc." Other proprietors turned to "colored excursion" parties after finding themselves crowded out of the whites-only market. Across the river from Collingwood Beach, in Prince George's County, Maryland, white businessman J. Harrison Johnson opened in 1890 a riverside resort catering to white Washingtonians on the fifty acres of woodland surrounding the old plantation home Notley Hall. He spared "no expense . . . in fitting out the grounds in a manner which places it far in the lead as a field for picnicking parties," including, "An elegant two-story café . . . mammoth pavilion . . . bowling alleys, a steam carousel, chariots, and horses, and other pleasing forms of amusement." Despite its advantageous location nine miles south of the Seventh Street wharf, which afforded guests a "grand view of Washington," Notley Hall was unable to compete with larger, more fanciful resorts downriver. After three unprofitable seasons catering to whites, in 1894 Harrison began soliciting black excursion parties.[14]

Like any good business, "colored excursion" companies evolved in relation to the structure of work and the culture of play among their customer base. Many boats specialized in offering moonlight excursions, which began in the evening and often lasted through the night and into the following morning. These proved an especially popular draw for persons who worked long hours. Domestic servants often carried "freedom bags" with them to work containing the outfit they planned to wear once the workday was done.[15] Young black men, likewise, donned their finest threads before boarding an excursion steamer.[16] For many, these moonlight excursions were one of the few stages on which they could figuratively (and literally) try on and wear identities that the long hours and humiliating racial conventions their jobs in the city's service trades denied. The moonlight excursion became, as one white reporter put it, an "institution the existence of which is not suspected by the white people." On board, young couples danced the "cake walk" to the sounds of ragtime, while groups of singers and musicians formed on the decks. As opposed to the select few who had "the time or money to go off an enjoy . . . a country retreat," the "river crowd" became, as one writer for the *Colored American* put it, "a faithful type of true democracy." The boats they boarded and the beaches where they landed, likewise, became formative spaces in the making of a modern, urban black public.[17]

The companies that owned these boats and resorts had little interest in supporting black social and institutional life. They wanted to make money, and entered into the "colored excursion" trade with a set of assumptions and strategies. White proprietors internalized and worked to prove stereotypes of African Americans as spendthrifts who were willing to part with their last cent on an ephemeral amusement. Most reported to prefer the "colored excursion" business since it was, as one operator described, virtually recession proof. Their business practices, in turn, reinforced the very prejudices about black leisure that justified segregation. Woolen and other white operators of "colored excursions" earned a reputation for their callous disregard for the desires and sensibilities of their clientele. They often purposely oversold tickets for black excursion parties (sometimes as many as twice the legal capacity), leading to disturbances that were often described as "riots." On several occasions, those holding worthless tickets attempted to storm the boat, resulting in the swift arrival of baton-swinging police squads. On board "colored excursions," parents, children, and preachers were crowded alongside hustlers and brawlers. One exasperated black clergyman reported that his church had tried to reserve a boat for an excursion, "with the express understanding that no tickets were to be sold to rough characters, that no gambling should be allowed, and that there should be no bar on the boat." The white manager instead sold tickets to all comers, dispensed alcohol on board, and looked the other way when gambling rings formed on deck. After the minister requested that he honor the wishes of the excursion party, the manager simply set up a "speakeasy and gambling joint in a less conspicuous corner of the boat." On a July 1888 trip to Collingwood Beach hosted by the Gleason Social

Club, young ladies and gentlemen shared picnics on the shore and in the surrounding woods while a party of young black men rolled dice near the beach. A fight ensued, sending guests ducking for cover and running toward the hills as combatants flashed knives and fired shots. While a "mass of struggling, bowling and brutal humanity" exchanged blows, one account described, "the women screamed and fled to places of safety, while a large number of men who had refrained from taking any part in the melee took refuge on the boat or at a distance." Such accounts of violence and debauchery aboard "colored excursions" became a popular item in the local press and emerged as a form of voyeurism among the city's white population, earning Collingwood Beach and Notley Hall the nickname "Razor Beach."[18] On boats and stretches of shore denoted as "colored," policing and surveillance veered wildly from bemused indifference to random and capricious acts of brutality.[19]

There was no shortage of black moral reformers who said that the excursion problem was of blacks' own making. Preaching that respectability and frugality could be a cudgel against racial prejudice and a ticket to middle-class upward mobility, advocates of racial uplift argued that the spending on excursions and the associated lavish displays not only confirmed negative stereotypes of black culture, but kept black communities impoverished. Following the 1888 "riot" at Collingwood Beach, the African American newspaper the *Washington Bee* wrote, "This is one of the causes that so much discrimination is made against the more decent class of colored people." "Every dollar spent for excursions, whiskey, foolish carriage rides and dress, together with other nonsensical displays," the *Baltimore Afro-American* warned, "is simply playing into the hands of the opponents of our progress." "Patrons of those disreputable Sunday orgies, in the South—called excursions," Edward E. Cooper, editor of the *Washington Colored American*, commented, "are not helping to solve the race problem. If killing time was a capital offense, the mortality among Washington's colored population would be something dreadful."[20]

Others argued that the deplorable scenes reported aboard "colored excursions" and at the so-called Razor Beach were the predictable outcome of an exploitative, white-controlled industry. African Americans *should* be ashamed about summers on the Potomac, they said—ashamed that they were lining the pockets of their white oppressors. The *Washington Bee* told readers that patronage of white-owned "colored excursion" boats enriched exploitative white businessmen and contributed to their own impoverishment and social and economic immobility. One of the more popular "colored excursion" boats, they charged, was "run by a company of white men . . . for the purpose of making money off of the very colored people whom they refuse to rent houses to except in alleys, whom they refuse to employ except in the most menial way and whom they Jim Crow in every possible way," but who also "make it a point . . . to distribute free tickets to a certain class of colored women who are usually joined at the boat by their male companions, and who spend Sundays down the river in every form of outlaw and intoxication." In Baltimore, black ministers and journalists decried a white-owned resort where "beer and whiskey are sold to minors . . . and various gambling devices [are] operated by white men." "Here we have a real picture of the Negro as a slave, and of the white man's master. . . . The white master, under the guise of giving blacks a 'good time,' is both filching them for their money, their brain power, and everything of intrinsic value, and when he has accomplished his purpose, hands them an empty lemon as a reminder of their present exhausted state." "For God's sakes," one organizer of an excursion for black Washingtonians gone awry begged, at least "permit [Negroes] to run their own boat and enjoy themselves upon their own grounds."[21]

Born in Richmond, Virginia, in 1870, African American John W. Patterson displayed, from an early age, a keen intelligence, a larger-than-life personality, and shrewd political skills. At age nineteen he moved to Washington and secured a job as a messenger in the Internal Revenue Bureau under the Benjamin Harrison administration. Following Harrison's defeat by Grover Cleveland in 1892 and the return of Democrats to power, Patterson was relieved of his position and turned to the pulpit, preaching at a church in South Washington while launching several unspecified, but ultimately unsuccessful, enterprises and earning a reputation in some circles as untrustworthy. With his handsome face, winning manners, and attractive personality, Patterson nevertheless deftly won the affections of his congregants and the attention of and influence over his fellow preachers. An article in the *Colored American* hailed him as "one of the most eloquent and profound men of his race," while the white *Washington Times* described him as one the city's many "shrewd, well-educated, light-colored negro[es]."[22]

Salvation, Patterson told his followers, would come through enterprise and incorporation. The 1890s witnessed the spread of stockholding and corporate investment among the American public. In an age of unprecedented corporate power, ownership of shares in a black-owned corporation promised individual enrichment and collective empowerment. Observers described the black neighborhoods of South Washington in the 1890s as a beehive of commercial activity and business investment set in contrast to the city's elite black establishment. "You will see in every direction corner groceries, notion stores, restaurants, saloons and undertaking establishments all operated and controlled by Negroes, while colored physicians, pharmacists and lawyers are waxing rich and prosperous." It was a place where risk and chance were woven into the fabric of daily life, and where political and economic activity was conducted within an "ecclesiastical galaxy" of preachers and prophets.[23] Indeed, for aspiring businessmen like Patterson, patronage and investment among the people necessitated the merging of the interests of the corporation with the interests of the race, and assuaging fears of past failures and lost savings.[24] Vesting the marketplace with a moral dimension, race-conscious corporate ventures responded to black Americans' past experiences while capitalizing on existing social and economic networks in urban black communities.

By early 1894, Patterson's Sunday sermons became increasingly laced with references to a prime opportunity awaiting his congregants to put the hopes and dreams of a rising race in motion. With an initial goal of $25,000 in capital stock and a mission to provide "transportation of passengers and freight in the interests of colored people between Washington and Norfolk," on May 4, 1894, the People's Transportation Company filed articles of incorporation and began selling shares in the company through the city's black churches. To woo prospective shareholders, Patterson offered more than hollow words. The corporate charter forbade any member of the board of directors from owning more than ten shares in the company, preventing a consolidation of power, ensuring the distribution of the company's profits throughout the community of investors, and promising each investor a voice in the company's operations. The People's incorporation and the drive to purchase a steamboat became, as with other major investment projects, a referendum on corporate investment as a means of economic empowerment. While Patterson's early partners confidently declared it to be a "sure thing," others expressed skepticism or declared "the concern to be a fraud" and warned the public not be "fooled."[25]

Patterson's big ambitions could not overcome the minuscule savings of his prospective investors. Sales of shares in the company fell $12,000 short of the target needed to acquire *Lady of the Lake*, an outdated steamboat retired by a white-owned company. The undercapitalization of fledgling black businesses led many to implement innovative and highly risky investment strategies. To meet the $25,000 capital stock threshold, shareholders in the People's Transportation Company signed promissory notes on their shares to Patterson, in effect taking out a loan in the amount of their shares in the hope that future dividends would cancel out this one-time loss. Without these notes, Patterson told investors, blacks' ownership of a steamboat of their own would remain an elusive dream.

Carrying the hopes (and dollars) of a race, the *Lady of the Lake* began running its route from Washington to Norfolk in June 1894. For excursion parties, Patterson leased the riverside landing at Glymont for the summer season. On the boat, he hired "Monty" Wells, an Irishman and "good fella" from a rough neighborhood in Southwest D.C. with ties to the Desmond Gang, one of the city's largest and most notorious crime syndicates, to operate the bar. Judging by the numbers of excursion parties and passengers that crowded onto the boat's decks that summer, the People's Transportation Company seemed to have exceeded the "most sanguine expectations" of stockholders and skeptics. By midsummer, shareholders eagerly awaited what, for most, was their first dividend check and first tangible evidence of the fortunes that awaited savvy investors.[26]

The large crowds underscored the riches that could be drawn from the pockets of black pleasure seekers, a fact that white steamboat operators had long been aware of and had come to depend on as a significant source of revenue. And as the People's Transportation Company worked to corner the market on "colored excursions" and make inroads into the freight hauling business, white-owned steamboat companies employed various forms of skullduggery to retain their market shares. The river's major steamboat companies colluded to prevent the *Lady of the Lake* from hauling any "colored" freight on the river by threatening dockworkers with the loss of jobs should they handle freight coming to or from the boat's pier in Washington. To hold on to their earnings from "colored excursionists," white steamboat operators reportedly offered black preachers generous donations in return for continuing to host events on their boats and at their resorts, and for disseminating warnings that, without blacks' continued patronage, these companies would cease offering service to blacks entirely.[27] Others scrambled to place black persons in prominent and visible positions within the company. After the Mount Vernon and Marshall Hall Steamboat Company designated the *River Queen* its "Negro excursion" boat, it hired Edward "Hop" Coates, a popular African American caterer, to manage the boat's waitstaff and to serve as the "Mascot of the River Queen." "To the socially inclined," a promotional piece on the boat's accommodations read, "no trip down the river is complete without one or more visits to Coates' department, where 'sunshine' is brought forward to order."[28]

As consumers, black excursionists were thus forced to choose between supporting a fledgling black-owned company whose accommodations were inferior and whose long-term viability was uncertain, or continuing to give their dollars to a more stable and familiar white outfit. Many opted for the latter, which, along with the loss of expected earnings from freight hauling, the high costs of operating a steamboat, and the usurious boat repayment scheme, left the company far short of the projected earnings on which Patterson's investment strategy depended on and which he had factored into the company's accounts. In late July, word spread among shareholders that, despite brisk business, no dividends would be forthcoming. Soon thereafter hundreds of shareholders received notices from Patterson that their notes were due and, without payment, they effectively forfeited their shares in the company. Few, if any, possessed the means or intention of contributing more of their savings to a venture that had promised immediate returns, and as a result, Patterson and his close associates' stake in the company grew exponentially. By August, Patterson, along with vice president Maria Jordan and secretary Mary Wilson, both schoolteachers, had amassed sixteen hundred shares in the company.

For investors, hope quickly turned to disillusion. In this age of false gods and confidence men, public opinion of the charming, well-mannered Patterson quickly turned negative. The acerbic and impetuous W. Calvin Chase, editor of the aptly named *Washington Bee* ("honey for friends, stings for enemies"), denounced the People's Transportation Company as "a gigantic fraud" and called for criminal proceedings against Patterson and his associates. "It is so strange," he sarcastically commented, "that some of the officers of the company are people who have been connected with all kinds of schemes." Moreover, he castigated fellow blacks for their susceptibility to "well dressed negro" con artists. "It is only necessary for some . . . fluent talker [to come to town] and that moment every negro in town will flock to him and call him the anointed. Before they are through the people's pockets are anointed and their money is weighed in balances and found wanting." For newcomers to the city, the experience provided cruel lessons in the new forms of entrapment and exploitation that awaited them in urban environments, and for the general public it served to sharpen distinctions between honest and respectable versus unscrupulous forms of work.[29]

But it also spawned, from the collective energy of hopeful investors, a collective sense of indignation and determination to seek justice and education in the workings of financial markets and corporate investments. In a hastily organized meeting at a Grand Army of the Republic Hall, 250 shareholders voted to appoint an internal investigative committee. Patterson's adversary, William H. Thomas, sought to have the *Lady of the Lake* placed under receivership after concluding that the company's accounts were rife with "willful speculations." Through ownership of shares, small-time investors, for better or worse, were navigating the urban political economy and becoming immersed in the overall structure and culture of corporations and financial markets. Like the churches in which these meetings were often held, shareholders, through their shared investments, shared sense of vulnerability, and shared determination to achieve opportunity in the marketplace in lieu of its denial elsewhere, formed political communities and acquired new identities as political actors. At shareholders' meetings, urban blacks reconstituted and put into practice forms of participatory democracy responsive to the impersonal nature of urban environments. At meetings, shareholders closely adhered to parliamentary procedure. Sergeants-at-arms stood guard to enforce discipline and order. Local leaders and unheralded citizens alike stood and spoke before their peers. Attorneys presented facts and explained the law, and individuals shared information and designed and voted on plans of action.

The company's president, meanwhile, struggled to extract himself from the web of debt his risky speculations had woven. On February 15, 1895, a fire that began in the boiler room of *Lady of the Lake* quickly spread to the rest of the boat, consuming it in flames within minutes and rendering the vessel a total loss. In May, authorities arrested Patterson on charges of arson after a member of the Desmond Gang claimed he had been hired to carry out the task so that Patterson could claim a $31,000 insurance policy and settle a $1,600 debt to the boat's bartender, Wells. A jury later acquitted him after finding the testimony of the state's witness unreliable.

Throughout the investigation into the finances of People's Transportation, Patterson told shareholders and the public that Thomas was allied with white steamboat operators who were determined to destroy this experiment in race enterprise. "The investigation," one reporter noted him saying, "was nothing more nor less than a conspiracy, and that the members of the committee had been hired by white men to wreck the colored steamboat company." One member allied with Patterson resigned from the committee in disgust, charging his fellow associates with "pecuniary motives" and claimed they were only "interested in these charges for what they can get out of it."[30]

Rather than lackeys for white business interests, Patterson's accusers sought to become his competitors. In April 1895 a group of disgruntled shareholders in the People's Transportation Company formed the rival National Steamboat Company, with $50,000 in capital stock divided into $10 shares. They acquired the elegant but aged *George Leary*, a 242-foot-long triple decker that could carry fifteen hundred passengers, and began running excursions to Glymont and Colonial Beach, along its route between Washington and Norfolk. To build popular support for the venture, the crew hosted a barbecue to end the 1895 season at Glymont, where a crowd of five thousand persons dined on freshly slain lamb and oxen meat and enjoyed unlimited, complimentary beer. That same summer, the National Steamboat Company's board of directors announced its acquisition of a stretch of undeveloped land on the lower portion of Cobb Island, about thirty miles up the Potomac from Chesapeake Bay, where it planned to develop a "colored Saratoga." The purchase, and the response that followed, exemplified a broader recognition of social rituals and places of social congregation as a measure of racial progress. "For years past," the *Washington Bee* remarked,

> the members of the race have been content to suppress the expression of their longing for the indulgence as a people in those golden hours of social and intellectual recreation which enter into the experience of the white race during the summer months, the "holiday season." . . . While the cultured and talented among them have been holding their summer Chautauquas, their teachers' institutes and their social and intellectual reunions at pleasant resorts the gifted members of the colored race . . . have

> schooled themselves to resignation and have not allowed them-
> selves to think that they, too could have their summer resort . . .
> and their intellectual gatherings if they just made up their minds
> to have them.

With the acquisition of land on Cobb Island, the paper wrote, the "colored race" now possessed a place "where there may be brought together
the educated and gifted people of their race . . . under the auspices of the
regulation character governing a high-class summer resort."[31]

Not to be outdone, less than a month after the destruction of *Lady of
the Lake*, Patterson acquired the *Jane Moseley* from a Baltimore businessman, Isaac M. Tibbert, and increased the company's capital stock to $60,000.
Like *Lady of the Lake*, the *Jane Moseley* was another ancient vessel that
had been replaced by newer models and whose sentimental value belied
its unreliability. He signed a lease with the owners of Collingwood Beach
on the Virginia side to run Negro excursions there throughout the summer, and renamed the destination Douglass Beach (after the famed abolitionist). To launch its second venture into the excursion trade, on May 19,
the People's Transportation Company provided complimentary excursions
to Douglass Beach aboard the *Jane Moseley*.

For the city's black population, the presence of two black-owned steamers and two resorts on the river signaled a monumental step forward in
their broader struggle for liberation from the humiliations and indignities
of summers in the Jim Crow city. As one writer later put it, "Then was life
a dream and the colored folks of this city no longer viewed with regret
and jealousy the river resort of the whites, but with supreme indifference
proudly sailed past River View and Marshall Hall—a veritable Charybdis
and Scylla of Negro pleasure seekers—to their own reservation, where they
could disport in the balmy air and enjoy 'merry-go-rounds' and red lem-
onade *ad libitum, ad infinitum*."[32] (See Map 3.)

Patterson's proclamations of the People's ownership of a new, more
commodious steamer were, however, more imagined than real. Unable
to secure a mortgage, Patterson instead had acquired the *Jane Moseley* on
contract. Under this arrangement, Patterson provided Tibbert a substantial down payment toward the purchase of the boat as well as regular
payments that were credited toward the eventual purchase. But Tibbert
held on to the boat's title until he had been paid in full, and until then
could exercise his authority over the boat's operation and pay schedule,

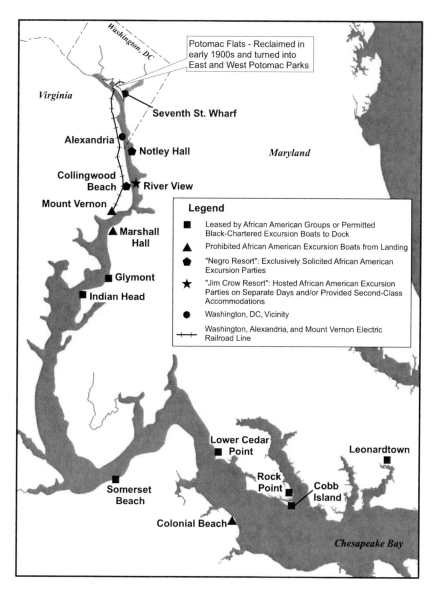

The following text appears within the map image:

Washington, DC

Potomac Flats - Reclaimed in
early 1900s and turned into
East and West Potomac Parks

Virginia

Seventh St. Wharf

Alexandria

Notley Hall

Maryland

Collingwood
Beach

River View

Mount Vernon

Legend

■ Leased by African American Groups or Permitted
Black-Chartered Excursion Boats to Dock

▲ Prohibited African American Excursion Boats from Landing

⬟ "Negro Resort": Exclusively Solicited African American
Excursion Parties

★ "Jim Crow Resort": Hosted African American Excursion
Parties on Separate Days and/or Provided Second-Class
Accommodations

● Washington, DC, Vicinity

+++ Washington, Alexandria, and Mount Vernon Electric
Railroad Line

Marshall
Hall

Glymont

Indian Head

Lower Cedar
Point

Leonardtown

Rock
Point

Cobb
Island

Somerset
Beach

Colonial Beach

Chesapeake Bay

Map 3. Potomac River basin, ca. 1900

and retained the right to reclaim his property (and pocket all of Patterson's payments) if Patterson failed to honor any part of the contract. Patterson might not have recognized or given much thought to these risks, or he might have been well aware of the risks but saw few other options.

With the vessel in his possession, Patterson quickly began booking groups for upcoming excursion dates, the biggest event slated for Decoration Day, when the Carroll Institute Lyceum of the St. Aloysius Church planned to host over three thousand persons on a holiday cruise. As the day approached, Patterson began to suspect that, in purchasing the *Jane Moseley* "on contract," he had been lured into a well-laid trap from which he had little hope of escape. The first sign that something was amiss came after an excursion on May 19, when the *Jane Moseley*'s Captain Kirby, described in one account as a "jolly old tar," refused to travel to or dock at Douglass Beach, saying that the waters there were too shallow and that offshore pilings had been driven too deep into the river, both of which rendered the location a dangerous risk to human life and property. Federal steamboat inspectors purportedly agreed. The claims were dubious at best. Other boats of similar size routinely landed there, and Patterson had arranged for a tugboat to safely ferry passengers to the shore and allow the vessel to remain in deep water.

On the morning of Decoration Day, expectant excursionists ventured to the wharf, "dressed in gay holiday attire" and "filled," as one account describes, "with provender, fishing tackle, and other necessary things to complete the pleasures of a day's outing down the Potomac." An aging butler for a foreign minister arrived on the docks to enjoy his first day off from work in over ten years. The night before, Patterson had made sure to stock the bar and concession stands in anticipation of high sales volumes. But at the announced time of departure, Kirby stepped out onto his perch and informed passengers that the boat would not be leaving the wharf. Anger and indignation rippled among the crowd. Some became "excited and demonstrative." All were disappointed. Kirby placed a riot call to the fourth precinct. Within minutes, over twenty police officers swarmed the wharf, prepared to suppress any hint of unruliness. Patterson arrived soon after and begged Kirby to journey to Douglass Beach, or, at the least, ferry the passengers forty miles downriver and back without landing. When he refused, Patterson told Kirby he was relieved of his duties. Kirby informed Patterson that, to the contrary, "until several more payments are made," he did not work for him, but rather for Isaac Tibbert, who under the terms of their contract had the right to "furnish the captain and the crew and command them." Moreover, his decision had the legal backing of federal steamboat inspectors, whom Tibbert had contacted in advance and instructed to prevent the boat from leaving the dock. Patterson and his associates were incredulous. Patterson's partner Frederick Dyson called it "an outrage to deprive these 3,000 people of their day's pleasure" and to deprive People's the right to conduct its business. A week later Patterson filed a $30,000 lawsuit against Tibbert, claiming over $2,000 in lost earnings and incalculable damage to his "reputation by the report that it was proposed to take . . . patrons to a dangerous landing." Kirby's refusal to dock at Douglass Beach was, Patterson claimed, "part of a scheme to prevent the company from doing business."[33]

The structure of the sale was a classic bait-and-switch frequently used to entrap and exploit the poor and politically impotent, and in this case to prey on Patterson's indefatigable desire to own and operate a steamboat. Tibbert had no intention of transferring title to the *Jane Moseley* to Patterson. He instead sought to secure a down payment and a summer seasonal payment of $4,500 from Patterson and subsequently make it impossible for Patterson to operate his business and make future payments, which would in turn allow him to initiate foreclosure proceedings and reclaim his assets while pocketing Patterson's previous payments toward the boat's purchase. Dyson said the scheme was motivated by pure "prejudice." In fact, the plight of People's could more accurately be described as stemming from the nexus of business calculation, personal prejudice, and structural inequality, just as Patterson's earlier scheme drew upon his intimate familiarity with the hopes and lack of financial education of his black parishioners. As jaded excursionists ate their picnics on the wharf and walked back to their cramped apartments, and as Patterson saw his investment go up in smoke, they all bore witness to the apotheosis of racial capitalism in leisure and transportation industries.

On June 2 the *Jane Moseley* sailed back to Baltimore under Tibbert's command. Patterson settled his lawsuit against Tibbert out of court for $1,000. The National Steamboat Company's lofty dreams of a "colored Saratoga," meanwhile, evaporated. Following two profitable and trouble-free seasons, the *George Leary*'s steam engine failed. Without its sole source of revenue, the company lacked the finances to make the needed repairs. In August 1898 a reporter found "the vessel . . . rusting and rotting away at a tumble down wharf . . . requiring only a bit of enterprise to put steam into the boilers." In 1900 she was sold, stripped, and converted into a lumber barge. Patterson, meanwhile, retired from the business world and opened a legal practice, specializing in real estate law.[34]

Following these failed ventures, "the Negro [continued to] sail the Potomac, and the pockets of the white man bulge[d] with coin." The companies' collapse and the further deterioration of black summer life on the river seemed to typify blacks' frustrated attempts to empower and uplift the "race" through the marketplace of leisure. Referring to the two steamboat companies, the *Baltimore Afro-American* wrote, "In business, the Negro suffers from the presence of a 'hoodoo,' which, while invisible, seems invincible." Commentators singled out these failed ventures for ridicule. Following the dissolution of the National Steamboat Company, the *Colored American* sarcastically remarked that "the colored boat company has gone swimming." "The boat companies organized and failed with such clock-like regularity," editor Edward E. Cooper commented, "that they became a joke and to talk 'boat' would cause the knowing ones to smile." "The odoriferous scandals emanating" from the People's Transportation Company, the *Baltimore Afro-American* commented, "caused a lukewarmness on the part of the colored people to subscribe to any further project of their nature."[35]

The likelihood of their failure was rather easy to predict. In each case, lack of capital and connections led aspiring race entrepreneurs to embark on innovative, but highly risky, investment strategies. Success and stability depended on a miraculous alignment of the galaxies, including a lack of unexpected expenses in an industry where mechanical failures were common, and the honest dealings of white business associates in a society where economic exploitation of black persons was endemic. Combined, these factors turned endeavors to uplift the race through enterprise into desperate attempts to salvage personal losses through exploiting fellow blacks. Confined to "petty trade at the margin of gain," the Negro businessman's success, Abram Harris observed, "must depend in a larger degree upon skillful exploitation of the Negro masses." The pursuit of profits and pride through the excursion boat business highlighted the structural inequities that conspired to virtually guarantee the achievement of neither.[36]

Lewis Jefferson, however, seemed destined to succeed where others had failed. Born in 1866 to a freedwoman from South Carolina, Jefferson was raised by his grandmother in Orange, Virginia, following his mother's death when he was an infant. He moved to Washington as a child and soon exhibited a taste for water travel. As a teenager, legend has it, he stowed away on the steamer *Jane Moseley* bound for New York. He enlisted as a seaman in the U.S. Navy at fifteen, after falsifying his age, and after two trips around the world secured an honorable discharge in 1887. After working for the U.S. senator and presidential candidate James G. Blaine in a mining company in West Virginia for a brief period, Jefferson moved to South Washington and joined the multitude of migrants from the rural South.[37] True to form, Jefferson tried his hand at various ventures, including work as a small-fry huckster, grocer, blacksmith, and coal and wood dealer. His business acumen quickly became apparent, and he rose to become one of the city's leading wholesalers of produce and fertilizer. "He was optimistic as well as industrious and persevering," Andrew Hilyer, editor of the 1900 Union League directory, a catalog of Washington's black professionals, wrote of Jefferson.[38] He was also keen to forge strategic ties with wealthy and influential whites. Jefferson befriended the aging banker, art collector, and philanthropist William Wilson Corcoran, one of the city's wealthiest men and owner of vast swaths of real estate in the District. Though it is unclear whether Corcoran sold or bequeathed the property, what is clear is that he facilitated Jefferson's acquisition of several hundred acres in the city's Southwest quadrant. By 1890 the twenty-four-year-old Jefferson was one of the largest real estate owners in the District, albeit of swampy, malarial land in an area of the city whites had steadily been abandoning since the Civil War.[39] Many of the rural black migrants that streamed into the city in the late nineteenth century found shelter in low-rent housing owned by Jefferson.[40]

Jefferson also established ties to the aforementioned Isaac Tibbert—the president of the Jane Moseley Steamboat Company and conductor of the contract sale that had driven John W. Patterson from the excursion trade—and in 1902 persuaded a team of black investors in Washington to incorporate and purchase the aging steamer. That same year the newly incorporated Freedman's Transportation, Land, and Improvement Company made a down payment on the purchase of the *Jane Moseley* and sailed her back from Baltimore to Washington. The terms of the sale were outrageous—$20,000, with an $8,000 down payment, and $2,000 monthly repayments under penalty of forfeiture, an arrangement that, as one report later concluded, was in excess of "its capital stock and the business done by the boat would justify."[41]

Upon the boat's purchase, the Freedman's corporation immediately embarked on an aggressive campaign to sell stock in the fledgling company. Advertisements for sale of ten-dollar shares in the company, payable in small monthly installments, implored readers not to miss the opportunity to get in on the ground floor of what was sure to be a "first class investment" in a "swift and commodious steamer." Jefferson reminded prospective buyers that the future of the race was tied to the future of race enterprises. And they took pains to distance this black-owned steamer from past failures. "The officers of this company are wide-awake, intelligent, aggressive men," one article read, "and they will leave no stone unturned to fit the bills to the fullest measure and to the pleasure and comfort of those who will run excursions down the Potomac the coming season." Later that summer, the white owners of Somerset Beach on the Virginia shore wined and dined Jefferson and his "party of colored capitalists" aboard their yacht *Bartholdt* during an inspection of the property, which Jefferson purchased. Such publicized accounts of Jefferson's exploits enhanced his status as a black power broker who enjoyed unprecedented connections with white capital. As one article described it, "When it was noised about that Lewis Jefferson was in the market, the agents of the mortgaged written land and river companies awoke as if by magic. The cloak of race proscription was put aside and everybody was looking for the dollar."[42]

The city's black newspapers worked tirelessly to drum up support for the Freedman's corporation and cast aspersions on its white competition. In the summer of 1903, a local social column claimed "The Jane Moseley is now the most popular excursion steamer on the Potomac," that "the River Queen is losing money," and "the Jane Moseley has outstripped all competitors." The following summer, the *Washington Bee* called for "a taboo [to be] placed on the River Queen by self-respecting colored people."[43]

It quickly became apparent, though, that the *Jane Moseley* was anything but a first-class investment. To scuttle the venture before it began, white steamboat operators instructed the Seventh Street wharf to refuse to allow the *Jane Moseley* docking privileges, forcing Jefferson to purchase a 135-foot wharf near O and Water streets, which the District subsequently condemned. (In response, Jefferson apparently dipped into his savings and paid for the $5,000 improvements deemed necessary to meet the District's code.)

Like its predecessors, the Freedman's Transportation, Land, and Improvement Company exemplified the precarious arrangements that grew out of turn-of-the-century black capitalists' lofty ambitions and glaring lack of credit or capital. The boat's costs of operation and exorbitant monthly loan repayments, not to mention competition from white-owned vessels, quickly drained the company of capital and optimism. After much fanfare, repairs forced the *Jane Moseley* to miss the first months of the 1902 summer season, leaving gossip columnists to wonder, "When will the steamer . . . appear upon the pellucid waters of the Potomac."[44] Continually plagued by mechanical problems, the *Jane Moseley* earned a reputation as unreliable, a fatal designation in an industry notorious for engine explosions (sometimes resulting in deaths of passengers) and mechanical failures that often left passengers stranded for hours (sometimes overnight) on the water.[45] As late as June 15, the boat had not enjoyed any business on the water, and lacking any cash on hand, Jefferson fell hopelessly behind on repayments. Despite a brisk July, business remained spotty. In August, at the height of the summer season, the *Jane Moseley* went two weeks without a single charter, before recovering later that month with two weeks of two to three trips daily "crowded with jolly excursionists." Despite such sales, by the end of summer the company had fallen three months behind on repayment of the loan, and Jefferson claimed he was buying additional stock in the company to prevent the boat's seizure and pay the salaries of the crew.[46]

As the promise of quick returns on their initial investments gave way to Jefferson's professions of the company's insolvency, the company's minority stockholders grew wary of his management style and suspicious of his business practices. Rumors circulated that Jefferson was in league with the boat's creditors (his former employers and business partners) and was cooking the books to make the boat appear unprofitable. His calls for contributions to meet the August $2,000 repayment generated a paltry $200. Several unsuccessful attempts were made by the minority stockholders to oust Jefferson from the board's presidency and assume control of the boat's operations. While Jefferson professed his determination to keep the *Jane Moseley* afloat and the public's dream of a black-owned boat on the water alive, the company slid toward bankruptcy, and his fellow investors suspected he was partner to a scheme to defraud them of their investments. In August 1903, with the Freedman's company unable to meet its payments, the Jane Moseley Steamboat Company seized the boat and appointed Jefferson as its manager.

The minority shareholders did not go down without a fight. Suspicious of the "manner in which the affairs of the boat were being conducted," in September 1903 the Freedman's Transportation, Land, and Improvement Company's minority stockholders filed a bill in equity against Jefferson and the Jane Moseley Steamboat Company, asking for an injunction to prevent the vessel's return to Baltimore, and the appointment of a receiver to provide more time to make payments. In court filings, they alleged that Jefferson "disbursed the funds of the new company without rendering a true and just account thereof," that he misled the creditor into believing that the company could not meet its payments, and that his resumption of duties as manager upon the boat's seizure suggested a conflict of interest. The minority shareholders were clearly motivated by a desire to recoup what they felt were misappropriated investments, asking the court to either allow more time to make payments or have the boat sold at a public sale and the profits disbursed to the shareholders. The court rejected the petition, Jefferson retained management of the boat, and the Baltimore company resumed ownership. The following spring, the investors sued Jefferson for refusing to submit to an accounting and the Jane Moseley company to recover their $3,000 investment.[47]

During the legal battle over the *Jane Moseley*, Jefferson granted lengthy interviews to the *Colored American*, in which he reiterated his trustworthiness, publicly agreed to submit his accounts to audit by any auditor of repute or the District courts (though it is unclear if he did so), and appealed to fellow blacks' sense of racial pride. He denied any intention of defrauding his investors and reiterated his "earnest desire for our company and our race to try and save the boat as this business can successfully be carried on by our people and make both pleasure and money for our people."[48]

His publicity campaign paid off. While many investors parted with Jefferson penniless and embittered, Jefferson enjoyed and quite purposely cultivated a beloved status among the poor families of the city's Southwest. He was active in supporting the Colored Social Settlement and served on the board of Southwest Citizens' Neighborhood Improvement Association, a chief arena of political activity in a city where all citizens lacked the franchise.[49] He routinely tendered free boat rides to charitable organizations and to thousands of the city's impoverished black children. When his business seemed destined to go under, Jefferson persuaded over eighty churches in the city to invest in the boat and buy it back from the Jane Moseley Steamboat Company. By June 1904 the *Jane Moseley* was again plying the river as the city's only black-owned pleasure boat. The success of the *Jane Moseley* became seen as a gauge of the power of consumer politics. One article proudly noted that, "with almost unanimous consent the steamboats owned by white men in this city were tabooed," and cited the pleasure boat industry as evidence that "we can never hope to succeed in our endeavor for the uplift or our race until we are united in effort and purpose. Pulling this and that way, each going the way he thinks best with no regard to the other will never give us a standing where we need a standing most."[50]

For Jefferson, though, the rhetoric of race loyalty, while a useful slogan and rallying cry in times of need, belied his collaboration with white capital in stabilizing and growing his leisure and amusement enterprises. In the spring of 1905, Jefferson dissolved the Freedman's Transportation, Land, and Improvement Company, purchased the *Jane Moseley* outright, and began selling stock in a new corporation, the Independent Steamboat and Barge Company, a joint partnership with a white Jewish investor, Samuel Bensinger. With this enhanced capital stock, Jefferson and Bensinger went in the market for a second, smaller steamer and a riverside property suitable for the development of a large-scale black amusement park and resort. Jefferson and Bensinger settled on 240 acres of riverfront property in Prince George's County on the Notley Hall grounds, purchased for $50,000. To ferry guests on this short, ten-mile journey, they bought the smaller, swifter *River Queen* from the Mount Vernon and Marshall Hall Steamboat Company.

That summer, Jefferson opened Washington Park to much fanfare. Dubbed the "Coney Island of the Colored Americans," Washington Park was outfitted with "7,000 lights, [a] carousel, double-decker, with music attachments; a 5 and 10-cent theater; a penny arcadium; moving pictures; shooting gallery; a dairy lunch depot and buffet; dancing pavilion; [and] pool and billiard hall." Jefferson and Bensinger sold lots on the property for the construction of summer cottages. And they worked to ensure that order would reign on the park's grounds. To that end, they hired a black security officer to defuse tensions and prevent outbreaks of violence; Jefferson, as one observer commented, "conduct[ed his park] and boats with an iron hand." Jefferson became a master at converting the sting of prejudice into profit. "Before the construction of Washington Park," he reminded black Washingtonians, "absolutely no place of recreation was afforded the people of our race, and I proudly point to the fact that I have fulfilled the demands of the people in every respect. . . . By perseverance and enormous cash outlay I have done this, and now I ask you to show me that I have your hearty support by calling at once and making charters for the coming season." "It is time for us to rally," Jefferson later implored black Washingtonians. "In union there is strength, and always will be. We can only be recognized as a power and a people by pulling together. Great results will follow, I am sure. It is time for the colored people to show their white brothers that they are a race." In advertisements, Jefferson appealed to African Americans' sense of dignity and past humiliations, while his friends in the city's black newspapers equated blacks' continuing patronage of white-owned boats and resorts with racial treason. "There is no Jim Crow entrance and you are not subject to the humiliation of a practical quarantine," one advertisement read. "If the colored men and women of this city are inclined to patronize nearby resorts," another asked, "why not patronize one conducted by a member of their own race, rather than one conducted by a white man, a jim crow arrangement . . . with its separate wharf"?[51] The structure and strategy Jefferson and Bensinger deployed paralleled those used by fledgling all-black towns, which appealed to their targeted audience's racial chauvinism and grievances over past discrimination, and which invariably accentuated its black ownership while purposely obscuring the influence of white capital investment. Jefferson's name was prominently displayed in advertisements for Washington Park in black newspapers, while conspicuously absent was any mention of Bensinger. (Conversely, Bensinger served as the company's spokesman in correspondence with white-owned newspapers.)[52]

As a gathering place, Washington Park became a microcosm of the shifting dynamics of race, class, and color in the city and the nation. During its initial years, Washington Park attracted large and diverse crowds of the city's black population. Mary Church Terrell visited with her children during the park's opening summer. "The park," she wrote in her diary, "is well equipped with everything lending to amuse the people. The children enjoyed the Merry Go Rounds immensely. By the way it is the finest pier I have ever seen anywhere." In 1908, Booker T. Washington delivered the keynote address at the annual Frederick Douglass Memorial Day celebration held there, which attracted a crowd of many of the city's "distinguished men," including Judge Robert H. Terrell, assistant superintendent of schools Roscoe Conkling Bruce, P. B. S. Pinchback, and Charles R. Douglass. Jefferson hosted "testimonial excursions" to benefit individuals in need, at which local community leaders gave speeches in the park's pavilion. In 1909, Associated Charities, whose executive director, Charles Weller, penned the exposé of alley life, *Neglected Neighbors*, began hosting a summer camp there for poor black mothers and children. Campers followed highly regimented schedules, rising at 6 A.M. for a 6:45 assembly, followed by dips in the river, hikes around the property, and supervised play "along scientific lines." Jefferson used his resort to further ingratiate himself to Southwest D.C. Each summer he brought countless numbers of black children from the city's desperately poor neighborhoods to Washington Park, often providing free rides for up to fifteen hundred schoolchildren aboard one of his steamers down to the park for an afternoon.[53]

Jefferson's success compelled his white competitors to scrutinize the dynamics of black business activity and community formation more closely. Unnamed competitors enlisted Jefferson's former, disgruntled associates to cast aspersions on the clientele found on board his boats and resorts within the black community, tie his accommodations to the city's most disreputable elements, and steer black excursion parties to his white competitors. Vicious rumors spread that the *River Queen* "has been made at different times, a cock pit, and a prize ring," and that the park was no more than "a dumping ground for the roughs and riff-raff of Washington." One embittered former associate notified Maryland authorities of violence and debauchery at Washington Park so as to ensure police harassment of guests, while another, Jefferson claimed, approached Bensinger and attempted to "wean him away from me by saying something particularly derogatory to the women of our race." Since he began his operations, Jefferson claimed to have "been the butt of malicious and libelous stories from the tongue of one who in his eagerness to gain the colored man's favor, likewise his money, has left all scruples behind."[54]

Some of these charges were not without merit. On some occasions, as the *Jane Moseley* floated out of District waters, blood bespattered the deck, games of poker and "sweat" commenced, and roulette wheels were set in motion. Like many of his contemporaries, and like any good businessman engaged in the business of pleasure, Jefferson hosted boxing matches, operated gambling tables, and dispensed alcohol on board. "It was wide open" on the *Jane Moseley*, one guest aboard a 1908 trip down the river reported. "Everybody could choose between seeing the fights . . . or trying their mettle against the little god of chance." But in the context of the Jim Crow city, even the "slightest semblance of unruliness" became fodder for segregationists and proof of blacks' inborn degeneracy and criminality, stigmas that the city's black elite and aspiring were anxious to distance themselves from. In the summer of 1909, a local black chapter of the Masons shunned Jefferson's steamboats and resort in favor of segregated facilities aboard a white-owned steamer and Jim Crow service at River View.[55]

The decision earned them a stinging rebuke. The *Washington Bee* waged a sustained public campaign against African Americans who failed to support this and other black-owned enterprises. "Colored men and women, who have an ounce of self-respect and race interest," one article charged, "should show their disgust for the managers of the proposed Masonic outing by refusing to go." "The so-called 'big Negroes,' the big churches, the big societies, and other institutions," the *Bee* charged, "have no regard or respect for those who have toiled and worked for years to give them pleasure and comfort," and instead "went over to the enemy the moment the white people's leavings were thrown to them." "The man who cries 'wolf' should himself be watched and chained, because he is more dangerous to the community than any other animal. The so-called intelligent Negro is the first to cry out against 'Jim Crowism,' and the first to 'Jim Crow' his own race and discriminate against himself." By the summer of 1910, when Jefferson stood alone as the only proprietor of Negro excursions on the Potomac, the *Bee* chuckled, "The many secret and benevolent organizations that attempted to boycott [Jefferson] last year and patronize one that didn't care a penny for the colored people, find themselves eating crow this year." But, they added, "If there had been a 'jim crow' opposition excursion company, no doubt the colored people would have given it the same support they gave the one last summer."[56]

After having invested a substantial portion of his wealth in building a Coney Island for black Washingtonians on the Potomac, Lewis Jefferson struggled, throughout the 1910s, to keep his business interests afloat. In the spring of 1911, Bensinger sold his shares and withdrew from the partnership, leaving Jefferson as the majority owner and president of the company. Black Washingtonians hailed the move as a signal of black economic empowerment. A headline in the *Washington Bee* read, "Col. Lewis Jefferson Now in Charge—The Colored People Have Purchased the Entire Interest of Mr. Bensinger." But it seems unlikely that Jefferson welcomed the move. By then, he had, by his own and others' account, "lost thousands of dollars in his efforts to give his people boats to run upon the Potomac River for the[ir] pleasure." Following Bensinger's withdrawal, more of Jefferson's fortune sank to the bottom of the Potomac. Later that summer, the *River Queen* caught fire and was later dismantled and its machinery and parts sold. The following summer, Jefferson acquired the *Angler.* After the District Excise Board denied him a license to sell liquor on board the *Angler*, the harbor patrol charged him with operating a bar and serving intoxicating beverages during a trip to and from Washington Park on August 11, 1912, and imposed a fine of $250. Such minor setbacks paled in comparison to the fire that destroyed all of the structure and the entire grounds of Washington Park in February 1913. The fire, which Bensinger (who remained Jefferson's public spokesman with the white press) characterized as of an "incendiary origin," caused $30,000 worth of damage to the property, which was uninsured.[57]

An exceptional achievement upon its founding, following the fire Washington Park joined a growing list of black beach resort ventures across the country that had generated much attention and considerable financial investment, but that had ultimately succumbed to official resistance, internal dissension, or an act of terrorism in the 1910s and 1920s. In the spring of 1926, outside of Roanoke, Virginia, a group of black investors converted a swimming hole at Kessler's Mill into a "colored bathing beach." "Electric lights, lockers, and every convenience had been installed," the local newspaper reported. "Brilliant autumn foliage spreads in every direction. Nature had done her part in making this exclusive lake for colored bathers a place of charm." Located upstream from Lakeside, a popular white bathing resort, the "colored bathing beach" aroused considerable opposition from area whites. In the weeks leading up to the grand opening, the Roanoke County Board of Supervisors went "on record as regretting and opposing the use of said property for the purpose named, unless and until proper restrictions and safe guards were thrown around it for the protection of the neighborhood and the public." "Considerable objection against such use of the dam had repeatedly been expressed by farmers of the community and owners of a nearby pleasure resort, whose pool is fed by water coming over the dam," the black newspaper the *Norfolk Journal and Guide* reported. On May 26, 1926, three days before its scheduled opening, an anonymous band of assailants, suspected to be members of the local Ku Klux Klan, bombed the dam and vandalized the newly built facilities. "Sledgehammer tactics," the *Roanoke Times* reported, "apparently were used on the light plant and the lockers, where privacy was abundant for the colored physique. . . . An adult tornado would have been no less effective." A similar fate befell the Pine Crest Inn, another ill-fated attempt to open a black waterside pleasure resort in the Roanoke area. The inn, which "command[ed] a magnificent view of the mountains, valleys, orchards, and pinewoods," had been owned by whites and had, over the years, attracted a "select following," before diminishing sales compelled the owners to sell the grounds to a group of black businessmen, who refurbished and reopened it as a "Negro amusement center." But in September 1926, just months after the explosion at Kessler's Mill, the Pine Crest Inn was reduced to a "conglomeration of ashes" after a midnight assault. Neither the beach at Kessler's Mill nor the Pine Crest Inn was rebuilt.[58]

In 1925, Hal H. Clark, a white lawyer and owner of a seven-acre stretch of undeveloped property facing the Pacific Ocean in Huntington Beach, California, entered into an agreement with a group of African American investors from Los Angeles, headed by E. Burton Ceruti, a West Indian–born civil rights attorney, for the construction of an exclusive seaside resort for the West Coast's burgeoning black elite. Under the terms of the agreement, the newly incorporated Pacific Beach Club (with Ceruti serving as president) agreed to pay Clark $10,000 cash through $100 subscriptions. Clark, in turn, agreed to invest $150,000 of his own capital in buildings and improvements and would receive 86 percent of net profits from the resort during its first ten years of operation. In seeking stockholders, the Pacific Beach Club cast the ambitious venture as the "Last Chance for Our Race to Secure Beach Frontage Near Los Angeles." Articles and advertisements in the African American–owned *California Eagle* asked readers, "What will the little ones who do not hold the future in their hands, think of the present generation should they fail to take out membership and preserve a Southern California Beach for their use and future generations?" The Pacific Beach Club quickly raised $10,000 in subscriptions, and construction began in the summer of 1925. Upon completion, the resort would bear testament to the most lavish and ostentatious strivings of "the race." Plans called for a bathhouse that could accommodate one thousand men and six hundred women; a ballroom and pavilion that could fit two thousand on the floor at any given time; a clubhouse with reading rooms, billiard rooms, smoking parlors, sun parlors, and a theatrical stage; a restaurant capable of seating seven hundred diners; a small grocery store, drugstore, and concession stand; two hundred cottages; and a "board walk patterned after those found at Atlantic City." All buildings were to be finished with white stucco; the entire resort was to be surrounded by a white stucco fence. One reporter called it "the most pretentious amusement resort ever projected by members of the Race." A 1925 Labor Day event on the uncompleted grounds, which drew over ten thousand guests and jammed the coast with over two thousand automobiles, testified to black Angelenos' interest in the project's completion.[59]

As word of the project leaked out in the spring of 1925, neighboring white residents raised immediate objections. The Huntington Beach and Newport Beach chambers of commerce, along with other civic organizations, passed resolutions expressing their strong disapproval of the project. A citizens group formed and attempted to persuade the Orange County Board of Supervisors to condemn the property and turn it into a public (that is, for whites only) park. At every turn in the construction process, the Pacific Beach Club encountered resistance. The Pacific Electric Railway Company refused to grant the club a right of way across the tracks that ran along the resort's inland border. The first contractor, Charles E. Rowe of Long Beach, unexpectedly quit in the middle of the construction. Weeks before the grand opening, slated for Abraham Lincoln's birthday on February 12, 1926, a blaze tore through the unfinished structures and left the resort in ruins. The night watchman, A. R. Sneed, who testified that he witnessed two white males leap into an automobile and speed off moments before the buildings erupted in flames, was not surprised. "I thought she'd burn up, but I thought they'd start her with a bomb. . . . A bomb is what I've been expecting."[60]

Following the arson attack, Orange County officials stepped up their efforts to condemn the property, while Pacific Beach Club investors began to scrutinize Clark's motives and intents. Immediately following the fire, the Orange County Board of Supervisors announced plans to relaunch its "condemnation campaign . . . with new vigor, now that the removal of the buildings has made condemnation cheaper." (The timing of this announcement, and the rationale behind it, confirmed many black investors' suspicions that public officials orchestrated the arson attack.) After the fire, the Pacific Beach Club also learned that Clark, instead of investing his own capital in building construction (as stipulated in the contract), had taken out a $19,000 mortgage. For Ceruti and fellow investors, their only option to stave off foreclosure was to raise $25,000 to cover the mortgage plus interest; if they succeeded, the Pacific Beach Club would gain immediate title to the property through Clark's default on the terms and agreements in the original lease. For Clark (not to mention anxious white citizens and public officials dedicated to scuttling the project), this seemed like a very real possibility, especially as Ceruti launched a national campaign to solicit contributions to save the project. Clark, in turn, worked to stir up dissension among the Pacific Beach Club shareholders by appealing to their underlying fears of future attacks on the property and eventual loss of investment, offering dissatisfied investors a return of money invested plus 10 percent interest. While a core group of investors remained determined to resist any of Clark's overtures, one by one investors began to cash out, and efforts to revive the stillborn Pacific Beach Club came to naught. Following the collapse of the Pacific Beach Club, a black reporter in Los Angeles commented that the $1 million whites-only clubhouse and surrounding structures slated for construction on the grounds would "stand forever as monuments to the increduality [sic] of the Black American to progressive leadership."[61]

Assaults on privately owned, black-oriented beach resorts in various sections of the country reflected the extent to which the rise of a distinct summertime leisure culture—and leisure-based land development—along coastlines and even interior bodies of water in the 1920s fundamentally reshaped the difference black land ownership and black economic initiative (indeed, race itself) made. For some participants in the increasingly crowded waterfront real estate market, racial segregation was a means of market stability and an amenity provided to white customers. For others, both black and white, black exclusion from commercial waterfront resorts created a niche market in pleasure boats and resorts catering exclusively to black Americans. While physically separate on the water and on land, the fleets of boats and pieces of real estate that constituted these niche markets did not, despite the hopes of many investors and desires of pleasure seekers, signal the flowering of a black summertime culture and economy that existed apart from and in defiance of Jim Crow in early twentieth-century America. Rather, they often came to reflect the new forms of economic predation and exploitation that took shape in racialized consumer markets. As their rights under the law dwindled and access to credit remained scarce, African Americans who sought to provide their people with places of retreat became easy prey for predatory lenders and remained continuously vulnerable to the incendiary actions of white competitors and neighboring waterfront property owners who, following the logic of the market, understood black leisure space only in negative terms. The insidious power of Jim Crow was perhaps most in evidence, though, in those instances when corporate ventures founded upon high-minded, civic ideals ended in dissension and acrimony, with executives forced, almost by necessity, to exploit their own people in order to keep the dream of cultural and economic independence alive, leaving behind a trail of embittered investors bilked of their savings and turning an expectant black pleasure-seeking public into hardened skeptics.

Writing in the early 1930s, the black Washington commentator H. A. Clark warned, "Many colored leaders who are advocating racial cooperation and the establishment of businesses, should not be surprised when the rank and file fails to respond . . . in view of the fact that among the numerous and great financial losses were three deep-water steamboats . . . namely, George Leary, Jane Moseley, and Lady of the Lake." Indeed, decades after the closing of Jefferson's amusement park and the migration of pleasure seekers from the river to the city's burgeoning commercial and entertainment districts, many black Washingtonians had come to remember the heyday of excursion boating on the Potomac as more a cautionary tale for future black investors than a time of carefree, innocent amusement.[62]

2

A SANCTUARY BY THE SEA

His timing, they said, could not have been better. In the three years since Methodist bishop Robert E. Jones purchased a venerable seaside mansion once owned by the nephew of former president Andrew Jackson along with 300 acres of swampy, overgrown coastal property near Waveland, Mississippi, for $6,000, and secured a long-term lease on an adjoining 320 acres, in the spring of 1923, "This most attractive section of the Gulf Coast," a church organ boasted, "has greatly enhanced in value," to the tune of ten times its purchase price. There, Jones founded the Gulfside Chautauqua Association and began work on developing the nation's first noncommercial, religious resort for the "Negro race." "With his characteristic interest and foresight," Jones successfully "secured for the Negroes of the M. E. Church and others, a location on the Gulf coast as near as possible to New Orleans, and beyond the marshes on land high and dry with a beach second to none in all this country for both summer and winter resorting." And he did so, many noted, at a critical moment in the history of the race and the Methodist Church, when the rise of vacationing and pleasure travel sent coastal land values soaring and, not coincidentally, hardened racial barriers along once informal and negotiable shorelines, and when the promise of a racially egalitarian church gave way to white unification and ostracism of blacks. "Coming, as it does, at the psychological moment in our race life when we are being hounded and driven from God's great seashores everywhere," Jones, one commentator noted, "has demonstrated the fact that he is a prophet, a seer."

And a savvy investor. Jones's remarkable purchase of hundreds of acres of coastal property came on the eve of a major campaign for coastal development and the marketing of the region as an "American Riviera," spearheaded by New Orleans and Chicago capitalists and made possible by transportation and infrastructure development. Within a few years, the thought of African Americans acquiring six hundred acres of coastal property in Hancock County would have seemed virtually impossible. "There seems to be no doubt," J. Beverly Shaw, president of Haven Teachers College in Meridian, Mississippi, concluded, "that Bishop Jones was divinely led in the purchase, organization, and establishment of this training camp. So great has been the enhancement of property values on the Gulf Coast . . . that if Gulfside were not already in possession of our group its purchase would be beyond our wildest dreams." "Somehow the Negro has become a kind of Lucky Child of Destiny amid the vast development along the Mississippi Gulf Coast," a promotional piece read. "Through the guiding hand of Bishop R. E. Jones . . . the Negro is in possession of, without doubt, one of the finest tracts of beach property to be found on the entire Gulf Coast." "The summer resort of the former master," one piece proclaimed in reference to the Jackson House, "[has] now become the summer resort of the former slave."

But in contrast to commercial enterprises, this seaside resort "was not born in the hope of greed or personal gain." Instead, "the Gulfside Idea," as it came to be known, was grounded in the notion, articulated by future president Herbert Hoover and later repeated in organizational literature, that the future of civilization "is not going to depend upon what we do when we work, so much as what we do in our time off." For "over-worked teachers, ministers, doctors" and other middle- and upper-class black professionals, Gulfside sought to provide "an oasis in the otherwise drab existence of the Negro"; and for the "working classes" it offered a place where they "may spend their leisure time under safeguard of a wholesome environment," away from the temptations of the city or the tediousness of the farm. At Gulfside, a forsaken race would find "renewed vigor and life and cheer," and the importance of "recreation . . . in the scheme of racial uplift" would be demonstrated.[1]

Its founder and directors would also learn to navigate a changing coastal economy in which growth and prosperity became increasing tied to the physical containment of black populations and scripted public performances of race. Holding on to the land required them not only to outwardly play by white coastal capitalists' rules, but also to join with their white neighbors in working to discipline a dynamic, volatile coastline regularly subject to destructive storms and resistant to human attempts to fortify and develop. Domesticating the shore became, for this band of black ministers, congregants, campers, and visitors, synonymous with securing a fragile partnership with their white neighbors and fostering a degree of racial amity and "cooperation" necessary for their own survival. As they worked to build a sanctuary for race and religious leaders, a beacon of hope for the tired and weary, and a place of practical training and reform for the wayward, the project of coastal development became vested with a profoundly religious and spiritual dimension.

Settled by Spanish and French explorers, Mississippi's coast was, until the early 1800s, a sparsely populated land of big estates under the control of absentee landowners. Along the shore, stretches of grassy dunes were interrupted by numbers of freshwater inlets that fed into the Gulf. Oak and cypress trees grew along the high-water line. The shore had been shaped by and adapted to withstand the Gulf of Mexico's furies, retreating and replenishing and assuming new configurations with each season. The French government had encouraged settlement of New Orleans through doling out massive land grants along the coast, where settlers established large plantations worked by slaves while enjoying a life of leisure in the city. Following the American Revolution, numbers of British loyalists fled from their homes in South Carolina and Georgia and settled along the sparsely populated coast (now under Spanish rule), where they attempted, without much success, to introduce the highly sought-after strand of long-staple cotton that grew so prodigiously on the Sea Islands they came from.

As ambitious white settlers poured into the Deep South and extended the cotton kingdom west, hopes of replicating a plantation economy on the Gulf Coast were tempered by encounters with the area's enslaved and free black populations. Writing of his visit to the town of Pass Christian in the 1850s, William Peas observed a "colored population" unlike anything he had previously encountered. "They behave themselves with great decorum, and are treated with much courtesy by the whites. They are allowed to pass on without sneer or reflection, and we have frequently observed the 'white folks,' as they pass by in numbers, give them the sidewalk."[2] These curious social relations both reflected and were a product of the strange, fluid, and untamed nature of the land itself. Inland waterways snaked through the swampy fields that led down to the coast, and a line of long, narrow barrier islands ten miles offshore kept the waters of the Mississippi Sound warm, tranquil, and muddy, while the obstacles facing those who wished to navigate their way to the coast kept the region isolated and afforded its inhabitants a measure of autonomy unavailable elsewhere. (See Map 4.)

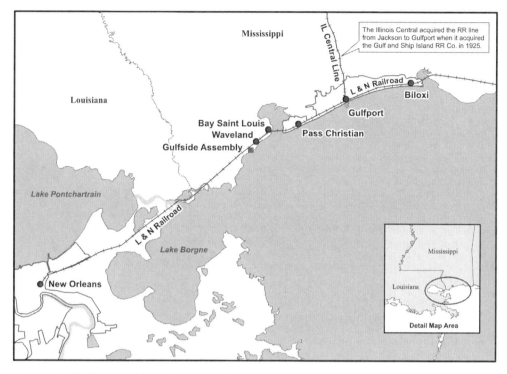

The Illinois Central acquired the RR line from Jackson to Gulfport when it acquired the Gulf and Ship Island RR Co. in 1925.

Map 4. Gulfside Assembly and surroundings, ca. 1923

By the early 1800s the coast had become home to a substantial and varied population of free persons of color, many of whom owned substantial portions of the rugged and mobile coastline. Typical among coastal land transactions was the passage of the lands that later became the town of Pass Christian from the widow of a French settler to her freed slaves. On a small peninsula that separates the Gulf from St. Louis Bay, New Orleanian Julia de la Brosse owned a small cattle farm operated by slaves from the 1740s to her death in 1800. In her will, de la Brosse deeded 680 acres of her 14,500-acre tract to her former slaves Charles and Madelon Asmard and their children, who farmed the land, harvested the Gulf's bounty, and eventually acquired their own team of slaves.

But while the coast's remoteness afforded this and other free persons of color a measure of landed independence, it also proved an attractive draw to the growing numbers of wealthy families from the neighboring city of New Orleans. By the 1820s, as New Orleans's population grew, persons of means fled from the city and its annual yellow fever epidemics and began constructing summer cottages on the coast, where mild climate and balmy breezes offered a stark contrast to the oppressive humidity and fetid air that wafted in the summer through the streets of New Orleans, a place where rates of death and disease rose with the temperature. As the ties that bound the Gulf Coast to New Orleans tightened, the ability of free families of color to hold on to their coastal lands began to unravel. One person who has examined land records for Hancock County (one of Mississippi's three coastal counties and the one located closest to New Orleans) during these years noted the emergence of several new players in the region's real estate market, as well as the rapid pace of acquisition and resale of beachfront lots. Many of these players were homegrown. Others came from out of town. In 1836, New Jersey lawyer and budding developer John Henderson, along with partners David Hughes and Charles Shipman, purchased for $20,000 some 15,500 acres on the same peninsula that was home to the Asmards. There they set out to develop what came to be known as Pass Christian into a summer community for wealthy planters and traders in New Orleans and the surrounding region. By the 1840s, several mansions, a string of summer cottages, and a few swanky hotels lined the town's coastline.[3] Between 1830 and 1850, the town's population tripled. In 1849 the region's first yacht club was organized there.[4]

Located in the center of the town's boundaries, the Charlot tract (as the Asmard lands were known) stood in the pathway of coastal development, and the free persons of color claiming ownership of it became a target of speculators and developers. Throughout his life, Charles Asmard successfully resisted attempts to wrest his property away. Following his death, however, Asmard's children steadily sold off their land claims, and today what was once the Charlot family tract occupies the center of Pass Christian's beachfront downtown district.[5]

Almost two centuries later, African Americans living along the Mississippi Gulf Coast still speak of the unequal transaction that give rise to Pass Christian as a harbinger of things that were to come:

> *Herman Melvin Cappie:* That entire [town of] Pass Christian at
>   one time was owned by blacks, the Charlot family.
> *Ruth Irene Cappie:* That family owned so much of the beachfront.
>   You know how white people take away the blacks' land? . . .
>   They sold it to them but, you know, they didn't get anything.[6]

In the decades following emancipation, coastal land values appreciated, aided by the completion of a railroad line linking New Orleans to the coast in 1869. Jefferson Davis lived out his final days at his seaside cottage Beauvoir on the Mississippi coast. Following his death in 1889, Beauvoir became a retreat for Confederate veterans. In 1890, New Orleans hotel operator Annie Allen purchased a home in Bay St. Louis and opened a "tourist court," with seaside gazebos that could accommodate up to one hundred guests. In 1896 the coast became connected to the state's interior with the completion of the Gulf and Ship Island Railroad Line from Jackson to Gulfport. By the turn of the twentieth century, the popular Montross Hotel in Bay St. Louis attracted people of "wealth and fashion from Memphis, Chicago, [and] Minneapolis. . . . Full dress dinners and elegant card parties were held, enlivened by Negro cakewalks and spirituals." During his presidency, Woodrow Wilson enjoyed a seventeen-day vacation at Beaulieu, an antebellum mansion in Pass Christian, later dubbed the "Dixie White House." By 1920 an estimated thirty millionaires, mostly from New Orleans, owned summer homes along the coast, ranging in value from $15,000 to $100,000.[7]

Steadily pushing blacks back from the sea became fundamental to the region's growing reputation as a fashionable vacation destination. One by one, white owners of coastal property fell in line and became agents in the establishment of a firm and impenetrable residential color line. After dividing his coastal landholdings into individual lots for sale to second-home buyers, Thomas Savage, a white minister from Michigan, instructed his local real estate agent, George P. Brandt, not to sell any lands fronting the Gulf to black buyers. "No Negroes on back street for me. Those lots north of the railroad might be sold to the negroes but nothing south of it. . . . People nowadays want all the luxuries especially when 'resorting' and at Boarding houses."[8] Among those luxuries were the absence of blacks as neighbors and their presence as servants and entertainers.

Blacks' desire to live where they pleased was just one of the threats to white seasonal and year-round residents' interests. Another threat to those interests was the coast itself. As the number of beachfront homes and hotels grew, the migratory shoreline turned from protector to nuisance. With each passing year, the shore moved in accordance with the inscrutable laws of coastal ecologies, consuming newly built docks, submerging landscaped yards, eroding the shell-covered Beach Drive, making a mockery of real estate boundaries, and rendering coastal property values highly unpredictable and large-scale development unfeasible. A massive hurricane that struck the coast in 1915 made mincemeat of a popular resort built on the mercurial sands of one of the Mississippi Sound's barrier islands, submerging the entire island and serving as a warning to those who hoped to halt the centuries-old movement of land and sea. But following each destructive storm, residents and public officials only grew more determined to tame the menace of the sea and minimize nature's liabilities.

Robert E. Jones was born in 1872 in Greensboro, North Carolina, to parents whose families' free status stretched back several generations and whose family trees contained more than a few white branches. "I'm black out of choice," Jones remarked to inquirers, sometimes in response to a conductor's request that he remove himself from the Jim Crow section of a train. As photos of him make abundantly clear, even the most suspicious eye would have been hard-pressed to identify evidence of Jones's African ancestry. Jones's racial ambiguity contributed to his tortured understanding of race. While, as a Methodist minister, he employed his ambiguity to secure gains for his congregants, and while he implicitly understood the social constructedness of race, Jones was also an outspoken opponent of social integration (which he distinguished from being "sociable"), harbored a deep distrust of the white "race" that belied his public professions of good faith and goodwill, and purposefully married a darker-skinned woman so that his children could, in his words, "know who they were."[9]

Jones ascended through the ranks of a Christian denomination whose own racial history was equally fraught with tension and contradiction. In 1845, southern Methodists split off from their northern counterparts over the issue of slavery. After emancipation, formerly enslaved Methodists fled these sanctuaries of white supremacy and formed independent African Methodist Episcopal churches. Between 1860 and 1865, two-thirds of all black members of the Methodist Church in southern states left their former masters' churches and formed AME congregations.[10] Those who remained were pushed into the segregated Colored Methodist Episcopal Church. Meanwhile, northern Methodist (ME Church) missionaries flocked to the war-torn region, seeking to compete with the AME and CME for the souls of newly freed slaves. In contrast to AME churches, which offered blacks total independence from white influence, the ME Church sought to win converts through its promise of equal standing in a racially egalitarian church.

As he reiterated throughout his life, Jones saw the ME Church as a bridge between two divided and increasingly hostile worlds, a forum for racial understanding, and a venue where the best of both races could come to understand each other better. While separate black churches matured and increasingly attracted black southerners away from the ME Church, Jones remained steadfast in the belief that "both separation by choice . . . and segregation by force . . . necessitated resistance if there was to be any hope for integration in either church or society." At eighteen, Jones enrolled in Bennett College, in Greensboro, North Carolina, one of the many Methodist normal schools founded in 1870s to educate freed slaves. Following graduation from Bennett in 1895, he enrolled in Gammon Theological Seminary in Atlanta, the leading seminary for black Methodists, and embarked on a career in the ministry. After graduating from Gammon in 1897, he began work at the *Southwestern Christian Advocate*, located in the ME Church's southern stronghold, New Orleans. In 1904 he was promoted to the editor's desk, a position he would hold for the next sixteen years.[11] The organ of black Methodism, the *Southwestern* weighed in on critical issues facing both the church and African Americans in New Orleans and the Gulf states.[12] In its pages, Jones focused on public health and practical education, stressed respectable conduct in public, and warned fellow blacks of the dangers of violent retaliation against white racism.[13] At the same time, Jones worked to extend social services and charitable organizations into black neighborhoods. He was instrumental in the formation of the city's first Colored YMCA, and moved the church's Bureau of Negro Work to address the environmental conditions of black neighborhoods that, in his estimation, corrupted black youth and reinforced racial inequality. By 1916 the *Crisis* called Jones a leader of "every big race movement in New Orleans for the past ten years."[14]

In 1920 Jones was appointed as the first stateside African American bishop in the history of the Methodist Church, serving the black congregations of New Orleans and the Gulf South, known as the Southwestern District. His election—on a separate ballot, his duties limited to black Methodist congregations—was emblematic of the church's tortured capitulation to Jim Crow and racialization of ecclesiastical governance in the first half of the twentieth century. Jones, though, never hesitated to work within and seek to influence an institution that most other blacks had judged as beyond redemption. That same year, he became one of two founding black members of the Committee on Interracial Cooperation, a comparatively racially moderate organization of predominantly white southerners dedicated to racial peace within a Jim Crow framework. Inherently paternalistic, the CIC's white leadership was greeted with skepticism by even the most conservative black southerners and denounced as a charade, at best, and a scheme to reinforce blacks' subordination, at worst. But Jones did not hesitate in working with the CIC, and throughout his career used his influence with southern white moderates and northern philanthropists to garner financial support and protection for black educational, recreational, and medical institutions.[15]

During his years in New Orleans, Jones spoke to friends and colleagues of his desire for "some spot on the shores of God's great Gulf of Mexico where his people could enjoy its refreshing waters unmolested and unafraid."[16] Jones had a Chautauqua-style resort in mind. Begun in upstate New York in 1874 and quickly sweeping across the United States over the next several decades, Chautauquas consisted of several days of lectures, plays and performances, instructional courses, games and exercise, and other forms of "productive" play conducted outdoors in a primitive campground setting. Participants were expected to follow a regimented schedule consisting of equal parts work, play, and study, and were to abstain from alcohol, gambling, and fornication. Their purpose was to vest Americans' penchant for play with purpose and weave values and skills into leisure activities. The popularity of Chautauquas in late nineteenth- and early twentieth-century America exemplified what the historian Cindy Aron identified as a broader ambivalence on the part of most Americans toward leisure during a time when work became, for a growing middle class, less time-consuming and more sedentary.[17]

The Chautauqua movement gained its most ardent support and participation from American Methodists. In 1921 Jones visited one such Methodist Chautauqua resort in Lakeside, Ohio. After watching white children worship and play in this bucolic setting, Jones mourned the absence of such places and programs in his own congregants' lives. Whereas white Methodists across the country flocked to lakes and seashores annually for recreation and inspiration, African Americans found no relief from the summer heat and few outlets for "inspired amusement." The congregants of his vast network of rural and urban churches spanning from Florida's western panhandle to eastern Texas, Jones concluded, desperately needed such a place of their own. He envisioned more than just a primitive campground, but a permanent, year-round institution that could serve as a vacation resort for families and groups, a training institute for ministers and laymen, a summer camp for boys and girls, a place of retreat for "tired mothers" in need of education in basic health, hygiene, and home improvement, and a working farm and vocational school for at-risk youth—in essence, a place that would address areas of primary concern to black social and religious reformers. "To provide a playground," a Gulfside member later wrote, "was not enough. It must be more than a playground. It must be a place where city pastors might go and learn something about the problems of city life, of housing and health; and of industry; where rural pastors could assemble and be instructed not only in the technique of saving souls but of saving lives; where tired mothers might go and rest and learn something of Home Economics and the scientific care of children." It would be, Jones hoped, an organic society in which those needing work and discipline would acquire it, while those needing rest and relaxation would find gratification. And where all would benefit psychologically from simply being outdoors in a pleasant, refreshing, and uplifting setting.

The challenge, though, was securing for fellow African Americans a piece of property that could fulfill that purpose. Jones cast his eyes toward the Mississippi Gulf Coast, where he traveled regularly to consult with ministers and visit his wife's family who lived in Bay St. Louis. During a trip from New Orleans to Bay St. Louis, a train porter informed Jones that the Jackson House—a large, antebellum-era mansion facing the Gulf and located just outside the town of Waveland—was on the market. Its owners, the Deblieux family, had acquired the mansion and surrounding property in 1876. It was an impressive building situated on a mostly undeveloped section of the coast. The massive, two-story structure included twenty-two bedrooms, a roof garden, and wraparound front porch. But by the time it was placed on the market in 1922, the mansion had fallen into utter disrepair after years of neglect, and the adjoining acreage had been ceded to nature. The house's bottom floor doubled as a barn for cattle, which grazed lazily along the wild shore. Slender pine and large, moss-covered oak trees so dense that one could not capture a glimpse of the Gulf from the balcony shrouded the front lawn. One person said that the "luxuriant and almost impenetrable" property "gave one the feeling of an African jungle."[18]

For Jones, it offered the perfect setting for the "Gulfside Idea" to take root. By the spring of 1923, he had raised $4,125 through personal donations from ministers and penny drives conducted in Methodist churches across the Southwestern District, enough for the down payment.[19] Short-term association notes issued to the Merchants Bank and Trust Company in Bay St. Louis bearing between 7 and 8 percent interest would allow Jones to finance the purchase.[20] Jones knew, however, that no amount of money could overcome the hard reality of the color line. So he used his skin color to circumvent the line. During his inspections of the property and negotiations with the sellers, Jones stealthily obscured his racial identity. A white Methodist minister accompanied him on his inspections of the grounds, leading the sellers to assume the two represented "white" Methodism. More important, Jones formed close partnerships with white bankers and civic leaders in Bay St. Louis and New Orleans, especially George R. Rea, president of the Merchants Bank and Trust Company. In April 1923 Jones acquired title to the land. Shortly thereafter, he transferred ownership to the Gulfside Association (of which he was president) "before," as one account later described, "the wave of protest could get well under way." Rea, who later served as a member of Gulfside Association's board of trustees, played a central role in squelching local white opposition and drumming up acceptance of Gulfside among the local business community.

In addition to the three hundred acres he purchased outright, Jones acquired from the Deblieux family the remaining twenty years of a ninety-nine-year lease on an adjoining 318-acre tract (much of which was uninhabitable swamps) owned by the state of Mississippi and known as "sixteenth section" land. Under the Public Land Survey System implemented by the state upon its admission to the Union in 1817, a portion of land in each county—the sixteenth section—was retained by the state and leased in the form of a trust, with the money collected in rent dedicated to public education. (See Map 5.)

"To have [purchased this land] with but a few minor hitches was a task worthy of highest praise," an account of the transaction later noted. Others greeted the acquisition with a mixture of amazement and skepticism born of remembrances of other big, grand projects that generated much attention and praise but eventually succumbed either to white racism, under-

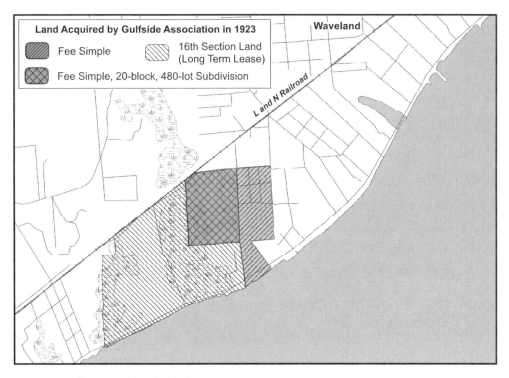

Map 5. Land acquired by Gulfside Association, 1923

capitalization, internal division, or some combination of the three. Even promotional material gave voice to these collective memories of loss and pervasive sense that an acquisition of such scale and ambition was simply too good to be true. Shortly after Gulfside's founding, one black commentator wrote: "A little band of colored folks down here, in some way, has gotten hold of some of the most valuable property along the Mississippi Gulf Coast. I don't mean just a little piece of it either, five or six hundred acres with about a mile and a half frontage is what I am talking about. And they have it alright, for I have seen it for myself and saw the papers, too. But, I just can't help from thinking this way about the whole big project: How long will they hold it?"[21]

While Jones and his fellow ministers began the arduous task of clearing the land and building a sanctuary from white racism and commercial amusements, Gulf Coast boosters were busy lobbying for the types of infrastructure and transportation improvements that would allow them to exploit the coast's commercial potential. Following another massive storm in the summer of 1916, calls for greater protection from the elements fixated on the salvation a seawall purported to offer. As their name implies, seawalls form a barrier between land and sea; their purpose is to protect coastal property from storm damage and halt erosion. But in attempting to hold back nature, seawalls damage and eventually destroy the shores they are designed to stabilize by preventing them from retreating landward and building seaward as sea levels and coastal currents change. Since the shore is cut off from interior inlets meant to absorb floodwaters, the coast as a whole becomes more vulnerable to violent attack. Artificial sand beaches placed in front of seawalls quickly disappear as erosion proceeds minus means of replenishment.[22] Only later, though, would those damaging repercussions become painfully obvious.

In the early 1920s, local municipalities along the Mississippi coast scrambled to raise funds for seawall construction. In 1923 Bay St. Louis completed work on a series of massive concrete steps rising from the shores of the town and up to the front yards of coastal residents' homes. In building the seawall, coastal engineers leveled sand dunes, tore out trees, and severed inlets from the Gulf. The final bill for the project, funded through a local bond issue passed by the town's voters in 1921, totaled $250,000. In 1924, Waveland voters passed a $225,000 bond to finance that town's own seawall.[23] That same year, seawall construction became a state matter when the state legislature formed a Seawall Commission and, through a special gasoline tax, authorized the construction of a seawall (completed in 1927) along the 26.5-mile-long shoreline of Harrison County.[24]

As seawalls were erected, coastal property values skyrocketed, and out-of-state developers and speculators increasingly eyed the Mississippi Gulf Coast as the next frontier in the burgeoning southern coastal real estate market. Northern speculators poured in, buying up dilapidated plantations and seaside mansions and converting the coastline into a winter playground for America's leisure class. Transportation made a quantum leap in 1925, when U.S. Route 90 (stretching from Jacksonville Beach, Florida, to Van Horn, Texas) replaced the old Beach Drive along the state's coast. Newly completed bridges connected New Orleans to the Gulf Coast, greatly shortening the travel distance by car or buggy. On December 2, 1924, the first standard train from Chicago to Mississippi arrived in Gulfport. Called "the Mississippian," the train marked the start of a joint ven-

ture of the Illinois Central and the Gulf and Ship Island Railroad companies. A trip from Chicago that once took up to two days and required a
change of cars in Mobile, Montgomery, or New Orleans now took only
twenty-three hours. Its arrival that morning was hailed as "an epochal day
in the history of the Mississippi Gulf Coast." Within months, the Illinois
Central filed an application with the Interstate Commerce Commission
for the purchase of the entire capital stock of the Gulf and Ship Island
Company.

Developers worked to ensure that beach frontage was "given solely to
the highest type of residential development . . . fine winter homes, broken
here and there by clubs, hotels and towns where the residents may shop."
In 1925 the Mississippi Coast Club, a conglomerate of local chambers of
commerce, successfully pressured the state legislature to authorize coastal
cities and counties to adopt comprehensive regional zoning and planning
regulations. The municipal zoning act of 1925 vested unprecedented powers in county boards of supervisors to regulate the types of buildings constructed within a given jurisdiction. Following passage of the zoning act,
the Coast Club consolidated its power through the formation of an all-
coast regional planning committee dedicated to the "orderly growth and
development" of the area. The *Sea Coast Echo* cheered, "There will be
no shacks, or forty-foot lots with a camp or tent on them. The idea is to
conform to the name that public opinion has given to the Gulf Coast, the
American Riviera." There would also be no excursion parties of "colored
people" from New Orleans prancing about town and picnicking along the
shore. In 1928, business and political interests in Bay St. Louis convinced
the Louisville & Nashville Railroad Company to discontinue its "Negro
excursions" from New Orleans to the Gulf Coast after "protests of [white]
citizens who objected to a large number of colored people coming to the
Bay for Sunday and utilizing the beaches."[25]

Throughout the mid to late 1920s the "clank of steam shovels, the whirl
of concrete mixers and the beat of the carpenter's hammer" could be
heard from Biloxi to Waveland. Stories shared by locals of fortunes made
overnight—of the beachfront cottage that sold for $5,000 in January, $20,000
in April, and $30,000 in July, or the beach frontage that jumped in value
from $75 a foot to $400 a foot following completion of a hotel nearby—
echoed down the coast. Bay St. Louis resident George W. Logan, for instance, was struggling to sell his home for $6,500 in 1924; a year later, it
sold for $16,000. By the spring of 1925, a reported $2 million in real estate

was exchanged each week, most of it among longtime residents who caught the speculation fever. In the two years following the Illinois Central's acquisition of the Gulf and Ship Island line, the *Chicago Tribune* reported, over $30 million had flowed from Chicago to the Gulf Coast. So dramatic was the influx of capital, Chicago developer J. F. Cornelius joked, the "natives . . . think God and Santa Claus come from Chicago."[26]

The coast's prosperity was fueled, in part, by booze. Prohibition turned the Mississippi coast into a terminus for rum runners from the Caribbean, with local distillers quick to add their products to shipments sent out across the country. By 1933 a reported one thousand stills were in operation in the state's three coastal counties. Gulf Coast producers supplied a fair amount of the alcohol for Al Capone's Chicago syndicate. Moreover, scores of white southerners came to the Gulf Coast to escape "drier" and more repressive parts of the country, fueling the rise of hotels, bars, dance halls, and casinos. Coastal Mississippians' laissez-faire attitude toward what their upstate neighbors called "sin" was complemented by their indifference to the laws of coastal ecology. In 1923 J. W. Apperson, owner of Biloxi's Buena Vista Hotel, opened a casino and dance hall on Dog's Key, one of the fragile barrier islands conveniently outside of federal jurisdiction. He renamed it the Isle of Caprice. Excursion boats ferried guests to and from the island twice a day.[27]

Social liberalism begat economic liberalism. Prior to the 1920s, the state's reputation as a no-man's-land for corporations was legendary. The same constitution of 1890 that effectively disenfranchised the state's African American citizens and set a blueprint for other states to follow had also placed severe restrictions on corporate power. A tangle of cumbersome laws took root and aimed to scare away outside capital. When he was not railing against public education for "field hands" or calling for the return of the state's black population to the shores of West Africa, Mississippi governor James K. Vardaman stirred the passions of his white constituents by vowing to fight any corporation that "seeks to oppress the people or to do injustice to the rank and file of our citizenship."[28]

Throughout the early 1920s, coastal developers agitated for the state to drastically alter its tax code so as to attract wealthy home-buyers and capital investment. New Orleans real estate agent James F. Trumbull told legislators that unless the state slashed taxes on income and inheritance, the Gulf Coast would continue to languish behind Florida. (Indeed, the absence of personal income and inheritance taxes in Florida played a large role in its becoming a haven for wealthy retirees and establishing a model of revenue generation reliant on perpetual growth that continues to shape the state's fortunes today.) "If Mississippi would change her laws relative to inheritance and income taxes," Trumbull said, "millionaires would buy property along the Coast to be used during their playtime, and good substantial people would buy here for permanent homes."[29]

Gulf Coast politicians and business interests increased pressure on the state legislature to liberalize corporate regulations and tax structures. "The laws on our statute books," state senator Harden Brooks charged, "makes [sic] it impossible for business to live." In June 1925 Brooks delivered a rousing speech before the State Merchants Association Conference in Biloxi, in which he assailed Mississippi's byzantine corporate laws, saying they constituted a "Chinese wall to investment in this State." Brooks called for repeal of the state's "confiscatory" income and inheritance taxes and raising the sales tax, the abolition of the office of revenue collection, repeal of the anti-corporation farming law and bank guaranty deposit law, and submission of a constitutional amendment that would prevent the state legislature from revisiting these new provisions. In 1926, members of the state legislature's Gulf Coast delegation sponsored a law seeking to repeal the state's income and inheritance taxes, but were only able to reduce the tax levy. They did, however, succeed in exempting stock in foreign corporations held by state residents from taxation, thus inducing residents of neighboring states (Louisiana, in particular) to take up residence along the Gulf Coast while continuing to do business in New Orleans. In addition, the state passed a five-year tax exemption on new industries, exempted hotels from taxation entirely, revised its tax code so as to tax corporations as individuals, added a gas tax to pay for massive appropriations for road construction and internal improvements, eliminated taxes on money deposited in banks, and exempted taxation on loans at 6 percent interest or less. By the summer of 1926, the *Wall Street Journal* happily reported that the state was shedding its irrational fears of outside investors and opening its doors for business. The *New York Times* predicted, "by the Winter of 1928 the 'American Riviera' will be as safely established on the Gulf as it is now on the beautiful real estate maps, and populated by America's prosperous Middle West in expensive period architecture." "The changed attitude of Mississippi toward capital and industry," Jackson, Mississippi, banker and real estate investor Edgar H. Bradshaw told members of the New York Stock Exchange, "should provide conclusive evidence to the rest of the country that Mississippi is now ready for progressive development which is already apparent in other sections of the South."[30]

The state's conditional embrace of capital-intensive coastal development did not entail a loosening of plantation power, which continued to dominate the state's overall political economy into the 1940s. It did, however, lay the groundwork for what historian James Cobb called the "selling of the South" in post–World War II America, accomplished in large measure through changes in tax codes favorable to corporations and lax environmental regulations that not only allowed industries to pollute at will but also encouraged developers to turn fragile coastal ecosystems into valuable real estate. It was in the 1920s that the idea of "progress" spread from the shores of Mississippi into the legislative and executive chambers of Jackson. In Mississippi, the marriage was consummated in the 1927 gubernatorial election, when Theodore Bilbo—the onetime foe of the carpetbagging northern capitalist—was quietly reborn, in northern investors' (if not his rural constituents') eyes, as a champion of enlightened thinking and free enterprise. In the following legislative session, Bilbo helped usher through the New Corporation Act, which dramatically liberalized the state's corporate laws. No longer would prospective corporations be required to advertise their intention of seeking a state charter for three weeks prior to their application. Directors were no longer liable for debts in excess of capital, nor were they required to file a nonfinancial annual statement. "Mississippi," a 1928 article in the *New York Times* cheered, "has abolished one of its dragons. There is a vacant stall in the official mythological stables of the State where once gambling, liquor, Sunday amusements and the corporation fed side by side upon the ignorance and prejudice of the commonwealth. The last has been turned out to shift for itself."[31]

The emergence of Gulfside from the wild shores of Hancock County seemed to embody the pro-development ethos and devil-may-care attitude toward coastal ecology sweeping the Gulf Coast in the early 1920s. Faith in the region's perpetual growth was reinforced by the ready availability of financing for those seeking to build on and "improve" coastal property. In 1925 Bishop Robert E. Jones secured a mortgage totaling

$10,000 at 8 percent annual interest from his friends at the Merchants Bank of Bay St. Louis to fund the refurbishment of the Jackson House and the construction of a twenty-eight-room dormitory, an academic building containing four rooms and an assembly hall, and tennis courts.

Jones sought no less than a wholesale transformation of Gulfside's 618-acre tract from fragile wetlands and dense forests to real estate for residential and recreational use. Soon after acquiring title, Gulfside designated a portion of the land for the construction of a summer cottage community consisting of five hundred lots laid out over intersecting streets. With sales of lots expected to help finance future building projects and meet loan repayments, Gulfside embarked on an aggressive advertising campaign targeting middle-class black professionals in the ministry and business community. Advertisements carried in the *Official Journal of the Mississippi Annual Conference* stressed that buying a lot and building a small cabin on the grounds would offer them the opportunity for "rest, study, and meditation" in a setting that was "quiet, calm, and restful—removed from the noise and heat of crowded cities." Promoters within the church also stressed that purchase of a lot was not just a spiritual investment, but also a safe financial one. "Lots are almost dirt cheap," one advertisement read, "and right near the beach. . . . If the colored people hold it, in time every investor will feel proud of this fine achievement on the part of the group. And if they eventually sell out, don't you know every person who has a lot paid for, will have to be reckoned with." Indeed, even if Gulfside failed, lot owners would still be in possession of property whose future appreciation seemed limitless. "The consistent and evident permanent advance in realty values are, with every assurance of perfect title, sufficient security."[32]

Like other real estate developers along the Gulf Coast, Jones designed the subdivision to appeal to a certain type of buyer. Each block in the twenty-block subdivision contained twenty-eight lots that were described as small enough to maintain an intimate, campground atmosphere in the spirit of the Chautauqua movement and also—as advertisements for the lots would point out—of sufficient size for planting gardens and fruit and pecan trees. Purchasers of lots agreed to abide by the association's strict rules and regulations on conduct.

Sales of lots were also expected to help finance Gulfside's ambitious social agenda. Among its first long-term initiatives, Gulfside instituted a vocational school for impoverished adolescent males. Initially called the Gulfside School for Retarded and Under-Privileged Boys, it drew children and youth ages twelve and up from areas wholly lacking in any meaningful schooling for young black people and brought them to Gulfside to gain a rudimentary, elementary education and acquire practical skills. The school operated year-round; students worked for half the day and took classes the other half. Their half day of work also helped Gulfside meet more immediate needs. Upon arrival, the "lost boys" (as they were called in Gulfside literature) got straight to work readying the grounds for the first waves of summer campers and building and maintaining the facilities during the off-season. They painted the interior and exterior of the Jackson House, academic building, and dormitory. They operated a farm that consisted of chickens, pigs, and cattle, and harvested shrimp and crabs from the Gulf. During the winter months, they cleared acres of farmland and in the spring planted a variety of vegetables for use in the hotel kitchen, including cabbage, snap beans, beets, carrots, onions, collards, and cucumbers. Some students worked as cooks in the kitchen, while others sold produce to passing motorists at a roadside market in Waveland. When guests arrived during the summer, the students carried their bags to their rooms and waited on them at meals. Other students focused on the building trades, pressing cement blocks for the new structures added to the campus in the coming years and assisting in their construction.

By the summer of 1924, campers and conference attendees were arriving in a steady stream. Gulfside established annual camps for boys, girls, and "tired mothers," and a school for rural pastors. At Camp Waveland, the girls' camp, the emphasis was on discipline and cleanliness. Campers were awarded prizes for neatest kept tent, and directors held inspections each morning. Ruth Sanders, who attended Camp Waveland as a child, described it as a boot camp geared toward behavioral modification; in place of carefree camaraderie, guests underwent, in her words, "rigorous religious instruction and recreation." Years later, she still vividly recalled "being awakened in what they called early morning, but it was still night." Camp Moorland for boys placed a strong emphasis on sports, competition, and character-building activities. With its campers hailing from New Orleans, a city where (as will be discussed later) drowning deaths among black boys neared epidemic proportions, the camp also devoted considerable time to teaching campers how to swim.[33]

As other scholars have noted, the early twentieth century saw the proliferation of prescriptive literature and advice manuals written by and directed at African Americans on subjects such as personal health and hygiene, the importance of a clean and well-kept home, and "proper" gender conventions and sexual behavior.[34] At Gulfside, these advice manuals were put into practice. Camp Rest-Awhile welcomed working mothers to Gulfside. Much of their time, though, was not spent resting but rather being told how to become better mothers and housekeepers, with daily schedules filled with lectures and demonstrations on subjects such as "Health and Happiness," "Making a House, Home," and "The Future of the Child." At the School of Practical Methods for Town and Rural Pastors, health experts and educators schooled rural ministers on basic health matters, including communicable diseases and milk, water, and food sanitation. They also taught them how to promote among their followers a "healthy organism," which required regular meals, fresh air and ventilation, elimination of waste from the home, and attention to hygiene and dental care, among others, and a "healthy personality," which demanded cooperation with fellow workers, respect for employers, and honesty.

Whether they came for training, instruction, or a vacation (or came expecting one but instead received another), first-time black visitors to Gulfside were amazed that African Americans could actually own a place of such splendid beauty. Robert N. Brooks, who later became Gulfside's director, liked to recount the story of an AME Church bishop's first visit to Gulfside. Heading east along the beachfront drive, the bishop peered out the window of his Model T Ford in search of a place that fit his mental image of a Negro resort. Two miles past his expected destination, the minister stopped at a filling station and asked a pair of black attendants the location of Gulfside, "whereupon the attendants pointed out, with apparent pride, the well-kept grounds which the bishop recalled having passed, but had evident suspicions it was under other auspices." Perhaps apocryphal, this story of a bishop who, quite literally, could not believe that blacks could own such an envious spot along the Gulf nevertheless captures the spatial ontology of white and black life on the "American Riviera," where blacks' ownership of a spacious, structurally improved seaside mansion, once owned by the family of a former president, had become virtually unthinkable. "I never expected to see the day when Negroes would own any such place right on the Gulf front," J. B. F. Shaw wrote Jones. "It does seem too good to be true," Chaflin College president J. B. Randolph remarked.[35] It is not too much to say that many blacks' initial encounters with Gulfside challenged the most hardened assumptions of race and space along exclusive shorelines.[36] For many children, the mere sight of open waters, much less the prospect of unmolested enjoyment of the shore and the land it hugged, sent many first-time visitors into a state of near delirium. "They'd scream and holler when they got out and saw all that water," Pat Harvey described the scene when groups of impoverished black youth came to Gulfside for the first time. "They were in a sheer panic. They had never seen the vastness." Juanita Doris Franklin brought busloads of children from the farther reaches of the Piney Woods and Delta regions—places where, as she described, blacks might cool off in "some mudhole, or some river," if they were lucky—for summer camps. "When you come there, you come around the curve on Sears Avenue and there's water ahead of you." That moment, she described, kids leaped from their seats, tugged on each other's shirts, and pressed their faces to the glass. "'Ohh, ohh, look at the water!' That's the kind of expressions you got."[37]

For ministers and laymen alike, Gulfside acquired a spiritual aura that reflected its visitors' long journey through the treacherous wilderness of slavery and Jim Crow to reach the coast. "Here God speaks through the giant, aged oaks, the flowing and ebbing of the tides, fishermen casting their nets from the shore, plying their trade from boats in the distance or toiling by night for flounders, the starry heavens above and moonlit waters of the sea," minister J. Leonard Farmer remarked. The journey to Gulfside, "in stuffy Jim Crow coaches," Brooks wrote, made the destination all the more gratifying. "There . . . was a laugh of triumph in the very waves as they broke playfully against the sea wall, resounding with shouts of exuberant glee. . . . Why, my very Bible seemed a new book as I pondered its pages by the shores of Gulfside!" "Gulfside," one guest wrote, "is more than a place. It is a spirit. It is more than acreage and cottage, dormitory and assembly hall, walk and grove; it is a living thing, that has breath, and warmth, and passion, and soul." "Something was there that was different, made you feel different," Franklin described. "You didn't have to be converted, saved, whatever the situation is. When you got on Gulfside ground, it made a difference in your life. You just knew you were in . . . a different sort of place."[38]

It should come as no surprise, then, that visitors often went back to their home churches devoted acolytes and proselytizers of Gulfside's social, educational, and recreational mission. The penny drives started by local churches to raise funds for the property's acquisition continued decades after Gulfside's founding. In small towns across the South, women formed

Gulfside Clubs, whose purpose was to educate local communities on the work being done at Gulfside, "promote the Gulfside Idea," solicit donations, encourage local organizations and groups to book their next meeting or conference there, and, as stated in Gulfside's charter, "become . . . enthusiastic and intelligent field agent[s] for the first and biggest venture ever started for any by colored people." Along with parishioners' independent efforts, throughout the 1920s the individual congregations within each of the Southwestern District's seven conferences annually contributed between $75 and $250 toward the Gulfside general fund.[39]

Their tireless support allowed Gulfside to get off the ground. But for Jones's ambitious social agenda to achieve long-term stability, and for Gulfside to be able to continue to grow its campus, they needed large donations from wealthy, mostly white, philanthropists. To that end, Jones toured the country giving his stock speech on the Gulfside Idea to white Methodist churches and before major donors. The story of the boys' schools and the children who came there figured prominently in Jones's speeches. The pathos he elicited from audiences as he described the conditions of impoverished black youth in the most oppressive corners of the Deep South reflected a fund-raising strategy geared toward pulling on liberal whites' heartstrings so as to untie their purse strings. He kept his ear to the ground for signs of wealthy whites sympathetic to the Gulfside mission. A mere mention by one of his associates of a "rich friend" interested in Gulfside sent Jones's heart racing and elicited a flurry of letters and telegrams.[40]

In order to persuade anyone, rich or poor, to support the Gulfside Idea, Jones had to convince them that a seaside resort situated along Mississippi's Gulf Coast, amid a growing number of white vacationers and in a state notorious for violent suppression of any signs of black initiative, could achieve a necessary level of acceptance and support. To quell such concerns, Jones stressed his good relations with the architects of Mississippi's coastal economy. Gulfside, he told potential donors, was not only aesthetically appealing but also, and perhaps more important, "sympathetically environed. We have not attempted to live apart of our neighbors. From the first we sought and secured cooperation and put our work to the front so that our purpose and program might be understood." A year after its establishment, the Gulfside Association placed a full-page advertisement in the *Sea Coast Echo* informing readers that Gulfside "seeks the good will, sympathy, encouragement, and helpfulness of all the citizens of Waveland, Bay St. Louis and the entire community round about, to the end that this project may become an outstanding development in the interest of the community and the welfare of the race." Out of this courtship, local businessmen, bankers, politicians, and law enforcement officials became some of Gulfside's most vocal supporters, always on hand to cut ribbons on a new facility or write a letter of endorsement to creditors and philanthropies. In addition to Merchants Bank president George R. Rea, a "man of high standing" in Hancock County, Jones counted Waveland mayor George Hearly, Hancock County attorney E. J. Gex, and *Sea Coast Echo* editor Charles G. Moreau among his local allies. Jones assembled a board of trustees that consisted of presidents of black Methodist colleges, local bankers and businessmen, and prominent national white supporters of African American education and institution development. In addition to serving as a trustee, Rea penned a letter that Jones included in solicitations of support testifying that white coastal leaders "have the greatest confidence as to [Jones's] ability and integrity. We think much good has been accomplished by this organization and they have our co-operation at all times."[41]

Gulfside cultivated a spirit of cooperation with local whites not simply by appealing to their sympathies, but by publicly positioning itself as an asset to the local economy. To railroad executives, Jones promised to bring upward of six to seven thousand "representative, progressive Christian men and women" aboard their trains each summer. Among the growing numbers of hotel and restaurant owners in the region, Gulfside's food preparation training programs and emphasis on "sanitation, food and health" were singled out for praise. The vocations taught at the boys' school were all uniquely suited to the needs of a building construction and service-oriented coastal economy. As an article in the *New Orleans States* commented, Gulfside "should be heartily supported for what it stands for and seeks to do to better fit and prepare men and women for life's work."[42] Northern investors also seemed to take notice. Articles in northern newspapers extolling the benefits of Mississippi coastal development stressed the region's cheap labor supply as a main selling point.

More fundamentally, Gulfside seemed to embrace the region's pro-growth ethos. Articles in local white newspapers pointed to the "rapid manner in which [Gulfside covered] its vacant spaces . . . with new buildings" as evidence of the "growth and material prosperity" Gulfside promised to contribute to Hancock County. The *Sea Coast Echo* called the enterprise "quite a credit to the colored mind and effort of Hancock County and Mississippi as well" and applauded Jones's efforts to ensure that the "material side of the enterprise rests on a foundation of permanence."[43]

On August 31, 1927, over two thousand African Americans arrived on special trains to attend the dedication ceremonies of the Gulfside Chautauqua and Camp Meeting Grounds. It was considered the largest single gathering of African Americans in the history of the Gulf Coast, and hailed by black newspapers across the country as a monumental achievement in the history of the race. Guests from the rural backwoods and small towns of Mississippi, Alabama, Texas, and Louisiana stepped off the train in Waveland, hiked through the woods that separated the town from the coast, and upon arrival stared out onto the gleaming waters of the Gulf, many for the first time in their lives. Bishop Wilbur P. Thirkield, the former president of Howard University, a Tuskegee trustee, and a longtime advocate for African American education, dedicated the grounds and praised Gulfside for its focus on fostering "peace, good will, and race adjustment." To "wave[s] of hearty applause" for their "support and cooperation," Jones introduced Hancock County sheriff A. J. McCloud and Rae. Gex spoke on behalf of the "responsible white business and professional men and women of Hancock County," professing their eagerness to help build and grow Gulfside. At this and all future interracial events, Gulfside observed segregated seating arrangements.[44]

Similar events in the coming years aimed to show for audiences of powerful white business and political figures both the desirability and necessity of the Gulfside venture. First staged in 1931, Song Fest brought together five hundred singers from several African American college choirs across the Deep South in an effort to display the talents and spiritual strivings of the Negro.[45] It proved enormously popular. An estimated twelve hundred of Gulfside's "white friends" were in attendance at the first Song Fest; the following year, the crowd swelled to well over two thousand, and in the coming years it regularly numbered well over five thousand. The audience consisted, as one account noted, of "bankers, mayors, other officials, and well-to-do residents of Biloxi, Bay St. Louis, Pass Christian, Gulfport, and New Orleans." White attendees described the performances as "the real thing," "unadulterated by refinements, close to its roots in the soil from which it sprang." "The humor and pathos of the negro race," one account described, "lifted many a white listener a little above the earth for a brief space." "The spirit of friendliness that characterized the gathering," an article in the white newspaper the *New Orleans*

Item read, "was a good mark of the work that Gulfside has been doing with the aid of its white friends." "The applause of nearly five thousand persons," a report to the Gulfside board of trustees proudly noted, "stamped indelibly the approval of friends." "These gatherings," another article read, "seem to . . . be doing excellent work in promoting acquaintance and sympathy between the intelligent and liberal white and negro people along the Coast." Along with Song Fest, Gulfside hosted an annual Goodwill Dinner for white residents of Waveland. For the 1933 occasion, students from the boys' school decorated the main dining room in the Jackson House and helped prepare the meals for seventy-five guests. A program of music and speeches followed dinner. This and similar events for white audiences were featured prominently in all of Gulfside's applications for grants and other funding sources.[46]

By the late 1920s Jones's national fund-raising efforts began to yield results. In 1928 Gulfside secured a $25,000 grant from the John D. Rockefeller fund disbursed over a five-year period; the following year, the Julius Rosenwald fund donated $6,000 disbursed in $2,000 annual payments over a three-year period.[47] During the years 1928 to 1930, donors from across the country contributed roughly $2,000 annually in additional funds. The late 1920s witnessed Gulfside's most rapid physical development, with the completion of the academic building and women's dormitory, as well as an additional ten new camp houses. In 1930 the county appraised Gulfside's total acreage at $102,780, and its buildings and improvements at $90,736, among total net assets of $192,240.

Gulfside's administrators hoped that the infusions of funds from philanthropies would provide a temporary stimulus to development as opposed to a long-term dependency. "Gulfside as a recreational center and assembly ground for Negroes of America can only be made secure as the idea takes root in the racial consciousness of the Negro. . . . The temporary help now being offered by philanthropists must and will be withdrawn in time."[48] And until it did stand on its own, Gulfside's programs and overall vision of racial uplift would remain subject to white approval.[49] Indeed, with white dollars came white scrutiny, and for Gulfside's administrations, a constant fear of embarrassment. This, in turn, made the project of domesticating and beautifying the land all the more urgent. For white trustees and influential donors, the state of the property was to reflect the hopes and dreams of "the race." "The buildings and the landscape should be beautiful," Committee on Interracial Cooperation president and Gulfside trustee Will Alexander told a roomful of white donors at a 1931 meeting in New York City. "They should symbolize a service to Negroes on a very large scale." In annual reports to donors, Gulfside listed among its chief needs funding that would allow it to drain the hundreds of acres of wetlands that covered the middle portion of the Gulfside tract. Home to a diverse range of coastal species, the wetlands stood as a silent reminder of an older coast, one in which human habitation was sparse and plant and animal life abundant. Through its social programs, Gulfside worked to remove what racial uplift reformers at the time characterized as vestiges of African Americans' slave past. The condition of its property was to be a reflection of those aspirations. Domesticating the land and taming an unruly shoreline became synonymous with uplifting the race and, more to the point, demonstrating to their white neighbors that they were equally dedicated to ensuring that the coast be well groomed and aesthetically pleasing. Gulfside should stand for "order, cleanliness, industry, courtesy, and usefulness. There are no sink holes around the place, no 'back yards.' Everything is beautiful, wholesome and sanitary." Failure to meet these standards merited a swift rebuke from white donors. Following one visit, Edwin R. Embree, Gulfside trustee and director of the Rosenwald Fund, upbraided Jones for the sorry "condition of the furnishings" in the Jackson House, reminding him, "The condition of furniture and cleanliness of the rooms is part of the education which any such project should give."[50]

While outside donations were trickling in during the late 1920s, some of Jones's investments were falling apart. The plan to sell lots for cottages proved a disaster. As soon as buyers acquired warranty deeds, conflicts arose over the administration of the property. Gulfside administrators struggled to enforce land-use regulations. Some lot owners attempted to run boardinghouses or rent out their cabins, and insisted on their right to use the property as they pleased. In the late 1920s the board of trustees voted to stop selling lots, while allowing those who purchased lots to retain their ownership claims. Gulfside's troubles, though, were far from over. To insure the timely payment of property taxes, Gulfside decided to pay all property taxes and later send bills to the owners. Seeking to avoid payments, lot owners argued that they considered property taxes to be included in the initial purchase price. Many of them refused to acknowledge the bills issued by Gulfside. Gulfside's administrators soon found themselves paying taxes on the entire property. As Jones put it, "instead of our lot sales being a help they . . . turned out to be a distinct liability." By 1928, records indicate Gulfside had already begun buying back the lots at the original purchase prices.[51]

When money was tight, Gulfside's identity as a noncommercial, religious resort similarly constrained its conversion of highly appreciated real estate assets into much-needed capital. To raise immediate capital, Jones tried to sell excess acreage. Trustees and benefactors objected to these sales over concerns that they could lead to the introduction of dance halls and other commercial amusements that "would demoralize the present quiet dignity of the place." "The experience of similar institutions," the Rosenwald Fund's Embree wrote Jones, "is that as time goes on they need more rather than less land and particularly they need control of a wide area so as to avoid undesirable developments near them. In the case of Gulfside this seems peculiarly important. Questionable hotels, dance halls, and other commercial activities might destroy the whole project."[52]

As America slid into the Great Depression, Gulfside's hopes for financial independence and self-sustainability dimmed just as white support plummeted. Across the Gulf Coast, the effects of the global economic depression were everywhere. Several hotels, including the Hotel Markham and the Inn-by-the-Sea, filed for bankruptcy, while funding for vacation home subdivisions such as the Spanish Acres subdivision in Bay St. Louis, begun in the summer of 1929, dried up prior to completion. Designed to attract "a man of ordinary means" wishing to "live decently and comfortably," Spanish Acres typified the oversaturation of the coastal real estate market by decade's end. Less than a year after winning approval from city commissioners to begin construction, its owner and developer, James E. Edmunds, ran out of cash, and the unsold lots were seized by the county and resold at tax delinquency sales. The notorious offshore rendezvous, the Isle of Caprice, was swept away—literally—by the changing of the tides; Apperson's decision not to rebuild suggested the changing of the coast's economic tides. By the early 1930s, coastal real estate values settled at roughly seven times the pre-boom value, down from a high of fifteen times in the mid-1920s.[53] Though developers' grandiose dreams for the American Riviera were tempered, the Great Depression did not bring financial devastation to a region that had only recently begun to enter the national market economy.

For Gulfside, on the other hand, the global economic crisis proved disastrous and nearly fatal. Carrying debts in excess of $24,000 by 1933,

Gulfside watched helplessly as its small but steady donations from African Americans dried up and its revenue from summer vacationers plummeted; formerly cordial and forgiving relations with local financial institutions gave way to more-exacting demands for repayment, and lastly, continued support from major philanthropies was withdrawn. Following the 1929 fiscal year, Gulfside struggled and eventually gave up trying to meet its annual fund-raising goals among area churches. In 1928, the Rosenwald Fund promised to match donations from local churches. That challenge yielded $2,337 in small donations, for a total of $4,674. Two years later, the Rockefeller Fund issued a similar challenge; donations from church members and supporters totaled $367.25. The hotel's receipts, which during the fiscal year of 1929–1930 topped off at $6,938, dropped steadily, to $5,705 the following year and a paltry $2,966 during the 1931–1932 fiscal year. The county's assessment of the land's value at $107,780 in 1930 added to the property tax load, which Gulfside's administrators—wary of the common use of tax liens to seize desirable land—habitually paid in full before all other debts. In 1932, George R. Rea was displaced as president of the Merchants Bank and Trust, and in his absence the bank immediately stepped up demands for repayment of outstanding loans, requiring Gulfside to reduce its capital indebtedness by 20 percent within a year. Payments on interest began to slide, while insurance premiums went unmet. In 1932, Jones wrote Edwin R. Embree to request the immediate release of the remaining balance of Gulfside's grant from the Rosenwald Fund so as to "help us in our now very embarrassing situation." But as the stock market plummeted, so too, did the Rosenwald Fund's endowment. By 1932 the foundation was spending its principal capital and selling portions of its stock holdings at ridiculously low market prices to meet immediate needs. And rather than meet Jones's desperate requests, the Rosenwald Fund instead cut Gulfside's annual appropriation of $2,000 in half, this after Jones had secured a $2,000 loan with the expectation of repayment upon receipt of the grant.[54]

To stay afloat, Gulfside scaled back all possible expenditures and pursued new avenues of support. Jones secured contracts with the Mississippi Department of Education to host a Summer Normal School for African Americans aspiring to become teachers in the state's segregated school system. Over the course of a five-week semester, Gulfside administrators and staff, under the supervision of state officials, instructed future teachers and administered the state entrance exam. Beginning in 1934, Gulfside secured a contract from the Hancock County Health Board to host an annual health conference directed at the area's black population. Gulfside had previously hosted similar conferences in which attendees listened to lectures on topics such as hygiene and sanitation, and received physical exams and consultations from black nurses and physicians.[55]

Other decisions made in order to balance the books backfired. Insurance on the Jackson House was reduced to only $5,000, less than one-tenth its appraised value, with no insurance carried on any other facilities or equipment. On September 30, 1935, the building mysteriously erupted in flames and burned to the ground. Though students at the boys' school and the school's teacher, Lillian Pugh, all escaped without injuries, the blaze consumed the building, all its furnishings, and supplies stored inside. "The chimney and pillars are all that remain, standing as fate-defying sentinels to protect the spot made sacred by its service to a needy group," one announcement read. "The furnishings, equipment, bed linen, dishes, keepsakes and collections for more than a decade, all in ashes." Though foul play was, of course, suspected, it seems as likely that the blaze was accidentally started by one of the students. The fire also consumed a considerable portion of the funds raised in the previous decade, which had been channeled to the mansion's refurbishment and beautification.[56]

Following the fire, Jones professed that this latest setback merely offered Gulf Coast blacks the opportunity to reaffirm their spirit of perseverance and rededicate themselves to the resort's interracial and spiritual mission. One brochure soliciting support for the rebuilding efforts read, "To many this destruction by fire was a tragedy but, IT MUST NOT BE! Anyone who has seen sunrise at Gulfside must have faith and everyone who loves sunrise must help. If the burning of this Jackson House seemed to be a crucifixion of yesterday's accomplishments, tomorrow must be a resurrection and a going forward to larger service." Serving a state in which its black residents suffered under the most inadequate and underfunded health and educational systems in the nation, a place where "misery and decay" touched every facet of blacks' lives, the "school for underprivileged boys," summer institute organizer Timothy B. Echols claimed, "alone justifies the expenditure of every dollar and all the sacrifices made during the past thirteen years, to say nothing of the numerous other projects included in the program at Gulfside."[57]

Gulfside's future looked bleak. Despite aggressive appeals to potential donors, the summer following the fire, Jones told an inquirer that contributions were "recently almost nil" and that Gulfside's only steady source of income was the penny drives. Lacking the money to rebuild, and in turn lacking the facilities to attract the types of groups that would provide a steady source of income, Gulfside remained locked within a self-described "vicious circle," forced to draw water from the rock of impoverished rural congregations to generate funds needed to rebuild the grounds in order to host the visitors and groups that generated revenue.

As Gulfside's future hung in the balance, so, too, it seemed, did the viability of African American–supported, not-for-profit social institutions in an age of commercial amusements. In a 1938 piece in the *Christian Advocate* titled "Shame on America," Gulfside administrator Henry J. Mason charged, "There's not a single desirable or even decent place, public or private, with adequate conveniences and facilities where Negroes may gather at will and give themselves freely to wholesome relaxation, rest and recreation. . . . What a travesty on our Christian civilization! . . . Is there no balm in Gilead? Can it be that men actually have no interest in their brothers' higher welfare?" Mason dismissed the numbers of seaside commercial ventures owned by or catering to African Americans as "not . . . [on] the plane on which it could attract the class of people who are in greatest need of wholesome recreation or offer the type of diversion desired." For Gulfside's supporters and administrators, blacks' exclusion from segregated shores was of secondary concern to the threat of their absorption into a morally hazy, for-profit world of cheap thrills. Without socially conscious, not-for-profit "outlet[s] for [the Negro's] pent-up energies and feelings," Mason warned, "there is a danger of producing a mental and moral pathological condition in the race that will become a menace to public welfare."[58]

Ironically, it was the unification of American Methodism—a moment that marked the nadir of black Methodism in America—that helped to save Gulfside from extinction and revitalize its mission.[59] By the early twentieth century, the northern and southern branches of Methodism commenced a long, tortured journey toward white reunification and black segregation. By the time of Jones's ascendancy to the episcopacy in 1920, the Methodist Church had entered into negotiations with southern Methodists over a plan to reunify the two branches through creating a separate, all-black jurisdiction (later dubbed the Central Jurisdiction) separate from and lacking any influence over white members. The plan of unification was ratified in 1939, with Jones reluctantly voting in favor.

Prominent black figures castigated the move. W. E. B. Du Bois called the attempts by the southern Methodists to stretch their "lean and bloodstained hands for [their] pound of black flesh" "one of the greatest crimes against the Negro race since slavery."[60] Jones's choice of acquiescence over resistance earned him the vilification of blacks inside and outside the church and, as one biographer noted, "cast a shadow over the accomplishments of his career." Upon hearing Jones's public endorsement of the plan, a dedicated white liberal Methodist reported being "never so disgusted in his life." Church members, especially younger members, protested en masse, issuing statements denouncing the church and questioning Jones's ability to speak for black congregants. With a headline that read "Bishop Jones Advocates Jim-Crowism," the *Pittsburgh Courier* charged that Jones "sold out his race to appease the demands of the rabid South," and in return received a mere "mess of pottage."[61]

But Jones saw more than a mess of pottage coming from this otherwise humiliating arrangement. The Central Jurisdiction, he argued, provided black Methodists an institutional identity and base of leadership training. It united over three hundred thousand black Methodists across the nation in a common struggle against racism and equipped them with an institutional infrastructure to wage battles.[62] On a more practical level, the Central Jurisdiction, in effect, formalized the arrangements that had allowed Jones's southwestern jurisdiction to control the allocation of its resources and internal fund-raising for Gulfside, and indeed, expanded its base of possible donors and, by extension, the constituents Gulfside aimed to serve. From a retreat serving local people and local needs, Gulfside became, under the Central Jurisdiction, a place and a symbol of black Methodists' resiliency, less a venue for appealing to whites' hearts and minds, and more a base of organization and inspiration in the black freedom struggle.

In 1946, Congress enacted Public Law 727, which "provided for federal assistance to construction for the protection of *publicly owned* shores against erosion by waves and currents." The law reflected the role of the federal government in stimulating coastal economies in the postwar decades and demonstrated the centrality of federal funds and federal jobs in the building of the Sunbelt. More immediately, it spoke to the federal government's interest in a safe, secure shoreline hugging one side of U.S. Route 90, which had become an increasingly vital commercial and military route connecting Florida and California in the decades prior to the creation of the federal highway system. The summer following passage of Public Law 727, a massive hurricane struck the Gulf Coast in August 1947, inflicting over $18 million in damage. When the waters subsided, the seawall that had promised to fortify the shore in perpetuity, along with much of the coastal property it had helped to create, had been reduced to piles of rubble, along with long stretches of U.S. 90. (At the time, Harrison County still owed over $900,000 on the original seawall.) By then, much of the sand that had been placed in front of the seawall after its construction had long since washed away; actual beaches along the coast were virtually nonexistent.[63]

The seawall's demonstrated incapacity to defend coastal property from massive destruction, and indeed its role in the rapid erosion of the shore in the decades prior, did not, however, inspire any public soul searching or raise questions of environmental sustainability, but instead led public officials to redouble efforts to fortify the coast with the assistance of an empowered federal government. In 1948 the Mississippi state legislature approved Harrison County's proposal to solicit federal funds for refortifying the shore. And in 1951 the Army Corps of Engineers began work on a twenty-six-mile-long, 100-to-150-foot-wide sand beach—much wider than the previous artificial beach and designed to be regularly replenished with sand pumped in from the Mississippi Sound. Over one-third (or over $1.3 million) of the funds for the project came from Washington. As part of the federal government's agreement to provide assistance, Harrison County "assure[d] perpetual ownership of the beach and its administration for public use."[64]

Under the direction of Bishop Robert N. Brooks, who became Gulfside's director in 1944, Gulfside also adopted measures to secure its long-term viability, embarking on a fund-raising campaign that aimed to modernize the facilities and, following the 1947 storm, rebuild the grounds. Brooks, like Jones, sought to use the Central Jurisdiction as a tool of self-empowerment, positioning Gulfside as a national retreat for black Methodists and tapping into a national network of black districts for donors, conferences, and events. Gulfside officials fanned out across the country, telling the "Gulfside story" at church services and to pastors and district superintendents, and tying the fate of Gulfside to the fate of black Methodism in the Methodist Episcopal Church as a whole. By the late 1940s, Gulf-side had established fund-raising ties to conferences in Northern Ohio, Oregon, Southern California, Arizona, Kansas, Wisconsin, Philadelphia, Pittsburgh, and North Georgia, among others, as well as to small and large congregations across the country.[65] In 1955, Gulfside raised $11,772 in donations. In 1958, it secured from a wealthy white philanthropist from Ohio a $25,000 bequest, which the board of trustees used to purchase the twenty adjoining acres owned by Jones so as to maintain control over this land following his death. At the time of Jones's death in 1960, the Gulfside Association had paid off all its mortgages, possessed over $200,000 in assets, and carried only $15,000 in debt.[66]

Through these coordinated efforts, Gulfside constructed a thousand-seat auditorium, a chapel, an administrative building, and a one-hundred-room hotel with a two-hundred-person dining room. It installed electric refrigeration as well as a gas or electric stove in each cabin, and drilled a new well. The "thrilling transmutation," as one visitor described, of Gulf-side's physical facilities reflected the significance of this place of retreat in the wake of blacks' all-but-official ostracism from the Methodist Church. "We would have been like fish out of water, floundering, like a person with no moorings" without Gulfside, church historian Jessie M. Robinson contends. "[Gulfside] became our moorings, a rock and an oasis where we could go for renewal. If we had not had it, we certainly would not be able to function."[67]

To function, black visitors to Gulfside had to learn to navigate the new Jim Crow landscape that the Army Corps of Engineers had helped to build. Upon completion, the pristine, white-sand beaches provided an im-mediate stimulus to the coastal economy and beleaguered real estate mar-ket, and demonstrated the region's continued pursuit of economic stability amid ecological instability. Between 1950 and 1992 the amount of devel-oped land along the coast tripled, while the amount of marshlands de-creased by 40 percent.[68] As federal assistance allowed marshlands to be-come waterfront real estate, it also inspired property owners and public officials to redouble efforts to inscribe clear lines of racial division along the refurbished shore. Along Biloxi's beachfront, areas that once were shared informally by white and black bathers and fishermen with little incident suddenly became bastions of white supremacy jealously guarded by violence-prone white teenagers and trigger-happy white police officers. "They wouldn't allow black[s] to swim in the Gulf or be seen on the beaches," Lydia Robinson-Cyrille remembers, "because that was a source, that was where their tourism came from. . . . The families could go and work in the hotels as cooks, as domestics, as maids, but they could not lounge or enjoy some of the same activities as, say, a tourist would enjoy." The actions of public officials and private businesses along town beaches were compounded by the actions of wealthy white beachfront property owners along the rest of the shore, who hastily drove "no trespassing" signs into the sands in front of their homes and erected physical barriers that extended into the waters. "You'd go up and down the beaches," Ed Moultrie remembers, "and on the waterside see these long docks . . . and on the front of the dock [was] a door [that] was locked [so that] you couldn't get around it to access the beach."[69]

"We couldn't go no farther than the railroad tracks," Genevieve Gordon recalls of childhood summers spent on Gulfside's grounds in the 1940s and 1950s. If you were black, Raymond Breaux said, "You didn't go idly walking on the beach." You stayed on the Gulfside grounds and avoided trouble. The freedom of the sea that Gulfside provided increasingly seemed like a place of confinement. "You could come here and go all over this place," Gordon added. "Now just as long as you stayed in front of here, now. . . . You had to stay within that realm. Nobody said 'don't go,' but you just knew." Still, within that realm, African Americans created a community defined by its sense of mission and grounded in a deep attachment to place. Year after year, individuals, families, professional organizations, ministers, and whole congregations came down for a weekend or week by the sea and under the oaks. There, they reunited with old friends and met new ones, worked to strengthen their faith and exercise their bodies and minds, and expand their own and others' sense of possibility.[70]

For those who had built, rebuilt, and continually struggled to keep this sanctuary by the sea alive through the storm of Jim Crow, finding and securing Gulfside's place in an emergent Sunbelt coastal economy would be their next test of faith.

3

BUILDING BLACK PRIVATOPIAS

Nostalgia courses through the veins of longtime owners of summer cottages in Highland Beach, Maryland. For Charlene Drew Jarvis, a former Washington, D.C., city councilwoman and the daughter of the renowned medical research pioneer Dr. Charles Drew, Highland Beach epitomized the ironic fruits of segregation for elite black Americans. In barring persons of color from popular white summer vacation destinations, Jim Crow, Jarvis remembers, gave rise to elite black summer enclaves noted for a "high density [of] very talented people all in the same spot." Racial segregation, in other words, begat class congregation. Highland Beach, longtime summer resident Ray Langston remembers, allowed "educated people" of color the opportunity to "get away from segregation, to get away from degradation, [to get away from] the poverty in the city." "There we had to walk on eggshells. Here we were taught that we were not inferior to anybody." "Just growing up in this place," John Moses, whose family owned a cottage in Highland Beach, remembers, "it was a paradise."[1]

It was, to borrow a term coined by the political scientist Evan McKenzie, a "privatopia," and was not, its founders stressed, to be confused with those commercial resorts frequented by "common" Negroes.[2] Writing for a mostly white audience in 1901, the writer, poet, and frequent Highland Beach visitor Paul Laurence Dunbar took pains to make this distinction clear. "There is a long distance between the waiter at a summer hotel and the man who goes down to a summer resort to rest after a hard year as superintendent of an institution that pays him several thousand a year. . . . In aims and hopes for our race, it is true, we are all at one, but it must be understood, when we come to consider the social life, that the girls who cook in your kitchens and the men who serve in your dining-rooms do not dance in our parlors."[3]

By the late nineteenth century, it became increasingly hard for privileged and distinguished persons of color to maintain those distinctions during the vacation season. Founded in 1893, at a time when private summer resorts and seaside retreats introduced strict racial segregation policies in place of a more negotiable color line that accounted for class, Highland Beach promised to gratify elite blacks' sense of status and cultural sensibilities, provide a place of rest and relaxation, and help to solve the "problem of summer." By the early 1920s, the numbers of privileged African American families living in cities in the mid-Atlantic eastern seaboard grew. So too did the accessibility of beachfront property along the Chesapeake shores. From a small cluster of cottages at the turn of the twentieth century, Highland Beach quickly grew into a sizable seasonal community and a source of pride, envy, and emulation for a wider black public. Its establishment as a permanent fixture along Maryland's Western Shore both reflected and stimulated demand among middle- and upper-class black Americans for their own places of vacation, and spawned the development of similarly planned beach resort communities in Maryland and across the nation during these years. In Great Migration–era cities, the growth of black landownership in burgeoning vacationlands gave weight to those who spoke of the "promise of development" in the larger struggle for cultural freedom and economic empowerment. The hearts of the "simple-souled Negro folk," the sociologist Kelly Miller wrote in 1934, "swell with pride over the achievement . . . [of] even such small enterprises as a successful watering resort . . . [and] show how earnestly we long for political, economic, and social structure built on our own foundation."[4]

The "simple-souled Negro folk" of Washington and Baltimore in the 1920s, though, might have questioned their admiration of the achievements of Highland Beach's founders as they drove back to their respective cities, clad in dry bathing trunks, dripping in sweat, and stewing in indignation, after having been turned away by the village's gatekeeper for lacking an invitation or, as many suspected, the requisite skin tone and social pedigree. Indeed, a closer look at this particular elite black summer cottage community reveals just how fragile, contested, and contentious that foundation was. In the high-stakes and artificially high-demand market for black vacation home real estate, success was measured by a real estate developer's ability to provide African American second-home owners both a vacation from Jim Crow and a vacation from the "Negro masses." For many, the two problems were inseparable and indistinguishable.

The segregation of outdoor places of leisure in Jim Crow cities, the growth of urban black populations, and the emergence of whites-only real estate markets along developing shorelines outside of the city from the 1920s through the 1960s widened the gulf between black demand for outdoor leisure space and availability and made property in existing black vacationlands both highly desirable and, to its owners, acutely vulnerable—both to an invasion of black Americans and, not unrelated, to exploitation and expropriation at the hands of white coastal capitalists. As a result, the status, desirability, and long-term viability of a given summer community were seen as dependent on the establishment and mainte-nance of structural and interpersonal mechanisms of exclusion of those identified as social inferiors. From these contests over who controlled and who could enjoy access to elite black beaches, the very meaning and con-tent of class and social standing within black America were being remade and redefined, and as the following chapter examines, a distinct political ideology grounded in notions of privatism and property rights began to take root within communities of black landowners.

On a summer weekend in 1890, Charles Douglass, a Civil War veteran, Treasury Department clerk, and son of the renowned abolitionist and statesman Frederick Douglass, boarded a train in Washington, D.C., with his wife, Laura, bound for the "Queen Resort of the Chesapeake," Bay Ridge, located south of Annapolis on Maryland's Western Shore. The Douglasses had visited the exclusive resort in previous summers and ar-rived expecting that, given their family name, his position in the federal government, and their reputation as esteemed persons of color among Washington society, the resort's proprietor would not dare to draw the color line. Indeed, Douglass's decision to vacation at Bay Ridge in the first place—and his expectation of dignified treatment—underscore the seem-ing permeability of the color line for distinguished, "exceptional" persons of color at places of leisure frequented by the upper class. In the decades following emancipation, privileged families of color purchased cottages and established close-knit summer colonies in many of the popular sum-mer destinations in the Northeast and mid-Atlantic states, including, among others, Saratoga, New York; Cape May, New Jersey; and Harpers Ferry, West Virginia.[5] Here, nationwide networks of distinguished and "cultured" black Americans took shape. As much as the property one owned, the schools one's children attended, and the church one belonged to, where a family vacationed spoke volumes about its place in the highly stratified social hierarchy of late nineteenth-century black America. Moreover, as A. K. Sandoval-Strausz points out, privileged blacks saw their acceptance in hotels and resorts as "a barometer of acceptance and citizenship in the United States."[6] On the afternoon the Douglasses arrived at Bay Ridge, that barometer forecasted that the menacing storm of Jim Crow would soon engulf even the "better classes" of colored America.

The Douglasses were denied entry. Following their rejection, they decamped to a nearby boardinghouse operated by the family of Charles and Charity Brashears, African American farmers and owners of forty-eight acres situated along the Chesapeake. The couple had inherited the farm from Charles's father, William Brashears, who had purchased the land along with his freedom from the children of planter Howard Duvall following Duvall's death in 1855. For the next half-century, the Brashearses farmed the sandy soil and fished the Chesapeake. By the time the Douglasses arrived, Charles Brashears was eager to sell the farm. Douglass, still smarting from the incident at Bay Ridge, was thinking about starting his own summer resort so that he would never suffer such an indignity again. At his wife's urging, Charles Douglass purchased forty acres of the Brashears tract for $5,000 cash and set out to develop the "first . . . seaside resort owned and controlled by a colored man in America."[7] Douglass surveyed the land and divided it into 104 lots measuring 50 by 150 feet, laid out over six streets and eleven blocks. He gave it the name Highland Beach. Streets were named after noted Reconstruction-era politicians, some of whom would later become lot owners. In a letter to his father on May 15, 1893, Charles expressed confidence in his ability to "get . . . rid of a number of lots this season" and added, "I have no doubt of the success of the venture. I am quite sure nothing will be lost at any rate and that a handsome profit will be realized on that investment."[8]

Douglass had good reason to be so optimistic. Few cities at the time offered a more fertile market of persons of color capable and desirous of vacation home ownership in an isolated and class-exclusive setting than Washington, D.C. In the decades following emancipation, the District of Columbia became home to a "colored aristocracy," consisting of educated, business savvy, and politically ambitious persons of color. Many came to the city during the era of Reconstruction and secured comparatively well-paying positions in the federal government during the nearly unbroken string of Republican administrations from the 1860s through the 1910s. Others operated successful businesses in the service trades. Many were fair-complexioned and descended from white slave-owning families, which they were often quick to note in recounting their genealogy. Possessing a distinguished lineage was one of several criteria for membership in Washington's colored aristocracy and a means of setting oneself apart from the "vicious," "degraded," and "submerged" Negro masses whom they professed a commitment to uplift, but with whom they shared little direct social contact. Members of Washington's colored elite lived in immaculate, tastefully decorated homes, where they hosted card parties and exclusive, dignified social affairs and prominently displayed libraries filled with the classics of Western literature and collectables from around the world. They sent their children to many of the same private academies in New England.[9] And they vacationed together.

In the wake of Reconstruction's downfall, social relations among whites and distinguished persons of color in the nation's capital deteriorated, and the treatment of upper-class blacks in public places grew more hostile and humiliating. As witnessed along the Potomac River during these years, waterside landings suddenly refused to book parties of elite blacks, while excursion steamers denied them access to first-class accommodations. By the turn of the twentieth century, the options available to elite blacks along this particular shoreline were limited to those Negro resorts and excursion steamers associated with an emergent black public and characterized by the types of more relaxed social conventions and expressive forms of leisure abhorrent to the black elite. W. E. B. Du Bois described this dilemma: "Where as a colored person can I go? If I go among white people, how much rest is there going to be under real or fancied or nonexistent but anticipated discrimination? If I go among colored people, what kind of colored people are they going to be? Am I going to meet educated and well-bred folk, or am I going to run into gamblers and makers of eternal whoopee?"[10] Seeking to avoid both the sting of prejudice and the indignity of forced association with the social inferiors of their race, the city's "colored aristocracy" increasingly sought shelter from racial proscription by withdrawing from public spaces and fashioning a private—and privatized—social world.

Highland Beach became one of these places. This beach, Charles Douglass assured those friends he sought to persuade to buy lots, would be strictly reserved for "our group." Among that group of early lot buyers were Reconstruction-era Mississippi senator Blanche K. Bruce, Virginia congressman John Mercer Langston, Judge Robert and Mary Church Terrell, the prominent Washington physician John R. Francis, former Louisiana governor P. B. S. Pinchback, Washington hotel proprietor James Wormley (whose Wormley House was considered one of Washington's finest hotels, in no small measure because it barred blacks as guests), and the celebrated Baltimore caterer George T. Bowen, who at Douglass's urging opened the first boardinghouse at Highland Beach. Among the first cottages constructed on the grounds was one facing the Chesapeake that Charles Douglass built for his aging father. Named Twin Oaks, it included a turret facing the water, so that Frederick Douglass (in his own words) "as a free man, could look across the Bay to the Eastern shore where I was born a slave." He never enjoyed the opportunity, dying just months before his cottage's completion in 1895.[11]

Early lot buyers came to the Chesapeake shore to reward themselves for a lifetime of struggle and adversity and to find relief from the burden of race. In the first summers, lot owners embraced a primitive lifestyle and communal spirit as they worked to establish Highland Beach as a permanent presence on Maryland's Western Shore. Families slept in tents and worked by day building cottages, digging wells, and planting fruit trees and gardens. On summer weekends, Bowen's nine-room house filled beyond capacity, with some guests forced to sleep in the adjoining barn. A building boom followed a fire that destroyed the Bay Ridge Hotel in 1914, as lot owners used salvaged lumber to build their cottages.[12]

With each lot sold or cottage completed, Douglass earned back a portion of his initial investment, while he and his peers gratified their sense of accomplishment. As Dunbar described, "there was a general flocking to one place taken up entirely and almost owned by ourselves. . . . There is, perhaps, an exaltation about any body of men and women who gather to enjoy the fruits of their own labor upon the very ground which their labor have secured to them."[13] But by Charles Douglass's estimate, not enough persons were experiencing that feeling of exaltation. Lot sales remained sluggish through the first two decades of the twentieth century. By 1920, Highland Beach consisted of 129 lots, but only 34 of them had been sold.[14] That same year, to drum up interest in the fledgling summer village, he persuaded Richard Ware, a shoe merchant from Washington, to buy several lots along the village's southern edge and open a hotel capable of hosting events and attracting prominent black families from cities along the eastern seaboard.[15]

Before Ware had even secured title to these lots, property sales began to accelerate. With the automobile making the Maryland shore more accessible, and with African American migration to Washington and Baltimore in the 1910s contributing to the growth of the cities' black professional classes (contemporaneous with the continued hardening of the color line in places of leisure), the numbers of families who desired and could afford to buy a lot at Highland Beach grew. Between 1920 and 1923 nineteen persons acquired one or several lots and began constructing summer cottages. Soon, others looked to develop neighboring property for African American buyers. In 1922, O. T. Taylor, a retired government clerk and Highland Beach property owner, acquired thirteen and a half acres of undeveloped land wedged between Highland Beach and Oyster Creek that had been abandoned by the children of William Brashears. Taylor paid the delinquent taxes, secured ownership, and then divided the property into fifty-five lots and began advertising real estate at what came to be known as Venice Beach. Between 1923 and 1929, Taylor sold two or more lots to eighteen separate buyers. Lot buyers at Venice Beach hailed from the same privileged circles of black America as their neighbors. Both in their physical features and the social standing of their summer residents, the two adjoining villages were indistinguishable.[16] (See Map 6, p. 98.)

The growth of Highland Beach and the surrounding area in the early 1920s signaled the emergence of a niche market in African American planned vacation communities. White and black developers, in various degrees of collaboration and competition, perceived and worked to capitalize on the formation of a black business and professional class in urban centers and the growing popularity—and feasibility—of leisure travel and vacationing. In Chicago, a pair of white developers, William Terrell and Walter B. Anderson, purchased twenty-seven hundred acres of cut-over timberland on a lake in Lake County, Michigan, in 1914 and founded the summer resort Idlewild.[17] After dividing the land into lots measuring fifty by two hundred feet, they launched an aggressive advertising campaign, aimed at black professionals, in newspapers across the Midwest, soliciting testimonials from celebrities such as Madame C. J. Walker, as well as esteemed Chicago black professionals such as attorney Beauregard Mosley, Alderman Louis B. Anderson, Provident Hospital founder Dr. George Hall, and Dr. Daniel Williams. They hired African Americans to organize excursions of prospective buyers to travel (at their own expense) to the remote lake in central Michigan. These local agents organized lot owners' associations in cities, and generally worked to make, as one observer put it, "lot ownership at Idlewild into a status symbol in the local Negro community." Promoters of Idlewild stressed the area's lack of prejudice and the freedom of movement and association a weekend or summer there afforded. "When you stand in Idlewild," one promoter boasted, "breathe the fresh air, and note the freedom from prejudice, ostracism, and hatred, you can feel yourself truly an American citizen."[18]

Idlewild was one of many black resorts founded during these years. In 1924 a group of white developers purchased a swath of land along the south shore of Fox Lake in northeastern Indiana, founded the Fox Lake Land Company, and began aggressively advertising summer homes to black professionals in Fort Wayne, Toledo, Indianapolis, and other nearby cities, touting the fresh air and freedom from prejudice families could enjoy in this rural oasis. The developers converted an old farmhouse into a hotel, turned a barn into a restaurant and dance hall, and rented out a cluster of lakeside cottages.[19]

For enterprising African Americans, the "promise of development" outside of the city was contagious.[20] In 1925, John Stewart, an African American funeral home director in Washington, D.C., collaborated with Lansdale Sasscer, a prominent Maryland real estate developer and later U.S. congressman, to acquire a swath of farmland along a wide stretch of the Patuxent River in the southern corner of Prince George's County, Maryland. There, Stewart and fellow investors plotted out one thousand lots measuring twenty-five by one hundred feet and founded the village of Eagle Harbor. In selecting the property and plotting the land, Eagle Harbor's investors leaned heavily on the services and expertise of E. S. Hine, a white Washington real estate developer who specialized in the growing market for summer colonies.[21] To promote sales, Stewart hired Michael "Casey" Jones, a silver-tongued, energetic African American real estate salesman, who worked out of a storefront on U Street in Washington.[22] Half-page advertisements appearing in black newspapers appealed to readers "who know and appreciate the value of vacation in modern life," telling them they could purchase a lot—and boat, bathe, and fish along a four-thousand-foot-long sandy beach and among "the better people"—for as little as twenty-five dollars with a five-dollar down payment and forty equal weekly payments. Jones and his team of salesmen stressed Eagle Harbor's accessible location thirty miles from Washington, on "fine roads." They organized bus trips from the U Street storefront to the undeveloped site for prospective buyers.[23] Within months, over seven hundred lots had been sold, and a small cadre of black families, most of them teachers and federal employees, began clearing the land and building small cottages. The apparent success of the Eagle Harbor venture inspired a separate group of black investors to purchase land on the opposite side of the river and found Cedar Haven. Hotels and clubhouses soon dotted both sides of the river, many of them collaborative endeavors by groups of investors.[24] On summer weekends, Cedar Haven became, as one dispatch put it, "a miniature Atlantic City," where a "fashionable gathering reclin[ed] in the easy chairs and view[ed] the host of bathers . . . splashing in the salt waters."[25]

Race began to assume a certain spatial structure and logic in areas undergoing the transition from rural agricultural to vacationland in the 1920s. Given the cold reception (if not outright hostility) African Americans could expect to receive at beaches and resorts frequented by white Americans, the development of distinctly black and spatially separate places of leisure was both desired and necessary for black vacationers who, after all, were seeking fellowship and relaxation rather than confrontation and potential humiliation. However, vast swaths of land in developing coastal zones were (in fact if not in law) simply unavailable to black vacationers or developers of black vacation properties. In these places, African Americans' presence, in anything but a service capacity, was seen by developers and homeowners as a potentially fatal market liability necessitating extreme measures of suppression. African Americans' ability to purchase summer vacation properties was, like housing in cities, severely limited by obstacles such as racial covenants, discriminatory real estate agents and lenders, and—when all else failed—the white mob. Likewise, the desire of African American entrepreneurs to convert fellow blacks' demands for vacation properties into profit was matched only by their naked vulnerability—to usurious, predatory lenders, and public officials beholden to white constituents and real estate interests.

Among the more common discriminatory devices used by public officials to suppress African American landownership perceived as a threat to future development in burgeoning vacationland areas and elsewhere was the property tax assessment. In areas not covered by racially restrictive covenants, where African Americans successfully purchased property in defiance of neighbors, planners, and developers, the discriminatory assessment of property values emerged as an effective mechanism for removing unwanted persons and land uses. Administered on a local level and shrouded from public scrutiny by layers of bureaucracy, property taxes were uniquely prone to corruption and manipulation.[26] As African Americans poured into northern cities during these decades, public officials relied on property tax assessments to relocate black persons and liquidate black property after other barriers had proven ineffective.[27]

No sooner had Eagle Harbor's initial settlers constructed their cottages on the shores of Maryland's Patuxent River than Prince George's County tax assessor James H. Shreve reassessed tax rates from $20 to $300 annually on lots that sold for between twenty-five and one hundred dollars. The new assessment notices reached owners one day after the expiration date for appeals. E. S. Hine accused the county tax assessor of deliberately overassessing the properties because he was "opposed to colored ownership" and intended to use injurious taxation as a means of "driving [black] owners out of the county." As proof, Hine compared assessments of properties at Eagle Harbor to the neighboring white development, Carmody Hills, in which lots were selling for $200 to $300 apiece but were assessed only $15 annually.[28]

In December 1920 Highland Beach's founder and de facto "mayor" Charles Douglass died.[29] In his will, he granted title to all unsold lots in the village's eleven blocks to his sons, Haley Douglass, a schoolteacher at Washington's Dunbar High School, and Joseph Douglass, an accomplished violinist. The two brothers subsequently assumed control over the family's business in African American vacation home real estate at a moment of rapid and uncertain change. Owners of dozens of lots exclusively available to African Americans in a vacation village along the Chesapeake, the Douglasses were keen to capitalize on the benefits of the discriminatory real estate market for owners of summer lots for "colored" buyers. As the numbers of interested buyers grew, Haley Douglass's concerns about breaking even on his family's investment dissipated, and he could instead focus strictly on selling to those persons who "belonged." In this mission, Highland Beach contended with another by-product of this separate-and-unequal summer home market. As was witnessed along the Patuxent River, where Cedar Haven followed close on the heels of Eagle Harbor, when a group of investors succeeded in securing coastal or waterfront acreage and developing a vacation village for African Americans— thereby establishing the area as "colored" in the eyes of whites—speculators and developers rushed to acquire adjoining property and market it to black buyers. In response, developers and marketers of properties in the

established black summer community often worked to scuttle these competing developments or stamp them with the mark of inferiority.

As the number of lot owners at Highland Beach grew in the early 1920s, it
became abundantly clear that a more formal structure of governance was
vital to the village's long-term viability. Lacking any means of revenue collection, the Douglasses and other leading families were forced to take up
collections among lot owners just to complete routine maintenance. Sanitation, fire protection, and security—services that buyers of summer homes
during these years were increasingly coming to expect—were out of the
question.

Enter incorporation. To lower the overhead on infrastructure development of coastal resorts, real estate developers had long used the powers of
municipal incorporation, which allowed for the construction of public
utilities with tax-free municipal bonds. For fledgling black summer cottage communities, incorporation as a municipality also offered residents
greater control over planning, zoning, and property taxation. Indeed, one
year after receiving their outrageous property tax bills, the residents of
Eagle Harbor petitioned the state of Maryland for the right of incorporation.
With the sponsorship of Lansdale Sasscer, then a state senator representing Prince George's County, the General Assembly granted Eagle Harbor
the power to vote to incorporate. On July 21, 1929, residents of Eagle Harbor voted overwhelming to incorporate and establish a five-person board
of commissioners. The following year Eagle Harbor was granted a charter
from the state of Maryland.[30]

In 1922 Haley Douglass and a group of fellow Highland Beach property
owners secured a charter of incorporation. Incorporation enabled Highland Beach to institute a commissioner form of government vested with
the power to adopt regulations and ordinances, levy and collect taxes, and
maintain public services. The following year, the board of commissioners
chose Haley Douglass to serve as board chairman—in effect, the village
mayor.[31] In Maryland and across the nation, African Americans who
themselves could only dream of owning a home, much less a second
home, saw the incorporation of Highland Beach—not only the first all-
black town in the Old Line State but also the first independent black vacation resort town in the nation—as a source of inspiration and a model for
future political action. During a time when the growth of urban black
populations further exacerbated racial inequities in municipalities' revenue collection and service distribution, the idea of municipal incorpora-

tion strongly appealed to many black Americans. Crowded into segregated neighborhoods, forced to pay exorbitant rents on inferior housing, taxed for services they seldom received, blacks saw neighborhood secession and municipal incorporation as offering, in a narrow sense, a partial realization of black nationalist goals and strategies. But while many were receptive to the idea of municipal incorporation, they were equally skeptical of the motivations of Highland Beach residents, who were notorious for their clannishness and disregard for the dire conditions average blacks faced. "All over the country," the *Washington Tribune* wrote, "the experiment is being watched. People are anxious to see how Negroes of superior intellect, and descended from those stalwart fighters for equality, are able to manage a town, and to know their attitude to friends and visitors of the same Race."[32]

Highland Beach's growing summer population, though, was not of one mind on the purpose and implications of incorporation. Among the village's older, "aristocratic," and more culturally conservative elements, incorporation simply ensured a more efficient process for raising revenue for infrastructure improvement and for providing services such as fire protection, sanitation, and policing. But it in no way altered the village's status as a private, secluded, and exclusive community, a belief that came to shape an overall governing philosophy characterized by an expansive view of property rights, a narrow interpretation of what constituted public space, and dedication to restricting access to residents and invited guests. Others, especially many of the younger property owners, however, saw incorporation as allowing for a more open and democratic social environment at Highland Beach, for newer residents and visitors alike, and as opening the possibility for commercial exploitation of the beach's appeal to a growing black middle class in neighboring cities. For the town's de facto mayor, Haley Douglass, it seemed, incorporation as a municipality provided him with another tool to manage the area's racialized real estate market to his best advantage and to ensure that prices for lots in the exclusive summer community remained artificially high.

In their capacity as owners of the village's available lots, the Douglasses were eager to play the role of judges and protectors of Highland Beach's cultural standards. However, in 1925 Edward Bradford Johnson, a white minister from Annapolis, surveyed and plotted a fifty-two-and-a-half-acre property located just behind Highland Beach, and advertised in area black newspapers the sale of lots at what he dubbed Bay Highlands.

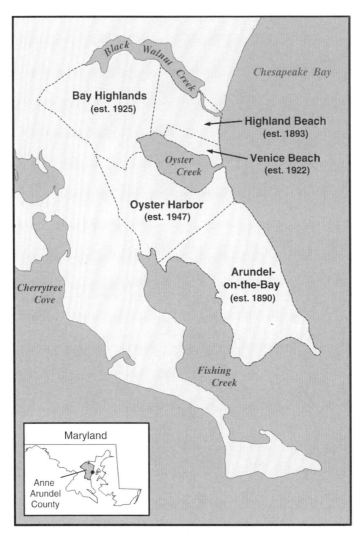

Map 6. Highland Beach and surrounding communities

(See Map 6.) Advertisements deliberately obscured the difference be-tween Bay Highlands and Highland Beach.[33] The proposed Bay High-lands development not only threatened to change the character and social composition of the area's summertime community; it also threatened the profitability of Joseph and Haley Douglass's real estate enterprise by open-ing the area market to additional black buyers. In response, Haley Doug-lass used the tools of government at his disposal in service of his real estate interests. He did so, in part, through sowing existing fears among property owners of a coming invasion of "undesirables." As one of his first acts as the Highland Beach commission chairman, he attempted to use village funds to purchase the Bay Highlands tract, claiming the measure would help ensure that the area would not become populated by a "less desirable set of owners." When that proved unsuccessful, he served notice that "any person buying lots from this white man will not be permitted to use the beach."[34] (Bay Highlands did not have its own beachfront.) Going one step further, Douglass claimed that his father, in deeding to his sons all unsold portions of Highland Beach, also deeded the beach itself, thus making it the private domain of the Douglasses and their invited guests. The legal claim was dubious, to say the least. The Maryland Supreme Court, in addition to interpreting the Public Trust Doctrine to mean that all land below the high-water-mark line belonged to the public, had previously ruled that "the recording of a plat of waterfront property, and conveyance of lots by preference thereto, has the effect of devoting the beach to the public as an avenue."[35] Undeterred by such legal niceties, in 1926 town commissioners passed an ordinance that levied a ten-dollar fine on bathers and picnickers caught on the beach without a formal invitation from one of the town's property owners.[36] In addition, they blocked all areas that could serve as public parking spaces, and removed picnic tables, locker rooms, and waste bins from the beachfront. (Such indirect methods of exclusion became an increasingly common and unremarkable feature of exclusive beach resort towns over the course of the twentieth century.)

In all instances, Douglass and fellow town commissioners disclaimed any attempt to simply punish rival developers or influence local real estate markets. Rather, they sought to protect all homeowners in the area from the threat of the black "criminal elements" that were seemingly multiplying on the streets of the Great Migration–era black metropolis. The specter of black strife-makers and lawbreakers on their shores became a favored justification for numerous policy decisions. The racist logic that fueled the rise of the broader Jim Crow real estate industry thus came to inform the ideologies of elite black landowners, while constructions of poor and working black Americans as culturally "deviant" and their forms of leisure as degraded and immoral became the language and the instruments through which privileged African Americans sought to advance (and obscure) their own interests as holders, investors, and marketers of real estate.

Make no mistake, though: the "problem" of trespassing was, if not so critical among elites, all too real for the great majority of black Americans. Lack of privacy was an everyday aspect of being black in Jim Crow America, especially—and perhaps most frustratingly—in places of residence. Whether it be a shotgun shack on a sharecropping plantation, or a cramped apartment in a ghettoized city, having a place you could truly call your own was a rare commodity, and one that its possessors were willing to go to extremes to protect. For African American owners of waterfront property, the racial enclosure of urban and rural shorelines and segregation of outdoor public places of play made their beaches attractive and comparatively safe destinations for black persons seeking a place to bathe and picnic. While many black owners of beachfront properties (as will be discussed in subsequent chapters) worked to capitalize on this void created in part by segregation, at Highland Beach, property owners came seeking freedom from forced association with unfamiliar people, and desired law enforcement to protect those interests. But they were under no delusions that such help would come from outside. Similar to the policing (or lack thereof) of ghettoized urban black neighborhoods, Anne Arundel County sheriffs exhibited a profound disregard toward criminal activities occurring within Highland Beach's borders, which in effect made it a magnet for both whites and blacks seeking temporary sanctuary from the law. Residents complained of recurrent acts of vandalism by "drunken revelers" who treated the town as seemingly outside the scope of legal authority, and frequently implored the sheriff's department to patrol the area at night, to no avail. In defending the village's extreme measures of exclusion, Haley Douglass expressed elite blacks' simmering resentment at the pernicious effects of segregation laws on them: "The failure of large cities to provide adequate bathing and recreational facilities has placed upon us the burden of protecting our property from roving trespassers whose ignorance or lack of self respect permits them uninvited to impose upon residents who bought their homes for the benefit of their own families and friends."[37]

But while the fear was real, its use as justification for public policies was often cynical and duplicitous. Douglass invoked the specter of "trespassers" and "undesirables" to scuttle several public works initiatives and to reinforce his claims of private ownership of public lands. In the mid 1920s a group of residents of Highland Beach and Venice Beach raised funds for the construction of a pavilion on the beach, using proceeds from entertainment shows, bridge parties, and raffles. Douglass denied them the right to build the pavilion on "his" beach, arguing that the pavilion would attract undesirables, obstruct the views of waterfront property owners, depress property values, and give the impression that the beach was open to the public. While incorporation promised to provide residents the ability to exert greater control over their tax dollars and raise revenue toward infrastructure improvement, there were few signs of Highland Beach tax dollars at work. The village's streets were a nightmare for motorists. Under the pretext that "good roads would be too inviting to an 'irresponsible' public," many residents purposely allowed trees to grow in the middle of the road in front of their lots and resisted any attempts at their removal, claiming that the road itself was included in their deed. When one town commissioner attempted to remove a tree from the middle of a street, the lot owner threatened to sue the town commissioners under the State Forestry Act. "Outside of the appearance of the homes," one black visitor sarcastically remarked, "the rest of the town that I saw looked as though it was cared for as some of the slum districts here in Baltimore are developed." While underdevelopment of their neighborhoods reminded the black urban poor of their second-class citizenship, at Highland Beach it became a sign of the village's exclusivity. For Douglass, in particular, it was a mechanism for adding to his real estate holdings. Trees remained in the middle of some streets because Douglass planned to subdivide and sell the land that was the street, a violation of the village's charter of incorporation. Douglass's attempts to reconvert public avenues into private property that he would sell for personal profit enraged neighboring property owners, who bought with the understanding that their lot faced a road, and led to suspicions and, later, formal charges that he was misappropriating public funds to further his real estate interests.[38]

In place of good roads, Highland Beach did devote public funds to good guards and good fences. In 1928 the town hired a black private police officer to stand guard at the village's entrance and turn away those unable to give the name of a person they were registered to visit, another new ordinance adopted by the town commissioners. Later, the town hired Frank Meyer, a white former ice hauler, to patrol the entrance, after concluding that black intruders would not "obey a peace officer of their own." The officer's salary reportedly constituted over one-tenth of the town's annual budget.[39]

Haley Douglass went to great lengths to block pathways connecting Highland Beach and Venice Beach and physically divide the two communities.

On the morning of July 4, 1929, he erected a five-foot-tall barbed-wire fence along the village's boundary with Venice Beach. He said the fence was meant to protect Highland Beach from the "throng of persons who journey to the beach for week-ends; some of whom . . . don bathing suits in autos or in the shrubbery, and otherwise misconducting themselves." Venice Beach residents castigated the move as a "gratuitous insult to their intelligence and pride" designed to "stigmatize the Venice Beachers as undesirable." After a day of celebrating the nation's birthday, Venice Beachers "exercised the independence day spirit and like the compatriots of 1776" tore down the fence.[40]

Indeed, the politics and culture of exclusion proved mutually reinforcing, sowing resentment among neighbors, visitors, and "trespassers" and exacerbating the very nuisances Highland Beach residents ostensibly aimed to combat, all of which in turn justified additional reactionary measures. The absence of locker rooms, removal of parking spaces, picnic tables, and trash bins, and overall criminalization of activities associated with non-resident recreation did not solve the "problem" of trespassing, but instead resulted in reports of strangers disrobing in public and leaving trash on the shore. "They undressed from their cars, threw broken liquor about the beach and grounds, got drunk, accosted the children and insulted the women," one resident said of intruders. Another resident detained and secured the arrest of a group of black teenagers from Annapolis he found changing into swim trunks underneath his front porch.

More often, though, calls to the county sheriff's office did not yield much, if any, response. And this, too, came to be seen by residents as one of the many underhanded tactics designed to drive them from the shore. Following the town's incorporation, a group of white developers challenged the legality of the town's charter. As land values along the Chesapeake's Western Shore rose in the 1920s, rumors spread of white developers enlisting African Americans to serve as front men in attempts to purchase property in Highland Beach and divide and displace the community. Throughout the late 1920s and early 1930s lobbyists representing waterfront developers continued to pressure the state legislature to repeal the town's charter. In February 1933, they nearly succeeded in sneaking a bill into the final legislature that would have done just that. By the early 1930s, Highland Beach was forced to hire a lawyer in Annapolis to "keep a constant watch" on the state capitol and keep town officials abreast of the maneuverings of Anne Arundel County real estate interests. Every ma-

neuver by state and county government was treated as a potential mechanism of displacement. A road construction project proposed in 1930 that
would have made the area more accessible to motorists from Annapolis
would, black property owners charged, first "throw open the community
to the general public and destroy protection of the community against the
invasion of criminals, brawlers, strife breeders, law-breakers, and all other
undesirables," and then, after having destroyed the character of the area,
it "would [have] permit[ted] the whites to enter, take possession of the
beach and ultimately force the colored inhabitants from the waters of the
Chesapeake Bay." Douglass and fellow town commissioners never missed
an opportunity to invoke these sets of fears when responding to their critics. Those who questioned the town's methods of governance were, Douglass charged, "inspired by commercial interests [seeking] to discredit the
authority of the Commission Board."[41] A Highland Beach resident who
penned a series of damning exposés in the *Washington Tribune* under
the pseudonym Eula G. Brown was later accused by two town officials of
being a "traitor" and pawn of "white land owners of the vicinity who
[sought to] destroy Highland Beach."[42]

Haley Douglass's dismissal of criticisms of his style of governance as the
work of outside meddlers obscured but could not extinguish the growing
divisions among Highland Beach property owners and mounting hostility
toward Douglass's use of his elected office to dispense favors to his friends,
punish his enemies, and advance his business and real estate interests.
Newer property owners complained of arbitrary and discriminatory assessment of property taxes by county assessors, who worked directly with town
commissioners in assessing village property values. Unsold lots were uni-
formly assessed at $50. Upon purchase by new lot owners, the lots were
immediately reassessed at $200 or more, before any improvements had
been made. While some of the choicest lots with cottages owned by longtime property owners such as the Terrells, Murrays, and Francises were
assessed between $100 and $350, other residents who had built on their
lots saw their property assessed as high as $5,000. Those paying the most
in taxes were often those most interested in the improvement of roads and
addition of lighting, piers, and pavilions, and other services and amenities, further exacerbating tensions among property owners.[43]

Contests over property rights, governance, and taxation became inseparable and at times indistinguishable from contests over the village's social
character and cultural identity. It was no coincidence that those property

owners most determined to resist change were those who found fun "in bridge, in meals, in gossip, in politics, and in sleep," and who wanted to keep the village private and exclusive, while those property owners targeted for discriminatory treatment by town commissioners were those who "want[ed] fishing, boating, swimming, dancing, tennis, and games," and who were receptive to the idea of leisure-based commercial activity.[44]

Among those property owners singled out for censure was Richard Ware, whom Charles Douglass had cajoled into buying several lots in 1920 and opening a hotel that, Douglass hoped, would draw in additional lot buyers. Opened in 1925, Ware's Hotel sported a ballroom, a restaurant, seventy-five rooms, and a basement "Grotto" with pool tables and slot machines. On Saturday evenings, Ware's nephew Dick Hall and his Jazz Night-hawks entertained guests on the patio and in the ballroom; gambling and bootlegged alcohol allegedly flowed freely inside. Ware advertised his accommodations liberally (a short drive from Washington, Baltimore, or Annapolis, "on good roads," one ad read) and emphasized that he "cater[ed] to the public without regard to their station in life." Ware's Hotel quickly emerged as a favorite summertime destination among Washington and Baltimore's fashionable sets. On summer weekends, it was not unusual to find local and national black celebrities barreling down Anne Arundel County roads toward the village's shrouded entrance, cruising past the row of waterfront cottages, and pulling into the hotel's parking lot. Their arrival at Ware's Hotel signaled the arrival of the New Negro, and the black expressive culture of Washington and Baltimore's "Stroll," at this citadel of the black aristocracy.[45]

Residents who bought lots and built cottages at Highland Beach so as to escape the city and find peace and quiet were less than enthused at the prospect of throngs of pleasure seekers bent on making what Du Bois described as "whoopee." Highland Beach, one resident grumbled, "was never designed to become a commercial summer resort for the accom-modation of the general public. . . . At the rate we are going, it will not be long before sheer gravitation will transform the place into an open, over-crowded, unwholesome public resort." A handful of dedicated opponents of the hotel conducted a concerted campaign to drive Ware out of busi-ness. Rumors about the conduct of hotel guests were spread via "back porch and card table gossip." Town commissioners passed ordinances that prohibited automobiles except for those driven by persons visiting resi-dents and banned music or dancing after midnight. An anonymous call was placed to the state health inspector charging Ware's Hotel with violating state sanitary laws. Finding the hotel in compliance, the state health inspector expressed his anger at "being sent out on what was . . . a 'spite' job." Ware called these brazen attempts to drive him out of business an assault on his property rights. Moreover, he and his supporters charged, they were conducted not in the interests of upholding community standards but rather as a result of Douglass's desire to maximize profits and accumulate wealth. Instead of buying a lot and constructing their own cottage, many families from Washington and Baltimore opted instead to rent a room at Ware's Hotel for a weekend or extended stay; thus Douglass saw the hotel's popularity as a direct threat to his real estate enterprise. Dire predictions of the village becoming a rendezvous for gamblers, bootleggers, drunkards, and "loose women" were, one critic charged, mere "camouflage and smoke screens and dead herrings [sic] . . . used by henchmen to becloud the real important matters. The open town legendary fear . . . helps keep the real issues in the background." Among those real issues, the writer argued, was Douglass's abuse of power and determination to ensure that "if any money is to be made in the place, he is the only one to make it."[46]

In 1929, Richard Ware ran for a seat on the village's board of commissioners. (He had previously fallen two votes short of election.) In response to an anonymous tip, on the eve of the election Anne Arundel County sheriffs arrived at the hotel bearing a warrant to search the premises for liquor and gambling devices. Despite an exhaustive search, they only found two nickel-slot machines. But the ploy had fulfilled its purpose. Ware failed to win election to the commission board; overall, opponents of plans to turn the town into what they described as a "wide-open commercial resort" won by a two-to-one margin. Following the election, Haley Douglass passed ordinances designed to "preserve good order, health, and beauty within its corporate limits," including a strict building code and required preapproval of the board of commissioners for proposed structures, annual licensing of businesses, a ban on all "public picnics or excursions," and restrictions on visitors to include only "house guests of a householder."[47]

Incendiary tactics completed what administrative maneuvers had begun. The following off-season, on the evening of January 20, 1930, flames engulfed the Ware Hotel, destroying the structure and a neighboring cottage owned by Ware's sister-in-law Sarah Hall. "Only the ashes and crumpled iron beds and springs remained," one report noted. There was little doubt that arson was the cause and that, given the makeup of the commissioner board, a permit to rebuild the hotel would not be granted. Ware did not even bother submitting an application to the board and instead rebuilt a smaller hotel on a lot he owned in Venice Beach that abutted Highland Beach.[48]

For a growing chorus of African American critics, town officials' deliberate efforts to force Ware out of business exemplified elite blacks' abandonment of the principles of democratic governance and embrace of dubious and at times blatantly illegal strategies to maintain their isolation from the wider black public, tactics that bore a striking similarity to those employed by white residents of "sundown towns."[49] "Notwithstanding its incorporation," writer Louis R. Lautier commented, "[town] commissioners have decided that they have the right to deny to any persons whom they term undesirable the use of town streets just as colored persons are denied the right to live in some southern towns under the admonition to 'read and run; if you can't read, run anyhow.'" "Residents of Highland Beach," Fred B. Watson charged, "have erected a social barrier almost as insurmountable as any the white race ever dreamed of." "No one who subscribes to this condition," he added, "could ever kick when at Atlantic City [New Jersey] and elsewhere white people, who think all of us are 'undesirable,' attempt to keep us completely off the beach or confine us to small segregated areas."[50]

On the streets of Washington and Baltimore, reports circulated of persons being turned away at the Highland Beach gate "because of a lack of ancestry, color, or social standing," and rumors spread that a person first had to pass the "brown paper bag" test to gain entry to the town. Critics singled out for rebuke the presence of a white police officer whose primary duty was to keep out African Americans who did not conform to residents' standards. "It is sickening and disgusting," one person turned away wrote, "to drive into the town and find a cheap, jobless poor white man empowered by the present council to insult the guests of some of the residents there. . . . Had I not been with my family, I would have given the town officials their first real case." "Why," Ralph Matthews wondered, is it "necessary to have a special invitation or have someone vouch for your pedigree before you can cool your toes in that large expanse of water that God permitted to flow past this excluded plot"? "Volsted [the Volstead, or National Prohibition, Act] made it illegal to use anything but water. Highland Beach made it illegal to use water. If those guys had their way a bird would have to bootleg to get a bath." A reader wrote to the *Baltimore Afro-American*, "Frederick Douglass would turn in his grave were he able today to see the town that he and his children had founded." *Afro-American* commentator "Professor Fudge" denounced the "inhumanness of the inhabitants" of Highland Beach. "When you ask for bread, they give you one of those sharp rocks out of the water and when you ask for a drink they call the constable." John W. Rudisell of Washington called for a boycott of the doctors, lawyers, and business owners who owned summer homes there. John E. Harris cited the controversy as further proof of how the arbitrary attribute of light skin was deployed by both the white ruling class and the light-skinned Negro aristocracy to divide and subjugate dark-skinned people. "When ever we blacks learn to hold our heads up and drop much of our color sensitiveness . . . whenever we show to the world that we honor and love our black women with their black skins and short hair, then, and not until then, will mulattoes and whites and Indians stop sneering at us when they pass us on the street." For some, the battle over Highland Beach crystallized the underlying sources of prejudice, rooted, as one writer commented, in a human desire to concentrate power, resources, and connections. "Perhaps," he wrote, the saga

> would give all of us a better understanding of the thing we generally term racial prejudice—not the barbarous or savage kind, of course, but the kind which instinctively impels human beings and groups to seek to hold such as they have achieved—if we come to realize and understand just how this same kind of prejudice is playing its part in our own advancement—or our retardation. . . . Highland Beach, a little incident in itself, therefore gives us a good chance to view our own human tendencies—and to some of us a chance to discover human tendencies within ourselves which we have lambasted in others.

Alongside expressions of outrage and calls for organized protest were bitingly satirical dismissals of elite blacks' claims to status and supremacy. "In order to be actually recognized in Highland Beach upper crust, and you'll admit they have a lot of crust," Ralph Matthews joked, "you either have to possess a fadeout complexion or plenty of filthy lucre and the less you have of the former the more you have to have of the latter. . . . You would think . . . from the way some of them put on the dog that they could trace their ancestry back to the 'Mayflower.'" "Without a doubt," black Washington resident W. R. Tillman wrote, "they are what we call 'the fays,' or the Negroes with light skins, who seek superiority over others. . . . Here is one of the reasons why the white man can laugh in our faces when . . . we complain of being segregated by him."[51]

A sign of black Americans' strides toward political independence and self-determination upon its founding in 1922, by decade's end Highland Beach had become, for many black observers, a source of outrage and embarrassment, and the profit-driven corruption of its elected officials evidence that the future of the race could not be entrusted to its most privileged members. One black writer from Washington, D.C., asked, "Is Highland Beach proving that Negroes are not yet intelligent enough to govern themselves?" Or, "Would the town's affairs be handled better if there were more commonplace people living there?"[52]

In the midst of these debates, Haley Douglass put forth a bold proposal. Instead of the uncertainties and contentiousness that came with representative government, why not dissolve the village's charter, unincorporate, and reform as a private homeowners' association? First outlined in 1898 by Ebenezer Howard, father of the British Garden City movement, and utilized in the United States by developers of luxury subdivisions in the first decades of the twentieth century, homeowners' associations established a common set of covenants, conditions, and restrictions on land use that were written into property deeds. Rather than a fluid and evolving set of rules and regulations on land use enacted through democratic procedures, homeowners' associations established a clear definition of a community's physical features and social characteristics that property owners were legally compelled to abide by or risk being sued by fellow association members for violation of the terms of their land contract. In place of popularly elected officials, homeowners' associations were governed by boards of directors charged with enforcing established regulations and legally empowered to operate outside the constitutional restrictions placed on elected governments. Participation in the governance of the homeowners' association was limited strictly to property owners, who in return for relinquishing rights to use their property as they wished were relieved of the threat of rogue neighbors violating community standards with impunity, or the introduction of persons and land uses that threatened to alter the character of the community and depreciate property values. Covenants barring racial and ethnic minorities from purchasing homes in a given neighborhood were the most notorious—but far from the only—type of restriction found in most homeowners' associations. As a 1928 study of deed restrictions in eighty-four high-end subdivisions found, prohibitions against property owners conducting business activity or using their property for anything but residential purposes were the most common restrictions, with racial covenants found primarily in areas with large minority populations or those experiencing high rates of black migration.[53]

Dissolving Highland Beach's town charter and reforming as a homeowners' association, Douglass argued, offered a more effective means of protecting the village from undesirable persons and land uses. For many residents and fellow commissioners who had quietly opposed Douglass's heavy-handed tactics and suspected him of harboring profit-driven motives, the idea of unincorporating was the last straw. The other four members of the board of commissioners openly denounced Douglass and signed an open letter that likened the abandonment of democratic governance to a return to slavery.[54] But while residents and town officials publicly distanced themselves from Douglass and placed the blame for the village's bad reputation at his feet, many shared his governing philosophy and worked to convert the village from municipality to homeowners' association in fact if not in name. In 1933 the town adopted a new charter (approved by the Maryland state legislature) that mimicked many of the features of a homeowners' association, including provisions that restricted voting rights to individuals owning real estate of no less than $200 in value, a prohibition against the establishment of businesses or engagement in commercial activity, a permanent moratorium on the dedication of any land for public use, and a provision that all future amendments to the charter or proposals for incorporating Highland Beach with any surrounding area must arise by a petition signed by over 50 percent of taxpaying residents and then approved by over two-thirds of voters in a general election.[55]

It is more than a bit ironic that the fire-bombing of Ware's Hotel was the only suspected case of arson in an area that experienced, in the years following World War II, sudden and dramatic changes in its racial demographics. During these years, legal breakthroughs in the workplace quite literally expanded the size and earning power of the black middle class in

Annapolis, Washington, and Baltimore. In 1939 the young NAACP lawyer Thurgood Marshall successfully argued, in *Mills v. Lowndes et al.*, for the equalization of salaries for African American teachers in Anne Arundel County.[56] The decision in that case constituted a pivotal victory on the road to the U.S. Supreme Court's 1954 *Brown v. Board of Education* decision, and was part of a growing wave of legal rulings, executive orders, and direct actions against hiring and pay discrimination in the public sector in the 1940s, all of which contributed to significant increases in many black families' incomes.[57] In particular, Marshall's successful litigation of the *Mills* case led to an immediate spike in the salaries of black teachers in Maryland's segregated school systems and afforded many families the means to move up and out of overpriced rental units in ghettoized urban neighborhoods.[58]

The market for black waterfront home development had never seemed more fertile. In 1939, Washington real estate developer G. Edward Moul formed the Columbia Beach Company, acquired just over eighty-eight acres of coastal real estate in southern Anne Arundel County, and divided the land into 359 lots laid out over fourteen blocks. In 1940 the Columbia Beach Company began marketing lots to African Americans. By 1950, 253 families and individuals had purchased a single lot or combination of lots in the development. Aside from the names given to the streets, which paid tribute to important figures in black history (twice in the case of Booker T. Washington, with parallel streets named Booker Road and Washington Road), the design of Columbia Beach was virtually indistinguishable from whites-only private beach communities under development during these years—as were the property deeds, which contained a detailed list of covenants and restrictions to be enforced by the Columbia Beach Property Owners Association.[59]

Whereas the governing structures of vacation communities such as Highland Beach founded in the late nineteenth century evolved slowly and contentiously, by the 1940s developers of planned communities adopted, almost without exception, the property owners' association model. In 1949 William Schlusemeyer, a successful real estate developer and owner of a thoroughbred racehorse farm in Virginia, purchased one hundred acres of undeveloped, forested land along Fishing Creek in the municipality of Arundel-on-the-Bay from a defunct land development corporation (which had acquired the property in 1941 but failed to raise the capital necessary to begin work).[60] Schlusemeyer cleared and subdivided the swampy, wooded area into eighty-eight lots laid out over fourteen blocks, and dredged and bulkheaded the creek so as to allow large watercraft to access the bay from the cove, a feat of civil engineering that would devastate the local ecosystem and hasten the shore's erosion. Oyster Harbor Inc. aggressively advertised the sale of lots to African Americans in neighboring cities. In Washington, D.C., Oyster Harbor Inc. hired a young black man to flood storefront shops in the city's black neighborhoods advertising lots that cost between $1,000 and $3,000.[61] Purchase of a lot came with a list of restrictions on the use of the property included in the deed, along with automatic membership in the Oyster Harbor Property Owners Association. Lots at Oyster Harbor sold fast. Between May 1950 (when lots were first offered for sale) and December 1953, 147 African American individuals and couples (the vast majority year-round residents of Washington, D.C.) purchased single or multiple lots at Oyster Harbor.[62] (See Map 6, p. 98.)

The appeal of property owners' associations was contagious, especially among whites who owned summer homes that bordered new African American planned communities. Following Oyster Harbor's completion, the white property owners of Arundel-on-the-Bay quickly moved to fortify their own status as a private community by dissolving the town's charter and, on June 3, 1949, reforming as a private homeowners' association.[63] Coming as it did after the U.S. Supreme Court's *Shelley v. Kraemer* (1948) decision that ruled racial covenants on real estate unenforceable, the newly private community would have to rely on its residents' racial solidarity to ensure the village's homogeneity. But only months later, that solidarity began to crumble. Over the objections of their neighbors, who complained that the design obstructed their view, in the summer of 1949 Arundel-on-the-Bay waterfront property owners William and Margaret Jamar completed work on a two-story cottage facing Chesapeake Bay. Completion of the home led to the Jamars' being ostracized by their neighbors. The Jamars retaliated by placing their home on the market— for "colored" purchase only. On November 12, 1949, black Baltimore caterer T. Randolph Waters purchased the Jamars' newly completed summer home.[64]

The Waters purchase immediately transformed the vacation housing market in Arundel-on-the-Bay. Before the Waterses had finished unpacking, white homeowners were scrambling to sell their properties. Later that month, Dr. Francis Dyer, an African American doctor in Washington, purchased a waterfront home from Jack and Sophia Ahrens.[65] In February

1950, William LeRoy and Lillian Berry purchased the Theodore and Rose Fifer family's three-lot summer home on Fishing Cove. Local real estate agents leapt into action. Annapolis real estate agent Joseph D. Lazenby, Kay Realty Company, and Newcombe Realty Company handled several homes being sold by white families and marketed specifically to "colored famil[ies] that can afford a fine home."[66] Black Annapolis realtist Carroll Hynson coordinated and profited handsomely from the process of racial succession, working with white sellers to identify black buyers who fit the social profile he, as the owner of a newly built waterfront home in the village, sought to establish, and working with area lenders to secure mortgages for prospective buyers.

Within three years after the Waterses purchased the Jamars' summer cottage, over forty black families had purchased summer homes in the village at prices ranging from $15,000 to $30,000. "There was almost a complete changeover from white to black," black summer resident Aris T. Allen recalled. "The whole community went in about a year, year and a half," resident John Moses remembers. "It flipped over completely. Massive white flight. But hey, if you're black, that's fine. You want a place to live." In a nationally syndicated column, former Highland Beach commission chairman Edwin B. Henderson crowed, "White people are leaving some of the most beautiful vistas and summer colonies as enterprising colored buyers moved in. . . . Some remain to find their neighbors are as refined and property-respecting as they."[67] Indeed, the irony of white flight from Arundel-on-the-Bay was that the African Americans who moved in were as much if not more dedicated to the principle of privatism and exclusion—and the benefits of privatized governance—as the whites who left. By 1954, African American property owners Theodore H. Johnson and Delores C. Hunt had been elected president and secretary, respectively, of the Arundel-on-the-Bay Property Owners Association, governing internal affairs and representing collective interests in a manner similar to their white predecessors. Oyster Harbor's Property Owners Association, similarly, served primarily as a vehicle for the protection of property interests against the public. Following a couple of unannounced visits by busloads of poor black children from Washington in the early 1960s, residents of Oyster Harbor installed a fence around their beach and twenty-two feet into the water.[68]

By the early 1960s, the areas surrounding Highland Beach had grown into an archipelago of distinctive black privatopias. "Arundel," a reporter for the *Afro-American* remarked, "has drawn the chic younger crowd that goes for swanky homes." In contrast to the consciously rural, rustic cottages in Highland Beach, most homes in Arundel-on-the-Bay enjoyed plumbing and electricity. "These are not casual cottages designed for 'roughing it.'"[69] Oyster Harbor, meanwhile, attracted a mixture of middle-class vacation homeowners and year-round residents. While bloodlines still mattered at Highland Beach, at Oyster Harbor "there might have been a plumber, electrician, doctor, teacher, [and] postal worker [owning cottages there]."[70]

African American children who grew up in post–World War II America and spent their summers at these enclaves along the Chesapeake remember them as an "an oasis in a parched environment." While poor black children remained confined in the sweltering city, forced to use the street as their sandbox and the fire hydrant as their swimming pool, at Highland Beach, children spent their summers playing on the beach and bathing in the Chesapeake. "You get up in the morning and had a little something to eat and out you went. We swam, we played games, we had boat races, all kinds of recreational activities. We literally lived outdoors." Here, parents strove to create a world where the only sting a black child learned to fear was that of a yellow jacket or a jellyfish. Summer residents arranged with local farmers and grocery stores to truck milk, bread, fruits, and vegetables to the town each weekend during the summer. "We didn't go into Annapolis, we stayed here," Ray Langston remembers. Instead, a worker from a nearby general store "came to the village to take orders so we didn't have to come in [there] and run the risk of having to get into it with some of those rednecks." Here, work was meant to build character, and the absence of shoes on one's feet was by choice, not circumstance. "I remember we had a few chores," John Moses recalls, "and then we could go out and just run and race and we didn't have to wear shoes because a lot of the roads were dirt. You could ride your bicycle and play in the woods and . . . [build] forts." You could let your imagination run wild. Sharon Merrick remembers the striking visual contrast between Oyster Harbor and her family's year-round place of residence, Harrisburg, Pennsylvania. "[Harrisburg is] an all-brick city. . . . When you came down here, people had white houses, they had green houses. [One neighbor] had a pink house. . . . And you had lots of woods. . . . It was a very different environment."[71]

For most blacks living in Jim Crow America, it was an utterly unfamiliar one that could be as hostile and uninviting as the streets of lily-white suburbs and the boardwalks along white beach resort towns. For those fortunate enough to secure a piece of land in one of these privatopias, class homogeneity in places of leisure reflected the natural sorting out of persons according to their tastes and social preferences, not the product of mechanisms of exclusion, stigmatization, and criminalization of nonresident "trespassers" enacted and enforced over the previous several decades. While much was wrong with the world outside, behind these gates, they told themselves, things were as they should be.

4

SURVIVING THE SUMMER

For Peter "Chuck" Badie, the sights and sounds of childhood summers in New Orleans in the 1930s and 1940s remain seared in his memory. The black son of a domestic worker and a numbers bookie, Badie lived in a shotgun house in a section of city's Uptown district bordered by St. Charles Avenue and the Mississippi River, where he and his siblings slept on the porch during the summer months, waking to the sunrise and to a body covered in mosquito bites. To help support his family, Badie would caddy for white golfers at nearby Audubon Park, the crown jewel of the city's world-renowned parks system. On his way back home, he and his friends would occasionally stop to catch a glimpse of the white children swimming in the park's Olympic-size swimming pool. "I'm peeping through them hedges and looking at them white boys and white girls swimming, wishing I would be in that pool." One time, a mounted park patrol officer sneaked up from behind. "I couldn't hear him coming . . . and that horse . . . reare[d] back [and went] 'rrrrrrgggg,' you know, he'd pull him back [and said], 'Nigger, don't you know you on these white folks' grass?' And then we had to haul ass"—back to the four-block area in Uptown whites derisively dubbed "Niggertown," where the anguished cries of a grief-stricken mother became, during the summer months, an all-too-familiar refrain. "Never forget," Badie said of the summer afternoon in 1948 when his childhood friend "Tee-Tan" Rousseau went under while swimming in the dangerous currents of the Mississippi. "We all ran out on that levee. They found him a few days later, but them shrimps had 'em. His face was the color of that [white] bottle on the table, that bottle of medicine right there. You know when shrimps get hold of you after a couple of days your face look just like the flesh of a catfish. He was about thirteen, fourteen years old."[1]

For New Orleans's black poor, it did not take a rising tide for the bodies of water that snaked around and through the Crescent City to remind them of the existential threats posed by the city's natural and built environment. And unlike the wealthy white families they lived alongside and served, for them "surviving the summer" was not just an expression. It was a lived reality. For New Orleans's nearly 150,000 persons of color, the city provided, as late as 1953, a single swimming pool at the Lafon "Colored" Playground in Uptown, described by the black newspaper the *Louisiana Weekly* as "little more than the size of a large bathtub, and which children must pay to use, for even an hour or two." Exclusion of African Americans from places of recreation extended far beyond the city's public swimming pools and beaches to include even an undeveloped portion of the lakefront, where, in response to a local charity's request to hold swimming lessons for Negro children there in the summer of 1947, the Orleans Levee Board warned they should expect to be "driven away, should they be discovered." As a result, the city's rivers and canals became, for poor black children, a makeshift playground and, for many, their final resting place. By the early 1940s, the NAACP estimated an average of fifteen black children drowned in the city each summer. Newspaper reports and anecdotal evidence suggest those numbers were far higher. Simply knowing how to swim, black New Orleans native Keith Butler recalls, was itself a marker of status. It meant "you had opportunities that others didn't."[2] The drowning deaths of friends, family, and neighbors became, for many African Americans, a cruel companion of rising temperatures, and a fundamental aspect of living—and dying—in the Jim Crow city.

The shocking numbers of African American drowning deaths in early to mid-twentieth-century cities was closely tied to changes in the spatiality of race, real estate, and recreation, changes that, in turn, profoundly shaped the urban black poor's interaction with nature—and nature's actions on them. As cities worked to reengineer urban shorelines in the interests of commercial and residential development, and as access to urban leisure spaces became a key determinant in local real estate markets, the total exclusion of persons of color from developed shorelines and safe, supervised places of play became incorporated into models of urban segregation, contributing in a direct and unambiguous manner to an increase in the exposure of urban black populations to environmental hazards and the deterioration of their overall health and safety during the summer months. As working black mothers prayed for their children's safe return each summer evening, growing numbers of black civic leaders in Jim Crow cities across the nation pressured public officials to address the summertime crisis that grew out of blacks' exclusion from public places of recreation and forced relegation to dangerous and polluted waters. In response to grassroots mobilizations for civil and environmental justice, white public officials scrambled to designate areas of urban shorelines for "colored" use and to fashion a sustainable model of summertime segregation. How certain places came to be selected as suitable for black bathers, and what considerations were factored into the decision-making process, reflected the shifting relations of power and influence among white populations and foreshadowed broader changes in the spatiality and seasonality of segregation for urban black populations in cities that undertook environmental engineering projects and expanded urban recreational programs in the first half of the twentieth century. The following chapter tells the histories of public "colored" beaches in three cities—New Orleans, Washington, D.C., and Norfolk, Virginia—and the struggles of urban black populations to survive the summer.

"Before the sea wall went through we did have a place where we could enter the cooling waters of Lake Pontchartrain," a 1928 editorial in the black newspaper *Louisiana Weekly* commented. But since completion of the seawall, "the pure waters of Lake Pontchartrain [are] forbidden to us." Before the Orleans Levee Board completed the seawall that made lakefront development and the city's northward expansion possible, the diverse collection of people classified by the state of Louisiana as "colored" had more than a few places on Lake Pontchartrain they could expect to retreat to without fear of harassment or expulsion. During the city's first two centuries, the southern shore of the vast lake to the city's north remained mostly free of inhabitants and peripheral to the regional economy. Marshes and dense forests extended a mile inland and served as a receptacle for the lake's routine floodwaters. To most residents of the still-"crescent" city, the lakeshore was no more than a place for fishing and crabbing. Development consisted of the resorts of Milneburg, Spanish Fort, and West End, where New Orleanians boarded steamers for their summer cottages on the Mississippi Gulf Coast or across the lake in Mandeville. For those who could not afford such luxuries, the southern lakeshore became a popular summer destination and refuge from the specter of yellow fever. It also became a haven for outcasts and eccentrics, and fostered the formation of working-class, bohemian subcultures. Squatters' camps dotted the shore, built upon pilings of driftwood. By the late nineteenth century, Milneburg housed a small, racially and ethnically diverse community of fishermen, woodcutters, dairymen, laborers, and barkeepers, and played a critical role in the evolution of jazz music, as captured in early jazz recordings such as "Milneburg Joys" and "Bucktown Blues" by Jelly Roll Morton, and "West End Blues" by Clarence Williams. With its saloons, lovers' lanes, and an "illicit atmosphere which is vaguely enticing," as one observer put it, the area became affectionately known as the "poor man's Riviera."[3]

The seeds of the lakefront's transformation from remote swamplands to suburban frontier were planted in 1873, when New Orleans city surveyor W. H. Bell first proposed the idea of fortifying the lakeshore, draining the swamps, and making the area suitable for development. Bell proposed the erection of an artificial levee and the pumping of sediment behind the wall. The proposal languished for the next two decades until 1893, when the city council passed an ordinance that called for a comprehensive drainage system from the city to the lake. The New Orleans Drainage Plan, completed in 1895, called for the construction of a system of canals that would divert water and sewage from Lake Pontchartrain into Lake Borgne. Construction began in 1896.[4] Reclamation of the lakeshore received a significant boost in 1897 when A. Baldwin Wood, an engineer with the New Orleans Sewerage and Water Board, invented an improved screw pump, a major breakthrough in the city's efforts to drain the swamps. In the coming decades, innovations in the design and function of the screw pump allowed the city to significantly improve its capacity to drain surface and underground water and sped the drainage of the swamps along the lake.

These early initiatives and technological advances laid the groundwork for the emergence of a new arm of political and economic power in the city and the state. In 1890 the Louisiana General Assembly established the Board of Levee Commissioners of the Orleans Levee District—known as the Orleans Levee Board—an agency charged with the construction, control, maintenance, and repair of the parish's levees. In total, the state legislature created twenty-one levee districts, deeded them thousands of acres of swampland, and granted unprecedented (and liberally interpreted) powers to accomplish their stated mission of flood protection. Vested with the power to levy taxes and maintain police forces, and with their board members appointed by the governor, levee boards became, in effect, po-

litical institutions unto themselves and a source of revenue elected officials were quick to manipulate.[5]

Levee boards enjoyed sweeping powers over land and people. They not
only created land where none previously existed (and pocketed the profits
from its sale) but also possessed the power to take land from private citizens
and give nothing in return. Unlike eminent domain, which required the
state to compensate property owners, under Louisiana's riparian servitude
statute, the state could appropriate waterfront property without compensation in the interest of flood protection, a practice upheld by the U.S.
Supreme Court in its 1896 decision *Eldridge v. Trezevant*.[6] Levee boards'
role in protecting Louisianans from floods gradually became indistinguishable from their role in creating and marketing new real estate, and no more
so than in Orleans Parish. During the period from 1893 to 1915, the state
legislature made several amendments to the constitution that expanded
the power of levee boards to manage and market property created by flood
control projects, the profits of which would flow back into levee board
budgets. In 1916 state officials appropriated $1 million for the construction
of seawalls and embankments along Lake Pontchartrain. In 1921 the state
amended its constitution to confer on the Orleans Levee Board the power
to "acquire any private property by donation, purchase, or expropriation in
a designated area along the lakefront from the Jefferson Parish line east-
ward to Little Woods." In 1928 the state legislature granted complete authority to the levee board to improve and manage the area, including the
power "to dedicate, construct, operate, and maintain public parks, beaches,
marinas, aviation fields, and other like facilities." The act, in effect, solidified
the board's role as an agent of residential and commercial development.[7]

As the levee board graded and paved new roads leading to the shore,
throngs of whites poured out of the city to dip their toes in the city's future. In the summer of 1932, a reported three thousand persons filled to
capacity the traffic lanes leading to the lake. Completion of the lakefront
redevelopment project had an immediate and lasting impact on the city's
physical environment. (See Map 7.) The implementation of subsurface
drainage pushed the water table below the soil surface, which in turn led
to a noticeable increase in the city's average yearly temperature. In addition, draining the swamps caused the city to sink even farther below sea
level, leading to an increased danger of flooding, the need for higher and
higher levees, and, consequently, an increasingly powerful levee board.[8]

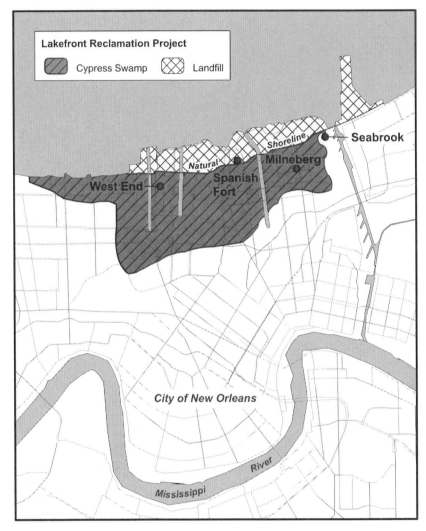

Map 7. New Orleans before and after the Lakefront Reclamation Project

The effects of the new lakefront on the city's social environment were equally profound. With its broad expanses, open fields, cool breezes, and sweeping vistas ripe for modern, suburban development, the new lakefront offered a striking contrast to the cramped, muggy, and proudly anti-modern neighborhoods that hugged the riverfront. City and state officials were on hand to cut the ribbon on the Lake Vista residential development on September 29, 1936, the first in a series of "garden city"–style residential developments planned and implemented by the levee board over the following years. "For more than two score years," Mayor Robert S. Maestri declared, "the people of New Orleans have visioned [sic] a development on this lake front which would enable them to enjoy its fullest possibilities for both recreation and better living. The work on the Lakefront Development Project was another and a vitally important step toward the full realization of this dream." "Gone are the Jerry-built camps, the scattered light poles, and the danger of rising water," Lake Vista developer Hampton Reynolds cheered. "In its place is a new development of high land providing adequate protection from the lake water, a major residential as well as recreational area open to all New Orleanians."[9]

Or, rather, *some* New Orleanians. Lakefront residential developments employed racially restrictive neighborhood covenants on a scale never before seen in a city where, as the geographer Richard Campanella found, pockets of black populations in majority-white districts were common.[10] The relationship between technological innovation, environmental engineering, and the racialization of space in the city was strikingly evident. The urban and environmental planning scholar Daphne Spain called the screw pump "an unwitting agent of residential segregation in New Orleans."[11] It was also an agent of recreational segregation and, in particular, the forced exclusion of African Americans from the new lakefront. Upon completing work on the seawall at Spanish Fort (a section of the lakeshore "given over to the negroes" at the turn of the century), the levee board implemented plans to convert the area into a modern, whites-only beachfront amusement park, named Pontchartrain Beach. (In response, blacks began bathing at Milneburg; two seasons later, however, the whites-only beach was relocated from Spanish Fort to Milneburg, and blacks were summarily excluded.) Operated by businessman Harry Batt, Pontchartrain Beach featured roller coasters and other rides, concessions, and a nearly half-mile-long, nicely manicured, white-sand beach (2,300 feet long and 400 feet wide), with the sand hauled in by barges from Horn Island in the Mississippi Sound. Pontchartrain Beach provided, as Batt described, "low-cost summer fun and pleasant, seasonal outing-opportunity for low and middle-income bracket families in New Orleans," those who were unable "to seek and to pay for the more-expensive types of entertainment, found elsewhere." It aimed to provide "the type of entertainment that helps the worker to escape from his work-a-day world; to make his children happy; and, to be with his family out-of-doors." Though they could not gain admission to the city's exclusive resorts or yacht and country clubs (nor would have felt welcome even if they could), at Pontchartrain Beach, these white "low and middle-income bracket families" enjoyed a taste of the good life, and a shared sense of racial privilege.[12]

During these same decades, the nation's capital was using similar techniques to transform its own waterfront from a place people avoided to a place they would flock to. Throughout the nineteenth century, the banks of the Potomac River in the District of Columbia had served as the refuge for gamblers, pugilists, and hustlers of all stripes. The Potomac Flats, some four hundred acres of wetlands that absorbed the tidal river's routine floodwaters, attracted what one public official described as a daily crowd of "10 cent gamblers and crap shooters," where the area's heavy overgrowth, and a team of "spotters" stationed around the margins, helped to keep authorities at bay. Following a massive flood in 1881 that nearly reached the front steps of the White House, the federal government stepped up its efforts to reclaim the Potomac Flats and construct, in their place, secure embankments, a sewer canal, and a tidal reservoir "to be forever held and used as a park for the recreation and pleasure of the people." The sediment dredged from the river became the foundation for the creation of the West Potomac Park, comprising 621 acres and stretching one mile west from the Washington Monument on the land that today also includes the Lincoln Memorial and the East Potomac Park, an island that stretched two miles south. The east and west parks surrounded the newly created Tidal Basin.[13] (See Map 8.)

An area deplored by city officials and avoided by the "respectable" classes was set to become the centerpiece of a broader transformation and reconceptualization of public space in both the city and the nation. The McMillan Plan (as it came to be known) called for, among other changes to the city's physical landscape, a "Washington Common" centered on the park's Tidal Basin, with permanent facilities for water sports. Plans for a large, well-manicured bathing beach with permanent structures, and a filtration and chlorination system that would rid the basin of dangerous microbes, were put into motion. In 1920, Congress appropriated $191,498 for the construction and maintenance of a new bathing beach. Carloads of sand were trucked in, and a commodious bathhouse erected. A chlorine plant that aimed to clean river water was installed at the inlet bridge where the waters of the Potomac passed through. When this system proved wholly ineffective, a boat was enlisted to circle the edges of the Tidal Basin and dump chlorine directly into the water. On June 13, 1920, a crowd estimated at over twenty thousand men and women dove into the waters off the new beach on the Tidal Basin. Throughout its opening summer, the beach attracted daily crowds of between four thousand and ten thousand, the numbers of guests "being limited solely by the accommodations the bathing beach affords." Swimming and canoe races dotted the summer schedule, along with female beauty contests. One urban-planning historian called East and West Potomac parks "the most elaborate experiment in recreational park functions" ever undertaken by a public entity.[14] In its final form, the newly redesigned waterfront and Potomac parks exemplified the City Beautiful movement's emphasis on unified, orderly urban spaces conducive to a healthy social order and its faith in the ability to enhance public health, and thereby reshape society, through improving the environmental conditions of the city.[15]

Few needed a bathing beach more than the growing numbers of desperately poor black migrants crowded into the city's back alleys, where running water was virtually nonexistent, fresh air in short supply, and unpaved streets the children's playground. But in Washington, as in New Orleans, African American exclusion was encoded into the DNA of redeveloped and beautified urban shorelines. Following his appointment as the District of Columbia's superintendent of public buildings and grounds by President Warren G. Harding in 1921, Clarence O. Sherrill embarked on a concerted campaign to introduce segregation into the District's new recreational facilities just as the nation's capital was emerging as a tourist destination for an increasingly mobile American public. Along with the Tidal Basin beach, Sherrill instituted whites-only policies at the newly built baseball diamonds, golf course, and tennis courts in the Potomac parks.

But the exclusion of persons of color from public places of play constituted only part of the story and, for many of the African Americans affected by these policies, a comparatively insignificant form of discrimination in itself. Of far greater concern for urban black populations than their ability to swim alongside hostile whites was the disappearance of their own informal gathering spaces—and the deterioration of remaining ones into cauldrons of death and disease. This too was the direct result of

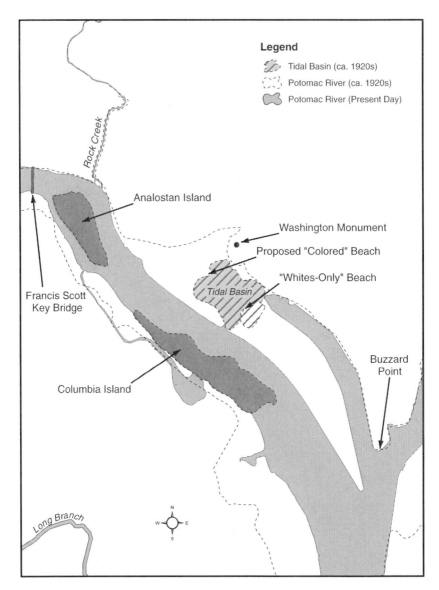

Map 8. The Potomac River waterfront in Washington, D.C., 1920s

improvements made to urban shorelines for the benefit of others. And in this respect, the places along urban shorelines African Americans were pushed *to* proved as significant in shaping the summertime experience of Jim Crow as the places they were excluded *from*.

In Washington, that place blacks were pushed to was Buzzard Point, a former dumping ground where the Anacostia meets the Potomac River, at the time located three blocks downstream from a sewage plant. It was here where, in response to black Washingtonians' demands for access to safe, supervised places to cool off during the summer months, Sherrill proposed, in 1923, to locate a separate "colored" bathing beach. Earlier proposals included locating the beach either on Analostan Island (now Theodore Roosevelt Island) or Columbia Island in the Potomac River. Both would have required black bathers to pay to board a Jim Crow trolley and cross over into Virginia. Analostan consisted entirely of "dry mud pumped up recently from the bottom of the river" during the construction of the nearby Francis Scott Key Bridge. (See Map 8.)

Any of the sites would have exposed African Americans to dangerously high levels of pollutants. Beginning below the Great Falls above Washington, the Potomac River slows and its waters become brackish. From here to the Chesapeake Bay, the river could more appropriately be described as an estuary, more influenced by ocean tides and winds than stream flows. As a result, the effects of urban and industrial pollution are far more pronounced and more difficult to eradicate. As the District and the neighboring towns of Arlington and Alexandria grew, so too did levels of pollution from raw sewage, joining the industrial runoff from plants and coal mines in Maryland and West Virginia, all of which, as one report noted, "stay[ed] right" where it was, "drift[ing] on and below the surface . . . giv[ing] off foul gases and pil[ing] up on the river bottom." The lack of stream flow rendered efforts to dredge the river's bottom futile. One study conducted in the early 1950s found that over ten feet of raw sewage sludge rested on the river's bottom in the area between the Key Bridge and Fort Washington. In the hot, humid summer months, "disgusting smells" wafted from the fetid waters. By the 1920s, high oxygen levels had decimated native shad, oyster, and lobster populations, leaving behind carp, catfish, and other bottom feeders. A 1925 study by the District's sanitary engineer found that the section of the river that ran past the District of Columbia, Arlington, and Alexandria was "teeming with the germs of typhoid fever, cholera and other diseases," and condemned it as a "public nuisance" and a "menace to health . . . unfit to be used for [bathing] purpose[s]." Subsequent studies called the "foul, stinking, filthy river," among other things, a "cesspool," "open sewer," "lagoon of sewage," and "disgrace." "The Potomac River," as writer W. M. Kiplinger put it, "has its place in the history books, but it does not do for Washington what the Thames does for England, or the Seine for Paris, and the Rhine for Germany, or the Danube for those countries in the Balkans. To Washingtonians the Potomac is noted chiefly for being 'too dirty to swim in.'" Kiplinger was being too kind; in certain parts, the Potomac had become too dirty to even come near. A report by the Interstate Commission on the Potomac River Basin noted, "Boating on the Potomac is unpleasant and potentially hazardous. . . . The air is heavy with the stench of the river, and even the spray is foul." So foul, it added, "that it spoils the enjoyment and menaces the health of the picnickers, strollers, cyclists, and motorists who . . . visit both its shores." Indeed, it was the rising levels of pollution that had inspired District officials to construct the Tidal Basin bathing beach and to fortify it with various forms of protection from the germs resident in the river.[16]

And it was these same waters that public officials deemed appropriate for the District's black citizenry. Not merely unsightly and remote (located one mile from the nearest car line, with the final one-fourth mile on bad, unimproved roads), Buzzard Point posed potentially fatal consequences for anyone who dared to swim there. Sanitary tests, even Sherrill acknowledged, proved that the water at Buzzard Point was "very foul." Given the site's former use as a dumping ground, the shoreline and river bottom were littered with bottles, cans, and other "dangerous pieces of refuge [sic]." As one of the city's black newspapers remarked, "A more inaccessible and unsuitable, and probably unsanitary location could scarcely be found. Brazos Bottoms [in Texas] would not be much more inconvenient."[17]

Nor less expensive a piece of waterfront real estate. Obtaining a site on the cheap Buzzard Point land, far from any future residential development, was the predictable corollary of ensuring distance from white bathers and pleasure seekers. That this "considerable tract of land could be acquired at low figures," Sherrill remarked, proved that it could become "an ideal park . . . not only for bathing, but various other recreational activities for the colored people." To direct attention toward its promising future, and obscure the gross inferiority of the site (as evidenced by its name, which predated its designation as a "colored" bathing spot but nevertheless was laden with racist connotations), Sherrill renamed the site Jones's Point, and in discussions with black civic leaders insisted on referring to it as such.[18]

In response to District officials' cynical solutions, African Americans and their few political allies in Congress moved to implement a qualified form of integration of the Tidal Basin as a strategy of equalization. In 1924, Representatives Frederick Zihlman of Maryland, the chair of the House Committee on the District of Columbia, and Martin Madden of Illinois, the chair of the House Committee on Appropriations (and representing an increasingly African American district of Chicago's South Side that would, following his death in 1928, be represented by Oscar DePriest, the first post-Reconstruction black congressman), appropriated funds for the construction of a second, implicitly "colored," beach on the western side of the Tidal Basin, directly across from the white beach. Opposition was immediate, with opponents raising the specter of blacks' supposedly diseased and hypersexualized bodies mingling alongside white boys and girls. These expressions of anti-black racism were often coupled with concerns of urban aesthetics and the maintenance of ideal leisure landscapes. Mrs. John B. Sherman, president of the General Federation of Women's Clubs, called the drive around the Tidal Basin "one of the most celebrated in the world," and one that should not be "marred" by the presence of beaches that, as another critic noted, served the "entire population of the District." Rumors circulated that the construction of the "colored beach" would necessitate the removal of some of the three thousand ornamental cherry trees that lined the northern side of the Tidal Basin. Congressman Joseph Byrnes of Tennessee advanced a bill that cut off additional funding for any beach on the Tidal Basin, which would effectively scuttle the "colored" beach project while leaving open the possibility of reopening and refurbishing the whites-only beach at a later date. Madden, though, called Byrnes's bluff and, prior to final passage, inserted into the bill additional funds for "the removal of the bathhouse and bathing facilities on the east [i.e., white] side of the Tidal Basin." The bill passed, and an era of sanctioned bathing in the Tidal Basin ended.[19]

Black Washingtonians hailed the closing of the whites-only bathing beach as a "surprising victory" in their struggle to dismantle Jim Crow. But while the removal of all swimmers from the Tidal Basin might have constituted a symbolic victory of sorts, it did little to solve the crisis of summer in the city's impoverished black neighborhoods. And in the coming years, the already shockingly high rates of drowning deaths among black youth in the city would continue to rise. The Anacostia River became the watery grave of countless numbers of black youth, among them twelve-year-old William "Bud" Dent, who drowned when he and friends took a dip on a hot June afternoon in 1928. He was, the local black newspaper noted, the "first victim of the vacation season." (Presumably, more were expected to follow.) New Deal public-works projects more often exacerbated rather than alleviated the yawning racial disparities in safe, supervised recreational facilities while firmly linking white privilege to public services and infrastructure improvements. In Washington, swimming pools constructed with WPA funds in the 1930s bypassed the poorer neighborhoods of the Southwest district, which remained without a single swimming pool and which experienced the highest rates of drowning deaths in the District. In response to African Americans' lobbying for swimming pools in their neighborhoods, District officials invariably said in response, as one black resident put it, "'Oh, just turn a hose on them.'" As a result, for many children of the nation's capital, running from the police in search of a place to cool off became, in itself, a form of recreation. As one black Washington teenager recounted:

> We go down an' swim in the pool down at the Lincoln Memorial. [Of] course we know we ain't got no business in it, but that's why we go in. The police, he say to come on out a there [or he'll arrest us. So] we swim over to the center of the pool where he can't catch us, an' we say, "Good old Abraham, [can we] swim in [your] pool[?] . . . Mr. Lincoln, you won't let him bother us will you . . . ?" Then, one of us boy's'll say, just like Mr. Lincoln, "No, indeed, you all stay down in there an' swim 'till you get ready ta stop." Then, we all say, "Thank you, Mr. Lincoln." Then, when the policeman go to get somebody else we crawl out an' run.[20]

In a city where bodies of water served aesthetic and symbolic—rather than practical—purposes, the sight of black children being forced to cool off in large, ornamental fountains could have served as a monument to the city's—and the nation's—mockery of justice.[21] But it more likely served as further confirmation for the white public, and white public officials, of African Americans' supposedly delinquent, criminal natures, and a clarion call for more repressive measures of containment.

✦

New Orleans also had a difficult time keeping its black citizens in place during the summer season. City and levee board officials' efforts to manufacture a prosperous lakefront real estate market were in tension with African Americans' persistent use of the shore for bathing, picnics, and fishing, and their incessant demands for designation of a decent, well-equipped, and safe place of their own. As development proceeded along the southern lakeshore in the 1920s and 1930s, the city's black population gravitated to a small stretch of undeveloped land known as Seabrook (see Map 7, p. 120), where the lake met the Industrial Canal, and following the opening of the whites-only Pontchartrain Beach, they began calling on the city to equip, improve, and guard the grounds. After the usual delays and equivocations, in 1929 the levee board concluded that the Seabrook location "provide[d] the very best facilities for negroes at the least expense and annoyance to the citizenship of this city." To no fanfare, in 1929, the city begrudgingly, and conditionally, conceded African Americans' right to fish, bathe, and picnic at Seabrook.[22]

The decision to allow blacks to use the Seabrook area generated sustained protests. Members of the city's real estate board, chamber of commerce, and neighborhood improvement associations in five of the new lakefront subdivisions flooded the February 19, 1929, levee board meeting to protest any attempts to allow persons of color to mar the beauty and value of lakefront property. H. J. Prevost of the real estate firm Victor and Prevost Inc. spoke for ten minutes on the harmful effects of the beach's location on home values and the levee board's long-term plans. Homeowner W. S. Bender argued that "property values will be decidedly decreased in [the Seabrook] neighborhood," and "the development of that section . . . will come to a decided standstill." He and others promised that residents would fight the proposal "with all means at their command."[23]

As part of their arsenal, opponents advanced alternative locations for a "colored" beach, including a proposed site on Lake Borgne, over four miles from the city's downtown. The site was so remote and inaccessible that it would have cost the levee board $200,000 just to construct a road through thick marshlands to reach it. Lakefront homeowners, real estate agents, and developers, however, agreed that it would be worth every cent if the beach succeeded in ensuring that real estate and recreation on the lakefront remained a whites-only affair. Prevost even went so far as to secure verbal commitments from property owners for rights-of-way for construction of the road leading to Lake Borgne, "in order," he said, "that an amicable solution to the problem might be reached."[24]

Steering a course toward a more "moderate" solution, city and levee board officials opted instead to make the Seabrook site as undesirable—and as impermanent—as possible. The city failed to equip the site with lighting, lifeguards, or concessions, and even resisted attempts by enterprising blacks to provide those services for a fee at the site. In 1929, black businessman E. J. Lamothe applied for a permit to build a bar, restaurant, and bathhouse on the site. The levee board begrudgingly approved a scaled-down version of the plan, minus the dance hall, and forced him to build it nearly a half-mile down the shore from the beach. In addition, they refused to enter into a lease and reserved the right to demolish the structures at their pleasure. With the start of each summer, levee board officials declared, for dubious reasons, the site closed to swimming, until members of the Louisiana League for the Protection of Constitutional Rights and the Urban League appeared before the board and threatened lawsuits unless the board relented and granted access to the site for the upcoming summer. Chuck Badie summarized the city's attitude toward the Seabrook site as compared with the modern, whites-only Pontchartrain Beach down the shore: "'As long as you don't go in the water down [at Pontchartrain Beach], here's a little spot for y'all.' Not a special thing out there. No refreshment stand. No nothing. Nothing but darkness."[25]

The gross inferiority of Seabrook as compared with Pontchartrain Beach was obvious to all who ventured there, and was directly related to the privileges whites enjoyed. The seawall that made lakefront habitation possible also led to the rapid erosion of the lakebed and formation of dangerous sinkholes offshore, both of which threatened to suck bathers under and behind the seawall. The artificial sand beach that extended into the waters off Pontchartrain Beach ensured the safety of white bathers, but it also sped the process of erosion on both ends of the beach, thus making Seabrook (located only blocks east of Pontchartrain Beach) one of the more dangerous places to swim on the lake. Soon after opening, reports of children and adults drowning or nearly drowning at Seabrook circulated. In the summer of 1935, thirty-seven-year-old Jesse Williams was seized with cramps while swimming at Seabrook. With no lifeguard on duty, he went under for several minutes before his friends dragged his lifeless body to shore, but were unable to revive him. Herman Melvin Cappie remembers Seabrook as the place "where we went swimming and got drowned. . . .

No lifeguards, no nothing." "The worst, you know, the worst," his wife, Ruth Irene Cappie, added. "It had holes and all that. It was terrible for the blacks." "Once you stepped off that seawall," William Garibaldi remembers, "you could get sucked under." "I almost lost my life out at Seabrook," Chuck Badie remembers. "You could drown in a drop of a hat. You see that seawall, and that slime there. You got no grip. Just suck you under."[26]

Attempts by black leaders to force the city to implement protective measures for bathers at Seabrook generated swift opposition. Following a meeting between levee board president A. L. Shushan and a delegation of black ministers in July 1932, the levee board agreed to provide lifeguards and police protection at Seabrook the following season. In response, a group of seventy-five whites marched on the levee board's headquarters, carrying a huge banner that read: "We Do Not Want the Negroes on Our Lake Front." A spokesman for the Edgewood Improvement Association announced that his group sought no less than the complete expulsion of non-white persons from all sections of the lakefront as well as all surrounding neighborhoods, since, as he put it, their mere presence gave visitors and tourists a "bad impression" and "depressed . . . realty values."[27] In response, the city backed out of its promise to provide protection at the site.

Black New Orleanians nevertheless persisted in their efforts to turn Seabrook into a viable and permanent community space. E. J. Lamothe, owner of the Sea Side Inn, hired a team of lifeguards to perform the duties the city neglected. Churches held picnics on weekend afternoons, and groups of students from area schools went on field trips to the site. An organization dedicated to offering swimming lessons and water safety instructions to black children and decrease the number of black drowning deaths hosted a summer Life Savers and Swimming Club there.[28] Those who owned a car or truck earned extra money during the summer as a shuttle driver. Badie remembers a man in his Uptown neighborhood named Wallace Comber, who drove through black neighborhoods on summer afternoons offering rides to Seabrook on the back of his truck. "For two quarters, he'd put about fifty of us on that raggedy old thing," Badie remembers. "We'd go out there and stay a couple of hours and he'd bring you on back."[29]

Going to Seabrook was a special occasion, however, and on most days the city's canals or the dangerous currents of the Mississippi were where young black males went to cool off. Like seventeen-year-old David Smith, who drowned while swimming in the Mississippi near Napoleon Avenue in July 1936, the second drowning death of a black youth at that location in a week. In one week alone in the summer of 1939, three black children drowned in the New Basin Canal on three separate occasions. Among the dead was sixteen-year-old Joseph Scott, who could not (as his obituary read) afford the fee to enter the "large bathtub"–size Lafon Playground swimming pool (the lone public pool for blacks in the city). The following summer, the city's waterways claimed four young blacks' lives in one week: ten-year-old Eugene Lazard, whose lifeless body was pulled onto the Seabrook shore; James Mitchell, who was claimed by the Mississippi while fishing for his family's dinner; and Roosevelt Campbell Jr. and Alvin Preston, ages twelve and thirteen, who drowned in the Mississippi after swimming into the waves of a passing boat.[30]

New Orleans was far from the only Jim Crow city to witness a rapid appreciation in waterfront real estate in the early decades of the twentieth century followed by more-determined efforts by white homeowners and real estate developers to draw lines of segregation in the sand. In Norfolk, Virginia, an explosion in the city's population during World War I contributed to the spreading of residential development from the urban core toward the Atlantic and Chesapeake shores during the 1920s. During these same years, Norfolk embarked on an aggressive campaign to expand the number of outdoor public spaces for residents, turning undeveloped areas into spacious, well-equipped public parks, and sections of the beachfront into public places of recreation. As with most public places in the city, Jim Crow rules applied, and blacks were barred from all beaches and parks with the exception of a tiny, remote area of one of the city's parks.

Simply keeping black people out was not enough. Of greater concern to white homeowners and public officials were African Americans who operated independent and popular summer resorts on their own property, and groups of investors who sought to acquire beachfront property for separate black coastal developments. In 1915 black Norfolk businessman Lem Bright opened Little Bay Beach, a "colored resort" and hotel located on his property on Little Willoughby Bay. "Being the only place of its kind near," the resort became, by all accounts, enormously popular. During its first season in operation, forty-seven different school, church, social, and fraternal groups held outings there. At one gathering, a reported twenty-five hundred people crammed into Bright's three-acre tract. Five years after opening, Bright invested in additional features to the grounds, including a merry-go-round, a shooting gallery, concessions, a dining room, and a dance hall. He hired a full-time manager "with seasoned hotel and amusement experience," and employed a jitney car service to run from black neighborhoods to the resort. "The beach is known practically wherever the city of Norfolk itself is known," the *Journal and Guide* claimed, thanks in no small measure to the newspaper itself, whose editor, P. B. Young, held a financial stake in the business and whose offices served as the resort's booking agency.[31]

Its fame, though, was short-lived. In February 1928, a fire widely believed to have been started by white neighbors consumed all but one structure on the property. At the time, the Norfolk City Council was considering an offer from the Bright family estate to sell the Little Bay Beach property to the city for use as a public beach resort for "colored" citizens. When black businessman W. H. McCoy and a group of investors leased the property and began rebuilding efforts in the spring of 1930, white neighbors pressured the Norfolk Board of Zoning to deny the group a building permit. At a hearing before the board of zoning appeals, white property owners offered a host of arguments for "keeping the black, dirty scoundrels out of our section," as one white resident put it, including claims of depressed property values, "sensational" accusations by a white woman of having been "insulted by Negroes returning from the beach resort" in previous years, and ostensibly race-neutral arguments that the site "was not naturally suited to development into a resort because of its poor beach, dirty water, and remoteness from transportation facilities." Speaking on behalf of the black investment group, P. B. Young told the zoning board that denial of the permit to rebuild constituted a brazen assault on African Americans' "property rights." Tellingly, Young's assertion that blacks also enjoyed rights to use their property as they saw fit was "met with derisive laughter from the property owners who were objecting." The permit was denied.[32]

Public officials similarly worked to scuttle any attempts by African Americans to purchase undeveloped beachfront property. In 1926 the Norfolk Beach Resort Corporation, formed with the explicit intent of acquiring beach space for black citizens and waterfront residential development, began negotiations to acquire a forty-seven-acre tract on the water and easily accessible to the city's black population. Seeking buyers of their

$12.50 preferred stock, the developers pitched the resort as both "easily accessible" *and* "secluded-from-interference" from hostile white neighbors, "in-every-way-desirable." Along with a bathing beach and seashore cottages, the developers proposed to include a tourist camp, hotel, and picnic grove. "Every Race man and woman can afford and should feel [a] compelling urge to cooperate in this last chance for a desirable, near-by waterfront resort, and subscribe to at least one or two shares. It's worth it just to have somewhere to go." Like other land developers before and after them, the Norfolk Beach Resort Corporation nourished dreams of instant and self-perpetuating wealth, of the opportunity to reap untold profits from the land through savvy investments instead of sweat. One advertisement for shares in the company read, "We know of no issue today available to our folks which presents such opportunity for QUICK PROFIT . . . and the probability of long-continued INCOME." Blacks' segregation and exclusion from the rest of the region's shores seemed to support such promises. "Based on extremely desirable Real Estate and a very acute RACIAL RECREATIONAL NEED, the element of RISK is practical [*sic*] ELIMINATED." But as Norfolk Beach Resort Corporation worked to sell enough shares to purchase the coastal tract, city hall successfully scrambled to purchase the land so as "to keep it from falling into the hands of colored people."[33]

The thoroughness of white Norfolk officials' efforts to drive blacks from every portion of the city's twenty-six miles of shoreline was breathtaking. By 1926 the city owned or controlled twenty-one parks for whites and none for blacks, and following the closing of Lem Bright's Little Bay Beach, there was not a single body of water in the city formally designated for African American use.

The absence of outdoor space for black Norfolk's working poor became not merely another indignity but also a civic emergency. Black neighborhoods within the city's limits suffered from overcrowding and an absence of infrastructure development. In 1920, black neighborhoods constituted 1 percent of the city's total area but housed one-eighth of its population. The death rate among African Americans in the city (already double that of whites) rose to shockingly high levels during the summer months. In the city's crowded black slums, typhoid fever, influenza, and tuberculosis ran rampant. Blacks' cramped living quarters, poor ventilation and sewage, inadequate shade, and the dust from unpaved streets rendered the summer heat all the more intolerable. Each summer, scores of African Americans (many, if not most, of them lacking the basic swimming skills increasingly being made available to white youth through social service agencies) drowned while seeking relief in dangerous, unsupervised bodies of water. In the summer of 1932 alone, the *Journal and Guide* reported that "26 colored persons lost their lives by drowning in the Hampton Roads area."[34]

The city's "Negro beach" problem presented a challenge to Norfolk's upper-class white establishment and threatened to tarnish its members' self-fashioned image as paternalistic, racial moderates, especially as drowning deaths mounted and white efforts to prevent the formation of independent black beaches grew more flagrant and extreme. By the late 1920s, newspaper editors Louis Jaffe of the *Virginian-Pilot* and Douglas Gordon of the *Norfolk Ledger-Dispatch* had joined with upper-class white female social reformers in calling on city council members to provide black citizens a decent, accessible beach of their own. The city's failure to fulfill this "commanding moral obligation" to "provide an adequate bathing beach for the city's Negro population" was, an editorial in the *Ledger-Dispatch* read, "a sharp and humiliating reflection . . . upon the white people":

> Here we are surrounded by many miles of deep-water front, of which an uncalculated portion is now put to no use whatever; . . . here we are, from time to time, lamenting sporadic migrations of Southern Negroes to the North; here we are holding ourselves out as the only people who truly understand the Negro; here we are claiming to be the best friends, the only real friends, of the Negro. And here we are, or here we have been, too selfish or too indifferent or too callous or too arrogant or too fearful of some vague bugaboo to make any effort to provide more than one-third of our population with facilities which the poorest of our white people are able to enjoy at a trifling cost.

Ada Walke, described as "one of the most prominent and highly esteemed white women of the city," became a tireless advocate for the welfare of the city's black population. She pleaded the case of black citizens' recreational needs in council meetings and in local newspapers, and served as a liaison between white and black power brokers in the city. Local merchant John J. Pitt also lobbied city officials and appealed to the whites' conscience. In a letter to the editor of the *Virginia-Pilot*, he wrote, "When the black man's flat-roofed house becomes unsufferably [sic] heated by the to-rid [sic] summer sun during dog days and the kerosene lamps during the mosquito-infested nights he seeks a bit of fresh air, not under the cool trees in some public square or restful park—there is none to bid him come—but on the doorsteps of his little home in a treeless street." A local interracial committee, led by Jaffe of the *Virginian-Pilot*, formed and worked to sway white public opinion by warning of black unrest and by highlighting the racial amity this small gesture of goodwill would ensure.[35]

The debate over public expenditures on beaches and parks for the city's black population played out against the backdrop of a shifting labor market following the war. The dependence of shipbuilders on black labor led them to adopt forms of welfare capitalism aimed at cultivating a contented workforce. Many employers provided black workers with separate recreational facilities as a deliberate strategy to decrease labor unrest. And with good reason. The shipbuilding industry's large pool of cheap labor evaporated in the years following the war, as many of the migrants who poured in from the rural South continued their journey north. Those who stayed behind grew increasingly militant as their bargaining power grew, and corporate leaders became more likely to push cities to undertake modest measures to make life under Jim Crow more tolerable for African Americans. Norfolk mayor S. Heth Tyler warned his white constituents that a bathing beach for colored citizens constituted a necessary measure to ensure social and economic stability. "We must face this fact or take the economic implications resident in such migration. The Negro is entitled to reasonable recreation. . . . It is required by humanitarian, social, and civil reasons."[36]

But in this burgeoning coastal metropolis, the anxieties of one industry ran headfirst into those of another, and one segment of the corporate-political establishment's dependence on black labor was countered by another, emerging segment—the real estate industry—and its dependence on blacks' isolation and invisibility. As the region's real estate industry grew in relation to the boom in population and growth of middle-class homeownership, industry leaders lobbied Norfolk's city council members to select sites that rested outside the boundaries of their long-term growth projections. Numerous proposals were rejected, council members later noted, because they lacked any "natural barriers" between the proposed Negro beach and nearby white residences. But as black Norfolkians persisted in their demands for beachfront access, and as the threat of economic destabilization grew, certain areas of the coast came to be seen, by civic leaders and corporate interests, as more expendable than others.[37]

In 1930 the city of Norfolk announced it had reached an agreement to purchase eleven acres owned by the Pennsylvania Railroad Company in a section of Ocean View for the construction of a "colored" bathing beach (later named City Beach). The place, in Mayor Tyler's words, offered "minimum possibilities for . . . friction." It was located on a remote, isolated stretch of the coast, near the Pennsylvania Railroad terminal, outside the city limits, ten miles from the center of the city's black population, in an area chosen for its lack of "contacts with white developments." It was "this one or nothing," as Tyler put it. City councilman J. D. Wood, who fashioned himself as a racial moderate dedicated, above all, to creating a climate favorable to outside investment, joined Tyler as a vocal proponent of the project and the proposed location.[38]

Though cast as a remote, forsaken stretch of shore suitable only for "coloreds," Ocean View had experienced, over the previous decades, a steady influx of people and infusion of capital investment. Following the city's extension of a streetcar line to the area in the late 1890s, a growing number of hotels, cottages, and pavilions dotted the shoreline. In 1904, real estate developer Otto Wells purchased and refurbished the Ocean View Amusement Park, a self-described Coney Island of the South. In the early 1920s, Wells sank $1.5 million into a housing development in Ocean View and marketed his balloon-frame houses to working- and middle-class families. Ocean View became typical of other planned communities under development in the 1910s and 1920s, where proximity to water and green space, and public and commercial recreations, played a significant role in determining property value and occupants' sense of status. For the white families of these new seaside housing developments, their property and sense of ownership of the area's beaches were integral to their racial and class identity.

Following the announcement of the location of the "colored" beach, Ocean View homeowners and investors mobilized in opposition. Area real estate developers, led by S. G. L. Hitch, Fay Garrett, E. A. Page, and W. G. Maupin, stoked fears among the area's white homeowners that competing real estate interests planned to use the presence of black bathers to depreciate land values in the area and shift future development away from Ocean View. And they worked to translate those fears into political action. Page organized the Ocean View Property Owners committee, serving as its chairman, while Maupin was its lead counsel. Ocean View residents formed the League for the Development of Ocean View, which they used as a vehicle to pressure the Norfolk City Council to abandon the project. Members flooded city council meetings en masse and circulated petitions to rally sympathy and support among the city at large. A January 15, 1930, hearing on the colored bathing beach drew more than fifteen hundred protesters, many of whom gathered around the municipal building hours before the meeting. Reports described the throngs of protesters as one of the largest crowds in the city's history to attend a public hearing. The meeting had to be moved from the city council chambers to a nearby auditorium, where what one reporter described as a four-hour "battle royal" ensued. During the hearing, an endless line of speakers protested the "raw, rotten deal" the city had dealt Ocean View. Women shook their fingers at the councilmen, who were hissed as they walked onstage, and threatened retribution in the upcoming election should the referendum pass. At the meeting, the Ocean View homeowners' association presented the city council with a petition protesting the site of the proposed colored beach. Signed by 1,442 Norfolk residents, the petition claimed that the beach would "tend to destroy the popularity and development of the Shore Drive . . . which is fast becoming an attraction to thousands of tourists and summer vacationists." The petitioners cited, among other things, the "crowding of portions of the highways with negroes clad in bathing suits."[39]

Though the proposed site was two miles from the nearest white development, opponents argued that it would nevertheless have a "depressing effect" on all property values, especially the undeveloped tracts adjacent to the site being eyed by area speculators. "Our property will become valueless," one resident charged. "OUR beautiful shore will become a spectacle." "We have nothing against our darkies, but we can't have this 'nigger' resort in that section." Besides, one person added, "They pay only negligible taxes." The colored bathing beach, Ocean View homeowner R. W. Turner claimed, "would mean that the property of 10,000 people would be confiscated. If this thing is put over, it will mean that those who have bought property in that section might as well throw it away." The three thousand unsold lots at Ocean View would remain unsold, while those who could, would move.[40]

Enacted in 1934, the National Housing Act promised to provide a jolt to the homebuilding industry and stability to the mortgage market through regulation of the home financing system and federally backed mortgage loans. As federal interventions into the mortgage lending industry aimed to stimulate housing construction and promote home ownership, the physical location of African Americans—as numbers of scholars have observed—emerged as a central concern of lenders and buyers, and a key battleground in the struggle for civil rights.[41] The places where blacks played were of no less importance than the places where they lived—indeed, the two were entwined. In New Orleans, the lakefront became the site where this federally backed process of recovery and growth came to fruition, and where, by decade's end, the levee board began what the local chapter of the NAACP called a "determined effort to force Negroes from the lakefront."[42]

In the summer of 1940, reports emerged of police officers patrolling the Seabrook site, rounding up and running off black bathing parties. On June 18, 1941, detective Joseph Brisbois arrived at Seabrook in response to a complaint from the nearby army base "that the negroes in swimming, were creating a disturbance by loud outcries, and that several of these swimmers were not attired in a proper manner, for swimming, and that several of the negroes were dressing on the seawall, in full view of the female fishermen." "Seeing that trouble would ensue between the negroes in swimming, and the Soldiers and Fishermen," the officer's report read, "the negroes were advised to leave this location, and go to the beach at Little Woods, La."[43] Black New Orleanian Louise Marion Bouise recounted her family's first confrontation with this new policy after years of swimming at the site:

> Not having transportation it was the habit to go, you'd get a truck and you'd go to the lake front. And somebody there, I think my father knew who had a truck, took members of my family and some of our friends to the lake front to go swimming. . . . And after they got there the truck driver left them on the lake front and . . . told them a time he'd be back. . . . But they weren't there very long when policemen came along and told them they couldn't swim on the lake front, that they'd have to go. They couldn't even stay on the lakefront and wait for the truck driver to come back to pick them up. They walked from the lakefront home which was on St. Bernard and Broad. And in the party was one of our friends, a teenager or he was ten by that time. He

had a deformed leg. But these policemen . . . said you'll have to move. And this young man with his brace on his leg walked all that distance home. . . . They threatened to arrest all of them if they did not leave that lakefront.[44]

Speaking before white members of New Orleans's Protestant Ministers Union in 1940, Rev. R. W. Coleman, pastor of the city's oldest black Baptist church, said that the absence of any safe bathing facilities for the 180,000 black children residing in the city, even as "provision is made for ducks and geese," made it "hard for us as ministers to teach our children Christianity." Imploring the city's white Protestant ministry to adopt a resolution urging the city to designate Seabrook for Negro use, Coleman ended his speech with the warning: "Christianity in America cannot maintain if we continue to allow race prejudice, discrimination, and color bars [to] destroy the principles of our fellowship and brotherhood of man. . . . If we preach and teach religious doctrines, why can't we practice it?" The ministers unanimously adopted the resolution and sent copies to the mayor, city commission, levee board, and governor's office. Such appeals to public officials' sense of moral decency held little sway. Expulsion of black bathers from Seabrook continued without interruption, and in 1943 the policy was written into law. That July, the city's commission council passed Ordinance 16542, which explicitly banned swimming at the Seabrook site (as a matter of national security) and threatened violators with a twenty-five-dollar fine or fifty days in jail or both. Later that summer, Robert E. Fullilove, a black doctor, and his wife drove to the area to park and sit on the seawall. A group of white civilians was there catching crabs. Moments after arriving, Fullilove reported, he was "summarily ordered from the area" by an MP, "and, over my mild protest that I was not swimming and that numerous white persons were nearby engaged in catching crabs, I was told that the rule did not apply to white persons, and, quite bluntly, that no colored people were to be allowed on the lakefront."[45]

Even donning a swimsuit and boarding the wrong bus put blacks at risk of arrest or assault or both. In the summer of 1943, seventeen-year-old Bernice De Latte, her sister, and a friend hopped aboard a city bus headed toward the lake dressed in their swim clothes. Noticing the "colored" section full, the girls moved the screen up one row, as was the custom. In the front, a plainclothes police officer used the action as an excuse to violently eject the passengers. As De Latte testified, the officer struck her in the back, stated that he would "knock out her brains with the screen," and hauled her off to the Fifth Precinct jail. Similar reports of abusive treatment of black passengers on the Seabrook-bound buses circulated through the city's black neighborhoods that and subsequent summers. The bus's destination, and the girls' attire, were not lost on black observers and commentators. One reporter called the incident part of a "crusade of brutality" against young blacks' pursuit of "wholesome recreation."[46]

Along with this "determined effort to force Negroes from the lakefront" came efforts to push them to a more remote location. In 1938 the levee board acquired 2.3 acres of lakefront property in a section east of the Industrial Canal known as Little Woods from the international fruit magnate Sam "the Banana Man" Zemurray, who parlayed a fortune extracted from the jungles of Honduras into a second career as a real estate developer. In 1934 Zemurray had acquired the five-thousand-acre tract, which had previously been the site of a failed attempt to plant orange groves and sell lots as truck farms, and planned a residential subdivision on the site. As his plans languished (he eventually abandoned the project altogether and all his acreage in 1954), Zemurray, who also fashioned himself as a philanthropist and political power broker, donated a portion of his lakefront property to the levee board, so that it could construct a permanent Negro beach on Lake Pontchartrain. Like many other public facilities designated for blacks during this time, it was named after the Great Emancipator, Abraham Lincoln.[47] (See Map 9.)

Lincoln Beach, though, was far from ideal. Unlike the whites-only Pontchartrain Beach, sited at the end of a streetcar line, Lincoln Beach was located fourteen miles from the center of the city, far removed from the bulk of the city's black neighborhoods, and virtually inaccessible by public transportation. Railroad tracks separated the beach from Hayne Boulevard, requiring visitors to dodge oncoming trains to make it safely to an area one observer described as a "reptile-infested portion of the lake." Rocky groins extended into the water on both ends of the small stretch of shore. Though ostensibly aimed at preventing erosion of the beach, the groins, for many blacks, typified the levee board's concerted effort to isolate and contain them. As Chuck Badie put it, "they made sure to put us out there so far nobody would see us but us."[48]

Black bathers were not the only real estate market liability designated for relocation to the eastern lakeshore. In conjunction with the decision to close Seabrook and develop Lincoln Beach, the levee board also canceled

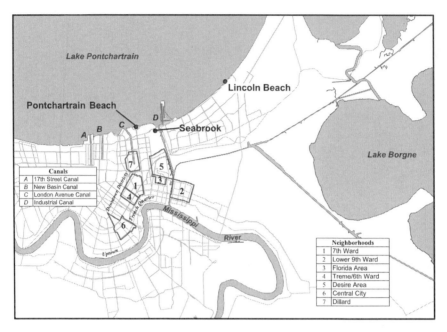

Map 9. African American neighborhoods of New Orleans in relation to canals and beaches

the leases on all fishing camps located on the southern shore and offered new leases for the stretch of shore adjacent to the proposed Lincoln Beach site. The impetus to remove and relocate the fishing camps stemmed not only from their unsightliness, but also from the large amounts of raw sewage campers dumped into the lake's waters. As a result, by 1941, over 175 fishing camps emptied raw sewage in the lake within a three-mile radius of the Lincoln Beach site.[49] The vast majority of these camps were relocated to the stretch of shore west of the Lincoln Beach site between Little Woods and the Lakefront Airport, which, given the counterclockwise circulation of the lake's waters, exacerbated the levels of pollution that washed onto Lincoln Beach's shores. On June 19, 1941, Dr. J. M. Musser of the state health department, citing a May 1941 report by the city's health director John M. Whitney that found the waters "grossly contaminated," suggested an injunction be filed to force the closing of the beach.[50] The high concentration of fishing camps in one site, combined with the pollution flowing from the nearby Citrus Canal into the lake, rendered the waters off Little Woods a virtual cesspool, wholly unfit for bathing.

But not, as levee board officials concluded, unfit for the city's black population. After years of neglecting the safety of bathers at Seabrook, the levee board built a bathhouse with lockers, hired lifeguards, and placed police on guard at the Lincoln Beach site. They secured a corporate partnership with a local brewery, which placed a large beer sign at the park's entrance on Hayne Boulevard. And, over the applications of black businessmen, they hired a notorious white racketeer who reputedly operated "the biggest Negro gambling joint in town" to operate the concession stands.[51]

Other cities' attempts to designate sections of waterfront for "Negro recreation" followed a similar pattern and logic. In 1930 the city of Charleston, South Carolina, responded to black citizens' demands for a safe and enjoyable place of summer leisure by constructing Riverside Beach on the Wando River. Few visitors during its opening season, though, mistook Riverside for a beach, and only the most cynical public official could call the place either safe or adequate. While sand was in short supply, thick marshes were in abundance, covering much of the area. Across the river from the site the city of Charleston dumped its sewage along with the wastes of the city's industries and manufacturing plants. African American ministers and activists condemned the so-called beach and warned fellow blacks to avoid swimming there.[52]

While public officials equivocated in the face of black protest and white homeowner resistance, growing numbers of enterprising white businessmen worked to capitalize on the crisis of summer in urban black neighborhoods by opening private, for-profit Negro bathing resorts. In Norfolk, W. W. Consolvo, John C. Davis, and Joseph Nelson opened Ocean Breeze, a seventy-five-acre beachfront resort on a remote stretch of coast near the opening of the Chesapeake Bay onto the Atlantic Ocean, in 1933. (See Map 10.) The owners hired the genial George W. Banks, a white retired army officer, to serve as the resort's manager and make guests feel "at home." For a ten-cent fee, guests could dip their toes in the Atlantic and enjoy the resort's fifteen concession stands and a bathhouse that could accommodate five hundred persons. The resort offered a six-hundred-foot-long boardwalk, a dancing pavilion, games of chance, a seafood restaurant, and cottages for rent by the day, evening, or weekend. For the 1936 season, the managers hired Fats Wallace and His Rhythm Aces to perform through

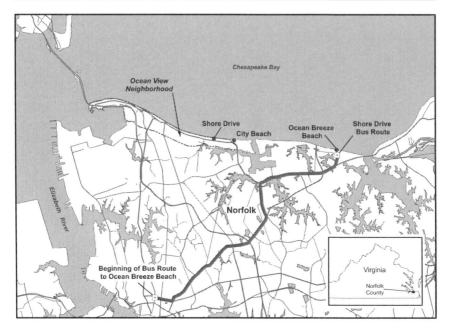

Map 10. Norfolk, Virginia, 1920s

the summer season. The business partners contracted the Norfolk Southern Bus Company to transport beachgoers from downtown Norfolk to the beach for thirty-five cents round trip. During the opening season, the beach hosted Sunday school and social club picnics, bathing beauty contests, and Boy Scout camps, among other groups and events. Finally, the *Journal and Guide* noted, "The Negro population in Norfolk, Tidewater Virginia and nearby North Carolina need have no worry over sweltering in the summer heat already forecast by the weather man."[53]

A trip to Ocean Breeze did not, however, offer a respite from harassment, humiliation, and exploitation. Sheriffs in Princess Anne County routinely stopped black motorists on the road leading to Ocean Breeze and charged them with petty offenses, a move understood as a continuation of the fight to keep blacks from the shore and to drive the bathing beach and amusement park out of business. Ocean Breeze vice president John C. Davis publicly defended the rights of his clientele, many of whom, he noted, "are highly educated colored people, including educators, doctors, lawyers, and preachers of the gospel." In a letter to the state's motor vehicle commissioner, Davis wrote, "There has always been a great deal of resentment in this section towards Negroes having access to the waters of the Chesapeake Bay. . . . Negroes who behave themselves have a perfect right to go to our bathing beach and bathe themselves in the waters of the Chesapeake Bay, and they have a perfect right to use the public highways."[54]

But while the beach's white proprietors publicly defended their right to operate a "colored" bathing beach, they privately collaborated with law enforcement to suppress any attempts by black petty entrepreneurs to profit from the site. Following complaints from the Norfolk and Southern Bus Corporation of lack of patronage due to competition from black-run jitneys undercutting their thirty-five-cent fare, the Princess Anne Sheriff's Department set up a sting operation to entrap black motorists into violating the state's livery laws. The department hired Chester Smith, a young black man from Oakwood, to stand along the road leading to the beach and attempt to lure black motorists into offering him a ride and then insisting on paying for their service. On June 30, 1933, John R. Lofton slowed his automobile to the side of the road and offered Smith a ride to the beach. During the ride, Smith insisted Lofton accept fifteen cents for his trouble. After a fellow passenger accepted the change and as Lofton approached his destination, Smith waved to a nearby squad car, which pulled Lofton over and demanded to see his for-hire license. Smith later testified that he had already performed the same stunt eight times that day, but had only succeeded in giving money to five of the drivers.[55]

There were other forms of entrapment that lined the road leading to Ocean Breeze, including a "round robin" racket organized by a filling station that dealt in bootleg whiskey, and the sheriff's department. As black motorists filled their tanks, station attendants, unbeknownst to drivers, slipped bottles of whiskey into the automobile's backseat and then notified a sheriff down the road of the oncoming motorist. The twenty-five-dollar fines levied against guilty parties, it was alleged, were split between the filling station, the arresting officer, and the justice of the peace. "Afterwards, it is said, the confiscated liquor is 'turned back in the business' to be used as bait for another unsuspecting victim."[56]

The corollary to this push to maximize profits from black visitors was the minimization of expenses. Ocean Breeze's shore was noted for its unpredictable currents, shifting depths, sinkholes, and strong undertow. Despite these dangerous conditions, Ocean Breeze neglected to regularly staff the beach with lifeguards or equip the site with lifeboats and rafts. The consequences of these policies quickly became apparent. In August 1933, James

Allen, a thirty-three-year-old chauffeur who days earlier had secured a job in New York City and made arrangements to move north, drowned off the shore of Ocean Breeze. At the time, no lifeguard was present. It was the twelfth drowning death of an African American in the city that summer. The following summer, the *Journal and Guide* recorded nineteen drowning deaths of African Americans by mid-August. And in the summer of 1935, a reported eleven African Americans drowned by mid-July. While many of these deaths were the result of the absence of safe and supervised places of play in the city, which led black youth on an endless quest for summertime relief in the area's numerous rivers, bays, and inlets, Ocean Breeze seemed, to most, equally as dangerous. Black Norfolkian Flossie Branchcomb recalled that both her brother and a cousin lost their lives swimming at Ocean Breeze. The underlying cause of this seemingly endless string of tragedies was, to many, painfully obvious. "The beach, being privately owned is operated solely for gain," visitor E. L. Cook complained. "The people are paying all charges fair or unfair and paying well. . . . What if someone should become suddenly ill? Is there an emergency kit, rest room, and a suitable person whose duty it is to render aid? It is absurd to expect people to pay hundreds of dollars, and on some occasions the receipts run into the thousands, and not receive even visible means of protection much less active and qualified."[57]

Along with inspiring a host of schemes and swindles, the opening of Ocean Breeze also added new opponents to the Ocean View public beach plan. Before long, it became hard to tell the Ocean Breeze proprietors apart from the Ocean View resident opponents. Speeches before city council meetings denouncing the Ocean View proposal became full-throated endorsements of the amenities available to blacks at Ocean Breeze. J. H. Cofer, who introduced himself as merely a resident who was not speaking on behalf of the owners and operators of Ocean Breeze, described for the council "the natural beauty of the Ocean Breeze site, its 'rolling hills, beautiful natural scenery, ideal location, and easy accessibility,'" before arguing that the public "colored" beach would inevitably become deluged with bootleggers and "other underworld denizens," and that there was "no room for two colored beaches." Afterward, John C. Davis told the council that he had sunk $120,000 into the Ocean Breeze venture and that he was in danger of losing his investment "if we are faced with any real competition."[58]

As delay tactics by opponents of the Norfolk public "colored" beach mounted, black protests grew louder and more sustained. A February 1932

meeting of black citizens at the Bank Street Baptist Church to discuss organization options was "filled to overflowing," and the roster of speakers
promised "the fight for the beach is going to be a fight to the finish." As in
Washington, protesters couched their demands for recreational equality
in threats to force the integration of whites-only sites. During a speech
to the city council, black attorney J. Eugene Diggs reminded them, "The
Negroes have always waived their rights [to use public beaches] because
they have wanted to live in peace with the white people [but that there is
nothing] to stop the Negroes, being citizens and tax-payers, from going on
[them] . . . nothing, except their desire for peace." The health and safety
of all Norfolkians, they reminded white officials, was at stake. The development of public recreational space for black citizens, black Norfolkian
E. E. Edwards predicted, would lead to the "decrease in the local murder
rate." "Wholesome recreation provided in part by the city," William M.
Hubbard added, "is a natural crime deterrent." To white residents' arguments against tax dollars being spent on recreational facilities for poor
blacks, blacks reminded them that the lack of recreational outlets led to
poor health, juvenile delinquency, moral derelictions, heavy court dockets,
full jails, and overburdened charity wards, "all of which constitutes a heavy
burden upon the tax payer." "Thus recreation is a thing bought and paid for
whether it is provided or not."[59]

After seven years of acrimonious debate, inexplicable delays, and re-
markably predictable acts of dissimulation and duplicity, on March 5, 1935,
Norfolk's city council convened for what was expected to be the final vote
on the Ocean View "colored" bathing beach issue. The various interested
parties crammed into the council's chambers. This time, discussion was
kept to a minimum, with only two women afforded time to speak, and two
letters from civic organizations read aloud by the city clerk. The vote was
not in doubt, nor were the motives of its supporters and detractors. By a
three-to-two vote, the council approved plans to move forward with the
construction of a public "colored" beach in the Ocean View section of the
city. As the votes were cast, a polite applause emanated from a group of ten
businessmen and developers from the neighboring town of Virginia Beach
in appreciation for the crucial "yes" vote from councilman J. D. Wood,
who, like them, held significant financial interests in the burgeoning resort town in neighboring Princess Anne County.[60]

Across the aisle, jeers and catcalls, and the promise of retaliation, rained
down on the elected body from residents of Ocean View, and spilled out

into the hallway following the meeting's adjournment. Profanity and threats of violence were in the air. A veteran of the Great War asserted that Wood "should be defeated for reelection, and, if this proved impossible, tarred and feathered, and shot with a shot gun." He and others called the decision nothing more than a plot hatched by Virginia Beach's business community designed to lower property values in Ocean View and thereby boost their own future prospects. They promised to retaliate against their opponents using the same weapons that had been wielded against them: black bathers. The Ocean View VFW, a war veteran shouted to the Virginia Beach corporate community as they exited city hall, planned to acquire property adjacent to the famed Cavalier Hotel on Virginia Beach's beachfront and operate a "Negro bathing beach . . . free of charge."[61]

Opponents in Ocean View nearly succeeded in running out the clock. As the city's option to purchase the property neared expiration, attorneys representing Ocean View residents filed an injunction preventing the Pennsylvania Railroad Company from cashing the $10,000 check issued to it by the city. With less than twenty-four hours before the option expired, Norfolk Interracial Committee members raised $10,000 themselves through soliciting small and large donations from black and white supporters. (When the injunction was later lifted and the city funding made available, donors were reimbursed.)

Opened in 1936, City Beach initially included a bathhouse, recreation hall, and boardwalk, built at a cost of $40,000, paid for by a local soft drink bottling company, which subsequently assumed management of the facilities. After two seasons of high volumes of visitors but little revenue, the company canceled its lease with the city, which subsequently leased the site to the black-run Norfolk Community Hospital. After assuming managerial control, the hospital's board of directors worked to establish the beach as a site for and symbol of race pride and community control, hiring an all-black managerial and work staff and lifeguard force. But lack of capital prevented the hospital from making necessary repairs and improvements to the beach, and by the time the hospital withdrew from the lease in 1949, City Beach had slid into a state of decay, which the city's Recreation Bureau, now placed in charge of the site, seemed content to allow fester. Storms that struck the coast in previous summers had destroyed the bathhouse, recreation hall, and boardwalk. In their place, the city built a single cinderblock structure that housed toilets and a twelve-by-twelve-foot lounge area. Four plywood shelters and a few scattered picnic tables

served as gathering places. With no waste cans and only minimal maintenance by the Recreation Bureau, bottles, trash, and other refuse littered
the beach. Without locker rooms, visitors changed into bathing suits in
their cars or on the beach. With a small, sand-filled parking lot capable of
holding only forty cars, many drivers were forced to park along the road,
where Princess Anne County sheriffs, in collusion with a local wrecking
company, established a thriving summer business through ticketing, towing, and impounding automobiles. On one summer weekend day in 1956,
a reporter for the *Journal and Guide* found, over one hundred cars attempted,
unsuccessfully, to park in the lot, which was often filled to capacity well
before noon. Many cars got stuck in the lot's knee-deep sand. Others took
their chances along the side of the road, where sheriffs on patrol were said
to deliberately mislead drivers into believing that they could park there.
After visitors exited their cars and headed toward the beach, sheriffs
hailed one of the three tow trucks on site that afternoon, which charged
violators fifteen dollars to retrieve their car. (By 1961 the towing fee was
up to thirty dollars.)[62]

While white sheriffs and tow truck operators profited handsomely, more
than a few black bathers died because of the beach's glaring inadequacies.
Owned by the city of Norfolk but located in Princess Anne County, City
Beach initially received fire and ambulance services from neither. On one
occasion, thirteen-year-old Alfred Emanuel Sears was pulled unconscious
from the beach's waters as a bystander placed a call to the Norfolk fire department for the pulmotor squad. Adhering to an order not to leave city
limits, the fire department refused service. By the time the pulmotor squad
from Princess Anne County arrived, Sears had expired. Upon assuming
management, the Recreation Bureau slashed the lifeguard crew, placing
one guard on weekdays and two guards on weekends in charge of several
hundred yards of beachfront. On the beach's eastern edge was one of the
subsidiary arteries of the Hampton Roads waterway and harbor. Large
waves and backwash generated by the hundreds of ships that passed by the
beach daily, combined with the dearth of trained lifeguards on shore, led
to several drowning deaths throughout the beach's years of operation.[63]

The unnecessary drowning death of a black child was often the spark
that lit protests. In Little Rock, Arkansas, the drowning deaths of three
black children along a "steep and dangerous slope" of the Arkansas River
"hidden from view by weeds and heavy thicket" in the summer of 1949,
parents and activists charged, were the product of the city's unresponsiveness

to years of pleading for safe and supervised recreational facilities for black youth. "While the subject of a park equipped with swimming pool for Negroes is debated, denounced, contested, promised and forgotten . . . while the city of Little Rock twiddled its thumbs and yawned in stark indifference," a local black reporter charged, "three little children died." In Monroe, North Carolina, it was the drowning death of a black child in a swimming hole in the summer of 1957 that sparked protests, led by civil rights activist Robert F. Williams, demanding that the city construct a separate swimming pool for blacks or allow blacks part-time use of the city's public swimming pool. On June 22, 1952, during an oppressive heat wave in Washington, D.C., an African American boy's body was discovered drowned in a whites-only pool in the Rosedale neighborhood. (He had sneaked in after the pool closed.) Protests, altercations between white and black youth, and arrests followed.[64]

In New Orleans, as the toll of drowned black youth continued to mount throughout the 1940s, the city's management of Jim Crow steadily unraveled, and—not unrelated—divisions between the city's black and Creole elite and the working poor over goals and strategies widened. In the summers of both 1943 and 1944, a reported ten black children and adolescents drowned in the city. By July 1945 six persons had already met an untimely death "seeking relief in the canals of the city from the torrid rays of sun." For black New Orleanians, outrage over the drowning of black children, and the city's duplicitous attempts to manufacture consent toward the Lincoln Beach site, fueled citizen activism and helped coalesce citizens and organizations into a movement for environmental justice (in fact if not in name). In the summer of 1939, the levee board circulated a petition signed by a "representative committee of colored people" that requested the removal of the bathing beach at Seabrook and its relocation to the Little Woods site. The petition called for the Little Woods site "for the best interest of both groups" and said that it would "enable the greatest good to be derived from the money spent and will permit close contact with the waters of the lake by a large number of Negroes." The letter also promised the levee board that the petitioners could "amply take care" of the needed capital for the project. This endorsement of the levee board's plans by a group of so-called black leaders sparked immediate outrage. Though blacks were accustomed to being "sold out" by those who claimed to "speak for the one hundred and fifty-six thousand Negroes who live in Orleans Parish," an editorial in the *Louisiana Weekly* noted, "the resultant cry was not as long nor as loud as in this matter of bathing facilities on the lakefront." While several of the signers of the petition disavowed any knowledge of its contents and claimed that their signatures were forged, the resultant fallout confirmed what many had long suspected: that middle- and upper-class blacks actively collaborated with public officials and real estate industry leaders to rid the southern shore of the black poor in the hopes of securing a residential and recreational subdivision of their own along the lakefront. "Certainly it seems that we have been sold out and away from the sea-wall, and it does not take a soothsayer, and diviner, tea-cup reader, or palmist to read the apparent motives which causes [*sic*] the sale."[65]

Such suspicions were not unfounded. Throughout the stages of lakefront development, the city's insular "colored" Creole elite (hailing predominantly from the Seventh Ward) and the more politically conservative and equally clannish black professional class had quietly leaned on politically influential friends and allies in public office and the private sector to secure a section of the lakefront for the development of a separate, exclusive residential subdivision on the undeveloped acres near the Seabrook site. Prospects for securing a place on the developing lakefront seemed to brighten in 1946 with the election of deLesseps S. "Chep" Morrison as the city's mayor. Morrison had run on a platform of business progressivism and racial moderation, the latter of which he pursued through measures designed to address the immediate concerns and interests of the city's most influential "colored" citizens. And indeed, the following year, Morrison began outlining plans for the construction of a residential subdivision with golf course, baseball diamonds, and playgrounds exclusively for the "Negro race" near Seabrook.[66]

The construction of a planned middle-class black residential neighborhood near Seabrook also intended to end further agitation by black leaders over designating the area as a public beachfront by providing them with their own incentives for keeping the "Negro masses" from the lakefront. By the early 1940s, young blacks periodically staged wade-ins at Seabrook, leading to tense, at times violent, confrontations between police and bathers. From the press and the pulpit, blacks pressured each other to reject Lincoln Beach because "as long as Negroes accept and use Little Woods, no progress will be made in getting a better place nearer town." "The passing years have seen Negro bathers pushed first from West End, then from Milneburg and now from Seabrook," an editorial in the *Louisiana Weekly* read. "A definite stand for bathing facilities should have been made when the West End 'push off' took place, and certainly this was the time for leaders to come forward." The New Orleans Urban League marshaled scientific evidence to prove that Lincoln Beach was unfit for bathing, and if opened could lead to the spread of diseases by the black persons who labored in whites' homes and cooked whites' meals. After a report from the city's sanitation department revealed the water off Lincoln Beach to be "polluted and unsanitary," Secretary Clarence A. Laws had warned Morrison's predecessor, "an epidemic may result from persons bathing in this water which may seriously threaten the total health of the community."[67]

Morrison sought to quiet summertime insurgencies by expanding the number of "colored" recreational facilities.[68] In his first two years in office, he authorized the creation of five swimming pools and three parks and playgrounds in African American neighborhoods. As the *Louisiana Weekly* kept a running tally of the number of drowning deaths of black youth each summer, in April 1951 Morrison and the levee board announced a $500,000 plan to refurbish Lincoln Beach and make it, in Morrison's words, the "equal of Pontchartrain Beach." Unlike in the past, this time the city and levee board backed up words with actions. Barges dumped white sand along an expanded shoreline, and fill was used to expand the site to seventeen acres, from its previous two and a third acres.[69] A two-thousand-locker bathhouse, a restaurant, and a pavilion were added. To render complaints over the lake's polluted waters moot, the levee board constructed two swimming pools, which were specifically designed to be equal in size to those at Pontchartrain Beach. Upon completion of the improvements, the levee board leased Lincoln Beach to Paul J. Lacassin, whose company equipped the grounds with an arcade, a Ferris wheel, roller coasters, and numerous other rides. On May 8, 1954, Morrison, along with a host of other local and state dignitaries, including Louisiana governor Robert Kennon, were on hand for the Lincoln Beach dedication ceremonies. Kennon pointed to the gleaming new rides and swanky clubhouse as evidence of white Louisiana's commitment to "all of her citizens." Several black ministers, civic leaders, and even a prominent local civil rights activist were also on the dais. Ernest Wright, head of New Orleans's People's Defense League, told the crowds gathered that the refurbished Lincoln

Beach constituted a "step forward in the Negro's fight for first-class citizenship."[70]

For the city's black and Creole middle class, it also seemed to mark the final step toward completion of the residential subdivision near Seabrook. During his speech at the dedication of Lincoln Beach, Morrison promised that the city would honor its commitment to finish construction of the middle-class residential subdivision. Named Pontchartrain Park, the neighborhood was finally completed in 1956, after years of contentious debate and bitter opposition from residents of the Gentilly Woods neighborhood located south of the development and foot-dragging by city hall. Tellingly, one white homeowners' association that was opposed to the subdivision's location on the southern lakefront suggested the undeveloped lands adjacent to Lincoln Beach as an alternative. Instead, the city turned Pontchartrain Park into a virtual fortress. Streets that ran north through Gentilly Woods stopped at Pontchartrain Park's southern border. The only entrance faced toward the lake and away from the city. New homeowners routinely encountered harassment and threats of violence from whites as they tried to navigate their way safely into the middle-class compound. Once inside, though, black homeowners entered a neighborhood virtually indistinguishable from other suburban enclaves built during the postwar decades. Three-bedroom, ranch-style homes lined winding streets where children rode bicycles without fear of traffic. Fathers played golf at the neighborhood's nine-hole course on weekends. Women hosted social club meetings from their living rooms, where picture windows faced neatly cut lawns, or prepared dinners from kitchens that looked out on fenced-in backyards. And fresh breezes blew in from the lake, where residents could hike to and enjoy a picnic, now without fear of harassment or expulsion. It was, for many, the fulfillment of a dream. By 1962, all one thousand homes in the subdivision had been purchased, at an average price of $17,000.[71]

And it was a dream whose fulfillment was predicated on the exclusion of the city's black poor. Of the many ironies of Pontchartrain Park, a neighborhood designed to uphold segregation and completed just as the legal foundations of the Jim Crow housing market began to crumble, perhaps most ironic was how indistinguishable property politics in Pontchartrain Park were from those of their white adversaries in neighboring subdivisions. A local development firm's request in 1963 for a rezoning permit to build a multifamily apartment unit in Pontchartrain Park "brought down the wrath, fury, and unification" of residents. In the coming weeks, residents of Pontchartrain

Park waged "a concerted, determined" campaign to scuttle the plan, which they conducted through their own neighborhood improvement association. In less than forty-eight hours, the improvement association gathered more than sixteen hundred signatures in opposition. City Councilman John Petre commented that he "had never witnessed such results in such a short period of time."[72] The development firm subsequently dropped its bid. The class homogeneity of the southern lakefront was preserved.

And, for the city's segregated black working poor, the crisis of summer continued. In the years following its reopening, Lincoln Beach hosted a number of summer camps for underprivileged black youth in the city, where children were taught, among other life skills, how to swim. The vast majority of black children in the city, though, had few opportunities to visit the amusement park. "Lincoln Beach," Lower Ninth Ward native Warren Brown remembers, "was too far for many of our parents, most of whom did not own cars." "We did go out there for a while after it was opened," John Harold Boucree recalls. "But it was a distance that you had to travel to get out there, no public transportation at all through that area." Brown and his childhood friends, instead, waited for summer rains to turn ditches and empty lots into "splashing pools and little rivers."[73] In New Orleans's Desire housing project, a place one historian described as an "archetype of despair," seventeen thousand minors shared a single, flood-prone public park.[74]

For these children, beating the heat still meant taking one's chances in the dangerous currents of a nearby canal. And for their parents, the long, hot summer months remained a time of worry and consternation, when the threat of a tragedy visiting them or a neighbor seemed to rise with the temperature, and when a year's worth of injustices came into focus. In his 1966 script for a dramatic play on black poverty in the Desire housing project titled *Ghetto of Desire*, writer, playwright, founder of the Free Southern Theater, and New Orleans native Thomas C. Dent directed audience attention to the Florida Avenue Canal, described as a "large, muddy ditch half-filled with foul, garbage-infested water," which snaked through the project. "Last summer," the script read, "several children from the project drowned in the bounding ditches attempting to swim after heavy rains." "Some day, possibly very soon," Dent predicted, "the city of New Orleans will hear an explosion, and no one, not the political 'leaders,' the police, the 'good' Negroes with the game all this time in exchange for personal favors—no one will understand why. A particularly provoking arrest . . . another death in the ditch— who can tell what will trigger the fuse."[75]

A real estate office located on North Beach, the tourist section of Corpus Christi, Texas, being reclaimed by the sea, 1939. Russell Lee, photographer. (Library of Congress)

SHELL ISLAND BEACH—TEN MILES FROM WILMINGTON, N. C. THE ONLY SUMMER RESORT EXCLUSIVELY FOR THE COLORED RACE

Postcard of the Shell Island Beach Resort, an African American resort located near the popular white vacation town Wrightsville Beach, North Carolina. The resort opened in 1924 and closed in 1926 following a series of arson attacks. (Courtesy of Hampton University Archives)

Parties arriving at the entrance to the Gulfside Assembly, an African American
Methodist resort in Waveland, Mississippi, on the Gulf of Mexico, ca. 1928.
(Photographs and Prints Division, Schomburg Center for Research in Black Culture, New York Public
Library, Astor, Lenox and Tilden Foundations)

Visitors to Gulfside bathing in the Gulf of Mexico, 1920s. (Photographs and Prints
Division, Schomburg Center for Research in Black Culture, New York Public Library, Astor, Lenox and
Tilden Foundations)

View of Gulfside from the end of the pier. (Photographs and Prints Division, Schomburg Center for Research in Black Culture, New York Public Library, Astor, Lenox and Tilden Foundations)

Haley Douglass, the son of Highland Beach founder Charles Douglass, and the town's first mayor following its incorporation in 1922. (Highland Beach Historical Commission)

A group of young boys preparing to ride their bicycles through the sandy, unpaved streets of Highland Beach, ca. 1950. (Highland Beach Historical Commission)

Aerial photo of the southern shore of Lake Pontchartrain taken by the Army Corps of Engineers, ca. 1946. (Louisiana Division/City Archives, New Orleans Public Library)

Pontchartrain Beach, a whites-only beach and amusement park in New Orleans.
(Louisiana Division/City Archives, New Orleans Public Library)

Aerial photo of Lincoln Beach, New Orleans's separate "Negro beach," located along a heavily polluted section of Lake Pontchartrain in a remote, sparsely populated area far outside the city. (Louisiana Division/City Archives, New Orleans Public Library)

Frank and Lulu Hill and a team of laborers at work constructing Monte Carlo by the Sea on the Freeman family's oceanfront property. The building was completed and opened in 1951. (Courtesy of Cape Fear Museum of History and Science, Wilmington, North Carolina)

Members of Freeman Beach's Surfing Club hit the waves as crowds gather on the beach. (Courtesy of Cape Fear Museum of History and Science, Wilmington, North Carolina)

Mosquito Beach, on James Island, South Carolina. (Photo courtesy of the Avery Research Center for African American History and Culture, College of Charleston, Charleston, South Carolina)

Jennie Brown and Vinnie Drake lounging on Bay Shore Beach, outside Hampton, Virginia.
(Rare Book, Manuscript, and Special Collections Library, Duke University)

Baltimore numbers king William L. "Little Willie" Adams (third from right) and a group of associates pictured leaving a Baltimore police station after submitting statements to the police following the bombing of Adams's tavern in 1938. (Courtesy of the Afro-American Newspapers Archives and Research Center)

A group of four young women posing in front of Annapolis, Maryland, deejay Hoppy
Adams's Cadillac convertible at Carr's Beach, ca. 1956. (Collection of the Maryland State Archives)

Unidentified teenage boy posing in front of a backdrop to Bay Shore Beach outside Hampton, Virginia, at the resort's photo booth.
(Rare Book, Manuscript, and Special Collections Library, Duke University)

Jazz pianist Milt Buckner and his band performing at Club Bengazi, the nightclub at Carr's Beach, ca. 1958. (Photograph by Thomas Baden Jr. Collection of the Maryland State Archives)

Poster advertising the opening of Bay Shore Beach for the 1952 summer season.

(Courtesy of Hampton University Archives)

Annapolis deejay Hoppy Adams, at left, posing with two unidentified musicians on the bandstand at Sparrow's Beach, ca. 1955. (Photograph by Thomas Baden Jr. Collection of the Maryland State Archives)

Anne Arundel County deputy sheriff and Carr's Beach chief of security George Phelps patrolling the area around the Carr's Beach music pavilion, ca. 1960. (Courtesy of George Phelps Jr.)

Phelps's special deputies arresting a man who had attempted to sneak onto the Carr's Beach grounds by wading past the chain-link fence that divided Carr's and Sparrow's beaches. (Courtesy of George Phelps Jr.)

The last days of
the Marshall Hall
Amusement Park,
ca. 1975.
(Courtesy DC Public
Library, Star Collection,
© Washington Post)

The ruins of the former Lincoln Beach in New Orleans, ca. 2010.
(Photo by Amy Pia; used with her permission)

Adolph "A. D." Brown's model for a proposed high-end condominium development to be placed on a tract of heirs property on Hilton Head Island, South
Carolina, 2006. (AP photo/Mary Ann Chastain)

5

FAMILY TIES

In the 1850s, as white southerners feverishly fought to extend the institution of slavery across the continent and into Central America, the free black couple Alexander and Charity Freeman accumulated 180 acres along the Myrtle Grove Sound in coastal North Carolina. In the decades following the Civil War, their son Robert Bruce Freeman continued to buy more—from failed whites seeking a new start elsewhere and from absentee owners looking to cash out. The going rate at the time for coastal property in New Hanover County was 15 cents an acre. By 1900, he had become one of county's largest landowners. Among his holdings were the Sedgeley Abbey plantation, described as "the grandest colonial residence of the Cape Fear," and the Gander Hall plantation, together totaling twenty-five hundred acres. "He never went to school—couldn't read or write—but he had a lot of sense," so the legend passed down by his ancestors goes. "He bought a lot of property."

Where he bought a lot of property was a good indication of the geography of slavery and freedom in the antebellum South. Indeed, if you were looking for a free, landowning person of color in the slave South, these sandy, windswept lands facing the furies of the Atlantic would be the type of place you would go. Those trends continued in the decades following emancipation. In New Hanover County, like many coastal counties stretching from southeastern North Carolina to Florida, the collapse of slavery was quickly followed by the rise of black landownership. Their human capital emancipated, their properties in ruins, and their coastlines blockaded, plantation owners in the Lower Cape Fear River region fled the area and relinquished efforts to tame the environment to suit the needs of a capitalist economy. In their place, freedpeople poured in, applying their own knowledge of the land and water to carve out a measure of autonomy, build a new economy, and secure their freedom through land acquisition. Between 1860 and 1870, the number of "colored" or "mulatto" households in Federal Point Township (where the Freeman landholdings were located) grew from eight to forty-four, or from roughly 10 percent to 50 percent of the total number of households in the township.[1]

The Freemans and other coastal black landowners worked to develop a subsistent household economy based around fishing and small farming. Black landowners often became builders of black institutions.[2] Robert Bruce Freeman donated one portion of his land for a "colored" public school and gave another to an African American church in Wilmington for use as a religious campground. Within months after his donation of land for the religious campground, a reported three thousand blacks from surrounding towns and rural districts attended a camp meeting there.[3]

As families remade the land to suit their interests, the land remade families. With the rise of coastal leisure economies, the commercial potential of waterfront property grew as families' ability (and, not long after, desire) to maintain subsistence economies and independence from white-controlled capital markets shrank. Using the one asset they had in abundance—the land—African American coastal black property owners worked to capitalize on—rather than fall victim to—shoreline engineering and development and an emerging mass entertainment culture along the coast. While their ancestors searched for freedom by the sea, the extended Freeman family of the first half of the twentieth century worked to turn their location by the sea into a marketable commodity, and came to exemplify a broader movement among African American coastal and waterfront landowning families to convert their spatial power into economic power, and their family property into business holdings.

At the time of his death in 1902, Robert Bruce Freeman left to his eleven children from two marriages over five thousand acres. In his will, Freeman dictated how the more valuable farm and timber land on the interior of the Myrtle Grove Sound was to be distributed among his heirs. The status of the uncultivable, unruly, and seemingly uninhabitable beachfront acres between the sound and the Atlantic, on the tip of the Carolina Beach Peninsula, was left unmentioned.[4] Freeman's death came in the midst of a wave of racial terrorism sweeping across the state. Beginning in 1898, white supremacy campaigns laid waste to the state's experiment in interracial democracy. In Wilmington, a racial pogrom resulted in the forced removal of black elected officials and the death of scores of black citizens, followed by the unsettling calm of Jim Crow segregation and black political disfranchisement. Along the Carolina coast, historian David Cecelski found, the white working poor—themselves displaced by economic downturns—"fostered an atmosphere of racial intimidation" that worked to drive many blacks from commercial and subsistence fishing.[5]

Conversely, these years also witnessed a broader movement among rural blacks to consolidate landholdings and create self-sustaining communities enjoying limited—and mutually beneficial—contacts with white and black neighboring communities.[6] From their family compound, the Freemans sold granite, clay, timber, and bootleg whiskey distilled on the premises.[7] They also sold excess property. Among several transactions, one stood out. In 1913 the siblings sold 772 acres of the Old Homestead site to Alexander W. Pate, D. N. Chadwick, and Joseph Laughlin of the Southern Realty and Development Company. The sale was remarkable not just for the amount of land sold, but also for what it foretold about the future of the region's economy, the ecology of its beaches and inland waterways, the legal status and treatment of black citizens, and, in particular, the relationship between black landholding families and their lands. The land transaction between the Freemans and the Southern Realty and Development Company gave the developers a controlling interest in the land lying to the immediate south of the Freemans' oceanfront property. It came on the eve of the extension of rail lines to the coast and the launching of an ambitious promotion campaign across the state's interior for the sale of seaside lots in the town of Carolina Beach. (See Map 11.) As part of that promotion, the newly formed Carolina Beach Corporation wrote into land deeds restrictive covenants that prevented the sale or lease of lots to "any Negro or person of African descent or other persons of color."[8]

To the north of Carolina Beach, the town of Wrightsville Beach similarly caught the summer fever as a new class of entrepreneurs worked to market the seaside village to white vacationers and mitigate the barrier island's exposure to social and environmental liabilities. Incorporated in 1899, the same year a massive hurricane destroyed virtually every structure within the town's limits, Wrightsville Beach became in subsequent decades home to a seasonal community of vacationing families and a small core of year-round residents. In both of these nascent vacation towns, the ability of local officials to determine where black persons could live and own land, and their ability to limit the presence of black persons on the

beaches and in vacation zones became central to their efforts to woo vacationers and attract additional capital investment. In 1933, Wrightsville Beach
passed a series of ordinances that prevented blacks from walking on the
beach, the boardwalk, or even in front of white cottages facing the ocean.
Persons of color pushing strollers or looking after a white child at play were,
of course, exempted. Later, the town instituted a "pass system" for blacks
seeking to enter the town through the lone drawbridge connecting it to
the mainland. As Margaret Rogers remembers:

> When you went to Wrightsville Beach you were stopped at the
> bridge tender shack until they really became familiar with you.
> If a colored person came to that bridge you were stopped and
> asked where you were going. You had to give a person's name
> and telephone number and they would call them to see if in-
> deed you were [expected]. And if that person said, "Well, yes, I
> know them but I was not expecting them today," you didn't get
> across that bridge. Or if they said, "Well, no, I have no idea who
> this person is," you didn't get across that bridge.[9]

The adoption of these extreme measures for controlling the movement
of black persons in Wrightsville Beach was, in a sense, a testament to how
real the threat of black vacationers and pleasure seekers was to the future
of this and other whites-only summer destinations, and an indication of
how determined African American landholders and capital investors were
in claiming a place in this emergent coastal economy. In 1923, C. B.
Parmele and Thomas H. Wright, the white president and vice president of
Wrightsville Beach, North Carolina's Home Realty Company, collaborated
with a group of black doctors, lawyers, and ministers to purchase Shell
Island, an uninhabited barrier island to the north of Wrightsville Beach
that local blacks had used as a bathing beach for decades. There they began
work on a $75,000 "Negro resort" development. They plotted fourteen
streets and 270 lots and outfitted the island with a pavilion, bathhouse,
restaurant, and landing pier. White contractor L. T. Rogers built the
$10,000 pavilion, while R. R. Stone built a pier to dock the Shell Island
Ferry, a small vessel that made four round-trips daily. Developers sold lots
to black professionals for the construction of private summer cottages, and
hired African Americans to operate the concessions and to serve as law
enforcement on the island. Promoters described Shell Island as "more
than a resort—[it] is a movement founded in the forethought of liberal

business men of the south who realize that the Negro's outlet for social and recreational development has heretofore been severely limited." But it was also less than a movement and more a business, as indicated by the substantial capital outlay from the Home Realty Company, along with the move by the Tide Water Power Company to construct a spur from their main line to the ferry landing (also built with white capital for the transport of black passengers to the island).[10]

The presence of black professionals enjoying their own leisure and entertainment at Shell Island sent whites in Wrightsville Beach into a panic. In a very real sense, they feared that its opening would wash all that they had worked to build, and the image they hoped to project, out to sea. As the Shell Island resort neared opening day, public officials in Carolina Beach circulated rumors that Wrightsville Beach had been ceded to the "colored race" in order to boost their own future growth prospects. The strategy seemed to bear fruit. "Now credulous persons in the upper end of the state are beginning to talk of other resorts for their summer vacation," the *Wilmington News* reported. The paper tried to dampen such fears, and assured readers that "racial lines are still observed." "The waters of the Atlantic ocean still beat against [Shell Island's] borders on all side[s], divorcing it completely, entirely and eternally from those fictitious drawbacks which the fertile imagery of Dame Rumor has woven."[11]

The enormous success of the Shell Island venture, however, did little to allay such fears. Several thousand people were reported in attendance for Shell Island's May 30, 1924, grand opening. During the first season, guests reportedly came from as far north as New York and as far south as Alabama. Throughout the summer, Frank W. Avant, a local African American doctor, booked touring college choirs such as the Hampton Harmony Six and jazz performers such as Lindsey Brown, "North Carolina's Greatest Tenor," and Morrow's Orchestra from Charlotte, to perform in the pavilion. Some weekends the managers reported having to turn away guests. The resort's instant popularity and high returns testified to the potential profits white investors saw in black leisure, while its sudden, and unceremonious, end underscored the perceived threat black leisure space posed to the regional economy. After three successful seasons, the facilities on Shell Island suffered a series of fires "of undetermined origin." Few doubted the origin and intent of these "mysterious" blazes. With most of its buildings destroyed, the investors cut their losses and, in the winter of 1926, abandoned the island.[12]

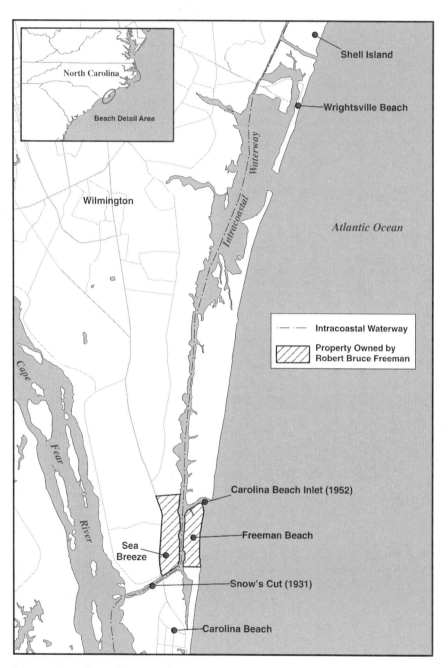

Map 11. Coastline of New Hanover County, North Carolina

The demise of corporate ventures such as Shell Island did not, as its opponents hoped, eliminate the market for black vacationing and seaside
amusement along the Carolina coast, but instead redirected it toward
those existing black-owned lands that had been held by families for generations. By the early 1920s the Freeman family's lands remained mostly
covered with forests and swamps, and were used by resident family members for fishing, oyster harvesting, and logging. But among this extended
family, some began to perceive potential riches to be made from refitting
and marketing its waterfront property to those black citizens who had been
turned away from whites-only leisure spaces and whose efforts to acquire
land and develop places of their own had ended in disappointment or disaster. In 1922, Roland and Nathan Freeman, two of Robert Bruce Freeman's children from his second marriage who owned clear title to sixty-
five-acre plots on the interior side of the Myrtle Grove Sound, formed the
North State Realty and Investment Company and divided their landholdings into small lots for sale. Development of what came to be known as
Seabreeze soon followed. The Freeman family's relationship with their
land—and with each other—was at this moment fundamentally and irrevocably altered. (See Map 11.) Formerly known as a wild bunch of rebels
and outsiders who lived by their own rules and openly expressed their
disdain for respectable black folks who lived in modest homes in Wilmington and Carolina Beach, the Freemans were now selling real estate
to those same persons for commercial and residential use and becoming
their partners in the building of a summer resort village on their family's
lands. In 1924, Tom and Victoria Lofton, a prominent black couple from
Wilmington, completed construction on a twenty-five-room, three-story
hotel, restaurant, and dance hall on the grounds. On their waterfront lot,
the Loftons built a cement walkway leading to the shore, along with a pier
for fishing and crabbing. Victoria Lofton arrived at her hotel in a chauf-
feured automobile and employed a crew of servants to prepare her meals
and wash her clothes and bathing suits during her stays. In May 1929 the
Russell Hotel opened with a performance by Frank Herring's seven-piece
orchestra. The Harlem-based, syndicated black columnist Geraldyne
Dismond reported, to her surprise, cottages that resembled a "trans-
planted Seventh Avenue tea room," "swank . . . bungalows," and a sporting crowd dressed in linen suits and driving roadsters. By the late 1920s,
weekend crowds at Seabreeze numbered in the thousands, and the resort
attracted numerous conventions of black business and civic organizations.

In 1934 Dr. Foster F. Burnett, a black physician from Wilmington, built a convalescent home and recreation center adjacent to the grounds. The following year, the North Carolina Utilities Commission granted a franchise permit to the Wilmington Bus Company to operate a bus line from Wilmington to Seabreeze.[13]

.✦.

Not all of the Freemans were interested in becoming coastal capitalists, and not all of the Freemans' land was deemed suitable for commercial development. While Seabreeze developed into a mix of commercial properties and private residences nourishing a vibrant seasonal economy, the rest of the Freeman family's interior lands continued to be used for farming, harvesting timber, and fishing and dredging oysters from the bountiful Myrtle Grove Sound. Across the sound, the dunes, marshes, and beaches facing the Atlantic Ocean remained undeveloped and were treated as a communal space shared by the Freemans and the rural black population alike. Persons freely used the windswept, marsh-covered peninsula to fish, hunt, and bathe. Its informal use reflected its legal status. Robert Bruce Freeman considered his beachfront landholdings so unproductive, uninhabitable, and inconsequential that he neglected to divide them among his descendants in his will. Upon his death, title to these lands dissolved; in its place, each descendant of Freeman, and their subsequent heirs, claimed an indivisible share in the land as tenants in common. Restoration of title to all or a portion of the land would subsequently require petitioning the New Hanover County Court for partition. The sandy dunes facing out on the Atlantic became known as "heirs' property," a type of arrangement that was common among African American landowning families in the rural South. When a person died intestate, it was left to a probate court to decide the manner in which the deceased's assets were distributed among the heirs. In the case of land, there were two options: joint tenancies, or tenancies in common. Joint tenancies distribute undivided shares in the property equally among the heirs, with those shares being redistributed among the surviving original heirs following the death of a shareholder, known as the right of survivorship. Joint tenancies thus have a consolidating effect. Over time, the number of persons claiming an interest in the land will decrease to the point that the single surviving heir claims title to the entire property in fee simple.

In tenancies in common (that is, heirs' property), the opposite is the case. When a co-tenant dies, his or her shares are not redistributed among the survivors but instead are inherited by the deceased individual's heirs, who now possess a fraction of the other, original heirs' shareholdings. Well into the nineteenth century, probate court judges tended to opt for joint tenancies. By the late nineteenth century, however, courts overwhelmingly favored tenancies in common, with some states moving to abolish joint tenancies altogether and others eliminating its chief characteristic, the right of survivorship.[14] As a result, the amount of land in heirs' property arrangements—and the numbers of persons with an interest in an heirs' property—grew exponentially. Over time, as the number of persons with an interest in the land multiplies, the legal standing of each shareholder (regardless of the size of his or her holdings) remains constant, creating situations in which persons with no personal connections to the resident co-tenants (that is, the persons actually living and working on the land) or role in the land's management can play a disproportionately influential role in determining outcomes affecting all co-tenants—resident and nonresident, large and small shareholder alike.

For many African American landowning families in the rural South, this type of arrangement might have been seen as preferable. On the Sea Islands of South Carolina and Georgia, where heirs' property arrangements were common, black landholding families had little access to legal advice and a deep distrust in legal institutions. But they also tended to adopt communal notions of land ownership, which heirs' property arrangements served to reinforce, since legally, no single family member could claim a personal interest in any portion of the land. As a legal form of dissimulation, the tangled web that constituted heirs' properties might have been seen by some as a means of fending off outside developers who preferred to handle clear title and individual owners, and suppressing individuals from within the family who might have sought personal gain at the expense of family interests. In other words, dissolving title to the land could be seen as a way of ensuring that the family unit—all united by shared interests in the land—could not be dissolved. As one study found, many black rural landowners believed that "heir property could not be sold or mortgaged," and saw the absence of title to the land as, paradoxically, "a means of retaining land in the family." Some have argued that African Americans saw in heirs' property ownership a source of collective strength, community cohesion, and cultural identity. More likely, most simply saw little to be gained from messing with racist and corrupt courts for a piece of paper with little practical value in a society where legal distinctions were applied only to their detriment. Indeed, among the primary reasons for clearing title is to secure a loan to build or improve the land, which, in the Jim Crow South, was often unavailable regardless (or available on highly usurious terms). Since many flocked to the coast to escape from Jim Crow justice, it should come as no surprise that black coastal landowners often developed patterns of ownership and inheritance that operated outside and in defiance of southern courts of law, in particular, and the classically liberal notions of private property ownership enshrined in American jurisprudence, in general.[15]

Spreading ownership of the land among descendants, though, led to problems of all sorts. With each passing generation, the number of persons claiming shares in the land multiplied, while the possibility of clearing title and dividing the property equitably among shareholders dwindled. After several generations, the shares of interest in a farm could become quite fragmented. Often the people who remained on the land had only a small fraction of an interest in the land, while many others, sometimes living far away, had little connection to the land but an equal share in determining its fate. Over time, fewer and fewer of these absentee shareholders even knew that they held interest in land down south, and if they did, their interest in the land was often for what meager money they could make by selling their interest.

In the coastal South, the decline of heirs' property owners' means of subsistence and self-sufficiency led many to sell their shares to parties outside the family or use them as collateral in securing a loan. The acquisition of shares by persons outside the family could have disastrous consequences for the family by exposing them to legal challenges to land claims adjudicated in Jim Crow courtrooms. Such was the case with the Freeman family's heirs' properties when, in 1940, Ellis Freeman sold his shares to the Home Real Estate Realty Company as part of a settlement on a defaulted loan. With these shares in hand, this group of white developers gained entry into the "family" and used their power as shareholders to seize ownership of some of the Freemans' increasingly prized beachfront. Immediately after gaining possession of Ellis Freeman's shares, the Home Real Estate Realty Company filed for a partition of a portion of the beachfront commensurate with the number of shares in their possession. The following year, the Superior Court of New Hanover County granted the Home Real Estate

Realty Company title to a thirty-five-hundred-foot stretch of property
along the southern portion of the Freemans' beachfront holdings to the
immediate north of the town of Carolina Beach. The status of the remainder of the property was left unaddressed. After gaining title, the development firm successfully petitioned the town of Carolina Beach to annex the
property, and they subsequently began construction on summer homes,
hotels, and condominiums.[16]

The actions of the Army Corps of Engineers had a slowly pernicious, but
no less devastating, effect on the Freeman family's hold on the land. From
the time of the earliest settlement, the shallow, brackish waters of the
Myrtle Grove Sound had provided a bountiful supply of fish and oysters,
and into the twentieth century these waters remained off-limits to large-
vessel navigation and virtually unaffected by the ecological effects of the
region's maritime industries. Vessels traveling from Beaufort, North Carolina, to the Cape Fear River instead had to journey into the ocean and
pass around the volatile Cape Fear Shoals. Seeking to open up channels
of commerce, in 1930 the Army Corps of Engineers completed a series of
canals that linked Wilmington's port to the Atlantic Intracoastal Waterway
(ICW). Stretching from Annisquam Canal, twenty-three miles northeast
of Boston, Massachusetts, to Corpus Christi, Texas, the ICW provided a
continuous, protected waterway for commercial and pleasure craft unable
to navigate the open waters of the Atlantic.[17] (See Map 11, p. 160.)

The economic benefits of the ICW for Wilmington's economy were as
profound as the environmental damage it inflicted on the Myrtle Grove
Sound. By the 1930s, hydraulic pipe-line dredges were used to deepen
water channels, replacing cruder, labor-intensive excavation measures. As
part of the project, the Army Corps of Engineers dredged a twelve-foot-
deep channel, named Snow's Cut (after W. A. Snow, the project's super-
vising engineer) through the Myrtle Grove Sound and the Freeman family lands. Completed in 1931, Snow's Cut immediately altered the area's
geography, turning a shallow estuary into a deep, volatile, and flood-prone
artery to the sea. Erosion that resulted from Snow's Cut slowly ate away at
the small but growing summer community of Seabreeze. Most devastating, the project decimated the fish and oysters that lived in the waters off
the Freeman family's lands and had been a source of food and trade for
generations. As part of the civil engineering of the area's inland waterways, the Corps channeled polluted freshwater from the Cape Fear River
into the sound, resulting in the death of most of the sound's oyster beds

and fish nurseries. Both the Corps and the public were well aware of the project's potentially devastating effects on local fish populations and the area's seafood industries. A white fishing village located north of Wilmington protested against the original route of the ICW, which would have exposed their waters to increased pollution. So as to preserve and protect this area for white fishermen, Snow rerouted pollutants through the Myrtle Grove Sound and past Seabreeze.[18]

In 1921, a young couple, Lulu Freeman, the daughter of Robert Bruce Freeman, and Frank Hill, the son of one of Wilmington's most prominent black families, married and moved from their families' homes in New Hanover County to New York City. For a young, ambitious black couple, coastal Carolina at the time seemed like a graveyard of dashed dreams. So, "like Europeans . . . in search of a better life," their daughter Evelyn Williams later wrote, "my parents fled from the escalating atrocities of the Ku Klux Klan, from legalized segregation, and from the limitations imposed by both job discrimination and the types of jobs available to black people in the South."[19] They settled into an all-black neighborhood in Queens, where Lulu raised their two daughters and Frank worked as a truck driver and auto mechanic and dreamed of someday owning a small business.

Theirs was a journey shared by countless other children of southern black landowners. Beginning during World War I and accelerating in the following decades, young black men and women fled the rural South in unprecedented numbers, lured to northern and southern cities by the prospects of industrial jobs and political freedom, and driven from the rural South by exploitative labor relations, political repression, wholesale violence, and the seeming absence of opportunity. Indeed, as evidenced by the annual movement in the dead of night of sharecropping families from one plantation to the next, long before the Great Migration the structure of racial capitalism in the Jim Crow South had firmly linked social and economic with literal mobility. Such conditions invariably shaped understandings of the land itself. Booker T. Washington's admonition to black southerners to "cast down their buckets where they are" and resist the temptations of the urban North rang hollow for those who had struggled to acquire, hold on to, and reap profits from the land. This was no less the case for those who actually owned the land under their feet. Rates of migration among tenants and landholders in South Carolina low country, one study found, were virtually identical.[20]

Regardless of their feelings for the land they left behind, many migrants carried a tie to the land with them in the form of shares to heirs' property. For his 1932 study, *Sea Island to City*, C. V. Kiser interviewed scores of black migrants from South Carolina in Harlem. Invariably, he found, respondents told him that they owned an "interest in some" land back home.[21] Ironically, migrants' material interest in their family's homesteads down south grew in relation to their emotional disinvestment in these lands. As they established roots in northern cities, raising families and becoming steadily detached from the rural South, they increasingly came to see their family properties more as an economic asset and less as an ancestral inheritance and source of personal and familial identity.

The multiplication and geographical dispersal of claim holders to family lands increased the likelihood of intra-family disputes and, in areas witnessing an appreciation of land values, exploitation of these disputes by outside parties. On Mon Louis Island, located along Alabama's Mobile Bay, the Durrettes, a "colored" Creole family, had claimed ancestral ties to coastal lands dating back to the early 1800s, when the area was settled by the Revolutionary War veteran Negro captain Maximilien "Jack" Collins, who upon his death deeded his land to his free and enslaved descendants "with the injunction that they should sell none of it." For the next century, Collins's descendants fished in the bay and inlets, tilled the sandy Gulf Coast soil, and clung to their status as neither "white" nor "Negro," and their independence from the plantation economy. In 1932 Harry Moseby, a black man from Mobile who had married into the Durrette family, mortgaged his home on the island to pay back taxes on his wife's family's Old Homestead after his wife's sister, Clairice Durrette, who had inherited the home, moved to New York City and stopped paying the bills. Her delinquency occurred just as the area was experiencing a steady influx of white families from Mobile during the summer months, who bought cheap land and built summer cottages on the beach, and who disdainfully referred to their neighbors as "Nigger Creoles." "I didn't want to" pay her tax bills, Moseby later wrote, "but my wife and her Mother insisted that I do so to keep the White people from getting . . . the Old Homestead." With its wide, white sand beach shaded by centuries-old oak and pine trees, the Old Homestead was one of the most majestic spots on Mobile

Bay, and had the county placed a tax lien on the home, it would have quickly been bought by one of the many white developers scouting available land in the area.

Two years later, having received no payments from his wife's sister, and continuing to pay the property's taxes, Moseby secured from Durrette a quit-claim deed on the land. With the property now in his possession, Moseby did what any shrewd owner of a beachfront in the age of the automobile would do: he started renting his beach to groups from the city (Mobile) for picnics and parties. Only, in this case, the groups were black. Moseby was not the first black person on the island to perceive his beach's appeal to vacationers and excursionists. Down shore from the Mosebys, the Faustinas, a Creole family who also had considerable holdings on the island, rented out their beach for summer parties.[22] Its reputation as a summer haven for black Alabamians was known far and wide. An article in the *Chicago Defender* described Mon Louis Island as "one of nature's little miniature paradises—a little Coney Island minus the hot dog stands and other commercial schemes." Its renown was captured in song:

> Grab a bun
> On the run,
> Boun' for Mon Louis Island . . .
>
> Swim or sweat,
> Play or pet—
> 'S all the same on th' Island![23]

Perhaps it was after hearing a few bars of the "Mon Louis Island Blues" hummed on the streets of Harlem that Durrette returned home and demanded to reclaim title to her inheritance. And when Moseby refused and persisted in booking summer events at the Old Homestead, many of his new and old neighbors were more than willing to help Durrette redeem her inheritance and, as Moseby describes, "stop me from making any money down there." In particular, it was the Faustinas—who until then had cornered the market on black excursion parties—and new white summer landowners who collaborated in heightening racial tensions to their mutual advantage. As Moseby's first party of guests arrived in the spring of 1935, white neighbor Frank Roche visited the Old Homestead and warned Moseby against renting his beach out for future parties. After Moseby ignored this threat and proceeded to book reservations, his neighbors implemented more incendiary tactics. During a picnic for the Lily Baptist Sunday School, Moseby's white neighbors called the sheriff and "told him they were fighting and cutting up at Moseby's place." The local sheriff invaded the party and searched the premises for knives and liquor but came up empty. Two nights later, two anonymous white men visited Moseby's house, interrogated his mother-in-law about his whereabouts, and then lingered in front of his driveway until midnight. At the next picnic, hosted by the Stone Street AME Church, hooded Klansmen "traveled up and down the road [leading to the beach] trying to scare the people . . . shining flash lights on the trucks and taking license numbers." In the face of death threats, Moseby agreed to cancel his upcoming Labor Day picnic if his neighbors would agree to pay for "the expense [he] had went to advertising and preparing for it." Moseby was summoned to Roche's lawyer's office the following day, where he hesitantly signed some papers whose contents he did not fully comprehend, and received a check for fifteen dollars in return. But, as he later learned, Moseby had not just agreed to cancel the Labor Day picnic, but in fact had "release[d] permanently the right to use" his land for "picnics and bathing parties for negroes." The following summer, after the first group of guests arrived at the beach, the Mobile County Circuit Court judged Moseby in violation of the terms of his contract and issued an order against any use of his property for "commercial purposes."[24]

Well aware that he "havnt got a chance in an Alabama court against a white man," on August 12, 1937, Moseby sought the counsel of Walter White, secretary of the National Association for the Advancement of Colored People. "White people are trying to get control" of an island "founded by Colored People," he wrote. "Mon Louis Island is the only place we can go, and now they are trying to take this away from us." His adversaries, Moseby described, sought no less than to "keep us colored people out of the Bay. If they can crush me . . . they will do likewise to all colored people who might try and have a Bathing Beach. It is not the case of Frank Roche and others vs Harry and Nellie Moseby, it is the case of the white man trying to keep the colored man out of the Bay." If it was, it was a campaign dependent on the active collaboration of other black landowning families whose own commercial interests placed them in conflict with fellow blacks, and whose intra- and interfamilial divisions became, for others, weapons of intimidation and expropriation. And it was, like many attacks on black property owners, conducted by the letter of the law, and as such did not fit comfortably within the NAACP's legal strategies for dismantling Jim Crow. After reading Moseby's hastily written letter, White, assistant secretary Roy Wilkins, and assistant special counsel Thurgood Marshall all agreed that the case was "lousy" and "hopeless," and kicked it back down to the head of the Mobile branch, John T. LeFlore. Moseby's case died in the Alabama Supreme Court.[25]

By the mid-1940s, Frank and Lulu Hill had grown steadily disillusioned with the promise of freedom in the urban North. Frank bounced from job to job, always the last hired and first fired. To meet house payments, Lulu worked in a garment factory and rented out spare rooms in their house in Queens to boarders. After securing a job in a wartime industry, Frank saved enough money to start an auto repair business following the war. But finding themselves barely able to break even, the Hills turned their attention back home, to the undeveloped oceanfront property they shared in common with Lulu's relatives. Each summer, daughter Evelyn Williams remembers, the family made a pilgrimage to Lulu's family lands down in North Carolina, where they fished, crabbed, and dug for clams and oysters, and where Frank and Lulu mapped out their future. "We would park on the silky white beach and I remember how proud I felt as I gazed at 'our beach' . . . and listened to my parents plan to develop it for black people."[26] In 1945 Frank Hill initiated efforts to clear title to the land and claim the oceanfront property as Lulu's inheritance, where the couple planned to construct a seaside pleasure resort. But while the New Hanover County probate court had adopted a liberal interpretation of property law in awarding title to a portion of the land to the Home Real Estate Company years earlier, with the Hills' petition it was a strict constructionist. Citing the ambiguous ruling in the previous case dealing with the oceanfront property, the court ruled in favor of the neighboring white realty firm's incredible contention that it owned rights to the entire northern tip of the Carolina Beach Peninsula, and denied Hill's attempt to clear title to any portion of the land. The Hills persisted, though, and began making plans to develop the fragile sliver of sand for commercial purposes. But as the Home Real Estate Company continued to press its case in court and prevent the construction of a black pleasure resort next door, the Hills were forced to scramble to locate and compare land-grant maps to property surveys to prove that the property was indeed acquired by Robert Bruce Freeman and passed down to his heirs. Frank Hill's search for a lawyer as well as a surveyor in New Hanover County willing to accept his case against Home Real Estate came up empty, while the county, citing the absence of the Freemans' title to the land, denied him a building permit. Initially naive about the underlying motives behind these obstacles, in 1950 Frank and Lulu moved back to her family's homestead and began pounding the foundations for their seaside restaurant and pavilion into the sand.[27]

On July 4, 1951, while the nation celebrated its independence, crowds gathered on the Freeman beach property to commemorate Robert Bruce Freeman and the beautiful beachfront he had bequeathed to future generations. Guests hiked through the windswept dunes and marshes leading to the northern tip of the Carolina Beach Peninsula to celebrate the opening of Monte Carlo by the Sea, the crowning achievement in Frank and Lulu Hill's quest to commercially develop her family's coastal lands. When they got there they saw a gleaming, white cement structure, replete with a dining room covered in seascape murals that doubled as a dance hall, locker rooms, showers, kitchen, and takeout window, facing the Atlantic Ocean.

The road to opening day at Freeman Beach had come at considerable expense, and its future remained far from certain. Frank and Lulu had sunk their entire life savings of $30,000 into the project, and had spent countless hours knocking on the doors of law offices and digging through dusty records in the county courthouse in an ultimately futile effort to simply prove to a Jim Crow court that the land in fact belonged to them. On Robert Bruce Freeman Day, though, such concerns were momentarily washed out to sea. Following a few short speeches and the declaration of July 4 as Robert Bruce Freeman Day, the business of pleasure commenced. While parents unfurled blankets on the shore and kids rushed into the water, Lulu dipped breaded clams into boiling grease, granddaughter JoAnne stood behind the cash register selling bags of potato chips and pickled pigs' feet, and Frank set the stage for the evening music revue.

Crowds at Freeman Beach became a microcosm of black coastal Carolinian society. "All kinds of people would come to the beach," Assata Shakur (née JoAnne Byron, granddaughter of Frank and Lulu) remembers, "some with little money and some you could tell were real poor."

Families came with picnic baskets full of fried chicken, potato salad, and watermelon. "Some of them looked so happy you could tell they didn't get a chance to go to many picnics." One could identify the city from the country folks on the beach by the degree of shade covering their bodies. "Many would say," Shakur remembers, "'I'm too black already, I ain't goin' out in no sun.' . . . We looked at them like they were crazy because we loved the sun." "The umbrellas we rent[ed] went like hotcakes. Some people draped clothes and blankets around the umbrellas so that no light permeated whatsoever. One lady put a paper bag over her head and poked holes in it for her eyes. Some women refused to go near the water because they were afraid their hair would 'go bad.'"[28]

While middle-class city folks obsessively covered their skin from the sun and fussed over their processed hair, the rural working poor who labored in the sun all day, and who had saved their meager earnings for a single day at the beach, cared little how they looked at the end of the day and more about how their overworked bodies and minds felt. On summer weekends, truckloads of rural black farm laborers, crammed into broken-down jalopies, poured in from the countryside. Alongside them came groups of rowdy youth in search of a good time. "Their cars smelled like whiskey. They would dance a lot, eat a lot, [and] spend a lot on the piccolo" [i.e., jukebox]. On weekends, they came for live entertainment. The beach soon earned the nickname Bop City for the steady stream of local and national jazz and R&B artists, including Fats Domino, Nat King Cole, Chuck Berry, Little Richard, Bobby Blue Bland, and James Brown, who played at shows on Sunday afternoons and evenings. When "them [farm workers]," Shakur remembers, would "come out of that dance hall . . . they'd be wet from their shirt" dripping in sweat. "Many a time on Saturday evening, [especially] the Saturday before Labor Day," David Wade recalls, "[you would] start seeing country people—all of them had little money—come down." "These people, they would work on farms [all summer] for that one day, and you should [have] seen the trucks, truck loads of people just coming down," Mamie Wade adds. "Sometimes the floors of their raggedy old cars or trucks were half rotted out," Shakur remembers. "Usually a lot of little children were with them and they wouldn't have bathing suits. They went in swimming in whatever clothes they had worn to the beach, and half the time the kids wore nothing."[29]

For some, just enjoying the chance to stare out at the sea was enough. "One of the most moving things" Shakur remembers from her childhood on the beach, "was when someone saw the ocean for the first time. It was amazing to watch. They would stand there, in awe, overpowered and overwhelmed, as if they had come face to face with God or with the vastness of the universe." "One time a preacher brought an old lady to the beach. She was the oldest-looking person i had ever seen. She said she just wanted to see the ocean before she died. She stood there in one spot for so long she looked like she was in a trance. Then, with the help of the preacher, she hobbled around, picked up some mundane shells, and put them in her handkerchief as if they were the most precious things in the world." Freeman Beach, as Billy Freeman later described it, "had a therapeutic effect on us as a people."[30]

Billy's uncle Frank was less interested in providing therapy for victims of racial oppression and more focused on finding ways to make some money. As a result of Snow's Cut, persons seeking to venture to the beach could no longer wade across the sound (as family members and visitors to Seabreeze did in the past) but instead were forced to pass through the downtown district of Carolina Beach. Margaret Rogers described the experience of passing through the resort town in the summer as harrowing. "The parents would always say, 'Now you know we're getting ready to go through Carolina Beach, so let's be quiet. Let's not make any noise.'" "When you ventured" through Carolina Beach, Margaret Fredlaw added, "you really felt a high degree of not being safe. . . . You might hear rumors of somebody getting . . . a brick [thrown] at 'em or catcalls . . . or calling names." The local police, Billy Freeman remembers, "would harass [persons coming to Freeman Beach] so bad." Instances of blacks being arrested and charged with trespassing became common. On August 24, 1947, a group of fifty African Americans traveling from Washington, D.C., and Baltimore to Seabreeze were arrested and fined $5.90 each for "trespassing" after attempting to drive along Carolina Beach's beachfront drive to reach Freeman Beach. In response, Frank Hill began operating a ferry service from Seabreeze to Bop City to shield his guests from confrontations with local authorities. For a fee, passengers were transported across the sound in what was described as "nothing but a big open boat with a motor on the back of it," and "then . . . had to walk through the marsh grass and mud and stuff like that to get over to the beach itself." After town officials refused to extend a street from Carolina Beach's northern border to the resort, Hill trucked in red clay dirt and laid down a road and parking lot, where he charged drivers fifty cents to park.[31]

The more popular Bop City became, the more it drew the ire of local white residents and public officials. White folks in Carolina Beach, Shakur remembers, were enraged that Hill had "dared to build on the land and to start a 'colored' business." Within eyesight of the new hotels and resorts built on the Freemans' ancestral lands, Bop City was, as she put it, "too close for their comfort." As a result, folks "would visit us from time to time to express their disapproval." As Shakur acidly describes, groups of "red-blooded amerikan boys out for some good clean fun . . . would ride around the parking lot, spinning and skidding, while they shouted curses and racist insults. One time they fired guns in the air." Similarly, Hill's ferry service could not insulate his guests from the threat of assault on the paths leading to Bop City. As David Wade remembers, "White people [would] go down there and keep people from Seabreeze from going across [the sound to Bop City]. I'd seen them go over there and set the marsh afire." "But," he added, "that didn't slow us down. Well, it might've slowed us down, but it didn't stop us from going there."[32]

Instead, such crude acts of intimidation strengthened the Hills' determination to protect and defend their rights as property owners. After suffering repeated damage to the parking lot, the Hills constructed a gated fence at the end of the dirt path leading to the resort. In 1953 Frank Hill again attempted to clear title to the land in order to begin work on the second phase of his development plans: the selling of lots to black families for the building of seaside cottages. That April he solicited local white attorney John Bright Hill for help. Bright Hill readily accepted the case and reactivated the dormant land dispute. Unbeknownst to Frank Hill, John Hill's interest in the case stemmed from his ties to local real estate interests, and he used his position as Frank Hill's legal counsel to structure the lawsuit so as to divest his client of any claims to the land. In the suit, John Hill argued that the Home Real Estate Realty Company was a tenant in common with the Freemans and held shares in the coastal land tract—instead of making the case that the company owned no shares in the remaining property, since the county court had restored title to the portion they had developed in 1940 and, in effect, divorced their land claims from the other shareholders. To prove ownership to land lacking in title, Frank Hill relied on land-grant maps that outlined the area known as Grant 97, which was included in Robert Bruce Freeman's landholdings.

Well aware that the veracity of such evidence rested on the personal inspection of such lands by a surveyor, John Hill purposely called before the
courts a surveyor who had inspected the maps but not the property itself,
thus resulting in the dismissal of this crucial testimony. Since there was
no proof of joint ownership of the land Frank Hill sought to partition, and
since Frank Hill failed to establish "title to the land described in the petition," in 1957 Judge Malcolm Paul of the New Hanover County court
ruled he was "not entitled to recover the lands described in the petition or
any part thereof."[33]

The treachery did not stop there, though. In order to prevent an appeal,
the judge, in collusion with Hill's attorney and the clerk of court, back-
dated the decision, rendered on July 9, 1957, to June 18, 1957, past the ten-
day statutory period for filing an appeal.[34] Paul's judgment operated as a
legal prohibition against any future claims by the Freemans to their coastal
property and opened the door for Home Real Estate to file for the Hills'
eviction.

As the town worked to prevent the Hills from adding to their coastal
properties, civil engineering decisions designed to facilitate the growth of
the region's whites-only leisure and tourism economy were, quite literally,
eating away at Bop City. In the postwar years, commercial fishing and
pleasure boat services had grown alongside hotels and resorts to become a
major industry with an increasingly firm grip on local and federal purse
strings. In 1951 a group of investors and business owners in Carolina Beach
applied for a permit from the Corps of Engineers to undertake an environmentally reckless plan to create a four-thousand-foot long, six-foot-deep,
one-hundred-foot wide inlet connecting the Intracoastal Waterway to
the Atlantic Ocean at a location to the immediate north of Bop City. The
inlet would shorten the distance from the town's marina to the ocean by
sixteen miles and provide easier access for commercial fishermen and
pleasure boats to the waters of the Atlantic. In 1952 the Corps of Engineers
approved the plan and supervised its completion.

The inlet set in motion a rapid erosion of the northern tip of the Carolina Beach Peninsula. Shoreline erosion on the peninsula's tip jumped
from an annual rate of 0.6 feet to 2.8 feet. Between 1952 and 1969, the Army
Corps of Engineers estimated, the Freeman property suffered a loss of 1,135
feet of shoreline from westward accretion and a quantitative loss of 3.67
million cubic yards of beach sand. By the late 1970s, the initial one-hundred-
foot wide inlet had, as a result of erosion, widened to seven hundred feet.

Once the inlet was completed, Frank Hill remembers, the expansive beach that fronted Bop City "started rolling. We started losing the land." Completion of the inlet also led to the entry of the Cape Fear River's water into the ocean, which produced volatile currents at the Bop City beachfront and resulted in several reported drowning deaths. The river also deposited pollutants along the ever-shrinking shoreline, contaminating local fish populations.[35]

For the Hills, Hurricane Hazel completed the work that the Carolina Beach Inlet had begun. Striking the Carolina coast in October 1954, Hazel pummeled the eroding coastline and washed the structures at Bop City, and the ground they stood on, out to sea. The damage to Seabreeze was equally devastating. Hurricane Hazel also washed Frank and Lulu Hill's life savings out to sea, and their status as heirs' property owners, which prevented them from securing a loan to build Bop City, stymied their efforts at future development. Since heirs' property was held in common, and its ownership divided and uncertain, it was effectively ineligible for mortgages or disaster relief loans through Section 502 of the Housing Act of 1949. Administered by the Farmers Home Administration (FmHA), Section 502 provided low-interest loans to build modest homes or modernize existing structures in rural areas. Though the Housing Act did not insist on clear title, in practice the FmHA refused to consider applications from heirs' property owners and instead, as one study found, "encourage[d] blacks to find another piece of property on which to build," which was, considering that the land was often their most significant asset and only means of revenue, "invariably an impossibility." Heirs' property owners could find some relief in Section 504 of the Housing Act, which provided funds for structural repairs through promissory notes up to $5,000, thereby bypassing the need for a mortgage or proof of title. But, as the same study found, those able to secure these paltry loans often were unable to find a contractor willing to accept such a small job with little margin of profit. To add insult to injury, while the federal government and private lending institutions erected numerous obstacles that effectively nullified the ability of heirs' property owners to utilize their illiquid assets to secure credit, administrators of food stamp and Social Security programs counted heirs' properties as part of a person's assets, thus rendering many applicants ineligible for welfare assistance.[36]

As Bop City slipped into the sea, the Army Corps of Engineers took affirmative action to shore up Carolina Beach's coastal economy. Following

Hazel, the Corps implemented a sand replenishment plan along Carolina Beach's fourteen thousand feet of beachfront, designed to repair the erosion caused by the inlet and exacerbated by the storms.[37] Freeman Beach was not included in the Corps' sand replenishment initiative, and as a result suffered further erosion. At this point Frank Hill was under no delusion as to the underlying motives of this policy of benign neglect. "I think it was done purposely for the simple reason they didn't want us in business down there—period."[38]

While Frank Hill had successfully fended off attempts to evict him, and doggedly rebuilt after each storm, the literal disappearance of the land (and federal, state, and local officials' determination not to replenish this section of the coast) rendered his plans for residential development impossible and ensured that the fruits of the postwar leisure economy—and the dollars spent by a growing and empowered black middle class on vacationing and tourism in the desegregated South—would flow directly into the hands of large-scale, corporately owned hotels and resorts. Hill's final application for a permit to rebuild on the former site of Bop City, submitted in 1967, was denied on the grounds that erosion and high tides had rendered the site unsafe. His plans to rebuild Bop City dashed, Hill began work as a bell captain at the Blockade Runner, a high-class hotel on the oceanfront in Wrightsville Beach. In subsequent years, Carolina Beach granted a permit to Spinnaker Point LLC to build a row of luxury, oceanfront condominiums on lands claimed by the Freemans that were adjacent to the property county supervisors had deemed too damaged and eroded for Hill to build on, and, at the behest of commercial boats and fishermen, the Corps of Engineers approved plans to re-dredge and further widen the Carolina Beach Inlet. By then, the wrecked structures that had once constituted Bop City jutted out from the ocean's waters a hundred yards offshore, an idle curiosity to vacationing families as they hiked along the coast.[39]

6

SPINNING SAND INTO GOLD

Of the estimated seventy thousand persons who journeyed onto Maryland's Annapolis Neck Peninsula on July 21, 1956, to hear Chuck Berry perform at Carr's Beach, only eight thousand made it past the gates before the grounds were deemed filled beyond capacity. More than a few got in by swimming around or crawling under the fence that lined the property at the risk of apprehension and severe punishment by the team of African American special deputies hired by the beach's black owners to patrol the grounds and maintain order. Others turned away that night headed toward the Clover Inn or Do-Drop Inn, two juke joints located a mile and a half down the road. Few made it home before dawn. The following morning, the Anne Arundel County sheriff's department reported a five-mile-long traffic jam leading from the peninsula that did not empty out until nearly 4 A.M.[1]

By the summer of 1956, large numbers of African Americans streaming onto the Carr family's beachfront property on summer weekends had become a common sight for area homeowners and a telling sign of the meteoric rise of a black seasonal entertainment industry in the years following World War II. Over the previous decades, the Carr family farm on the Chesapeake Bay had gone from growing fruits and vegetables for sale in local markets to providing boarding accommodations and hosting families and groups on the family's beachfront property to becoming a lucrative corporate enterprise drawing in crowds (by car, bus, and foot) by the thousands from as far as New York City to play at the amusement park and midway, gamble at rows of slot machines, and watch a hot summer lineup of local and touring musicians and entertainers perform at the beach's large, open-air concert pavilion.

The crowds gathered on the shores of commercially owned African American beaches on summer weekends reflected the role of leisure spaces in nourishing postwar black Americans' dreams of freedom from Jim Crow and in transforming visions and expressions of black cultural identity. For a black kid growing up poor in Annapolis during these years, Carr's Beach made summers "something to look forward to—a chance to be among 'us.'"[2] Drawing persons of color from different neighborhoods, cities, and regions into intimate contact and fostering cultural exchange, the beach also came to reshape the very meaning of what constituted "us." For aspiring musicians and entertainers, the demanding audiences who crowded around beachfront pavilions made summers a chance to shine— whether as a contestant at a talent show sponsored by a local black-oriented radio station, as the opening act for a headline performer, or as one of the legion of touring musicians riding the coastal "chitlin circuit"—and made the beach a critical proving ground. For a growing web of white and black investors, proprietors, marketers, laborers, and regulators, Carr's Beach and other commercial beach resorts made summers an opportunity for work, innovation, and capital accumulation, a chance for some to pursue alternative outlets for earnings and possible freedom from wage labor, for others a means toward building wealth and exploiting opportunities created by a segregated leisure marketplace. For the beach itself, summers in postwar America became a time of intensive—and unprecedented—use and abuse, and of increasingly determined efforts to establish and police racial boundary lines. Built on the shifting sands of a Jim Crow marketplace, these seasonal enterprises facilitated the evolution and physical expansion of urban economies, and played a formative role in the making of black-oriented cultural industries and the unmaking of Jim Crow's cultural and economic foundations.

Frederick Carr came to the shore in search of affordable farmland on which he could grow fruits and vegetables and raise hogs and cattle. Born into slavery in 1847, Carr secured his first full-time job as a freedman working as a waiter and later a cook at the Naval Academy in Annapolis. In 1870 he married Mary Wells. After nearly fifty years of serving cadets, in 1902 Carr retired and purchased 66 acres of cheap farmland on the Annapolis Neck Peninsula. Three years later he acquired another 114 acres from a man named William Earickson, for a total of 180 acres.[3] There the Carr family (which included daughters Minnie, Elizabeth, Nancy, and Florence and son William Edward) grew crops and raised farm animals for subsistence and market.

Like many independent black farmers at the time, the Carrs found limited opportunities for monetary accumulation. On the streets of Annapolis, where Carr and other area truck farmers brought their goods for sale, white farmers utilized prejudice as a means of limiting competition, preventing his access to white individual and wholesale buyers and forcing Carr to deal with exploitative intermediaries in order to get his goods to market. Searching for ways to supplement the family's income and to put their land to profit, Carr hosted picnics on the family's farm and took in boarders. Evidence shows that as early as 1909 churches and organizations from Annapolis and Baltimore scheduled outings at Carr's Farm, where guests unfurled blankets on the sandy grass facing the Chesapeake Bay. By 1916, notices appeared in regional black newspapers from traveling families who reported staying overnight as boarders at Mount Pleasant Cottage on Carr's Farm, with daughter Minnie listed as the cottage's host and manager.[4] During those same years, an aged Frederick Carr took legal action to ensure that the land would stay in the family following his passing. In 1917, Carr conveyed to his children his entire real estate holdings, which included a plot of land in the city of Annapolis he acquired in 1890, to be held by them as tenants in common. Reflecting the new sources of revenue derived from the land, Carr specified that the children would receive a mutually agreed upon portion of the income from rentals and other commercial activities during the remainder of his lifetime.[5]

Most places that later became popular beach resorts had similarly inauspicious origins in the early twentieth century. Some, such as Mosquito Beach, on James Island, South Carolina, began as informal gathering spaces for farm workers, where area landowners earned extra income selling food and drinks or providing shelter. At the turn of the twentieth century, James Island was home to roughly one hundred African American independent truck farming families, many of whom had acquired land on the low-lying, marshy, and flood-prone former plantation of Solomon Legare in the decades following emancipation. There they grew tomatoes, cucumbers, watermelon, okra, and cantaloupe, among other crops, for sale in local markets. In 1923 an oyster factory opened on the island, providing jobs as harvesters, shuckers, and packers to black men, women, and children living in the area and from nearby Charleston. As workers assembled outside the factory after work, truck farmer Joe Chavis, who lived near the factory, began selling them beer, wine, and food. Soon the area around the factory became a popular gathering place for workers and island residents and, for Chavis, a much-needed source of income as the fortunes of independent truck farmers in the area began an inexorable decline toward extinction. When the oyster factory closed in the early 1930s, Chavis and his neighbor and eventual business partner Andrew "Apple" Jackson Wilder worked to ensure that the area known as the "factory" would continue to serve as a place of congregation and commerce. In 1953 they built a boardwalk pavilion on Wilder's property along Elijah Creek near the closed factory. The place came to be known as Mosquito Beach, and attracted a steady stream of blacks from Charleston during the summer months. The opening of the pavilion led other black landowners who were also struggling to make a living from oyster harvesting and truck farming to turn their barns into nightclubs, dining rooms into restaurants, and spare bedrooms into do-drop inns.[6]

Chavis and Wilder were fortunate enough to own waterfront property at a time when rising demand for leisure and entertainment among a segregated black public turned land once deemed useless and worthless into commercial assets. Other black-owned beachfront properties that became public places of resort were initially acquired for recreational purposes, but of the private, noncommercial kind. In 1890 a group of Hampton Institute administrators in Hampton, Virginia, were in the market for a stretch of beachfront property that could serve as a place for student exercise and athletics, and for the location of a hotel that could host out-of-town guests of the school and social events. They succeeded in acquiring one and a half acres from a viciously racist beachfront property owner (who kept a large sign on the beach that read "Niggers, dogs, and Chinamen not allowed on this beach") after a dispute between the owner and his neighbors compelled the former to sell his property to the most undesirable buyers imaginable. Apparently, a group of educated black professionals fit the bill. After acquiring the property, the group, headed by school administrator Frank D. Banks, pooled their funds for the construction of a four-room cottage. They named it the Bay Shore Hotel. They soon discovered that the beach itself could be used for more than student calisthenics, and along with booking rooms in the cottage, began renting the beach out to groups. Word soon spread that a black-owned stretch of shore in Hampton was hosting excursion parties. By the early twentieth century, trains and steamboats carried families, church groups, and professional organizations from as near by as Richmond and as far north and south as New York and Georgia to Bay Shore Beach on summer weekends.[7] Capital accumulated during its first two decades of operation allowed the Bay Shore Company to acquire an additional six adjoining acres and to construct, in the 1920s, a larger, seventy-room hotel with a pavilion, an amusement park, and a boardwalk along its 275-foot-long waterfront. By 1930 the beach generated $15,453 in annual income and held a reported $35,563 in reserve.[8] The growth and development of Bay Shore Beach paralleled and, literally, took place alongside that of the whites-only Buckroe Beach Amusement Park. As it did, Bay Shore inspired its neighbors to implement new mechanisms of segregation and expressions of white supremacy, in this case, a fence consisting of wood pilings that cut across the beach, separating white from black sand, and into the bay's waters.

On the Annapolis Neck Peninsula, white neighbors of the Carr family seemed less interested in segregation and more intent on expropriation. During the same years the Carrs worked to supplement their income through satisfying fellow blacks' desire for rest, recuperation, and recreation along Maryland's quiet Western Shore, outside interest in the family's waterfront real estate grew. In 1922 Carr and his daughters and their respective husbands sold several acres on the tip of the peninsula to the Eintracht Club, an incorporated body whose function and purpose was unspecified in extant land records but, based on location alone, was likely interested in the property for use as a marina and sailing club. Three years later, a group of white developers began work on Annapolis Roads, a posh vacation resort one-fourth of a mile down shore from the Carr family homestead, intended for the families of senators, congressmen, and professionals from the nation's capital. The plans called for a country club with a nine-hole golf course, tennis courts, a swimming pool, and summer homes with views of the bay. As surveyors began work on the Annapolis Roads project, developers and their allies in county government worked to acquire surrounding properties.

Following Frederick Carr's death in 1928, his widow, Priscilla, and children carried out the necessary legal steps to ensure that the land stayed in the family. In October 1929 Carr's children filed suit for the property's partition, a move that cleared title to the land through dividing the tract into lots to be held under individual ownership, ensuring that no one descendant could, due to debts or other legal liabilities, intentionally or unintentionally force the seizure and resale of the entire tract. After the property's partition into ten lots (five inland and five on the waterfront) of approximately fifteen acres each, and distribution among Minnie Dickerson, Elizabeth Smith, Nancy C. Mills, Florence Sparrow, and William Edward Carr, Carr's widow Priscilla released all claims to the farm in return for $5,000 and title to a home owned by her late husband in Annapolis. Shortly thereafter, the children acted on their different interests in the land. Between 1931 and 1937, Minnie and Nancy (both of whom had since moved to Baltimore) and William (who lived in New Haven, Connecticut) sold their lots to siblings Florence and Elizabeth, who along with their husbands William and Abram remained as residents and caretakers of the family's lands.[9]

For reasons that remain unclear, the two families got into the business of summer travel leisure accommodations simultaneously, but not cooperatively. Carr's and Sparrow's Beaches, as they would come to be known, developed side by side but remained separate business entities. (See Map 12.) By 1931, advertisements began appearing in black newspapers for board and lodging by the week at Mount Pleasant Cottage on Carr's Farm, located on the land owned by Elizabeth Carr, where guests were told they could enjoy a week of bathing, fishing, and crabbing, along with home-cooked meals. The following summer, William and Florence Sparrow built several cottages and cabins and graded three hundred yards along the waterfront for a beach on their property. The fledgling seasonal enterprises hosted churches, organizations, and day-trippers from nearby Annapolis and, in growing numbers, Baltimore and Washington. Guests came stocked with their own provisions, carrying picnic baskets filled with chicken, salads, and drinks down to the shore, perhaps, along with a deck of cards. The Sparrows provided the space; the guests brought whatever food and entertainment their budgets could muster.

Florence Sparrow's business savvy, which would later become legendary among black Annapolitans, took shape during these initial years of growth. While her husband William continued to farm until his death in 1941, Florence aggressively pursued strategies for exploiting the property's advantageous location for summer recreation. In collaboration with business manager French Burke, Florence constructed in 1935 a playground and baseball diamond on the grounds and purchased sets of beach umbrellas and chairs. She worked to establish annual events that would draw big crowds and revenues by observing the changing tastes and fashions

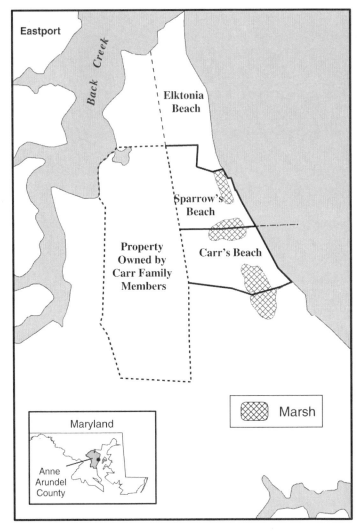

Map 12. Annapolis Neck Peninsula, Anne Arundel County, Maryland, ca. 1945

coming from nearby cities and working to channel that creative energy into events that would, she hoped, draw persons toward the beach during the summer and foment a distinctive summer beach culture and marketplace. Advertisements for the first annual Bathing Beauty Contest, held in 1936, showed an image of two shapely, fashionably attired young women

(one with cigarette in hand) posing on the beach's pier. She also appreciated the profitability of a good rivalry. A 1938 "Inter-City Amateur Contest" pitted "Washington's Best" against "Baltimore's Best" young talent in
dance and singing contests held on the outdoor pavilion. Sparrow offered
discounted group rates to churches and organizations, hired booking agents
to work the Washington, D.C., Baltimore, and Philadelphia markets, and
signed contracts with bus companies to shuttle groups from inner-city
neighborhoods to Annapolis and back. To accommodate the growing vol-
ume of traffic, in 1937 she graded and expanded the beach's parking lot
and hired area black youth to collect parking fees from automobiles and
chartered buses. She and fellow family members set up food stands where
fried fish and baked clams caught in the Chesapeake were sold, various
games and other carnival attractions for children, and rented out bathing
suits, an article of clothing few working poor blacks could afford to own
but most coveted to wear, if only for an afternoon. By the late 1930s, Sparrow employed roughly fifty-five seasonal workers—mostly teachers from
the Anne Arundel County segregated school system—and welcomed weekend crowds that reportedly numbered in the thousands. Church-sponsored
trips to Sparrow's Beach proved so popular in urban black neighborhoods
such as Washington's Deanwood in the 1930s and early 1940s that, as one
former resident recounted, "the community practically shut down on these
days."[10]

As with most black businesses of this era, big crowds often obscured these
places' undercapitalization, uncertain revenue streams, lack of access to
credit, and lack of adequate insurance—structural weaknesses a violent
storm churning in from the Atlantic exposed. In Hampton, a massive hurricane that struck the coast in the summer of 1933 destroyed the Bay Shore
hotel and the amusement park. The damage, estimated at $31,000, far
exceeded the resort's minimal insurance policy. In 1934 the corporation
applied for a $25,000 loan from the Public Works Administration. It was
granted $15,000. With only enough funds to rebuild the dance hall, reve-
nue declined sharply, and the company struggled to meet its repayment
schedule, eventually defaulting on the loan in 1940.

After seizing the property, the federal government resold it to a newly
reconstituted corporate body, titled the New Bay Shore Corporation and

carrying $10,000 in capital stock, and headed by Hampton Institute physical education professor and founder and director of the Hampton Institute Creative Dance Group, Charles H. Williams. That summer, the resort's operations consisted of a beer garden and food stand, which generated a minuscule $263 in sales over the course of the season. Plans for the construction of a new hotel and amusement park ground to a halt the following year, with the United States' entry into World War II and the virtual freeze on building and construction unrelated to the war effort. Not until 1947 did the New Bay Shore Corporation begin construction of a hotel and an amusement park and midway on the site, the latter consisting of rows of booths the company rented to various vendors for games and sales of food. Enterprising black men and women lined up for the chance to rent a booth. Months before the start of the 1947 season, Williams noted that he had already received "about a dozen applications for stands at the beach. . . . People came down last week and wanted to pay the money down now for stands. . . . We could rent every one and get a good price for them." A source of revenue for the company, vending booths offered enterprising blacks the otherwise elusive opportunity to earn extra income, through selling fried fish, reading palms, or operating various carnival games.[11]

Local and touring musicians, meanwhile, clamored for a chance to perform on the pavilions being built on the sands of black commercial beach resorts. In the mid-1930s, Florence Sparrow invested in the construction of an open-air pavilion, and signed a contract with Reese DuPree, a music promoter who did business in several East Coast cities, to begin booking bands, comedians, and other acts popular with black audiences.[12] By the summer of 1940, Sparrow's Beach attracted a steady stream of jazz bands to its Sunday afternoon "swing jamborees." For many bands and artists, Sparrow's was just one of many beaches they could expect to perform at during the summer months, as was the case in June 1940, when Count Basie followed his Sunday afternoon show at Sparrow's Beach with a Monday night performance at Bay Shore Beach.[13]

In providing a venue for popular black artists and local acts, places such as Bay Shore and Sparrow's beaches helped African American performers gain a measure of independence from a white-controlled and highly exploitative music industry, and facilitated the rise of a national network of black-owned concert venues at the center of an evolving infrastructure of promoters, managers, performers, and, increasingly, radio stations and recording labels. Collectively, these places, which ran the gamut from urban entertainment meccas such as the Apollo Theater in Harlem and the Howard Theater in Washington to informal and unregulated bars, taverns, residences, barns, or even an open field, came to be known as the "chitlin circuit."

The profits accumulated on the streets of burgeoning black metropolises became the glue holding this network of venues together. The growth and maturation of the various black-owned music and entertainment venues that became the chitlin circuit were made possible, in many cases, by the illicit profits of urban informal economies. Forced to live in overpriced, decaying rental properties in racially segregated neighborhoods, and with opportunities for advancement within white-dominated sectors of the economy closed to them, many enterprising African Americans in Great Migration–era cities instead applied their skills and channeled their ambitions toward mastery of illegal sectors of urban economies. Those same obstacles also made urban black neighborhoods thriving marketplaces for those in the business of selling illicit pleasures and peddling promises of instant riches. Of the high-income-generating illicit trades, the "numbers" stands out. Though its name and the rules governing its operation varied by city (in Chicago it was called "policy," in Miami "bolita"), the core characteristics of the "numbers" was fairly consistent across urban America and differed only in degree from what Americans today call the "lottery." Like today's lottery, playing the numbers appealed to, as it exploited, the hopes, frustrations, and limited resources of the poor, enticing players with the elusive dream of the big score while steadily draining them of their limited income.

Few persons living in neighborhoods where the game thrived would have called these so-called numbers kings pariahs. Instead, they were more often treated as folk heroes and saviors. Operators of illegal lotteries often assumed the role of lending institutions of the black metropolis, dispensing loans to fledgling black-owned businesses denied credit from banks, donating handsome portions of their earnings to local charities, and opening many businesses of their own.[14] As the foremost scholar of African American business history, Juliet E. K. Walker, notes, "Access to black policy dollars provided black communities with a privately funded, informal cash subsidy, which was used as venture capital in the promotion and support of black business."[15] They had good reason to be so generous. Aside from building trust and support with their customer base, loans to African

American small business owners helped numbers bankers launder their earnings and provided them with storefronts where their runners could collect bets, count earnings, and hand out winnings. Structural inequality forced talented and ambitious black men and women to become "criminals" under the law. But in providing tangible measures of support and playing a vital role in the social and economic lifeblood of segregated neighborhoods, numbers bankers came to be accepted by growing numbers of urban blacks for what they were: businesspeople.

Few blurred this line between "gangster" and businessman more thoroughly than Baltimore's William L. "Little Willie" Adams. During the same decades the Carrs worked to turn their beachfront property into a seasonal enterprise, William L. Adams rose from chopping cotton on a North Carolina plantation as a child to working as a rag packer on Baltimore's waterfront to becoming the head of Baltimore's numbers trade and, by the 1940s, the "undisputed mayor of Negro Baltimore." In 1929, at the age of 15, Adams left North Carolina and moved in with an aunt and uncle in Baltimore following the death of his father. There he worked a series of odd jobs before becoming a low-level numbers runner. His remarkable accounting skills and reputation as an honest broker who always paid out on winning number combinations allowed Adams to compete with the city's major white-operated numbers books and facilitated his quick rise to the top of the city's numbers trade. By the late 1930s Adams ran one of the city's largest and most profitable books from his tavern on Druid Hill Avenue, handling an estimated $1,000 a day in wagers. In 1938 Adams consolidated his control over the Baltimore's illicit economy after he successfully fended off a coordinated attack by white mobsters from Philadelphia seeking to take over the city's numbers trade, which included a fire bombing of his tavern.[16]

Adams was a cool, unassuming, and ruthlessly skillful black capitalist. In contrast to many of his competitors, Adams exhibited little desire to take part in the high-rolling, big-timing lifestyle associated with urban kingpins. He dressed conservatively, drove a modest automobile, married a schoolteacher, and was rarely seen out on the town. Perhaps most important, he did not simply dream of one day graduating from the streets and becoming a legitimate businessman, but saved and invested accordingly. As one profile of Adams read, while many of the new "barons" who jumped into informal and illicit economies in post–World War II cities "blew their wealth bigtiming," Adams "profited by others' experiences. [He] invest[ed] in property."[17] In 1940 he founded Adams Realty Brokers. By 1950 Adams owned over one hundred pieces of property in the city. With the high revenue from his real estate, he was able to start or buy a stake in numerous businesses. In the early 1940s Adams partnered with Henry G. Parks to acquire a sausage manufacturing company based in Cleveland, Ohio, which they subsequently relocated to Baltimore. (In 1969 Parks Sausage Company would become the first black-owned company publicly traded on Wall Street.) Adams's business investments both reflected and furthered the development of distinct black consumer markets, and consumer culture, in postwar America. In 1946 he opened the Sphinx Club, an exclusive, members-only social club on Baltimore's Black Main Street, Pennsylvania Avenue. In 1948 he opened the Charm Center, also on Pennsylvania Avenue, the first high-end clothing store in the city where black women could try on the latest fashions and be treated with dignity and respect. His wife, Victorine, managed the store and taught classes on social graces and etiquette to young black women. Similarly, Adams used his wealth to further the commercial commodification of black celebrities and entertainers, investing heavily in the Joe Louis Bottling Company—a venture started by the heavyweight boxing champion, a close friend and golfing partner of Adams—and contributing financially to the promotion of its soft drink, Joe Louis Punch.[18]

For fledgling black-owned businesses in Baltimore, Adams became, as one friend later described, a one-man "Small Business Administration." Kurt L. Schmoke, who would later become mayor of Baltimore, characterized Adams as "the most 'reliable bank' that African-Americans could go to in order to start and continue to operate businesses" during the 1940s and 1950s. A master of the Jim Crow marketplace, Adams dangled before desperate businessmen and women denied business loans from formal lending institutions the opportunity to access the capital necessary to grow businesses and generate profits. In return, they handed Adams a 51 percent stake in the company. By the late 1940s, Adams's effective control over black-owned businesses in west Baltimore was extensive—and virtually untraceable. As one chronicler of black Baltimore wrote, while "hardly a black-owned tavern in west Baltimore was not part of [Adams's] empire . . . all his properties were listed in someone else's name."[19]

As growing numbers of black Baltimoreans trickled out to the Carr family's beachfront during the summer months, Adams took notice. In 1944, Adams and business partners Chandler Wynn, Askew Gatewood, John

Neal, and Littleton Gamby formed the Oak Grove Beach Company and acquired the land on the Annapolis Neck Peninsula tip formerly owned by the Eintracht Club, where they built a cluster of five cabins on what they named Elktonia Beach (see Map 12, p. 184).[20] Adams's syndicate came to the shore not only to build vacation homes for themselves, but also to expand their commercial interests in black entertainment outside of the city and into the seasonal economy of summertime leisure. Following the death of Elizabeth Carr in 1948, her son, Frederick Smith, and his wife, Grace, inherited her 26-acre tract of land on the Chesapeake known as Carr's Beach. The moment was ripe for the property's commercial development, and Fred and Grace Smith's new neighbor, Willie Adams, was eager to provide the necessary capital for the beach's growth and expansion into a regional entertainment destination that would, in its attractions and events, appeal to a wide segment of the black public and generate large crowds and revenues from the months of May through September. Later that year, Smith, Adams, and a group of Adams's business partners formed the Carr's Beach Amusement Company and invested over $150,000 in buildings and improvements to the site. By design, the new Carr's Beach sought to appeal to young and old, families and young couples, daytime picnickers and nighttime partiers. The company constructed a string of booths along a midway for carnival games and cleared a portion of the property for the erection of amusement rides. While children waited in line to ride on the Ferris wheel or tossed rings at rows of glass soda bottles, parents and older adults could dump coins into one of the many slot machines lined up in a row by the beach. Young adults, meanwhile, were expected to flock to the front of the stage in the open-air concert pavilion that would play host to a steady stream of local and national music performers and entertainers, and during and after the show, retreat to the more intimate setting of the nightclub (originally named Club Bengazi, after a well-known club in Washington, D.C.) built on the grounds.[21]

The naming of the beach's nightclub after a place popular with high-rollers, entertainers, and celebrities in Washington was indicative of the extent to which the company worked to bring the culture and leisure-based economy of the postwar black metropolis to the shore, and to create a niche market for summertime entertainment that would complement those that Adams and others had helped to develop in the city. To that end, the company hired as the beach's manager Rufus Mitchell, who had cut his teeth as a music promoter in Baltimore and enjoyed extensive connections to bands and managers in cities along the eastern seaboard. Mitchell soon began booking a steady stream of bands from Washington and Baltimore and, increasingly, regional and national touring artists, to perform on Saturday evenings and Sunday afternoons.

Located near several major and mid-size metropolitan areas, and in between Baltimore's Royal Theater and Washington's Howard Theater, Carr's Beach became seamlessly woven into a burgeoning network of black concert venues on the East Coast, alongside other beach resorts and outdoor concert venues that filled soul and jazz bands' summer itineraries. The stage nourished local talent and provided a platform for aspiring bands and musicians to reach new audiences, and became a conduit for the sharing and spreading of musical and cultural trends and tastes that would constitute a postwar black American public. As it did, concerts at Carr's Beach came to have a multiplying and transformative effect on black-oriented entertainment industries and black consumer marketing as a whole.

Among others, the birth of black-oriented radio stations, the growth of independent rhythm-and-blues music recording labels, and the direct marketing of consumer products to African American audiences stand out. The same year Adams and his associates invested in the commercial development of Carr's Beach, Morris H. Blum made his own investment in black entertainment. In 1947, Blum, a native Baltimorean and son of Jewish immigrants, founded WANN-AM, the second of three radio stations that began broadcasting from Annapolis that year. The station's original format was a hodgepodge of music that spanned several genres and aimed to attract a wide range of audiences. Its motto was "Everything from Bach to bebop." The station failed to gain a following among fans of either Bach or bebop, nor did it attract much advertising revenue. Running a distant third in the local radio market, Blum looked to attract a following among the city's African American listening audience, first by adding an R&B show called *Savoy Swing Time* to the lineup (the city's first black-oriented music program) in 1948, then by adopting an all-black-oriented lineup in 1949. WANN became one of the first radio stations in the country to appeal directly, and exclusively, to an African American audience, following close on the heels of Memphis, Tennessee, radio station WDIA's adoption of an all-black-music format in the fall of 1948, the first of its kind. Blum began hiring young black men as deejays and on-air personalities, among them an Annapolis taxicab driver named Charles Adams.

Behind the microphone, Charles became Hoppy Adams, and with his boundless enthusiasm and exuberance, he quickly attracted a large following of listeners and became the face of the station. Blum, likewise, saw his revenues skyrocket as companies seeking to reach black consumers lined up to buy advertising space, and to have Adams promote their product over the air. Fledgling black-owned record labels in Baltimore and other mid-Atlantic cities competed for the chance to have WANN broadcast their latest singles.[22]

Hoppy Adams's skills in promoting musicians and products targeted for black consumers soon attracted the attention of Rufus Mitchell, who hired him to serve as emcee for Carr's Beach's Sunday afternoon music revues during the summer. Blum, in turn, purchased remote broadcasting equipment and began airing Carr's Beach Sunday shows live. At 3 P.M. on Sundays in the summer Adams stepped onto the stage at Carr's Beach pavilion and onto the front stoops of homes, row houses, and public housing in Washington, Annapolis, Baltimore, and beyond. Bands that had previously never been heard outside of small clubs in Baltimore and Annapolis were now being heard as far west as Ohio, thanks to the station's 50,000-watt tower. Growing up in 1950s Annapolis, Carl O. Snowden remembers hearing the sounds of Carr's Beach echo throughout the city's black neighborhoods. "You could walk blocks . . . and hear WANN being played on transistor radios or as people washed their cars." While other concert hall owners often turned down radio stations' attempts to broadcast their shows over the air for fear it would depress ticket sales, Carr's Beach's proprietors realized that WANN's *Bandstand on the Beach* program offered them hours of free advertising and an invaluable opportunity to showcase their product to a regional audience. Possessing the seductive power to turn little-known bands and musicians into stars, WANN helped to make Annapolis, a city with little black music tradition of its own, into a destination for aspiring bands and artists who clamored for the opportunity to perform over the air in the station's small downtown studio or to be heard over the air at Carr's Beach. The product of a variety of local, contingent circumstances—from the Carr family's ownership of beachfront property to Morris Blum's decision to save his business by switching to an all-black format—Annapolis's unlikely rise to prominence in the postwar East Coast black music scene was also indicative of larger trends. Across the postwar South, rock music journalist Preston Lauterbach writes, "cities and towns that had been inconsequential were growing into lively hubs, with nightclub work, recording opportunities, and strong connections to national talent agencies."[23]

The exponential growth of Carr's Beach in the postwar years also reorganized leisure-based commercial activity among the members of the extended Carr family who owned acres of land on the Annapolis Neck Peninsula. Following Carr's Beach's incorporation, Florence Sparrow changed Sparrow's Beach's business model to appeal to those seeking a quieter and less commercialized place of summer retreat. Rather than general admission, Sparrow's Beach offered group reservations for churches and organizations. Sparrow rented out cottages on the grounds for weekends or longer vacations. These cottages also served as overnight accommodations for touring musicians who performed at Carr's Beach. Other Carr family members converted plots of land on the peninsula into jook joints and roadside food stands that, they hoped, would capture a portion of the crowds headed to and from the beach.[24]

Like the owners of Carr's Beach, Bay Shore Beach's owners made substantial investments in improving the facility's accommodations and infrastructure. The company signed a contract with a local construction firm to build a new hotel and modernize the grounds at a cost of $113,375, and acquired a set of rides for the amusement park.[25] Along the boardwalk, a strip of seasonal businesses serving food, drink, and souvenirs took shape, including the Cameo Beach Club, the "400" Club, the PW&W Lounge, Joe's Place, Juanita's Cafeteria, the Seaside Inn, Liria's Inn, the Blue Bird's Nest, and the Bay Shore Photo Shop, where children and adults lined up for a photo in front of a painted backdrop of the beach and ocean and a memento from their outing.[26]

Along with residents of Hampton and the surrounding area, Bay Shore relied heavily on patronage from African Americans living in Richmond, who traveled to the resort aboard the C&O Railroad line that ended a short distance from the beach's entrance (see Map 13). Large employers of African American workers in Richmond annually hosted company picnics for "colored" employees at Bay Shore.[27] (Conversely, with no bridges or railroad lines connecting Hampton to Norfolk, Bay Shore was virtually cut off from the neighboring city's large black population.) Predominantly white organizations whose membership also consisted of African Americans called on Bay Shore to provide hotel accommodations for guests denied entry at white-owned hotels in Hampton, as was the case in 1956 during the Virginia State AFL-CIO annual convention, held at the Chamberlin

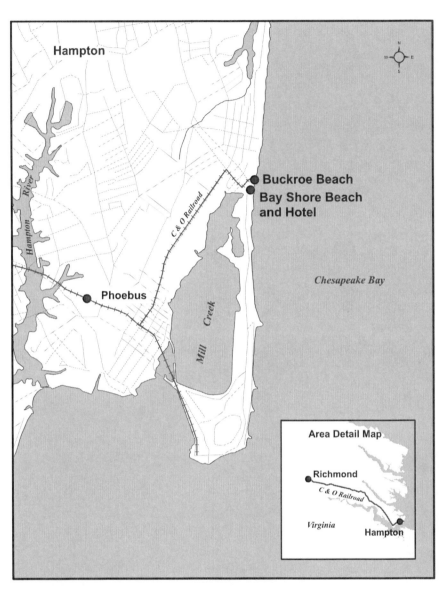

Map 13. Bay Shore Beach, Hampton, Virginia

Hotel in downtown Hampton, when Bay Shore provided rooms for the union leadership body's twenty-five black members. But while the hotel brought steady returns, it was during the beach season that the roads leading to Bay Shore became clogged with automobiles and the registers burst with bills and coins. Revenue from the beer garden and food and custard stands told the story. In 1947 the company reported $1,939 in gross profits at these seasonal businesses for the year. By 1951 that figure rose to $5,808, and in 1953 to $16,696. So, too, though, did expenses, growing from $20,000 in 1947 to $73,918 in 1953. By 1954 the company estimated that eating places, amusement rides, and beach facilities accounted for 80 percent of Bay Shore's business, with the remaining 20 percent coming from the hotel. Its payroll that year (before deductions) was $25,544 for roughly twenty-eight seasonal employees, most of whom were area schoolteachers and college students home for break.[28]

Among Bay Shore's more significant expenses were radio and print advertising. During the summer months, Bay Shore blanketed the airwaves of black-oriented radio stations in the Hampton Roads and Richmond areas. In 1956, for example, the New Bay Shore Corporation ran advertisements on stations WGH, WLOW, and WRAP (Norfolk). Beginning in 1954, Bay Shore paid station WLEE (Richmond) seventeen dollars per broadcast for the right to sponsor the station's Sunday news and public affairs program. In 1961 it spent a reported $1,784 on advertising.[29] Much of the advertising focused on the musical and entertainment acts and special events at the Bay Shore Beach pavilion throughout the summer. On Sunday night, emcee Botsy Swann stepped on the stage at 9:30, serenaded by Jap Curry and His Orchestra, for the first of two shows that lasted well past 2 A.M. On the playbill one found a mix of burlesque entertainment such as exotic dancers, local R&B bands, and a more nationally known group on tour.[30]

White corporations and commercial investors were equally bullish on the black beach resort and amusement park market during these years and, like numbers bankers, were quick to partner with and, often, assume control over African American businesses in dire need of infusions of capital. In Norfolk, Virginia, a group of investors headed by the African American dentist and self-described real estate developer Irving M. Watts formed the Seaview Beach and Hotel Company and acquired, for $45,000, fifty acres of beachfront property along an undeveloped stretch of shore in neighboring Princess Anne County in 1943. To construct a planned forty-room hotel, a five-hundred-person-capacity ballroom, a midway, and an amusement park, the corporation borrowed $200,000 from the Jewish amusement park mogul Dudley Cooper.[31] To observers, the new resort exemplified black upward mobility and the emergence of new avenues of opportunity for business success in postwar America. In 1947, *Life* magazine featured Seaview Beach in a summer feature section, including a photo spread and a description of its amenities and capital outlay. One longtime resident remembers seeing one of the resort's owners driving along the shore in a Cadillac. "He was in the money."[32]

Or so it seemed. The Seaview Beach Corporation's ambitious investment, and heavy indebtedness, far exceeded its projected earnings. Before the owners had even cut the ribbon on the resort, the group struggled to meet its repayment plan, and in 1947 ceded management of the park and the handling of its finances to Cooper. Cooper added Seaview to a business portfolio that included the nearby whites-only Seaside Park and Ocean View Amusement Park.[33] Cooper tried to remain attentive to Seaview's black clientele even as he worked to incorporate the "colored" amusement park into a white-dominated industry. When Cooper placed an order for posters for both the neighboring, all-white Ocean View Amusement Park and Seaview Beach, he asked the Globe Poster Company of Chicago if it was "possible to have the figures in the stock sheets [for Seaview] shown as colored perhaps in a light tan which would indicate to anyone seeing it at first glance that it was definitely for negroes." The Globe Poster Company replied, "We regret very much that we will not be able to give you the colored people effect on the posters. These are stock propositions and we are unable at this time to do that type of work for you."[34] While positive images of blackness mattered to Cooper and other whites in the business of black amusement, jobs for black people did not. Soon after assuming control over Seaview, he purged the park of its African American vendors and leased the restaurant, carnival booths, and food stands to his white friends and associates.[35]

The influence of white capitalists and white public officials over black beaches and resorts extended far beyond hiring practices and policing the color line, and came to play a dynamic role in the production of postwar black culture and racial segmentation of consumer markets. Following its refurbishing and reopening in 1954, New Orleans's Lincoln Beach became, despite its distance from the city, an increasingly popular summer destination for the city's working-class black population, due in large measure to the strategies white marketers employed to reach and retain black customers of their products. The white-owned, black-oriented radio station WMRY sponsored Thursday night dance parties hosted by deejay Larry McKinley, and a Friday night "Dance under the Stars" on the restaurant's outdoor roof terrace. Regal Beer, owned by the New Orleans–based American Brewing Company, annually hosted its Regal Hospitality Hostess Contest at Lincoln Beach, where young black women vied for the chance to become a spokesperson for the company in local bars, along with a $250 cash prize. Regal feted its loyal customers with the sight of "beautiful girls" and the sound of "good music," while offering their children free rides and prizes. Candy and soda companies partnered with the park's management to offer free admission to children bearing their wrappers and bottle caps. Sunbeam placed coupons for free rides inside packages of its loaves of bread. "On a summer day when it was hot," Roy L. Washington recalled, "you hustle your seven cent to get out there, you save your candy wrappers to get in the place. Five bottle caps or six candy wrappers would get you in. That's it. Period." White employers of black labor, similarly, worked to build loyalty among their workers through annual events at the beach. As a reward for working in the most arduous, dangerous jobs in the plant, Kaiser Aluminum provided its black employees a day of free rides, food, and entertainment at Lincoln Beach. "All the black employees would have their family day for kids out there," Willie Williams, whose father dodged live electrical wires in temperatures that rose well above 100 degrees in the pot room at Kaiser, remembers. "[Kaiser] paid for all the refreshments and food. It was exciting, we had a place to go ride rides. . . . We looked forward to it every year. The opportunity just to walk around the beach was beautiful."[36]

For many black New Orleanians, Lincoln Beach offered the chance to step outside the humble conditions of their work lives to showcase their talents and to pursue their ambitions. Joyce Bailey, for instance, worked as a housekeeper by day, then caught the bus out to Lincoln Beach to sing and perform at one of the many talent shows staged on the beach's pavilion each summer. The soul duo the Aubry Twins got their start at a Lincoln Beach talent show. In 1954 the levee board hosted the first annual Miss Lincoln Beach contest. That year's winner, high school senior June Foster, received a fifty-inch gold-plated cup, a dozen roses, a music scholarship, an assortment of gifts from local organizations, and perhaps most important, her picture in *Jet* magazine receiving a kiss from the master of ceremonies, Nat King Cole.[37] To close the 1956 summer season, the legendary Gospel singer Brother Joe May, the "Thunderbolt of the Midwest," gave a free show that drew forty thousand devoted followers. In between national tours, Fats Domino, the Neville Brothers, Irma Thomas, and other New Orleans R&B stars performed for their hometown fans at the beach.[38]

As the revenue from "colored" beaches mounted, African American business and civic leaders stepped up efforts to force cities to lease the grounds and hand over managerial control to local black businessmen and women. In Charleston, South Carolina, black citizens and civic organizations waged a multiyear struggle against the county's "Jim Crow rental" of Riverside Beach to white businessmen. In 1941 they succeeded in forcing the county to lease the grounds to local black businessmen P. J. Greene and Herbert Frazier. In the years that followed, Riverside emerged as a hub of black summer culture and seasonal enterprise in the city and the coastal region. Black families residing in the Scanlonville neighborhood, located adjacent to Riverside on land owned by blacks since 1868, operated food stands out of their kitchens, while others turned their homes into do-drop inns. Event promoters sponsored baseball games between the area's local Negro league teams on the park's ball field. Local churches conducted river baptisms there.[39] Radio stations sent their deejays down to the pavilion to spin records for the late-night crowds.[40] Neighboring black property owner Henry White turned his home into White's Paradise, a nightclub that would play host to performers like Augusta, Georgia, native James Brown, who got his start performing on Sunday nights on the bandstand in White's salmon-colored ballroom. By the late 1950s, clubs such as Hunt's Store, the Chitter-Chatter, and others competed with White's for the summertime beach traffic.[41]

They also competed for white people's dollars. The influx of young males from across the country to military training bases in the South during World War II turned the trickle of white youth who surreptitiously ventured across the color line into a flood. In North Carolina, white teenagers and enlisted soldiers stationed at Camp Lejeune near Wilmington flocked to Seabreeze to dance to the latest "race" records and see black performers. Along Hampton, Virginia's beachfront, white youth climbed over the wood pilings that separated the whites-only Buckroe Beach from Bay Shore and stepped onto the dance floor. "At night the whites would come over to our side, and party with us," Cora Reid recalls. "[White] folks heard the music just went on in there."[42] From these exchanges, crazes and fads were born. Along North and South Carolina's coastal towns, white devotees of black beach culture popularized a dance called the "shag" derived from their interpretations of dance moves observed at black beach resorts.[43] For some African Americans, the presence of white persons behind the color line was a sign of cracks in the culture of segregation; for others, it magnified their own lack of freedom and physical mobility. At Bay Shore Beach, Bill Carson recalled, "whites used to come down and listen to the music that's being played—Cab Calloway used to play down there—and they'd come to hear the music, but we couldn't go over [to Buckroe Beach]."[44] Of greater concern to most black beachgoers than the presence of whites was the intent. At Charleston's Riverside Beach, racial tensions came to a boil only after a pair of white businessmen attempted to acquire the resort's lease in 1948. Local blacks staged protests and threatened to boycott the place until the bid eventually was withdrawn.[45]

By the early 1950s, weekend crowds at Carr's Beach routinely exceeded ten thousand persons. Over the course of a summer season, hundreds of chartered buses from as far north as New York and as far west as West Virginia and Ohio carried entire neighborhoods to the beach. While kids ran toward the rides and games, many adults headed straight toward the rows of one-armed bandits. Throughout the first half of the twentieth century, the state of Maryland laid claim to being the "Sin Capital of the East Coast." In the counties of Charles, St. Mary's, Calvert, and Anne Arundel, slot machine gambling was legal and lightly regulated. By 1960, roughly two hundred establishments (from saloons to filling stations and grocery stores) in Charles County alone housed 2,338 licensed slot machines. The saturation of gambling devices in Anne Arundel County was no less pronounced. The revenue slot machines generated for commercial establishments augmented the political influence wielded by gambling interests in Annapolis. The state's tax code exempted slot machines from sales taxes and levied only a one-half of 1 percent tax on slot-machine receipts. As a result, a single slot machine in the state of Maryland generated an estimated fifty dollars per week in revenue. While small establishments might house between one and ten machines that supplemented primary sources of revenue, Carr's Beach and other waterside resorts offered well over fifty machines, which, along with the added gate receipts that came with gaming devices, served as a major source of revenue.[46]

Adams's investment in sanctioned forms of gambling at Carr's Beach was indicative of his broader efforts to graduate from the illicit economy of black Baltimore and become a legitimate and respected businessman. By the late 1940s Adams had effectively "farmed out" his numbers operations to business associates and devoted his energies to managing his extensive real estate and commercial interests. The timing was no coincidence, as Adams's prominence made him the subject of local and nationwide inquiries into organized crime. In 1951 he was called to testify before the U.S. Senate's Special Committee to Investigate Organized Crime in Interstate Commerce (known as the Kefauver Committee). In exchange for immunity from prosecution on federal racketeering charges, Adams confessed to his extensive involvement in illegal gambling and fingered several mobsters from neighboring cities. Following his testimony, though, Maryland authorities tried and convicted Adams on violating state lottery laws. Adams fought the decision to the U.S. Supreme Court, which in 1954 unanimously overturned the conviction on the grounds that his testimony before the Kefauver Committee was inadmissible in state court. Adams continued to be subject to police harassment throughout the 1950s and 1960s, but despite several close calls, he wielded his considerable political influence to avoid ever spending a day of his life behind bars.[47]

For Adams and others making the transition from gangster to respectable businessman, success in the licit economy demanded a healthy degree of law and order. Crowds at Carr's Beach grew so large that they threatened the business's long-term viability. Complaints from white homeowners about noise, trespassing, property damage, and low-level criminal activity at Carr's Beach accumulated on the desk of Anne Arundel County sheriff Joseph Alton Jr., and calls to crack down on the thriving enterprise began to escalate. As Carr's Beach's management worked to develop a security apparatus that could satisfy concerns of white homeowners, a young black war veteran came back to his hometown of Annapolis in search of a job in law enforcement. George Phelps Jr. had served as a military police officer in segregated units of the army during World War II. Upon returning home, he went to Alton's office to inquire about a position in the Anne Arundel County Sheriff's Department. At the time, neither Anne Arundel County nor the city of Annapolis employed any African Americans on the force. Phelps's hiring by Alton in 1950 yielded a typical reaction from white residents of the small, conservative harbor town. On Phelps's first day of duty, Alton remembers, "I said, 'George, walk around town and get people used to seeing you.' . . . I got a call before George even got to the bottom of Main Street. 'There's this . . .'—they didn't say *black man*—'walking down Main Street pretending to be a deputy.'" Few of Phelps's colleagues welcomed his arrival, either. Phelps described his early years on the job as an endless series of hazing, harassment, and humiliation. His tasks were limited to transferring prisoners to and from the county jail and policing the county's black neighborhoods. He could detain but not arrest white suspects; in one incident, he was beaten within an inch of his life when he pursued a white suspect into an all-white saloon in Annapolis. This was common. In Baltimore, black "special policemen" employed by the city could expect to be arrested if caught armed anywhere outside their designated location.

But mounting concerns over Carr's Beach offered Phelps a chance to wield authority, expand his duties, and create opportunities for other African Americans to secure employment in Jim Crow law-enforcement bodies. Phelps petitioned the sheriff's department to give him jurisdiction over the resort and the authorization to hire a team of part-time, deputized black officers. Alton granted him full authority to hire and deputize a team of officers, but little else. The sheriff's office provided, as Phelps describes, "no budget, no jobs, no nothing"—just the right to put a badge on the chest and a gun in the hands of black males, both of which, as well as the uniform, Phelps had to supply himself. Moreover, his jurisdiction extended only as far as the Carr's Beach property line. With this green light (minus any green), Phelps began combing the county for qualified black men to become what the sheriff's department dubbed "special deputy officers." With help from the YMCA, churches, and other organizations, Phelps interviewed candidates and enrolled qualified applicants (many of whom were also war veterans) in a training program he designed with the assistance of black training officers in Baltimore and Washington. He purchased used firearms from the Baltimore Police Department and raised funds for the purchase of uniforms. Whatever equipment Phelps could not secure through charity came out of the special deputies' pockets. As with any for-hire security unit, Phelps's officers were beholden to the proprietary interests of the businesses contracting their services, who paid their $1.50 hourly wage.

Despite negligible pay and nonrecognition from white sheriff's deputies, black men competed for the opportunity to join Phelps's force and to exert measures of authority denied by white America. At its height, Phelps's force included 255 special deputies employed in a part-time capacity, men whose talents and experience (as they were well aware) far outweighed their second-class status in the county's law enforcement community. Upon returning from eleven months of service in Korea in 1959, Howard Fuller took and passed the county police exam. "I waited and waited and finally they wrote back and said they did not accept blacks as policemen," Fuller said. "I thought to myself, 'I was on the front lines in Korea.' Have you ever heard of Pork Chop Hill? I've been there. Camp Desert Rock? I've been there." Fuller instead spent the next ten years working part time for Phelps.[48]

The formation of Phelps's special deputies unit marked a pivotal, transitional stage in African Americans' long struggle for police protection and community control over black businesses and institutions, and a telling example of the role of leisure and amusement spaces in the emergence of African American private policing and security forces. As witnessed along the Washington, D.C., waterfront at the turn of the twentieth century, Jim Crow police departments' wanton brutality toward black pleasure seekers suspected of disturbing, disrupting, or interfering with white persons and property was matched only by their utter indifference toward actions otherwise deemed crimes, when those actions were committed by black persons against other black persons or black-owned property.[49] Early twentieth-century urban Progressive-era reforms aimed at standardizing and professionalizing police forces quite perversely wove notions of race and crime into the fabric of cities, and aligned the policing of urban space with the value of urban properties and status of urban communities.[50]

The purging of African Americans from metropolitan police forces accompanied this broader "professionalization" of policing. Between 1900 and 1910, David E. Barlow found, the percentage of African American police officers in the police workforce fell from an already minuscule 2.7 percent to a virtually nonexistent 0.1 percent.[51] As cities rid police departments of persons deemed unfit to serve, they invariably assigned the least qualified or most egregiously violent and trigger-happy officers to police predominantly black districts. White officers assigned to police urban black neighborhoods, commercial districts, and public spaces during the age of police professionalization were not only often the most viciously racist members of the force, but also the most incompetent. "Colored" neighborhoods became the place where police officers cited for misconduct or deemed incapable of performing their duties by Progressive police administrations were often assigned. Once there, more than a few became heavily involved in the vice operations that had, by design, been concentrated in black districts, partnering with white ethnics and immigrants who, as historian Khalil Gibran Muhammad notes, "dominated the ownership and management of vice," or going into business on their own; in either case, they used their police powers to suppress competition.[52] Writing on the white-owned "colored" resorts located along Baltimore's waterfront, an editorial in the *Afro-American* wondered, "how much the gamblers at Westport, Shadyside Park, and other places along the 'Shore' are paying the Baltimore County Police to stay away from that section of the county while they are fleecing the foolish Negro out of his week's wages[?]" Indeed, reports of physical or sexual assaults by drunken, lecherous officers, and of their chronic indifference to black citizens' calls for help in emergency situations or in suppressing vice activities that targeted and profited from blacks, became common complaints emanating from urban black populations, and a reminder that African Americans' struggle to expose and combat police brutality, harassment, and corruption was—and remains—inseparable from the fight for police protection.[53]

African Americans' exclusion from police forces did not, however, result in the absence of uniformed black men in black neighborhoods or in places of interracial contact. White-owned leisure and entertainment venues located in black neighborhoods were among the earliest, and most prevalent, employers of African American private police and security guards. Correspondingly, city police departments actively enlisted African Americans to work for vice squads as informers on underground criminal syndicates. White owners of businesses dependent on appeasing a white clientele through careful management of the performance and spatiality of race, meanwhile, were known to hire black "special policemen" to handle "Negro affairs" in a peaceful and expeditious manner. In 1930, NAACP secretary Walter White called for a probe into the segregation policies of beachfront hotels in Atlantic City, New Jersey, following the forced expulsion of groups of black bathers from the city's beachfront by "special colored police [employed by the hotels] to direct colored people away from the beach in front of the hotels, to a less desirable part." These officers, White added, were "uniformed and paid by the hotels [and] had no authority to expel colored people from any part of the beach."[54] In contrast to the theories advanced by early twentieth-century white racial pundits that African Americans were predisposed to coddle black "criminals," white business owners catering to black consumers were well aware that privately employed black officers' loyalties were to those who wrote their paycheck.

Lacking protection from the state, or rights white law enforcement felt bound to defend, black land and business owners adopted measures to prevent their property from becoming legal "no-man's-lands"—places where whites and blacks could engage in criminal activity without fear of retribution from official authority—or, for those involved in informal illegal economies, from becoming even more vulnerable to the selective raids of vice districts conducted by corrupt police departments. Due in part to the long tradition of legally questionable activities being conducted behind the scenes at all leisure and amusement enterprises, and their added exposure to vice raids by racist police forces, African American owners and proprietors of turn-of-the-twentieth-century "colored" beaches and resorts proudly boasted of their reputation for inflicting swift and harsh punishments on disruptive or unruly patrons, and for implementing extreme (albeit legally dubious) security measures. George Brown, owner and operator of Brown's Grove, an early twentieth-century resort located outside Baltimore, personally patted down and searched for weapons and contraband all persons deemed suspicious, before allowing them entry into his amusement park or onto his excursion vessels—no doubt a familiar experience for many patrons, who increasingly found themselves on the receiving end of new methods of racial profiling being implemented by urban police departments at the time.[55] On his boats and at his park, Brown reportedly dealt with "loud or abusive" "troublemakers" by delivering a "haymaker right hand blow . . . to the unsuspecting loudmouth." George Bailey, manager of Shadyside in Baltimore, another black resort in operation in the early 1900s, claimed to have lived by the motto "Nothing beats a Jack but a blackjack" and took great pride in his pummeling of "lowbrows" who got out of line and threatened the bottom line.[56] In the process, men such as Brown and Bailey came to understand their rights as citizens—and the "problem" of Negro crime and disorder—through the lens of a business and property owner.

Those charged with enforcing discipline in black-owned leisure spaces gained a rare opportunity for work in law enforcement. Before many could hope to be hired by a city to police a segregated black neighborhood, aspiring black law officers could expect to find opportunities policing black private property. In response to the absence of police protection of patrons, and the hostile conditions that invariably arose when racist cops made an appearance on the beach, Bay Shore Beach hired and trained its own team of black private officers and provided them with a small headquarters on the grounds and a vehicle to transport persons to jail. Officials placed great emphasis on ensuring that officers were "properly uniformed and trained at all time so they will demand the proper respect," and drew up plans for the company to operate a training school for officers (though it is unclear if these plans came to fruition).[57]

For neighbors as well as guests, the presence of Phelps's special deputies at Carr's Beach was immediate and unmistakable, and for the Carr's Beach Amusement Company, it was indispensable. Phelps responded to white residents' complaints about traffic, noise, and trash, and helped to pacify any fears of crime and violence accompanying the tens of thousands of visitors who flocked to the beach for weekend shows. Before "we went to Carr's Beach," Phelps notes, "they were having all kinds of problems. . . . People in Annapolis Roads couldn't get in their homes. People parked in their driveways, all kinds of things. Somebody's throwing whiskey bottles [in their yards]. . . . But when we went there that ended all that." "By people realizing that we cared [about the problem of crime, noise, and property damage]" and that "we could handle it better than the police department, we became known and respected. . . . Letters to the police department [with complaints about Carr's Beach], they'd turn them right over to us, and we'd take care of them. . . . We took care of just about everything. We were the diplomats."[58]

Among African Americans, they were the enforcers. Phelps developed highly aggressive policing strategies and punitive measures toward patrons. At the beach's entrance, Phelps installed a loudspeaker that repeated the recorded message: "Welcome to Carr's Beach. We're here to protect you. If you're from Baltimore or D.C., I hope you've left your problems behind, because if there's any trouble here, we'll whip you so low to the ground, you'll need a stepladder to look over the end of a dime. Have a good day!" On the grounds, Phelps strolled, baton in hand, through crowds of youth, issuing the warning that, as he put it, "blood will flow like water" for those who stepped out of line. Along with fear and intimidation, Phelps adopted familiar and innovative forms of surveillance. He dispatched plainclothes officers to infiltrate low-level criminal syndicates and gather information on persons of interest. On a summer weekend in

1950, for instance, his deputies arrested four moonshine peddlers after learning their password: "See the doctor man." Foreshadowing the inner-city tactics of the drug wars, Phelps implemented what he called Operation Clean Sweep. "At a certain time, we would line up officers and we would sweep the beach all the way down to the gate. We were observing everything within sight and hearing. Had fifteen officers on the beach, people not in uniform. We had a communication network that was second to none." In the music pavilion, Phelps placed an observation booth on the bandstand, where an officer observed the crowds at shows and signaled to fellow officers stationed throughout the pavilion the exact location of an altercation within the sea of people.

Repeat offenders or persons or groups Phelps and management deemed undesirable became subject to harsh punitive measures for the slightest infractions. Zastrow Simms was among those whom management and Phelps's force observed closely and punished harshly. On one occasion, Simms recalled, a special deputy threatened to detain and assault him and a group of friends with a nightstick for loud talking on the beach. Simms was incredulous. "Here you got Ray Charles [performing on the band-stand], Ferris wheel, slot machines." But the deputies were dead serious. "We were going to jack him up," Phelps remembers.

Phelps's officers took a special interest in apprehending and punishing persons caught attempting to sneak onto the grounds without paying an admission fee. At the entrance, officers inspected automobiles suspected of smuggling nonpaying passengers in the trunk, paying particular attention to the rear suspension, for signs of extra weight. Upon discovery of a stowaway, Phelps's officers reportedly sprayed mace into the trunk, slammed it back shut, and left it closed for several minutes before removing the violator. To catch stowaways who made it past the gates undetected, Phelps stationed plainclothes officers in the parking lot, whose job was to nab passengers as they attempted to crawl out of trunks.

"You needed protection *from* them," Simms said of the special deputies. Customers caught in violation of park rules and policies were subjected to additional forms of cruel and unusual punishment. "They had a place they'd lock you up until the beach closed, which was filthy." Called the "shithouse," the makeshift detention facility was a trash and excrement-filled shed covered by a tin roof. With minimal ventilation, temperatures inside easily rose above 100 degrees on summer afternoons. "One time [in there] was enough for me," Simms described.

While black officers' personal motivations for committing acts of torture and brutality on others were complex and undoubtedly influenced in part by a desire to compensate for their own subject position in a Jim Crow society, the persons subjected to Phelps's disciplinary measures shared a common characteristic: their actions were detrimental to business profits and, by extension, Phelps's crew's job security. And given that the Carr's Beach profits came from the pennies and dimes of an impoverished but resourceful people, officers constantly struggled to discover and eliminate the innovative mechanisms employed by the poor to secure access to this private, commercial facility. Growing up in Eastport, a hardscrabble community of watermen and oyster factory workers, Larry Griffin and his friends got to Carr's Beach on summer weekends by swimming across the Back Creek with pairs of dry clothes tied in waterproof sacks. (See Map 12, p. 184.) Once on the Annapolis Neck peninsula shore, they would change clothes in the locker rooms at Sparrow's Beach or in a patch of bushes, and then sneak onto Carr's Beach through one of the many trenches that they and others had, over the years, dug under the barbed wire fence that lined the property. Others swam out from the shores of Sparrow's Beach and tried to come ashore at Carr's Beach. Their strategies of eluding capture and enjoying free entertainment evolved in relation to Phelps's methods of surveillance and punishment.[59]

The stationing of deputies along the property's boundaries was indicative of the place of Phelps's force in the beach economy. Paid by the proprietors, the security force's primary duty was to ensure that visitors' search for pleasure yielded profits for the resort—to squelch altercations before they resulted in general mayhem or property damage, ferret out individuals trying to sneak in without paying, snuff out bootleg whiskey dealers and direct thirsty patrons toward the bar, break up crap games and consequently boost returns from the one-arm bandits, and keep the parents and their kids coming back. Rather than rid the beach of crime and vice, Phelps's special deputies simply restructured business relations in a manner that proved mutually acceptable, and self-sustaining, for all parties. Peddlers chalked up the $500-to-$1,000 fines Phelps's forces meted out as a comparatively small cost of plying a trade that routinely netted in excess of $2,000 on a summer weekend. (With such money involved, as compared with the pitiful wages of special deputies, it should come as no surprise that many suspected that Phelps's deputies were "on the take" and susceptible to bribes.) In their efforts to foil Phelps, dealers employed a

growing number of "spotters" and developed increasingly elaborate methods for conducting their trade, which in turn provided temporary employment for young black males—added costs that were simply passed on to
the consumer. In contrast, the larger numbers of guests and steady returns
delivered to management allowed Phelps to employ additional officers on
the grounds each summer. The steady stream of persons hauled into the
Anne Arundel County courthouse on Monday morning for violations over
the weekend, likewise, reinforced among county brass the necessity of
Phelps's force.

The presence of Phelps's special deputies served a vital purpose in management's broader efforts to appeal to a cross-section of the black consumer
public. Promotional pieces stressed that the Carr's beachfront was "spic
and span" and that the atmosphere was "gay but orderly." And safe. Photo
spreads prominently featured comely young women perched atop lifeguard
stands, with a megaphone in hand and a round life preserver emblazoned
with a red cross and the words "Carr's Beach" by their side, simultaneously
selling sex and safety. Below a photo of the "highflying whirligig," a ride
consisting of eight two-person metal baskets extending out from a one-
hundred-foot-high tower and spinning at a high rate of speed, promoters
assured readers that this and other rides were "regularly inspected to comply
with State safety regulations." Along with police, the resort had its own medical tent staffed with a doctor and a nurse. In an interview with the *Baltimore Afro-American* in 1951, Rufus Mitchell stressed, "We have done everything possible to minimize all hazards. Our beach was patrolled by six
well-qualified life guards, and the grounds by a corp [*sic*] of special policemen, we will continue this policy with greater emphasis."[60]

By the early 1960s, as the black freedom movement dismantled Jim Crow
and desegregated (among other public places) whites-only beaches, the
future of Carr's Beach never seemed brighter. Crowds continued to jam
the roadways leading to the beach on summer weekends for performances
by artists who later became legends but to the crowds at the time were
simply seen as good dance music. A 1962 performance by James Brown
drew over eleven thousand; shows by Sam Cooke, Jackie Wilson, and other
national touring artists drew similarly large crowds. After the shows, fans
and would-be high rollers crowded around the entrance to Club Bengazi

(later renamed the Tahitian Port Lounge and decorated in a South Asian style wildly popular in the 1960s) for a chance to rub shoulders with musicians and their entourage, and to see and be seen among prominent black businessmen and celebrities. In the booths that lined the walls of the Tahitian Port Lounge, "big timers" in the numbers trade held court, flaunting their style and wealth while surrounded by young women handpicked from the crowds mingling around the grounds after shows. Young black men seeking to gain entry to the club "had to be somewhat in the know." Entry was determined less by one's occupation or reputation and more by one's dress, appearance, and desire (and ability) to consume. "Whenever I got a score" from his various hustles and petty thefts, Simms recalls, "you know I'd be there."

Others wished they could be anywhere but there, and dreamed of a widened horizon of leisure and vacation options. Reflecting back on summers spent at Carr's Beach, black Baltimorean Elizabeth Oliver commented:

> Those beaches were crowded with (you guessed it) the most unglamorous crowd of our folks in bathing suits of all kinds and descriptions. Some of the bathers splashing in those little backwater waves and on the sand littered with bottles and paper cups and plates, wore short dresses, the men in their underwear shorts. Not a jet-set bunch under umbrellas and keeping quiet, no sir! Beer was allowed and coke bottles were half-filled with gin and whiskey. A good time was had by all in the broiling hot sun. A good time including fist fights and more severe encounters.[61]

For performers who had struggled to survive under grueling schedules, miserable accommodations, and little pay on the chitlin circuit, freedom meant, among other things, freedom to negotiate for better performance contracts at higher-ticket venues. Indeed, as a host of large and small entrepreneurs continued to spin sand into gold, their patrons and performers dreamed of summers on other, perhaps more lavish and opulent, shores, and shows on other, larger stages.

7

THE PRICE WE PAY FOR PROGRESS

Charles Williams began his letter to Vincent J. P. Connolly dated April 10, 1973, as one might expect a person in desperate need of a loan would: he referred to their long-standing personal ties and his own personal struggles. "As you well know, I have been involved with Bay Shore for more than thirty years, some of which were good and some not so good. We have had to contend with storms, hurricanes, tidal waves, fire, and finally, integration." It was a sentiment that could have been expressed by any number of beach resort and amusement park proprietors in the early 1970s. Indeed, Williams's plight seemed, at first glance, indistinguishable from that facing Harry Batt, the white owner and operator of Pontchartrain Beach in New Orleans, who in 1966 reported a staggering loss of revenue that was, in his words, "a direct effect of the passage of Federal Civil Rights Legislation."

Williams, however, was an African American businessman, and his Bay Shore Beach had been, since its founding in 1890, a "colored" resort. And while Batt's fears of solvency stemmed from the prospect of white flight from integrated shorelines, inspiring him and other operators of formerly segregated places of play to do anything within their power to depress black patronage, Williams searched for ways to bring African Americans back to his place of business, his struggle a testament to fellow blacks' determination to taste the fruits of freedom in their moments of leisure and their refusal to turn back in the face of new, more insidious, forms of exclusion and intimidation that Batt and others adopted. Staring, from his desk in Hampton, Virginia, at stacks of unpaid bills and increasingly dismal revenue reports, Williams sighed, "This is the price we pay for progress. I have no complaints, but I realize ways must be found to meet these new demands."[1]

The "price" African American owners of property along bodies of water (or places that would become bodies of water) paid for the South's "progress" in the decades following the death of Jim Crow was, quite often, their land. The economic resurgence of the South did not so much pass them by as it exposed them to new and more aggressive forms of predation by those seeking to capitalize on the region's insatiable demand for water—the vital resource, the magnet for vacationers and pleasure seekers, and, for upwardly mobile homeowners, the ultimate sign of luxury living. The lands once owned by Edna Cole's family told this story of the modern, Sunbelt South. After years as itinerant sharecroppers caught within the cycle of Jim Crow capitalism, in 1949 Cole's parents secured a loan through the Farmers Home Administration and purchased a seventy-five-acre farm in Chatham County, North Carolina, located near the cities of Durham, Raleigh, and Chapel Hill. As a black child growing up in the 1960s, Edna Cole recalled her father (who lacked any formal education) telling her, "'I got nothing to give you, but I want you to take this land and make it do something for you. I don't want you to sell it. . . . Whatever you do, always keep it.' . . . He made me feel as if you had land, then your land, no matter where it was or what it was, it was just like white land. It didn't make any difference. . . . They can run you away from every[where] else, but if you pay your taxes they can't run you away from here."

As he imparted these lessons, the U.S. Army Corps of Engineers began drawing up plans for the creation of Jordan Lake, which would control flooding and provide the water necessary to accommodate the region's projected population growth—along with expensive, waterfront property to house its most affluent migrants—and catapult the poor, rural county from the tobacco belt into the Sunbelt. "I'll never forget," Cole recalls, "a man came to my dad's with a briefcase and telling him that Jordan Lake was going to come and part of the land in Chatham County was going to be used as a flood area and some of it was going to be for wildlife. . . . And he took the briefcase out and showed him some of the things that was going to happen and told my father that, you know, if he didn't sell it, they would take it anyway." Seeing little option, Edna advised her elderly father to sell the man 22.5 acres of their farmland for $5,000. Jordan Lake was completed in 1982.

"In later years we found out that this man [Russell Barringer] was not from the Corps at all, but he had inside information about what the progress was or when it was going to happen." Through examining courthouse records, Cole learned that Barringer later sold the Coles' farm to the Army Corps of Engineers for twice the amount he paid to acquire it. Along with

the land, Edna Cole lost her father's faith in its power to provide its possessors a measure of freedom and equality. "This America we live in, you
know, you never own anything because at any given time they can take it
back for whatever reason." In the end, she found a measure of comfort
mixed with resignation knowing that Barringer's act of deceit was just another chapter in a long history of "blacks' . . . land being taken, or finagled."
This, she remarked sarcastically, was the coming of progress to the
South—and "You can't stop progress."

If it was, Whitney and Barbara Irvin could be called the face of progress. As Whitney Irvin's date of retirement from his position at the Federal
Reserve Bank in New York City approached, he and his wife, Barbara,
yearned to relocate and live out their golden years far from the miserable
winters, bumper-to-bumper traffic, and seemingly endless suburban development of Westfield, New Jersey. "We wanted water and a boat," Whitney recalls. And, at the least, "a major university" nearby that would provide the cultural events and attractions they had grown accustomed to
enjoying in the Northeast. Flipping through an issue of the *New Yorker*,
they found, in the advertisements for real estate, what they were looking
for—a new, planned community, Fearrington Village, along the shores of
Jordan Lake, near the University of North Carolina at Chapel Hill and
nestled in the Research Triangle Park metropolitan area. They headed
down south and settled comfortably in their waterfront home alongside
young, highly educated professionals and wealthy retirees. Folks down
there seemed to share their political conservatism, which helped to smooth
any tensions with those who drove past their gated community in trucks
with bumper stickers on the back that read, "I don't give a damn how you
did it up North!" When Hillary Rodham Clinton was running for the
U.S. Senate in New York in 2000, Whitney joked with his new southern
friends of his plans to "move back to New York so I can vote against her."
Barbara, meanwhile, became immersed in the county's local history—in
her words, "an undiscovered gem"—and bemoaned the area's rapid development, which threatened to destroy all that had brought them there in
the first place.[2]

As both Charles Williams and Edna Cole could attest, in the modern
Sunbelt South, bodies of water *mattered*, and the ways they mattered could
profoundly shape the fortunes of people and places. They provided pleasure and enjoyment to people, attracted enormous outlays of capital, inspired both innovative and reckless attempts to stabilize and market, suf-

fered the most starkly visible effects of pollution and overdevelopment, and struck back with righteous fury at humans' futile but unending attempts to conquer and contain nature.

In a sense, the Sunbelt South grew up along the water, and its bodies of water came to embody its ethos and contradictions. Socially and ecologically, coastal zones experienced the most immediate and transformative effects of the Sunbelt revolution. During the 1970s, the U.S. Census found, the nation's fastest-growing counties were those that included "seashores, inlets, lakes, rivers, mountainsides, ski resorts, hunting preserves and other such places . . . of outdoor recreation and natural scenery."[3] In North Carolina, for example, four of the coastal counties, which until the 1960s remained among the state's most sparsely populated, gained residents at a rate two to six times greater than the rest of the state. These same counties also contained, by the early 1980s, two to three times as many houses as permanent residents. Both the U.S. Forest Service and Water Conservation Fund noted a rapid increase in prices for waterfront real estate (adjusted for inflation) during these years. "New names are appearing in the land ownership books in musty county courthouses," the conservationist Robert G. Healy and economist James L. Short reported in 1983. "Rural places long accustomed to stagnation and decline are experiencing a new inflow of people and money." "Whether on the ocean or on inland lakes," they found, water frontage was the most in-demand rural property at a time when the value of smaller recreational tracts in rural areas rose at a rate of 15 percent a year.[4] The rush to the sea led to a rush to privatize the shore. A 1974 congressional study of America's coasts concluded, "The shoreline of the United States has, in general, been relegated to private interests" and that a "seemingly boundless demand for a spot by the sea has sent land values skyrocketing."[5]

As with other sectors of the Sunbelt economy, federal policies and dollars played more than a passive role. Between 1936 and 1978 the Army Corps of Engineers conducted over seventy-five coastal protection and beach restoration projects, erecting seawalls and groins and undertaking other structural measures designed to preserve beaches and maintain high coastal property values, in defiance of patterns of beach migration.[6] In 1968, Congress passed the National Flood Insurance Act and established the National Flood Insurance Program, which underwrote private insurance policies on homes and businesses in flood-prone areas and accelerated an already robust coastal real estate market. Alongside legislation, judicial interpretations of coastal and property law steadily encouraged development in ecologically fragile areas, eased restraints on displacement of small landowners, and narrowly interpreted the public's right to access public spaces.[7] Between 1950 and 1980, coastal barrier islands, the first line of defense against nature's wrath and an essential element of coastal ecologies wholly unfit for human habitation, were developed at a rate of six thousand acres per year.[8] Septic systems, the traditional means of waste removal in remote areas, proliferated in booming coastal zones far beyond the soil's capacity, malfunctioning often, filling the air with putrid smells, contaminating oyster and clam beds, degrading estuaries, and threatening outbreaks of hepatitis. For many, it was a small price to pay to live away from it all—from the city and its problems, and from public spaces and places that had become *too* public.

As people and capital rushed to the sea, they encountered the limits of mass development on fragile shorelines. Along with deadly hurricanes that washed away homes and businesses, attempts to stabilize shorelines through erecting groins, building seawalls, and closing inlets accelerated coastal erosion and threatened the viability of an increasingly lucrative and influential segment of the American economy. Locked in this vicious cycle, coastal capitalists begged for—and state and federal officials (with rare exceptions) readily agreed to spend—tens of millions of dollars each year for dumping sand on eroding shores in desperate and ultimately futile attempts to halt the natural movement of beaches, hold back the sea, and protect coastal property. Inevitably, projects initially touted as long-term or permanent solutions to beach erosion were soon revealed as one- to two-year stopgaps. And as the sea quickly reclaimed its sands, wealthy homeowners and otherwise robust defenders of private property rights were reduced to desperate solicitors of federal assistance.[9]

What follows is a selective overview of formerly "colored" stretches of shore after the music stopped and the crowds dispersed and as a new coastal capitalist economy—and new spatial strategies of race management—took hold and spread. From this vantage, we can observe how changes in the political economy and ecology of coastal zones reflected and informed changes in the meaning and redistribution of power that accompanied the demise of Jim Crow and the rise of the Sunbelt.

✦

In the summer of 1960, the sand curtain that walled off the Mississippi Gulf Coast's white beachfront began to disintegrate. Following the expulsion of a group of black students from the Biloxi beachfront in 1959, and after years of requests for adequate beach space of their own falling on deaf ears, the city's African American population, led by Gilbert Mason, a physician and founder of the local chapter of the NAACP, conducted wade-ins on Biloxi city beaches. There he and others sustained brutal attacks from police officers and civilian defenders of white supremacy while sending local businesses and regional boosters—who came to understand the state's reputation as a hotbed for racial bigotry as a liability—into a panic. Mason's wade-ins coincided with and exploited the Mississippi Gulf Coast's ongoing efforts to attract new, high-tech industries and upper-middle-class families and retirees to the region, and to further distance itself from the state's interior.

Mississippi's Gulf Coast played host to both the decline of the Black Belt and rise of the Sunbelt. While the "closed society," as one historian famously called the Magnolia State during the civil rights era, scared away people and business, between 1959 and 1969, Hancock, Harrison, and Jackson counties (lying along the Gulf Coast) experienced a 26.9 percent population growth (more than twice the nation's average) and an influx of new money and new industries.[10] As new money poured in, coastal development accelerated. By 1969 an average of two thousand persons per square mile lived on the coast.[11]

Biloxi's was one of many wade-ins that civil rights activists staged along segregated beaches. Strategically, wade-ins sought to exploit the vulnerabilities of a changing coastal political economy. By stepping onto whites-only beaches and swimming in whites-only waters, protesters expected to generate an explosive reaction from the most ardent, and violent, defenders of Jim Crow. And that was the point. Staged wade-ins brought conflict and bad publicity to places whose economies were becoming increasingly oriented toward attracting vacationers and pleasure seekers and, as a result, reliant on a façade of pleasure and harmony. They pitted the interests of native, working-class white southerners against the interests of an emergent class of northern transplants and Sunbelt boosters. Reporting on the crisis that engulfed Fort Lauderdale, Florida, following a staged wade-in on the city's public beach in the summer of 1961, an NAACP field-worker noted that the action "has caused a hodge podge of confusion as to what should be done to eliminate the question of race . . . [and] has struck fear in the minds of The City Fathers as well as those who have invested millions in building attractions for the tourist's dollar."[12] Moderate white southern politicians in the Sunbelt mold were anxious to prevent these spectacles from taking place, and scrambled to come up with short-term solutions that might quiet black unrest. Not surprisingly, the state of separate black beaches in areas targeted by freedom fighters figured prominently in such discussions. In the summer of 1961, for instance, North Carolina governor Terry Sanford learned of plans by Freedom Riders to attempt to desegregate Carolina Beach's public beach during their stay in nearby Wilmington. Sanford's administrative assistant, Hugh Cannon, sent an aide to the coast to investigate and report on conditions on the ground. The aide wrote back to Cannon that "everything had been worked out to the colored peoples' satisfaction" after local officials had promised "some local financing for improvements at Freeman Beach." (Presumably, these improvements involved a promise to include Frank and Lulu Hill's beachfront property in future sand replenishment projects.)[13]

Wade-ins not only exploited the coastal South's changing demographics and its increased dependence on tourism dollars, but also its dependence on federal dollars and federal agencies to furnish the types of environmental and aesthetic amenities that visitors had come to expect. On the Mississippi Gulf Coast, federal funding of the 1951 beach replenishment project came with the stipulation that the beach would be dedicated to the public. (At the time, the "pubic" was understood to mean white persons.) But by the early 1960s, federal officials in Washington had come to recognize that the public included African Americans. After white officials and vigilantes prevented Gilbert Mason from integrating Biloxi's beach, the U.S. Justice Department filed suit against Harrison County in the United States District Court for the Southern District of Mississippi for denying citizens their constitutional right to access the Gulf of Mexico's foreshore.[14]

The same summer black Mississippians breached Biloxi's sand curtain, Robert C. Thomas, an investigator for the Mississippi State Sovereignty Commission (a state agency charged with surveillance and suppression of civil rights activities), was in neighboring Hancock County investigating the activities at Gulfside. After asking around the town of Waveland, he wrote back and assured state officials that, in the view of all local white officials he spoke with, Gulfside "is a very good thing" and had "never [been] out of line in the least bit." "The general public here was in sympathy with the folks that were running it."[15] Gulfside's long tradition of dissemblance and outward accommodation to "local customs" proved critical in allowing it to serve as a safe haven for civil rights workers. It was at Gulfside that Constance Baker Motley and Thurgood Marshall, among others, prepared to argue cases in southern courtrooms against segregated education. Thomas Dent organized and hosted summer retreats for the New Orleans–based Congo Square Writers' Workshop at Gulfside. In the summers of 1963 and 1964, Gulfside organized freedom schools, and in November 1964 it hosted a retreat for members of the Student Nonviolent Coordinating Committee, where members submitted position papers on the future of the organization. "Only at Waveland," civil rights worker and SNCC member Mary King commented, "was it possible for a racially integrated group to stay together and not trigger violence in Mississippi." It was, Gulfside alum Jerry Ruth Williams adds, "a place where integrated groups could meet and plan without the threat of being jailed."[16]

The prospect of going to jail was the least of Gulfside administrators' worries. As white-collar workers and their families streamed into Mississippi's coastal counties, buying up all the land they could in proximity to the water, Gulfside struggled to balance its lack of capital with its abundance of land. On several occasions it was forced to sell portions of its property so as to keep up with the rising taxes that accompanied regional development and to preserve what it saw as its nucleus—the land facing the sea. In 1959, Gulfside's board of trustees sold seventy undeveloped acres on the backside of the campgrounds, which had, as Robert E. Jones told the board, "fallen into what has become the 'white' section of Waveland." The following year, the board agreed to sell 175 acres of undeveloped swampland for $100 an acre to C. H. Fricke, a local real estate developer, as well as two lots near the Waveland railroad station for $1,000 cash. Through the mid 1960s, administrators and trustees argued bitterly over whether these sales threatened or strengthened Gulfside's long-term viability.[17]

With passage of the 1964 Civil Rights Act and, in 1968, dissolution of the Methodist Church's Central Jurisdiction, those essential functions were drawn further into question just as Gulfside's financial situation worsened and outside pressure to sell intensified. By the early 1960s, the Methodist Church had entered into the final stages of its plan of integration. In turn, black Methodists shifted focus from the fight to abolish the Central Jurisdiction to ensuring an equal voice and the protection of their assets

and institutions in a reconstituted church.[18] Under the initial plan of unification, the separate black conferences that composed the Central Jurisdiction were to be absorbed, along with their propertied assets, into their
respective, formerly all-white, state conferences. Casting a skeptical eye
toward the promises of white church leaders, black Methodist conferences
strongly resisted integration proposals that threatened to deliver them—
and their assets—into the hands of white southerners, and fought for implementation of a more just and equitable plan of integration. As both a product of the church's segregated past and as a highly valued asset, Gulfside
became both a site and a symbol of this larger struggle over the meaning
of equality and empowerment, and over the redistribution of resources and
power in an integrated church. As Gulfside's executive director William
Talbot Handy told the national church, "Gulfside is the one thing of great
import that we can take over into the Jurisdiction. It can be carried over
with dignity and pride . . . for the all-inclusive church." In the end, the
black conferences of the Gulf South succeeded in establishing a plan of
unification that preserved their administrative control over Gulfside and
black Methodist colleges and universities.[19]

The initial euphoria over these achievements was soon tempered by the
steady exodus of the people and groups who sustained these institutions
under Jim Crow and the corresponding diminution of funding and support from the United Methodist Church. While black Methodists maintained administrative control over Gulfside, they lost control over their
primary method of fund-raising: the collection plate. Those dollars and
cents now went to the United Methodist Church before trickling back
down to Gulfside. As one Gulfside member described it, under this new
arrangement, "Gulfside was just left to flounder." More so than ever, it
was dependent on hosting camps and conferences as well as vacationers
during the summer months. But, as a 1968 report on Gulfside's declining
finances noted, those groups and individuals were now "spending their
time in other places. This has resulted in an under-usage of the Assembly
grounds." Although the resort had attracted twenty-eight church and non-
religious groups the previous summer, and remained in constant use
throughout the year, the size of the groups dwindled, and rarely did the
number of guests approximate the campground's capacity. The continued
loss of groups and visitors paralleled the loss of the land. In the latter half
of the 1960s, the rent on the adjoining 326 acres of sixteenth-section land
that Gulfside leased from Hancock County on a ninety-nine-year lease

spiked. Some suspected this as retaliation for the organization's involvement in civil rights activities, but likely it was due to rising land values in
general and a desire among state and county officials to devote the area to
public recreational use and draw in additional summer travelers. Unable
to make payments, Gulfside ceded the land back to the county.[20]

✦

As early as the mid-1950s, Charles H. Williams, president of the New Bay
Shore Corporation and operator of one of the largest hotel and beach resorts catering to black Americans in the mid-Atlantic region, perceived
the challenges facing African American businesspeople in the leisure and
service trades as the black freedom movement chipped away at the foundations of Jim Crow in public accommodations. In a speech before a
group of black newspaper publishers in 1955, Williams predicted the
swift downfall of black-owned hotels following desegregation unless a
concerted plan of professionalism and physical improvements were implemented. For decades, "We had to bear [inferior] conditions, because
we had no other places to go, and some short sighted business people
have just been cashing in on the racial bar at our expense, and inconve-
nience. Their day of reckoning could well be at hand before they know it."
Indeed, it already was. Years before court-ordered integration of public
accommodations, a small but noticeable number of white-owned hotel
corporations entered into the Negro hotel trade. The emergence of
"competition [from] unexpected quarters," combined with the growing
dissatisfaction of a growing black middle class with the "inferior accommodations and indifferent service" of black hotel and resort operators,
meant, Williams warned, "Negro hotels and places catering to Negro patrons would have to improve or . . . be wiped out."[21]

With federal legislation forcing beaches, resorts, and hotels to desegregate close at hand, Williams began work, in the winter of 1964, on his own
"program of integration" for Bay Shore. Following a storm in the summer
of 1962 that inflicted over $33,000 in structural damage to the grounds,
Williams solicited the assistance of the Small Business Administration
(SBA) in securing a loan and growing his business. The SBA had been
founded in 1953 with the passage of the Small Business Act, its primary
function being to assist small businesses in accessing credit. Similar to
the Federal Housing Administration, the SBA assisted small businesses

through guaranteeing to lending institutions a portion of the loan against default on the condition the recipient follow the SBA's guidelines. Through the SBA, Williams secured a $15,000 loan from the Virginia National Bank.[22]

Williams expressed cautious optimism about the prospect of maintaining and perhaps growing his customer base. "It will," he predicted, "be sometime before we get white [sic] to patronize Negro businesses as Negroes patronize their business places because we do not have as much to offer." Yet Williams had precious little time to wait. Annual financial statements make it clear that the corporation was rapidly sliding toward insolvency as, in Williams's words, "Negroes left Bay Shore and carried their patronage to the top hotels where they got better service and accommodations," while whites, when they acknowledged it at all, saw Bay Shore as either a curiosity or real estate ripe for the plucking. Gate receipts for the beach fell from $19,234 in 1962 to $14,861 in 1966. Between 1962 and 1969, the hotel's cash receipts grew at an annual rate of $819, which, given the massive inflation of the decade, did not come close to meeting rising costs. This was underscored by the losses the company reported each year. In 1966 it reported a net loss $15,605. That figure grew in subsequent years, topping out at $25,554 in reported losses for the year 1973. Much of this was due to ballooning interest on a series of loans the company had taken out early in the decade to improve the grounds in the hopes of retaining black patrons and attracting white guests. A 1967 economic study of Hampton's waterfront by the Hampton City Planning Commission described Bay Shore's "buildings . . . to be in a fairly poor state of repair, and a hotel in definite need of rehabilitation." Focused on finding ways of turning this section of the shore into the "waterfront playground of Hampton," and attracting "upper-socio-economic groups who generally don't visit" the area, the drafters of the study envisioned and worked to promote the removal rather than rehabilitation of Bay Shore.[23]

As summer revenue plummeted, Bay Shore's finances, always shaky at best, assumed nightmarish proportions. In perusing Williams's unprocessed papers housed at Hampton University's archives, the most common items one can find are angry letters from vendors and advertisers demanding payment of outstanding balances, and delinquent tax notices from the city of Hampton and the state of Virginia. By 1968, Bay Shore Corporation owed $233,845 to the Small Business Administration, the Citizens and Marine Bank, various vendors, and the IRS. Following completion of a seawall along the Hampton shore in 1967, coastal real estate values skyrocketed. But for Bay Shore, that proved more a curse than a blessing. Subsequent reappraisals resulted in higher property taxes, which added to the mounting cost of maintaining ownership. (The addition of the seawall led the Bay Shore property's appraised value to climb from $432,275 in 1963 to $891,025 in 1967.) Despite this, Williams continued to believe that, given its ideal location facing out on the mouth of the Chesapeake, "with proper management and money, [Bay Shore] can become a multi-million-dollar project."[24] Lenders thought otherwise. And in 1974, sensing no signs of any plans for the liquidation of his debts, the Small Business Administration initiated foreclosure proceedings. Williams died in 1978. The same year, the city of Hampton assumed ownership of the property, which it later sold to a developer. Today, the area is known as Chesapeake Landing, a residential subdivision consisting of twenty homes (eight on the beach) on a cul-de-sac. All residents enjoy access to their own private beach.[25]

In recent decades, there has been a growing interest in the preservation and revitalization of black Main Streets and other economic and cultural centers of black life under Jim Crow. However, during the years these places were becoming a thing of the past, there was no such interest among the white public, much less white capital. Given widespread perceptions of what went on behind "the color line" and what whites could expect when they entered black leisure space, this should come as no surprise. "Most whites thought that if they came there they were going to get jumped," black Annapolitan Larry Griffin said of Carr's Beach. "Whites were listening to that music, they wanted to be there, but they had that stereotype that they couldn't come in without trouble." "I first fell in love with Tina Turner in the summer of 1961!" an unnamed white male who grew up in a subdivision located near Carr's Beach posted on an Internet blog. "Ike and Tina . . . were playing at Carr's Beach. . . . On a nice night you could hear the music from Carr's Beach in [the neighboring white subdivision] Victor Haven. However . . . no white kid with half a brain would go down to Carr's Beach by themselves. So I snuck into the woods near the beach and listened to Ike and Tina for half of the night." In her memoirs of growing up in postwar Washington, Caryl Rivers similarly recalls her fascination with the groups of blacks from the city motoring to Carr's Beach down the same roads her family traveled to get to the all-white Mayo Beach down the shore: "Sometimes, on the way to the beach cars would pass us—old cars crowded with black people, the car radios blaring Rhythm and Blues from a black station, the people drinking beer with gay abandon, oblivious of the car's fragility and the probability that a tire would blow before water's edge was reached. . . . I used to watch the cars drive by and hear the music and imagine that Carrs and Sparrows beaches must be places of rare exotica. They were not, of course, places to which I would think of venturing."[26]

Following the 1969 season, with attendance sagging, the Carr's Beach Amusement Company attempted to breathe new life into Carr's Beach by renaming it World Beach (in the hopes of creating an inclusive atmosphere that would attract an integrated audience) and booking rock-and-roll acts. The venture proved a dismal failure financially; white patronage was spotty, while young blacks, who in years past flocked to shows by Joe Tex, Funkadelic, and Percy Sledge, were less interested in paying to hear Rare Earth, Edgar Winter, or Led Zeppelin. The following summer, the grounds were leased to a group of young white concert promoters, who advertised as the Great McGonigle's Seaside Park. By then, the facilities at both Carr's and Sparrow's beaches had significantly deteriorated. In 1973 the park hosted its last show, a performance by Frank Zappa that reportedly ended in violence instigated by members of the outlaw biker gang the Pagans. "When [Carr's and Sparrow's beaches] shut down, we lost a lot," Larry Griffin remembers. "You learned a lot more than music there. You learned how to love people, get along with people. You got taught to be a man, to be a woman. It was a village. [Their closing] took a big piece of our hearts away."[27]

While Bay Shore and Carr's Beach struggled valiantly to remain afloat in post–Jim Crow coastal economies, other owners of African American commercial beach resorts simply cashed out. Shortly after passage of the Civil Rights Act of 1964, the black shareholders in Seaview Beach, outside of Norfolk, Virginia, moved to sell the property and recoup a portion of their initial investment. In 1965 they sold the 116-acre tract with three thousand feet of water frontage to Norfolk real estate developer David Levine for $500,000. The buyers subsequently embarked on a $50 million project to convert the property into what Levine described as a "series of alternating high rise hotels and motels along the bay front." Plans also included a commercial district and marina. Upon acquiring the land for what could best be described (certainly in retrospect if not also at the time) as dirt cheap, Levine proclaimed that "this tract of land is one of the most important in the future development of Virginia Beach." Irving M. Watts, an African American dentist and one of Seaview's founders and principal investors, made the best of his company's inability to hold on to this valuable piece of property, arguing that the closing of Seaview constituted a step forward on the road to equality. "Now that every place is open to Negroes, [Seaview's closing] is no loss to the community."[28]

White public officials charged with desegregating public recreational facilities, likewise, quickly moved to close "colored" beaches and liquidate any assets. In New Orleans, the Lincoln Beach Corporation invoked its escape clause and terminated its lease with the levee board immediately following passage of the Civil Rights Act of 1964. That summer, Lincoln Beach abruptly closed. Also closed in the summer of 1964, on the orders of Mayor Victor Schiro, were all the city's public swimming pools, ostensibly to avoid the possibility of racial violence. (This act was repeated in countless towns and cities across the South, as well as parts of the North.) "And so," the Louisiana Weekly read, "the coming summer has cast its shadow ahead," and the city's poor black children faced "the summer's searing heat without any relief whatsoever." As expected, "a rash of deaths by drowning in unsupervised waters" followed. By mid-July, eight black youths had drowned in the city.[29]

The now-desegregated Pontchartrain Beach, meanwhile, was refitted so as to dissuade black patronage. Prior to the park's formal desegregation on July 1, 1964, Pontchartrain Beach's owner, Harry Batt, constructed a fence around the grounds to ward off "troublemakers" and instituted a one-ticket-per-ride policy, in addition to a gate fee, to discourage underprivileged black youth from hanging around all day. (These, too, were common measures implemented throughout the amusement park industry.)[30]

They came anyway. Black New Orleanian Kenneth McGruder recalls his initial excitement at the prospect of visiting the once-forbidden amusement park. "It was a thrill . . . to go on the rides [whites] went on, the better rides, the better games, and the pretty beaches." And they came in spite of the violence and hostility they expected to receive. Throughout the latter half of the 1960s, violent assaults on black youth sporadically erupted on the park's grounds and along contested sections of the lakeshore. "When you went [to Pontchartrain Beach]," black New Orleanian Ethel Ellis recalls, "you had to be ready for a fight, you had to watch your back, because [whites] did not want us there. Integration said we had a right to go to your beach. That didn't mean they welcomed us with open arms to come to our beach. So you had to go with a crowd and watch each other's back."[31] What whites saw as dangerous, roving gangs invading *their* space, black youth saw as a necessary means of survival.[32]

"We were integrated by law in 1964," as white New Orleanian Mary Lou Widmer put it, "but that doesn't mean everybody accepted it. There was always a great deal of dissatisfaction about the [desegregation of Pontchartrain Beach] among whites, so whatever places you could stay away from, you did."[33] The prospect of desegregated swimming pools, beaches, and parks reinforced, for working- and middle-class whites, an understanding of civil rights for blacks as a "loss of rights for them." In the age of Jim Crow, these public facilities and resources had been, in effect, their private places of privilege. A process of desegregation led by pro-growth, more progressive southern politicians drew working-class whites' own unequal standing with other whites into relief, and fueled a sense of outrage and betrayal that constituted a core element of modern conservatism.[34] At Ocean View Amusement Park in Norfolk, Virginia, white patronage (and gate receipts) plummeted in the wake of desegregation and the growing presence of black youth on the park's grounds. In a 1970 letter to Dudley Cooper, owner and manager of Ocean View, white Norfolk resident L. J. Holstein gave voice to these sentiments and offered a prescient observation of changes in the culture and economy of summer leisure and coastal real estate development that soon followed: "Why don't you do away with the Ocean View Amusement Park and build two good motels there in it's [sic] place," Holstein advised. "The negroes have ruined the place . . . like every other public place they are allowed to go. Fences are not going to solve the problem so you might as well turn it into something that will be on a paying basis. Decent white people won't go there anymore." In 1975 Cooper did just that, closing the park and making plans to redevelop it as a private beachfront residential community.[35]

While owners fretted, black patrons simply played. By the 1970s, Pontchartrain Beach, once a forbidden citadel of white supremacy, became for the city's black youth the place to be in the summer. "We took our dates out there," Willie Williams remembers. "It was fun . . . [to] get on the roller coaster. We looked forward to every spring it would open." "In high school," Kenneth McGruder recalls, "that's where we gravitated to, because it was easy to get there. . . . It's where all the high school kids, black and white, met . . . so you kinda put Lincoln Beach behind you." In its place, "Pontchartrain Beach got to be the focal point for us."[36]

Not for long. In New Orleans, the migration of middle-class whites to suburbs in neighboring parishes depressed gate receipts and contributed to the deterioration of the park's facilities. The shrinking number of patrons at the park contrasted with the rising levels of pollution in Lake Pontchartrain. By the 1960s, a half-century of unmitigated lakefront development, and the rising levels of raw sewage dumped in the lake from the sprawling suburbs of Jefferson Parish (where the population grew rapidly in the years following the *Brown* decision), threatened to render Lake Pontchartrain, as one writer described, "a rancid carbon copy of the Great Lakes." In the coming decades, the lake, as one New Orleanian who fished its waters described, "traveled from one environmental disaster to another." Eutrophication upset the lake's normal plant and animal life. The absence of regulations on clamshell dredging resulted in the death of large swaths of the lakebed. Industrial waste further decimated fish populations. Along the shore, dead fish became a more common sight than sunbathers. By the mid 1970s, public officials deemed much of the southern shore unsafe for bathing. "All of a sudden everything was dead," John Hainkel remembers. "You couldn't catch anything. It was a cesspool. It was a disgrace."[37] It was, as it had been throughout the twentieth century, a mirror on the city it surrounded.

"It happened in such a subtle way," black New Orleanian William Garibaldi remembers. "We were integrated, then all of a sudden we were resegregated. When the smoke cleared, we looked up and said, 'Wait a minute, we're here by ourselves.'" Other historians have referred to integration as that "brief moment between segregation and retreat."[38] At formerly segregated beaches and amusement parks, the personal circumstances and ambitions of owners and proprietors went far in determining the duration and quality of that moment.

In 1958, Joseph Goldstein, the "dapper . . . son of [a] prominent Southern Maryland commercial and political family," purchased the concessions at Marshall Hall and the Wilson steamboat line that ferried white patrons to the segregated amusement park on the Potomac. Following

passage of the 1964 Civil Rights Act, Goldstein put in motion plans to redevelop the site as an exclusive, planned subdivision of single-family homes
and condominiums for thirty thousand residents with amenities such as
horse stables, tennis courts, a marina, and a golf course. His plans generated swift opposition from across the river, specifically the Mount Vernon
Ladies' Association, which was determined to slow riverfront development
and preserve and protect the "view enjoyed by George Washington."
Calling plans to develop the land directly across the river from Mount
Vernon a "monumental insult" to the father of the country, the MVLA
coordinated with garden clubs, homeowners' associations, and wildlife
protection and environmental preservation groups to lobby Congress to
designate 4,748 acres of river frontage stretching from Piscataway Bay to
Marshall Hall as a national park, which Congress authorized in October
1961. Following a lawsuit filed by the Interior Department to seize the
Marshall Hall property by eminent domain in 1970, Goldstein's financial
backers fled, and plans for a multimillion dollar resort evaporated. In 1972
the Interior Department ruled that Goldstein could not expand or rebuild
any of the rides or facilities at Marshall Hall, a move designed to hasten
the park's closure and the land's transfer to the National Park Service.

Determined to hold out until he could obtain the most favorable payment for the land, Goldstein came to rely on the patronage of working-
class black families and children in order to delay the process of condemnation, even as he placed the lives of those essential patrons at risk. In
August 1973, eleven people were injured when the center column supporting the chair plane ride collapsed. On July 21, 1977, the park's roller
coaster was reduced to a pile of rubble following a windstorm. By then,
most of the park's rides were inoperative, yet the park remained open and,
by one estimate, host to over one thousand children each summer weekend. Park-goers helped give cover for Goldstein in his efforts to keep the
Interior Department and a growing line of creditors at bay. Attempting to
prevent a court-ordered seizure of his excursion boats, Goldstein told
Judge Glenn Goldburn of the U.S. Bankruptcy Court for the District
Court of Maryland that the boats provided a public service to the thousands of impoverished children who came to the park each summer. In
response, the prosecuting attorney remarked that, since Goldstein carried
no liability insurance on the boat or the park, "Then it seems the school
children ought to be protected by keeping them away from the boats." In
April 1978 the court ruled against Goldstein. Later that summer the

amusement park officially closed, the grounds fell under the jurisdiction of the National Park Service, and all of the Wilson Line's assets were auctioned.[39]

On September 24, 1983, visitors passed through Pontchartrain Beach's turnstiles for the last time. For years, the levee board had been searching for a developer willing to lease the property and redevelop the site. After securing a deal with prominent local developer Stephen Kapelow, the levee board terminated its lease with Pontchartrain Beach owner Harry Batt and made plans to dismantle the crumbling amusement park. Before turning out the lights, Batt called all of his former white patrons back to the city for what the park promoted as "The Last Ride." The event was dripping with irony. White suburban families trickled back into the city to relive childhood memories. What they found, though, was a place that had been claimed by the city's black population in the wake of their absence. Headlining that night were legendary R&B artists Irma Thomas, the Drifters, and Fats Domino, performing before a mostly black audience. Years later, black New Orleanian John Howard Boucree still recalled the television commercials leading up to that final night:

> We'd sit and laugh at that commercial. . . . I say now you going to tell me to celebrate, to go back to Pontchartrain Beach! . . . And who do they get to sing those commercials? [Irma] Thomas and a whole lot of black persons. . . . That means nothing to me. You know, [when I was young] you couldn't even look at Pontchartrain Beach. "What are you doing in that area? You're not supposed to even be in that area."[40]

Where they were supposed to be during Boucree's childhood was out at Lincoln Beach. But at the time of Pontchartrain Beach's closing, the shuttered grounds of Lincoln Beach stood as another cruel reminder of the broken promises of civil rights. Its closing, like that of many other public "colored" recreational facilities, did not, as civil rights organizers and activists at the time had hoped, constitute the first step toward addressing and alleviating the crisis of summer in urban black America. By the mid 1970s, one study found, access to clean water for swimming and recreation had become more, not less, linked to economic status.[41] A walk along the shores of the former Lincoln Beach during those years told that story. Broken bottles, crushed cans, and abandoned refrigerators and other appliances littered the grounds. Concrete riprap jutted out from the severely eroded beach. Trash mingled with rainwater at the bottom of the emptied swimming pools. Condoms and hypodermic needles pressed up against the bottoms of graffiti-covered walls. Weeds sprouted through the pavement. Raw sewage dumped by the city and by the neighboring fishing camps continued to foul the lake water.[42] Only a rusting, deco-style sign, a broken-down carousel, and the shuttered restaurant and bathhouse testified to the area's former life. A 1979 report called it a "modern day ghost town." A house of horrors might have been a more apt description. With the site written off by capital investors, city and levee board officials seemed content to allow it to deteriorate into a haven for crime and drug use, with neither agency willing to claim policing jurisdiction over the site. To no one's surprise, Lincoln Beach became "a lovers' lane [and] a place where people would dump stolen cars [and dead] bodies." One person remembered it as "a cool place to go party and check out all the abandon[ed] rides. . . . We used to go there and target practice sometimes." An article in the *Times Picayune* described it as resembling a "bomb-test site." Another visitor described it as "a perfect set for a war movie." Nearby residents reported high rates of property crimes, which they attributed, in part, to the presence of this legal no-man's-land. By the early 1990s, most of the homes near Lincoln Beach on Hayne Boulevard had been abandoned or were barricaded with razor-wire fences.[43]

For the growing numbers of African American families who moved east of the Industrial Canal in the 1970s and 1980s, Lincoln Beach became, almost by necessity, their summer playground. On weekends the site came "alive with the smell of barbeque and the frolic of children at play." "Trespassers" trampled paths through the underbrush, across the railroad tracks, and down to the shore. There, children swam in the lake as parents took turns as lifeguard. A 1979 report of the property noted, "Even though the site is a debris strewn collection of abandoned buildings, it is actively used by the public for sunbathing, swimming, fishing, crabbing or just strolling . . . in spite of its unkempt and even dangerous condition."[44]

Beginning in the 1960s, beach communities founded by privileged African Americans in the Jim Crow era began to suffer from a different form of neglect. With only their skin color and not their incomes having limited their options in the past, younger middle- and upper-class African Americans increasingly looked beyond the cottage communities where their families owned property for a place to vacation. For them and for new entrants into the American middle class, there was a host of new places and vacation packages to choose from. While the summertime population of places like Highland Beach became noticeably smaller and older in the 1970s, the vacation home rental industry experienced a period of steady growth, as it expanded into previously marginalized segments of the American consumer public and introduced innovative strategies for capitalizing on middle-class Americans' insatiable appetite for luxury living.

The rise of time-share resorts offers an illustrative case of larger changes in coastal real estate markets during these years. First introduced in the United States in 1971, vacation home "time-sharing" quickly grew into a billion-dollar industry and a ubiquitous presence in coastal zones. Under a time-sharing arrangement, a person purchased a share in a condominium unit and enjoyed the right to use that property during a designated period each year. Prices for a share varied according to the time of year. Time-share resorts were often clustered around wealthy vacation destinations. Beach access became a determining factor in the marketability of time-share resorts. In 1975, time-share resorts could be found at only 45 vacation destinations in America; by 1980 American time-share corporations boasted 450 resorts worldwide. During those same years, the numbers of Americans owning time-shares grew from forty thousand to three hundred thousand.

Time-shares were marketed as providing the average American the chance to live like a king—for one or two weeks a year. For a down payment of roughly $1,000, a person could "own" a "two-bedroom, luxury vacation condominium, completely furnished, in [a] popular resort area." During the years in which the time-share industry emerged, vacationing and tourism by middle- and upper-class black Americans rose considerably and grew into a niche market among a growing circle of developers, agents, and promoters. African American vacationers were among the target audience for time-shares and travel packages. Lacking the historic baggage and continued residue of race-based exclusion of their more established, and expensive, competitors, modern coastal developments proved especially attractive to middle-class African American vacationers, as did the time-share model, which appealed to those eager to experience luxury living at a variety of America's most famous beaches and resort towns after a lifetime of having been confined to separate, "colored" shores.[45]

By 1990, over one million American families owned time-shares (a figure that would nearly double in the following decade) and paid an average of $7,500 annually for roughly one week in a three- to four-bedroom unit each year. In 1993, the industry recorded over $2.5 billion in sales. The time-share industry's meteoric growth far outpaced the capacity of regulators and watchdogs to examine its practices and sales techniques, which in turn contributed to its growth by allowing deceptive and manipulative sales tactics to run rampant. At vacation destinations, salespersons combed the streets, drawing potential buyers into their offices with promises of free vacations, meals, and other prizes in exchange for simply listening to their offer. Once inside, families were subjected to lengthy "grind sessions" in which agents deployed a host of high-pressure tactics. Among them were the deliberate withholding of a person's credit card under the pretext of conducting a credit report. A major marketing ploy was the opportunity for time-share owners to exchange their unit and designated period of use for another unit in another location via a "worldwide exchange network" of corporate-owned vacation time-shares, a process one industry puff piece bizarrely described as being as seamless as "musical chairs." A low-cost contract for the use of a unit on the chilly and deserted shores of Nags Head during the first ten days of February, for instance, could be made more palatable to prospective buyers if they were told that they could easily exchange those days for, say, the first ten days of April in Fort Lauderdale, Florida. Of course, this was rarely the case. Numerous time-share developments went under due to the improvidence or insolvency of the developer, with buyers—who often financed their purchase through the developer—forced to repay loans on a foreclosed unit. Reports of property mismanagement were common. The chairman of a Florida state committee that investigated the time-share industry described time-shares as a "very unregulated, chaotic form of merchandise in which there is virtually no consumer protection." In 1996 the Better Business Bureau "reported 18,570 inquiries into time-share companies . . . and 574 complaints."[46]

At Highland Beach and other summer resort towns, the dwindling numbers of young people on the beach each summer was just one of the many ironies of racial progress. Another was the declining significance of race to younger whites in search of vacation home property, and the passing of racial stigmas associated with this type of "colored" property. In the early 1950s, as whites in Arundel-on-the-Bay sold their summer cottages en masse, one Highland Beach resident wrote that, if those whites had only bothered to inquire, they would have found "their neighbors are as refined and property-respecting as they."[47] Decades later, whites finally began to make that discovery. Beginning in the 1970s and accelerating thereafter, the city of Annapolis and Anne Arundel County experienced a steady influx of wealthy retirees, many of them naval veterans attracted to the nation's "sailing capital," and young professionals working in and around the Washington Beltway. Between 1960 and 1994 the state's population grew from 3.6 million to 5.2 million. A rush to develop land within the Baltimore–Annapolis–Washington axis grew at an even faster pace. During the decade of the 1970s, the amount of developed land in the state of Maryland grew by 16.5 percent, more than double the percentage of the state's population growth (7.5 percent) during that time. The growing population of the Washington metropolitan area, combined with the extensive network of freeways connecting the Washington Beltway and neighboring counties in Maryland and Virginia, transformed Maryland's Western Shore from a rustic vacationland to a collection of bedroom communities.[48]

In this and other appreciating coastal real estate markets, construction often far outpaced the capacity of coastal lands to absorb more people and, in particular, more waste. Throughout the 1970s, according to one estimate, over one thousand acres of wetlands on the Chesapeake were lost annually to development.[49] In many of these places, the only mechanisms for waste disposal were septic systems. Notoriously unreliable, especially in places where the water table was near the surface, septic tanks for houses along Maryland's Western Shore were regularly inundated with ground water, with overflow seeping to the surface and spilling sewage into yards and down streets. By the 1980s, environmental scientists agreed that the large numbers of septic tanks along the shore as a result of rapid and uncoordinated development over the previous decades had become an environmental hazard wreaking additional havoc on the already ecologically fragile Chesapeake.[50]

For many longtime landowners, though, those malfunctioning septic systems were the only thing standing between them and corporate-financed developers. Arundel-on-the-Bay resident John Moses recalls that, beginning in the late 1970s, "the county [began] pushing the sewers, really pushing the sewers. And I thought about it, and said, 'Those sewers are not for the people who live here. Those sewers are for the [developers].' . . . They follow sewer lines just like ants follow a trail of sugar." And indeed, following the extension of water and sewer lines into the area, beginning in 1986, property values rose sharply—as did property taxes. Houses in Arundel-on-the-Bay that sold for $25,000 to $30,000 in the 1970s could, by the late 1980s, fetch between $109,000 and $575,000. Property assessments on some beachfront lots rose by as much as 1,000 percent. The extension of sewers into Oyster Harbor, Sharon Merrick recalls, "made all the difference in the world. If they didn't put sewers in, a lot of people wouldn't be interested in buying [here], but when they did, it became much more attractive." Regardless of their emotional attachment to their family's summer homes, many of the children who inherited these properties during these years had little option but to sell. Those who could afford higher property taxes found the windfall that came with selling the land hard to resist. New summer residents rarely moved into older homes, but instead bulldozed and rebuilt. Large-scale developers, likewise, replaced rustic cottages with clusters of cookie-cutter mansions that, as one real estate agent said, "cater to baby boomers in search of the shoreline." Of the roughly one hundred homes in Arundel-on-the-Bay in 2009, fewer than fifteen predated the 1980s.[51]

"I feel like I'm being strangled," Highland Beach homeowner Jean Wilder Cooper told a reporter in 1991 as they passed rows of new, multistory homes where small cottages surrounded by forests once stood. Next to Arundel-on-the-Bay, Maryland mega-developer Mark Vogel completed in the late 1980s the two-hundred-acre luxury-home development Fishing Creek Farm, where buyers paid up to $600,000 for undeveloped waterfront lots. In 1993, Anne Arundel County passed sweeping changes to zoning regulations that allowed for the construction of larger homes on small lots, including an increase in the percentage of a lot a house can cover from 30 to 40 percent, and a shortening of the distance between a house and the property line to seven feet.[52]

In these racially transitional communities, something as simple as a bookkeeping matter could draw old and new residents' separate understandings of power, the law, and the land into relief. At Oyster Harbor homeowners' association meetings, the African American man who served as treasurer, as Sharon Merrick describes,

> would go through great pains to make sure the records were straight and would . . . make sure everything was in sync with the rules . . . because if you did anything wrong, it could be taken away so easily. A lot of the newcomers were like, "No, you can do this," but . . . the older residents would be like, "No, you *have* to do it this way." Because if you veered away you could be so easily punished, so you have to go with what your experiences are. [We know] you might not be given a second chance if you're late with a payment. It can just be taken away. . . . You haven't experienced somebody coming in and su[ing] you just because they think you're stupid, or they feel like you're passive and therefore they may have an advantage. You haven't experienced that the land may be taken away for no really good reason. . . . Whereas with other people, it'll be, "Okay, catch up or do what you need to do. I'll give you a slap on the hand." You haven't experienced where it's just taken away. You haven't seen that.[53]

It should come as no surprise that shrewd speculators like Little Willie Adams, who had profited from "colored" property in the past, were among the first to detect the new sources of wealth buried in the sands of deteriorating, anachronistic black-owned beach resorts. By the early 1970s, Adams had emerged from the shadows of Baltimore's underworld to become one of the state's largest real estate developers and most powerful political brokers. Always dependable in rounding up the necessary votes from Baltimore's black voting districts on Election Day, Adams enjoyed close ties to Baltimore mayor Thomas D'Alesandro Jr. and governors Spiro Agnew and Marvin Mandel, which he used to, among other things, secure contracts for the construction of federally subsidized housing projects. Along with Theo Rogers, a young black Harvard MBA, Adams founded A&R Development, which they would grow into a multimillion dollar company. During the years when crowds at Carr's Beach dwindled and profits evaporated, Adams steadily accumulated portions of the Carr family's properties and then flexed his political muscle to dictate redevelopment of the entire peninsula. With only Florence Sparrow seemingly resisting Adams's overtures, in March 1971 Anne Arundel County executive Joseph Alton Jr. successfully sued to have 35.51 acres of the Sparrow's Beach site condemned in order to locate the Back Creek sewage treatment plant there. In October 1973 Adams purchased the Carr's Beach site (consisting of 15.83 acres) from Elizabeth Carr's children for $95,850 and turned out the lights on the once-vibrant summer resort.[54]

Following the closing of Carr's Beach, numbers of enterprising African Americans clamored for inclusion in any redevelopment partnership, among them the former head of security at the beach, George Phelps. In 1974 Phelps left the Anne Arundel County Sheriff's Department and founded Phelps Protection Systems Inc., a private security firm that employed many of his former special deputies. From his humble beginnings enforcing order at the beach and at taverns in the city, Phelps expanded his operations to include federal nuclear facilities, military research laboratories, banks, shopping centers, and housing developments in five states, eventually employing over 250 persons and operating a $3 million annual budget. Partnering with a group of black professionals and civic leaders, Phelps founded Investment Dynamics, a black-run, race-conscious development firm focused on acquiring the remainder of the Sparrow's Beach property (which remained under the ownership of Florence Sparrow) and partnering with Adams in the redevelopment of the entire peninsula. As Phelps described, "The plan was to get some money together, regardless of how little it was, to show an interest in the development of that property, since that's the way the winds [were] blowing. . . . Lots of other blacks were talking about [real estate development], but not doing it." Phelps's team drew up plans for a gated community consisting of waterfront condominiums affordable for middle-class families, a place where "policemen, firemen, [and] teachers had a place to live. Everybody—blacks and whites."[55]

Phelps's vision for black economic empowerment belied his comparative lack of capital and connections. In 1975 Adams orchestrated the sale of the remaining property owned by Florence Sparrow, along with the acres owned by the Carr's Beach Amusement Company, to Duck's Run Partnership, a development group headed by Baltimore mega-developer Jerome Parks. For her coveted piece of waterfront property, Sparrow received $290,802. Phelps's Investment Dynamics, much to his bitter disappointment, was not included in the deal. In September 1983 Duck's Run Partnership began work on the Villages of Chesapeake Harbour, a fifty-two-acre, 404-condominium development with a two-hundred-slip marina. Units were priced between $87,000 and $150,000, and all of them enjoyed an unobstructed view of the bay. In place of nightclubs and a rusted pavilion, the gated community provided a swimming pool lined with lounge chairs. A full-time tennis pro was to be on hand to assist residents five days a week, while a resident manager helped to organize committees on various social and recreational activities and events. Through its design and amenities, the development reflected and sought to satisfy middle- and upper-class Americans' retreat from public space and their re-creation of a more narrow and homogeneous definition of "community" behind gated fences. As one promotional newsletter read, "Add these community extras to the natural allure of a private sandy beach and front yard marina, and you'll know why Chesapeake Harbour's residents never have to leave the community to enjoy all the fun of a Maryland summer."[56] Following completion of the Villages of Chesapeake Harbour in 1985, a migration of the privileged to the peninsula began. (See Map 14.)

They came to live by the water and to enjoy its beauty every day from their front porch. But the desire to live amid "nature," which fueled demand for waterfront property, was one of many factors contributing to the ecological crisis facing the bay. In 1984 the state of Maryland passed the Critical Areas Act, which severely restricted development on land within one thousand feet of tidal waters. Jerome Parks praised the act for "help[ing] to] preserve the natural beauty of the Annapolis area which attracted many of our residents in the first place." In practice, the act did little to slow development, but instead narrowed the field of developers to heavily capitalized firms that could afford to navigate through the thicket of regulations. With mounting profits came growing influence over regulatory bodies. Three years after completing Chesapeake Harbour, Parks returned to the Anne Arundel County zoning board seeking a release from Critical Areas Act regulations and other existing zoning laws so that he could build a second condominium development on an adjoining wetlands area. Dubbed Chesapeake Harbour North, the plans called for forty-four town houses to be built less than one hundred feet from the water on a floodplain in front of the existing condos. The Anne Arundel County Office of Planning and Zoning approved the exemption, an indication of the inadequacies of the law. (Into the late 1990s, one report

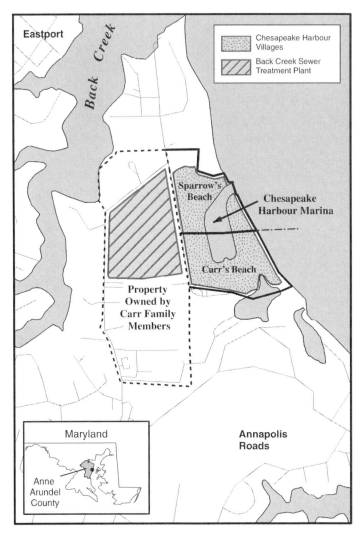

Map 14. Annapolis Neck Peninsula, Anne Arundel County, Maryland, ca. 2010

estimated, the Chesapeake continued to lose an average of eight acres a day to development.) In rendering a decision, officials indicated what aspects of the bay merited protection, expressing little concern with the environmental consequences of development on protected wetlands area, and instead framing the issue of preservation strictly through the lens of aesthetic value. "Existing features which would add value to residential development or natural or man-made assets of the County, such as trees, water courses, falls, beaches, vistas, historic spots," one report on the proposal read, "should be preserved." The rest, seemingly, was expendable. Including the unobstructed views of the bay Parks had promised to residents.[57]

As word of Parks's plans spread, residents of Chesapeake Harbour rose in protest, circulating petitions that criticized the proposal as environmentally unsound and a violation of Parks's verbal assurances "that their view of the water would not be obstructed by future development on this property." Like their counterparts on the planning and zoning board, residents shared a view of nature as an aesthetic asset. Robert and Anne Harbrant called the plan "outrageous! When we purchased our unit . . . as our retirement home we were told our view would never be spoiled." Moreover, residents learned that the sense of mutuality that Parks cultivated was merely another selling point in his quest to extract maximum profits from the land. "I fear I am being taught [that] Annapolis, even the state of Maryland, is not to be trusted," resident Margaret DeAnbough wrote to the planning and zoning board. "I was warned about moving here."[58]

In 2008 a land-development corporation appeared in the New Hanover County Circuit Court seeking to force the sale of the Freeman family's remaining 182 acres of beachfront property. Their move to force the sale of the land against the family's wishes was devious but legally sound. The company possessed shares in the property; as was their right under the law, they could petition to liquidate their assets. For the Freemans, it marked the end of a long, tortured struggle to hold back the entwined forces of nature and man.

Throughout the 1970s and 1980s the process of erosion instigated by the widening of the Carolina Beach inlet and exacerbated by beach replenishment down shore (on land Frank Hill claimed had been stolen by Spinnaker Point LLC) continued to consume the northern tip of the Carolina Beach peninsula at an alarming rate. The relationship between civil engineering decisions, local business and political interests, and her family's loss of land was not lost on New York City attorney Evelyn Williams, the daughter of Frank and Lulu Hill. Having watched her family's land steadily devoured by the sea so as to provide a shortcut for speedboats, in

1982 Williams represented her parents in a federal lawsuit against the Army Corps of Engineers for the damages incurred by the Carolina Beach Inlet. Few lawsuits before had so explicitly sought to demonstrate the relationship between black land loss and the environmental degradation of America's coastlines. In court proceedings, Williams castigated the Army Corps of Engineers for its "single-minded concern with the desires of private pleasure boat owners who have convinced them that easier access to the ocean for their potential customers is more important than the loss of over 100 acres of valuable land or the environmental quality of life." But while the leveling of such charges might land one in the history books, it rarely produces a favorable outcome in court, especially when the adversary is a powerful federal agency. The suit was dismissed on the grounds that the Corps anticipated such levels of erosion from the project's outset.[59] In 1986 the North Carolina State Court of Appeals dismissed Frank Hill's lawsuit against Spinnaker Point LLC over its seizure of Freeman family property without compensation. Local blacks watched these farcical proceedings with a mixture of disgust and resignation. "Of course . . . the white people . . . took what they wanted . . . and Frank Hill . . . never did get anything for it," Mamie Wade of Wilmington later told an oral history interviewer. "Just took it away." "They fought in the courts, but the money's what wins."[60]

Few legal devices better demonstrated this maxim than petitions to partition heirs' property. Beginning in the 1960s the numbers of forced partition sales of heirs' property and, more significantly, the number of sales resulting in outside acquisition rose sharply, with the vast majority of these cases occurring in areas with comparatively large numbers of African American landowners. In contrast to a partition in kind, in which each heir receives clear title to a portion of the land, at forced partition sales the entire property is auctioned to the highest bidder, with the proceeds from the sale (minus court costs and lawyers' fees) being distributed among the shareholders in proportion to their holdings. While most state statutes specify that the division of property among heirs is preferable to a partition sale, the percentage of heirs' property disputes resulting in a forced partition sale grew over the course of the twentieth century to the point where, today, it is ordered almost without exception. In part this trend reflects the fact that, by the 1960s (and even more so today), the multiplying numbers of shareholder interest in a given piece of property increasingly rendered division in kind impractical. But larger trends in property law are at play here, also. By the post–World War II era, courts increasingly rejected the notion that land holds unique values that cannot be measured in dollars and instead treated real property like any other marketable commodity. Under this paradigm, the "best use" of a given piece of property could be measured by the wealth generated from it. As a result, the tangled, antiquated, and precapitalist arrangements developed by heirs' property owners were increasingly viewed by judges as a problem in need of a solution. The forced partition sale thus became the means through which the property could be placed in the hands "of the party that values it most."[61]

For speculators and developers, forced partition sales allowed them to get a "foot in the door" on land previously off-limits. Conversely, for resident co-tenants seeking to retain their land, the partition sale opened the possibility (and in areas experiencing appreciating real estate values, likelihood) of putting them in a bidding war against a person or corporation with far deeper capital reserves. "At these forced sales," wrote one researcher for the Black Economic Research Center, an organization founded by the black economist Robert E. Browne in the late 1960s to stem the tide of black land loss in the South, "it is very rare, in properties that have value to [outside developers], to see blacks as purchasers. The chief benefactors of any laws to ease heir property restrictions would be your large development corporations, your corporate farmers and other land grabbing concerns." In putting desirable land back on the market, partition sales allowed well-connected, opportunistic speculators the chance to acquire it at far below its market value. (According to one estimate, properties acquired at partition sales were, on average, resold within one to two weeks at vastly higher prices.) This was due to the fact that property sold at partition sales was not publicized as extensively as commercial real estate, resulting in sales in which one or more well-connected bidders acquired title to lands at prices just beyond the purchasing power of the families living on the land.[62]

For a prospective developer or savvy, unscrupulous land speculator, the most expeditious way to force a partition sale was to simply buy a share in the property from an heir. Under heirs' property arrangements, any person possessing a share in the land reserves the right to sell that share to a third party, who in turn enjoys the same legal rights (including the right to force a partition sale) as heirs. In areas with high rates of black heirs' property ownership, it was common for predatory lenders to force borrowers to use their shares as collateral and, upon default, to initiate a sale. As the value of heirs' properties (especially those in coastal zones) appreciated, and as the numbers of shareholders multiplied, developers began actively searching for shareholders who could be induced to sell their stake in the land. By the 1970s, large-scale real estate developers and agribusiness increasingly employed a team of gumshoes whose job was to track down and acquire shares in heirs' properties from distant relatives. The price paid for a share was immaterial; acquiring one was the key. For the person charged with locating a compliant relative, the more persons holding claims to the land, the better. As one observer noted, "One-thousand heirs provide 1,000 targets to a person who really wants the land." Often, the persons who sold their share did not even know they possessed it beforehand, had little knowledge of the land's true value, and failed to appreciate the disastrous implications of the transaction for the persons still living on the land. Even if they did, such considerations were often overshadowed by the prospect of a onetime windfall. Indeed, it was no coincidence that "share hunters" targeted the most distant and destitute shareholders. In one particularly egregious, but not uncommon, example, a development firm acquired a seventy-nine-acre tract on Johns Island, South Carolina, through locating "a wino [living] in New York City." As one local observer described, "[the speculative agent] just walked up to him and said, 'I heard you own some property on Johns Island.' The guy thought he was kidding because he had never been to Johns Island. So he started laughing. [The agent] said, 'I'm serious. You get a witness and come with me and I will give you five hundred dollars for what you own.'" The ploy worked. The developer acquired a share in the land, forced a partition sale, and forced the family off the land.[63]

The lawyers who handled cases involving intra-family disputes over heirs' property were often more than passive observers. In most southern states, attorneys received a nonnegotiation fee for partition actions resulting in a sale. As a result, one study found, "Many lawyers do not encourage voluntary resolution of heir title problems because they often view their legal fees as being dependent on the sale of the property." More often, lawyers escalated intra-family disputes, pitting shareholders against each other and encouraging resolution through the courts. Given the dearth of black lawyers who specialized in real estate law in the South—a legacy of the Jim Crow era—black landowners often had little choice but to turn to lawyers who were, more often than not, working in collusion with developers and public officials. The Emergency Land Fund noted that its files were "filled with cases of heirs who, over the strong objections of the families, initiate partition suits to force the sale of the land," a practice, they found, that was "encouraged and frequently initiated by lawyers who wish to fill their coffers with the usual fee of ten percent of the sales price of the land." Similarly, "Judges, acting in concert with lawyers, often pursue a partition sale when a division of the property would be more appropriate, both legally and morally."[64] Ironically, it was the way in which these families had tied themselves to the land—through alternative property ownership arrangements that operated outside of the judiciary—that not only frustrated their attempts to become partners and beneficiaries of the region's booming economy—and thus secure their place in a changing coastal economy—but rendered them acutely vulnerable to an industry whose profits were so tightly bound to the exploitation of others' weaknesses and vulnerabilities.

On August 17, 1969, Hurricane Camille made landfall on the Mississippi Gulf Coast, with sustained winds of 190 miles per hour, to this day the strongest hurricane to strike the North American continent.[65] The storm claimed over 143 lives in Alabama, Mississippi, and Louisiana and inflicted over $1.42 billion in damage to properties and businesses. Camille swept out to sea or damaged beyond repair many of the stately antebellum-era summer homes that lined the coast. It ran roughshod over the cottage villages and quaint commercial districts that drew visitors to the coast each season. At the Gulfside Assembly, "the only word" that one reporter could find "to describe what [he] found there is a word which we have used many times—devastation. . . . Everything on the campus had been damaged or demolished." The storm destroyed twenty-six buildings on the campgrounds, heavily damaged the four that remained standing, and threw the property's future into further doubt.[66]

The Gulf Coast's struggle to recover from Camille was compounded by sharp declines in federal shipbuilding contracts at Biloxi's Ingalls shipyards, the rollback of NASA's budget under the Reagan administration, and increased competition for fisheries from Asian shrimp farms in the 1980s. In Camille's aftermath, economic recovery strategies centered on the exploitation of the region's recreational assets, and development proceeded in defiance of the destructive lessons of the past. "One after another noncompliant permit application was approved as a special exception," Ernest Zebrowski and Judith A. Howard recount, "and soon the improved building code [enacted after Camille] became a paper tiger."[67] The most egregious case took place on the fragile barrier islands that sheltered the Mississippi Sound from the Gulf. In 1980, Florida developer John Stocks purchased Deer Island and managed to acquire land on Petit Bois Island, a federally designated wilderness area that was part of the Gulf Islands National Seashore. At the time Stocks was facing a lawsuit in Florida for bulldozing sand dunes in violation of state environmental regulations. Stocks announced plans to construct four hundred "hurricane proof" condominiums on Deer Island and divide his Petit Bois Island holdings into five-acre lots. Even after the National Park Service filed eminent domain proceedings in 1980 in order to prevent Stocks from developing his Petit Bois Island holdings, he was still able to profit handsomely from the investment. In *United States v. 717.42 Acres of Land* (1980), Federal District Court judge Walter L. Nixon Jr. awarded Stocks $6.2 million in compensation; federal officials wanted to pay $330,000 for the land. The ruling prompted a grand jury investigation on possible bribery charges, which eventually led to Nixon's impeachment by the House of Representatives and removal from the bench by the U.S. Senate in 1986. His judgment in the case involving compensation for Stocks's Petit Bois Island lands was, however, upheld.[68]

Though scuttled, Stocks's reckless attempt to build on barrier islands with a long history of swallowing coastal capitalists' dreams—and the eagerness with which his plans were greeted by local officials—was a revealing sign of things to come. The Gulf Coast's dire straits in the decades following Camille was music to the ears of the casino gambling industry, which was in the early stages of deploying an unscrupulous but highly effective strategy of preying on the most economically destitute regions of the country for market expansion. Beginning in the late 1980s, as the effects of Reagan-era federal budget cuts trickled down to state governments, and as low taxes and fiscal austerity became a form of civic religion, state legislatures embraced, Robert Goodman argues, casinos as "magic bullets for dying economies. They had become the economic development strategies of last resort." On March 15, 1990, the Mississippi state legislature passed the Gaming Control Act, making the state the fifth in the nation to legalize casino gambling, and the first in the South.

The legislation legalized casino gambling in the fourteen counties along the Mississippi River and the Gulf Coast and required all casinos to operate on the water. The provision appeased the state's hidebound interior by ensuring that the industry remained confined to its margins, the most economically depressed counties (and, not coincidentally, those with a history of tolerance toward vice), and cloaked an otherwise unsavory industry in the romance and lore of the age of riverboats. As gambling industry officials understood, the more desperate the state, the more lax the regulations. Mississippi adopted some of the most industry-friendly regulations in the nation, placing no restrictions on the number of casino licenses (and charging only a nominal licensing fee), putting no limits on the amounts of wagers, losses, or days in a row a person could gamble, and taxing the industry at half the rate of other states. In 1992 the first casino "barge" opened in Bay St. Louis. Down the shore, Biloxi became home to a string of casinos that dominated the city's waterfront and, as *Rolling Stone* writer and Biloxi native Matt Taibbi later commented, became "a showcase city for a new . . . ethos of vice-funded political power in an era of vanishing manufacturing reserves." By 2004, twenty-nine vessels were tied to piers on the shore, employing twenty-nine thousand people in mostly low-wage jobs, generating $330 million in state tax revenue, accounting for 10 percent of the state budget, and further tying coastal ecological management (and environmental policy) to the exigencies of regional economic growth.[69]

Following the arrival of casinos on the Mississippi Gulf Coast, pressure on members of the Gulfside Association to sell the land intensified, and tactics to force its placement on the open market became more devious. One administrator reported receiving incessant calls from anonymous persons desiring a room for the evening. (Were Gulfside to operate its dormitories as a hotel available to the general public, and not strictly for group reservations, it risked losing its nonprofit status and experiencing a sharp spike in taxes, which developers well knew it could not hope to meet.) As they had throughout its existence, Gulfside's community leaders once again became schooled in the black arts of real estate speculation as a means of preserving a spiritual mission forged in struggle and sacrifice.

Seeking to secure a sense of permanency after years of decline and uncertainty, beginning in the early 2000s director Marion Martin campaigned and raised funds for the construction of a retirement community

on the grounds. The plans drew the ire of some coastal residents, who reportedly circulated petitions and appeared before planning and zoning
meetings decrying the traffic, disruption, and decline in property values the
retirement village would supposedly bring. "But Marion Martin wouldn't
give up on Gulfside," Gulfside member Ed Moultrie describes. "She went
on a crusade to have this retirement center built right on the front property, looking out on the Gulf." Along with the construction of the Ernest
T. Dixon retirement village, Gulfside launched a ten-year, $17 million capi-
tal campaign titled "Moving Forward," with a goal to become debt free
and self supporting, to establish a Head Start program, a writers' colony,
and a mission training institute, and to establish an archive and museum.
The fruits of these efforts were on display on August 15, 2005, when members gathered to dedicate the opening of Norris Hall and the achievement
of another milestone in Gulfside's program for permanency. "When we
built that," Moultrie said, his tone of voice capturing the tragic irony of
his words, "I think it finally opened the eyes to the community that Gulfside [was] here to stay." Nine days later, meteorologists upgraded a tropical
depression spotted over the Bahamas to tropical storm status, and gave it
the name Katrina.[70]

While Gulfside's members worked to protect their property from expropriation and incorporation into the Gulf Coast's leisure-based economy,
poorer communities in economically stagnant and environmentally hazardous coastal zones were fighting to be included in the bonanza of
corporate coastal development sweeping the South. Beginning in the
1980s, residents of the low-income neighborhoods along the eastern portion of Lake Pontchartrain's southern shore worked to drum up support
for the redevelopment of Lincoln Beach as a corporate-financed pleasure
zone. By the 1990s and early 2000s interest in Lincoln Beach's historical
significance grew—fueled in no small measure by those directly interested
and invested in its redevelopment—and calls to redevelop the site took on
a grassroots quality. Proponents of Lincoln Beach's redevelopment called
on city officials to recognize and capitalize on the site's "unique heritage
as a segregated amusement park." Proposals included plans for a museum
housing Lincoln Beach memorabilia as well as "interpretive murals, sculp-
tural representations, tile mosaics, entertainment stage and interactive
fountains to capture the excitement of the former amusement park." "When
we started learning about [the site and its history]," local activist Mary
Croom Fontenot described, "we realized this place is a jewel, it's just been

neglected. And so we decided, we not only want to clean it up and remove the threat of crime, we want to redevelop it . . . [and] restore it to its heyday."[71]

More to the point, proponents of Lincoln Beach's commercial redevelopment wanted, as one black New Orleanian described, "equity in the development of the lakefront," and a greater role in shaping the city's emergent leisure- and entertainment-based industries.[72] As with contemporaneous efforts to institutionalize, as the sociologist Michelle Boyd put it, "nostalgic vision[s] of black identity . . . in urban development policy and politics," proponents of Lincoln Beach's redevelopment sought to highlight its historic status—in a city where celebrations of cultural diversity and black culture had become firmly ingrained in the local tourism economy—as a means of channeling economic growth into black districts.[73] In New Orleans, nostalgia for Lincoln Beach grew in relation to the deterioration of the city's industrial base. In the mid-1980s a sharp drop in oil prices left southern Louisiana's petrochemical industry reeling. Industry insiders referred to the Gulf of Mexico as "the Dead Sea." Workers in petroleum industries suffered waves of downsizing, bankruptcies, and layoffs. The oil bust sent New Orleans's unemployment rate skyrocketing above 13 percent, and came on the heels of a decade of steady deindustrialization and decline in cargo transportation through the city's port.[74] When the dust settled, the city was more dependent on its leisure, tourism, and convention trades than ever, on the manufacturing of an image of cultural exoticism, racial amalgamation, and social permissiveness, and on cheap labor.

The return of Lincoln Beach—located as it was far from the French Quarter, in a section of New Orleans virtually uninhabited prior to the 1950s—did not, to say the least, generate much enthusiasm from public officials, capital developers, or historical preservationists. The promise of redeveloping the site at some indeterminate point in the future did, however, prove an effective political bargaining chip. In 1998 the levee board announced plans to devote $1.5 million toward the restoration of Lincoln Beach. In addition to the funds from the levee board, the federal Environmental Protection Agency agreed to earmark $2 million toward the restoration of wetlands and sea grass on the property. In announcing the decision, U.S. attorney Eddie Jordan proudly noted, "This agreement will enable our community to reclaim Lincoln Beach and transform a section of the lake, which once carried the stigma of racial discrimination, into a safer and cleaner natural resource which all members of our community can enjoy." The announcement, however, was later revealed to be no more than a ruse designed to compel the federal government to reduce a $29 million fine against the New Orleans Sewage and Water Board to $1.5 million. Once the levee board secured a favorable decision in that separate case, it rescinded its funding commitment to clean and restore the beach, claiming ownership of the property had effectively reverted to the city because of unpaid back taxes, thus making the levee board's efforts to fund development of the site unconstitutional—and in any case, the board added, the project did not serve the board's primary duty of flood protection.

The legal technicality was dubious at best; the claim that the levee board served only to protect Louisiana citizens from floods was an affront to the historical record. Following the decision, Linda Reed of the activist organization All Congregations Together (ACT) castigated the board for its disregard for "those citizens of New Orleans who are perceived as not white enough or wealthy enough to be of note" and reminded them, "Previous Levee Boards have spent our money like drunken sailors. Where have they spent it? They have spent it on the west end of Lake Pontchartrain . . . on sidewalks, fountains, statuary bridges to nowhere, etc. None of which is flood-control related." "We're not asking for anything extravagant," Reed told the board. "We just want the property to be made safe and usable, because right now it's a public nuisance and a blight on the community." New Orleans East councilwoman Ellen Hazeur-Distance added that her constituents sought little more than a levee board "accountable to all of the taxpayers that support it, not just a particular group," and, to that end, demanded proactive measures to redress a racial and class imbalance along the lakefront that was decades in the making. "If you look at the history of the Levee Board, when you look at the east end of the lake versus the west end, it's easy to see where most of its resources have gone."[75]

For those who lived through Hurricane Katrina, it was easy to see where the resources would go after the floodwaters subsided. Standing in front of the remains of his church in New Orleans's Lower Ninth Ward weeks after the storm, the Reverend Willie Walker warned, "They're going to take it all. They're going to bring in the developers, and this neighborhood is going to be gone." In his dire predictions, Walker was far from alone. As a black child of homeowners in the Lower Ninth Ward, Mary Croom Fontenot remembers hearing her elders say, "If they ever get a chance to take this city back, they'll flood it." So, "when the levees broke, everybody knew they were coming for the land." Following the storm, conservative think tanks such as the Heritage Foundation eagerly awaited the "opportunity" to apply what Naomi Klein calls the "shock doctrine" to the crippled city and rebuild it on a free-market model. While it dithered on rescue and relief efforts as thousands lay dead and dying, the Bush administration moved quickly to implement a plan of disaster capitalism, designating the battered region as the "Gulf Opportunity Zone" and suspending labor rights for relief workers. Vultures soon encircled the city in search of big and small ways to profit from disaster. The breathtaking dysfunction of federal, state, and local recovery agencies was matched only by shocking levels of corruption. That some politicians spoke openly of the storm as an opportunity to build a new, smaller, and implicitly richer and whiter New Orleans, only confirmed existing fears and suspicions of a "plan" of black removal, as did the geography of action and inaction in the region's post-storm redevelopment.[76]

In New Orleans, the abandoned shores of Lincoln Beach have come to symbolize the contours of the struggle to rebuild the city on a more just and equitable model. Following Hurricane Katrina, Nolatown Development Group, a black-owned and race-conscious development firm, introduced plans (and purported to possess the financing) for a massive, $300 million project on the site that included a forty-story, four-hundred-unit condominium complex, a casino, and a three-thousand-seat amphitheater. As of 2010, ACT and other grassroots organizations continue to pressure a highly skeptical city hall to endorse the proposal.[77]

Before reaching the coast, Katrina had veered east, sparing New Orleans a direct hit. In the initial aftermath, commentators and meteorologists exclaimed that the Crescent City had been spared the Big One once again. But in Waveland, Mississippi, where the eye of the storm met the coast, there were no momentary sighs of relief. The storm obliterated the small town and, with a single, thirty-two-foot storm surge on the morning of August 29, claimed the lives of fifty of its citizens. When the skies cleared, only a single oak tree at Gulfside's entrance remained standing.[78]

The state's gambling industry and its political allies quickly turned disaster into an opportunity. Following the storm, state and local officials in Mississippi worked to channel federal funds and subsidies toward rebuilding Gulf Coast casinos and away from small businesses and low-income homeowners, and rewrote laws that augmented the industry's presence on and influence over the coastal economy. Weeks after the storm, the Mississippi state legislature called a special session and passed a bill that waived the requirement for casinos to be anchored on the water and instead allowed for construction farther inland. Meanwhile, Governor Haley Barbour successfully lobbied the U.S. Congress to strip a provision from a recovery bill that specified that 50 percent of the funds for Community Development Block Grants be granted to low-income people. Such moves were indicative of a broader strategy to remake the coast through rolling out a red carpet for commercial developers while constructing innumerable obstacles for poor homeowners to return. In the mostly poor, low-lying, but highly coveted East Biloxi, located hundreds of yards from the Gulf Coast, displaced homeowners returned home to find pink flyers strewn throughout the neighborhood that read: "IF YOU OWN LAND IN EAST BILOXI AND WOULD LIKE TO SELL YOUR LAND TO A CASINO/DEVELOPER CALL (228) 239-__ " Given that new flood maps required East Biloxi homeowners—by virtue of their low-lying status—to construct new homes on eighteen-foot-high stilts at an average additional cost of $30,000, few saw any other option than to sell.[79]

Less than a year after the storm, the Silver Slipper, located a few miles down the shore from Gulfside, opened its doors. The swift return of this and other casinos seemed a harbinger of a new dawn. "God has come in and wiped the slate clean for us," Gulfport mayor Brent Warr exclaimed. "We have an opportunity now to make it an absolutely unique place." Indeed, a year after the storm, the *Wall Street Journal* concluded that Katrina "was a boon to . . . casinos, washing away old limits that had restrained their growth." To that end, the Army Corps of Engineers resumed what coastal geologists Robert S. Young and Orrin H. Pilkey called its "quixotic fight" to tame this unstable shore, proposing in October 2006 to construct a massive seawall along parts of the coast along with storm-surge gates, and to dump over fifty million cubic yards of sand on the barrier islands offshore (thereby threatening the islands' wilderness habitats) so as to protect coastal development. Coastal geologists roundly denounced the plan as wasteful, environmentally reckless, and futile.[80]

The state's reliance on its beaches as a source of revenue, and the environmentally disastrous policies that grew out of this marriage, were again on display in the summer of 2010. In the aftermath of the *Deepwater Horizon* well explosion on April 20, 2010, as oil continued to pour into the Gulf's waters, President Barack Obama addressed the nation on the crisis. Among his first words were directed to vacationing Americans: "Except for three beaches in Louisiana, all of the Gulf's beaches are open. They are safe and they are clean." Others were quick to echo these sentiments. "Come down and rent a condo, stay in a hotel, play golf," Alabama's governor Bob Riley urged Americans. While political leaders struggled to keep the engine of coastal capitalism running, British Petroleum (BP) was busy dumping chemical dispersants into the Gulf so as to minimize unfavorable surface appearances—to, in effect, keep the oil out of sight and, hopefully, out of mind, regardless of its potentially catastrophic effects on underwater species. That August, with the well capped, the Obama family traveled to the Florida Panhandle to vacation and, more importantly, swim in the Gulf. Back at the White House, his administration issued a highly questionable report stating that 75 percent of the oil released by the broken well "had been captured, burned off, evaporated, or broken down in the Gulf."[81] It will be decades before scientists are able to fully assess the long-term effects of the oil spill itself and the consequences on marine environments.

A disaster that grew out of humans' dependence on fossil fuels was due in large measure to the evisceration of regulatory agencies in the federal government, and was made worse—ecologically—by decisions made with coastal vacationers in mind. The Gulf oil spill of 2010 and its effects on the people of the Gulf Coast and the marine species of the Gulf and its environs offered a fitting testament to the exploitative, contradictory, but fundamental place bodies of water played in the making of the Sunbelt—and modern America.

EPILOGUE

Adolph "A. D." Brown came to Hilton Head Island, South Carolina, in 2006 with big plans. An aspiring real estate developer born and raised in New York City by a mother who had journeyed north from Hilton Head as part of the Great Migration, Brown was the living embodiment of the fruits of the black freedom struggle in the twentieth century. Like many families of the southern diaspora, the Browns maintained ties with their relatives back down south and others scattered in cities across the nation, ties that were bound to and inseparable from a parcel of twenty acres that Matthew and Teena Jones, the children of former slaves, purchased on Hilton Head for $225 in the 1880s. As was so common among black landowners at the time, Matthew Jones neglected (or consciously chose not) to leave a will, and, upon his death, his direct descendants became tenants-in-common of heirs' property.

In the extent of black-owned land lost to forced partition sales, and in the sheer mendacity and duplicity of speculators, lawyers, and developers engaged in the liquidation of heirs' properties, few regions of the coastal South could rival the South Carolina Sea Islands.[1] Real estate values along the coast escalated sharply in the years after visionary developer Charles S. Fraser carved the Sea Pines Plantation out of the forests of Hilton Head Island in the 1950s, which along with the state-funded construction of a bridge to the island turned this and other formerly remote and forsaken islands into one of America's preeminent vacation destinations, and unleashed a flood of speculation and predation.[2] On these islands would-be developers encountered African American families like the descendants of Matthew and Teena Jones, whose ties to the land extended back to the dawn of freedom and for whom possession of land had come to shape and reflect the very meaning of freedom. As developers descended onto the Sea Islands, within black landholding families conflicting views of land-as-community versus land-as-commodity, which had long been a source of tension, negotiation, and conflict, grew more heated as the resolution of these disputes became more tied to regional development.[3]

In the coastal Sunbelt South, competing claims to and uses of family property were conducted against the backdrop of a public-private growth machine dedicated to the manufacturing of a landscape aesthetic conducive to high-value real estate development and, conversely, the elimination of all nonprofitable (and unattractive) uses of land. Small black landowners, whose ability to remain self-sufficient deteriorated in relation to coastal land development, whose lands were caught in the trap of heirs' property, and whose disputes with family members multiplied with each generation and often in relation to the appreciating value of the land in their possession, became, by virtue of these changes in the coastal political economy, both a market liability (marring, in local politicians' and boosters' eyes, otherwise beautiful seascapes with clusters of mobile homes) and, for unscrupulous developers, a potentially lucrative opportunity. Heirs' property disputes that were initiated by a disgruntled family member or an indifferent distant relative who sold his or her share for a song facilitated the movement of high-value land onto the market (and poor people off the island), while providing highly capitalized investors the opportunity to acquire, for pennies on the dollar, parcels of land worth millions on the open market. Forced partition sales of heirs' properties constituted one of the primary mechanisms for land acquisition and redevelopment on Hilton Head and neighboring islands. As family properties became high-end hotels, private gated resorts, and golf courses, and savvy speculators and developers became millionaires, low-country blacks steadily became landless and dependent on the paltry wages of a service-oriented economy.[4] By the early 2000s, several legal aid organizations had formed and worked to educate heirs' property owners of their rights and responsibilities under the law, warn them of the various schemes developers used to fleece them of their wealth in land, encourage them to leave wills, and lobby the state legislature to pass laws designed to curb the exploitative excesses of the coastal real estate industry.[5]

But while legal nonprofits sought to protect, A. D. Brown promised to empower at-risk black coastal landowners, and awaken holders of shares in heirs' properties to the riches slumbering under their feet. After learning of his parents' possession of heirs' property shares in the Matthew and Teena Jones tract, advantageously situated along a section of the William Hilton Parkway that all motorists passed as they drove onto the island,

Brown, along with Charleston attorney Horace Jones, tracked down all 180 persons holding a share in the property and proposed that they clear title to the land and together form a limited liability company (LLC) with the purpose of building a twenty-six-unit condominium complex on the property. The project, Brown told shareholders, would generate an expected $16 million in annual revenue and make the descendants of Matthew and Teena Jones, including the roughly twenty-four descendants who lived and paid taxes on the land, fabulously wealthy.

Brown showered the heirs with hope and fear. He claimed to have secured a commitment of $14 million in financing from a bank for the project on the condition that he clear title to the property. To the families living on the land, he told them that, whereas under an heirs' property arrangement it only took one rogue heir to initiate a partition sale that would inevitably lead to their displacement, by forming an LLC no single shareholder could force them off the land. And he issued vague warnings of the city's intentions to claim the land via eminent domain unless they took proactive steps toward its development. It was now or never, he told distant relatives. Either grab the reins of the rapidly changing coastal economy or be trampled underfoot. "People have to understand that the world has changed, and it is no longer acceptable for them to do nothing."[6]

Despite sunny (and highly marketable) descriptions of black Sea Islanders' primitive culture and its direct links to West African traditions, African Americans' distance from the region's coastal capitalist economy was less the product of their own indifference and more the result of decades of calculated measures designed to stymie independent land development initiatives and ensure the susceptibility of black-owned lands to expropriation. As one researcher who studied African American land tenure and coastal development in the region described, "The maximization of economic profits for developers in the Lowcountry depends on the black community remaining uneducated about the economics of real estate [and] without adequate resources to clear property titles."[7] By the time Brown arrived, many native Sea Islanders had no doubt grown disillusioned after decades of witnessing failed attempts by others to grab a portion of the riches that snaked through the islands and out to the sea. Black coastal landowners' attempts to profit from the rise of vacationing and leisure economies on the Sea Islands emerged simultaneously with the more-celebrated story of Fraser's conquest of Hilton Head, as families owning beachfront properties opened seasonal enterprises of their own that catered to black families and groups from Charleston and Savannah.[8] In the 1950s and 1960s, Bradley Beach, Singleton Beach, and Burke's Beach, all located on Hilton Head Island and all owned by black families, welcomed excursion parties from Savannah, Georgia, on summer weekends, spawned numerous seasonal businesses, and became another stop for black musicians on the Atlantic coast's "chitlin circuit." Their heyday was not unlike those of many of the places visited in the preceding chapters.

As was their demise. Today, you will still finds signs pointing the way toward Singleton and Burke's Beach. But you won't find any Singletons or Burkes there. Instead, you will find a private, gated condominium development containing "some of the most luxurious homes on Hilton Head Island." For the wealthy vacationing couple or family, Singleton and Burke's Beach offers the "most elegant and comfortable accommodations on the island," including poolside patios, a private walkway down to the beach, and multiple master suites in each unit.[9]

Like many other African Americans sitting on valuable beachfront property, black Sea Islanders did not so much resist the rise of mass commercial and residential development in the 1960s and 1970s as seek to become partners and players in their own right. On Johns Island, native islanders responded to what one visiting observer described as a "conspiracy on the part of rich whites and municipal authorities to drive the blacks from the area and to convert this into a white tourist resort" by attempting to exploit the island's "golden beaches, lush vegetation, wildlife, meandering creeks and equable climate" to their own advantage. Working with nascent organizations dedicated to stemming the tide of black land loss in the South, beachfront landowners attempted, unsuccessfully, to raise the necessary capital to open their own hotels, restaurants, and condominium complexes, and to capture a portion of the region's sudden (and decidedly concentrated) prosperity.[10] The competition from deep-pocketed developers was, quite simply, too overwhelming, and the cash being dangled before them by real estate speculators often too much to resist—even though it was often a small fraction of the land's actual value. Along with the more familiar forms of predatory land speculation, those years also saw the introduction of increasingly deceptive strategies by developers to liquidate heirs' properties, which until then had been generally avoided by developers who lacked the patience to wade through the hundreds, sometimes thousands, of claims on the land, and who generally encountered fierce, coordinated opposition from those families living on the land. Instead of confrontation, coastal capitalists tried deception. Promising to liberate families from the burden of heirs' properties and equipping them with the tools to become partners in the island's booming economy, lawyers descended on black Sea Island communities and offered to assist heirs' property owners in clearing title to their land. In theory, clearing title would allow them to secure credit and realize their own dreams of development, but in actuality, it placed the land on the auction block where a deep-pocketed developer could easily outbid the previous owners. Such a tactic was first implemented in the mid 1970s, when Sea Pines Plantation Company established the notorious Land Title Clearance Program, which hosted clinics and informational sessions for heirs' property owners and was later denounced by the head of the local chapter of the NAACP as "a scheme to get black property in the disguise of help."[11]

As real estate values continued to escalate, growing numbers of enterprising African Americans descended on heirs' property owners looking to offer their "help" and using their racial credentials win the confidence of skeptical landowners. In 2002 the Space Company, which advertised itself as "Charleston's only full service, African-American real estate company," collaborated with the development firm Landmark Properties and Ben Smith, the nephew of Roges Brown (who occupied twenty-three acres of heirs' property on an enviable stretch of shore), to force a partition sale of Brown's land in 2002. The land was assessed at nearly $2 million; Smith successfully bid on the property at auction for $500,000, of which Brown received a little over $3,000, barely enough to cover his legal expenses. The following year, Smith sold the property to a North Carolina development firm for over $1 million, with Space Company brokering the deal. With his windfall, Smith purchased a home on the coast, at Hope Plantation, one of the numerous gated communities with golfing and waterfront properties.[12]

To many observers who had watched with alarm the shocking decline of black landownership in the coastal South over the previous decades, A. D. Brown's plan to convert heirs' properties into an LLC—and small landholders into shareholders—was nothing short of brilliant. A staff writer for the Associated Press, which had conducted a groundbreaking investigation in 2001 on black land loss in the South titled "Torn from the Land," penned a glowing piece on Brown's attempt to preserve his family's lands and "reap millions" in the process.[13] The heirs who actually lived on the land were more familiar with the long, sordid history of duplicitous black coastal capitalists, working independently or in collaboration, and wielding their racial bona fides as a tool of personal profit to dispossess small black landholders of highly valued coastal property—and more skeptical. Inside their mobile homes (ubiquitous on heirs' properties due to the inability of shareholders to obtain financing for home construction), they recounted numerous stories of total strangers appearing in court claiming to hold shares to their land and successfully petitioning for partition; of distant relatives from "up north" who came back home promising to deliver families from poverty only to leave them landless and penniless; of supposed good-Samaritan lawyers and policymakers whose strategies for untangling the mess of heirs' properties turned out to be little more than another, more sophisticated, predatory scheme; and of a honest black lawyer murdered, many said, for refusing to do a northern developer's bidding.[14] Fear and distrust of fellow family members (especially those living in distant cities) were pervasive.[15]

Nevertheless, Brown's hard-sell tactics succeeded in convincing all 180 heirs (including the 24 who lived on the land) to form the Matthew and Teena Jones LLC in 2004. Brown appointed himself the company's president. He simultaneously founded Gateway Development LLC, a firm dedicated to turning minority-owned land from a liability to an asset and, as stated in its charter, "dreams into reality." He leased an office in the Sea Pines Plantation alongside the area's largest development firms. But as the coastal real estate market crashed along with the global economy in 2007 and 2008, any dreams of collective empowerment through real estate development shared by the extended Jones family quickly vanished, and a power struggle between two vastly unequal factions ensued. After financing for the condominium project (if it existed in the first place) evaporated, Brown proposed to the shareholders spread across the country the sale of the property and liquidation of shares. The proposed buyer was the city of Hilton Head, which offered Jones LLC $4 million for the twenty-acre tract with the intention of simply clearing the unsightly mobile homes from the highly visible property and "preserving" it as open space. The city's offer did not come without reservation. After feeling the sting (if ever so slight) of bad publicity over the wholesale removal of black families from the island (without fair compensation) over the past several decades, city officials were hesitant to enter into an agreement that would lead to another instance of poor blacks being forcibly removed from their homes. Brown assured city officials that all the family members supported the sale, and that those still living on the land were, as one of them described, "squatters." Despite his professed desire to keep the land in the family, Brown was not in violation of the legal contract that bound the family together. Indeed, Brown was correct in saying to the families living on the land that no *one* heir could force their removal; he did not, however, bother to add that a majority of the heirs could vote to have the land sold and them removed. The decision to sell was overwhelmingly approved by the shareholders, most of whose investment in the family property was strictly financial. In a cruelly ironic fulfillment of longtime Hilton Head Islander Emory Campbell's prophecy that black coastal landowners, as an "endangered species," would eventually become extinct, the city used funds dedicated to land preservation to purchase the property.

In the spring of 2011, the city began the process of forcibly removing the twenty-four persons living on the land. For sacrificing their homes so that vacationers could enjoy uncluttered views of marshlands as they journeyed toward their destination, and so that distant relatives could finally make some money off their inheritance, the families living on the Matthew and Teena Jones property received roughly $34,000 each. (Meanwhile, some of the larger shareholders' onetime capital gains were in the six figures.) With the gentrification of the coast nearly complete, $34,000 afforded displaced residents few options for relocation. "I have no idea where I'm going to go," Chante Ellison told a reporter. "Can't afford to move my mobile home, can't afford to buy a home." "We're out here naked! We have nowhere to go! No one came to our rescue. Nobody!" Thelma Byas cried to me over the phone just as this book went to press. "We've been had, we've been stepped on, we've been walked all over. Like a stampede."[16] "The cousin [Brown] who had the great idea," relative and displaced landholder Gloria Simmons Murray commented sarcastically, "he saw he could make a bulk of money and he is making a bunch of money [but] nobody else is getting any money." For the families torn from the land, and pushed from the beach, the future is bleak.

Despite what some might characterize as a shameful act of betrayal, Brown was unapologetic. "Change is hard because of its uncertainty, but change is a must and it's inevitable." Having inadvertently introduced and later voted to approve the measure on the belief that all family members were in agreement, Bill Ferguson, Hilton Head's lone black councilman, tried to represent his constituents (and save face) by leveling charges of racism against the city. Indeed, the source of the city's interest in the property seemed apparent to the displaced families. "They [Hilton Head] don't want us there," Byas told me, "because it's an eyesore for people coming onto the island." But town manager Steve Riley was quick to respond to critics: "We did not go to them, they came to us." Brown confirmed the city's account, and added, "This has nothing to do with race."[17]

In a narrow sense, it never has. The capacity to convert others' vulnerabilities into gain, while instrumental in the production of racial inequality, can operate as effectively and as ruthlessly in the absence of any personal malice or prejudice, no more so than today, in our supposedly "color-blind" society. For better or worse, persons like Adolph Brown are not so much race traitors as inheritors of a distinctly black capitalist imagination, one that grew out of the same conditions that inspired more-democratic and egalitarian understandings of land and property, and which has proved no less influential in shaping and frustrating the long struggle of persons of color in America for freedom from oppression and exploitation. Indeed, the strength and resiliency of racism is derived, in part, from its capacity not merely to turn targets of past exploitation into agents in its reproduction but also, almost if by necessity, to turn fellow victims into future targets. Like the futile but nevertheless unending quest to engineer shorelines to suit human needs, the profound—and, for most, disastrous—effects of modern coastal capitalism on African American landholders and coastal communities alert us to the coercive and manipulative measures that went into the making of that moment when a vacationer dips his or her toes in the water, or a family closes on a vacation home by the sea.

The fact that African American beaches and coastal landownership grew in number and extent in the decades today referred to as Jim Crow, and have steadily eroded in the half-century since, should be, this book argues, less a matter of historical inquiry and contemporary concern than the *manner* in which black coastal landownership disintegrated and *how* such lands became incorporated into modern coastal economies. Indeed, the desegregation of beaches, the de-racialization of coastal real estate markets, and the closing of those stretches of shore that provided black Americans shelter from a century-long storm is a story of progress, albeit a bittersweet one for some. The hubristic dreams of pleasure and prosperity that fueled ecologically devastating efforts to stabilize fragile and mobile shorelines, and the forces that led to the demise of black coastal landownership and contributed to the corporate consolidation and privatization of

America's shores, in contrast, force us to confront a more troubling set of issues, and complicate more-comforting narratives of America's long—but supposedly inevitable—journey toward equality. Fundamentally, the human and natural histories of America's shores remind us that the making of a more sustainable planet is inseparable from the making of a more just, equitable, and democratic society. Perhaps fittingly, that work begins at a place where we go to forget about the problems of the world and to wash our troubles away: the beach.

NOTES

PRIMARY SOURCES

ACKNOWLEDGMENTS

INDEX

NOTES

Abbreviations Used in Notes

AACS   *Anne Arundel County Sun*

AC   *Annapolis Capital*

ADW   *Atlanta Daily World*

AN   *New York Amsterdam News*

BAA   *Baltimore Afro-American*

BaS   *Baltimore Sun*

BERC/NYPL   Black Economic Research Center. Records. Schomburg Center for Research in Black Culture. Manuscripts and Archives. New York Public Library.

BTV/RBMSC/DU   Behind the Veil Collection. Rare Book, Manuscript, and Special Collection Library. Duke University, Durham, NC.

CA   *Washington (D.C.) Colored American*

CCP   *Charleston (S.C.) City Paper*

CD   *Chicago Defender*

CHW/HU   Charles H. Williams Papers (unprocessed). University Archives. Hampton University Museum. Hampton University.

CPC   *Charleston (S.C.) Post and Courier*

CSM   *Christian Science Monitor*

CT   *Chicago Tribune*

DCCA/DCPL   Artificial Collection of Rare Items for District of Columbia History, ca. 1791–1990. DC Community Archives, Washingtoniana Division. District of Columbia Public Library, Washington, DC.

DCOVAP/ODU   Dudley Cooper and Ocean View Amusement Park. Papers. Special Collections. Perry Library. Old Dominion University, Norfolk, VA.

DMC/NOPL   DeLesseps S. Morrison Collection. Louisiana Division, City Archives and Special Collections. New Orleans Public Library.

EFF/MSRC	E. Franklin Frazier Papers. Moorland-Spingarn Research Center. Howard University, Washington, DC.
FST/ARC	Free Southern Theater. Papers. Amistad Research Center. Tulane University, New Orleans.
GAS/NYPL	Gulfside Association Scrapbook. Schomburg Center, Manuscripts and Archives. New York Public Library.
GTS/NCSA	Terry Sanford, Governor's Papers, 1959–65. North Carolina State Archives, Raleigh.
HNL/TU	Howard Newton Lee Papers. Howard-Tilton Library. Tulane University, New Orleans.
JRFA/FU	Julius Rosenwald Fund Archives. Special Collections and Archives. Franklin Library. Fisk University, Nashville, TN.
KHP/TU	Kingsley House. Papers. Special Collections. Jones Hall Library. Tulane University, New Orleans.
LBVF/NOPL	Lincoln Beach Vertical File. Louisiana Division, City Archives and Special Collections. New Orleans Public Library.
LDR/MDAH	Land Deed Records. Mississippi Department of Archives and History, Jackson, MS.
LW	*Louisiana Weekly*
MBCC/ARC	Mosquito Beach Community Collection, 1953–1990. Archives, Avery Research Center for African American History and Culture. College of Charleston, Charleston, SC.
MCC/UNO	Marcus Christian Collection. Louisiana and Special Collections. Earl K. Long Library. University of New Orleans.
MCTP/LOC	Mary Church Terrell Papers. Manuscripts Division. Library of Congress.
MM/NOPL	Mayor Marc Morial, Records. Louisiana Division, City Archives and Special Collections. New Orleans Public Library.
MOHP/USM	Mississippi Oral History Project. Center for Oral History and Cultural Heritage. University of Southern Mississippi, Hattiesburg.
MPDDC/NA	Metropolitan Police Department of the District of Columbia. Records. National Archives, Washington, DC.
NAACP/UNO	NAACP–New Orleans Branch. Louisiana and Special Collections. Earl K. Long Library. University of New Orleans.
NJG	*Norfolk Journal and Guide*
NLD	*Norfolk Ledger-Dispatch*

NOAC/UNO	New Orleans Association of Commerce. Records. Louisiana and Special Collections. Earl K. Long Library. University of New Orleans.
NOBC/NOPL	New Orleans Building Corporation. Records, 2000–. Louisiana Division, City Archives and Special Collections. New Orleans Public Library.
NOPD/NOPL	New Orleans Police Department. Clippings, 1944–46. Louisiana Division, City Archives and Special Collections. New Orleans Public Library.
NOTP	*New Orleans Times-Picayune*
NVP	*Norfolk Virginian-Pilot*
NYT	*New York Times*
PBVF/NOPL	Pontchartrain Beach Vertical File. Louisiana Division, City Archives and Special Collections. New Orleans Public Library.
PC	*Pittsburgh Courier*
PGCHS	Prince George's County Historical Society. Archives. Glenn Dale, MD.
PSR/NOPL	Paul Sens, Records. Louisiana Division, City Archives and Special Collections. New Orleans Public Library.
PT	*Philadelphia Tribune*
REJ/ARC	Robert Elijah Jones Papers, 1872–1965. Amistad Research Center. Tulane University, New Orleans.
RJD/UNO	Robert J. Drueding Collection. Louisiana and Special Collections. Earl K. Long Library. University of New Orleans.
SCE	*Bay St. Louis (MS) Sea Coast Echo*
SOHP/SHC	Southern Oral History Program. Southern Historical Collection. Wilson Library, University of North Carolina, Chapel Hill.
SSC/SHC	Sallie S. Cotten Papers. Southern Historical Collection. Wilson Library. University of North Carolina, Chapel Hill.
SWCA	*Christian Advocate, Southwestern Edition*
UMCA/GCAH	United Methodist Church Archives. General Commission on Archives and History, Madison, NJ.
VHS/NOPL	Victor Hugo Schiro Collection. Louisiana Division, City Archives and Special Collections. New Orleans Public Library.
WB	*Washington (D.C.) Bee*
WP	*Washington (D.C.) Post*

WSJ *Wall Street Journal*
WSN *Wilmington (N.C.) Star-News*
WSP/SHC William R. Savage Papers. Southern Historical Collection.
Wilson Library. University of North Carolina, Chapel Hill.
WT *Washington (D.C.) Times*
WTr *Washington (D.C.) Tribune*

Introduction

1. E. B. Furgurson, "Carr's Beach Reunion Concert Sunday," AC, June 26, 2009, HometownAnnapolis.com, http://www.hometownannapolis.com/news/top /2009/06/26-18/Carrs-Beach-reunion-concert-Sunday.html?ne=1 (accessed August 17, 2010).
2. "Carr's Beach Party Pictures," July 4, 2009, Life in Chesapeake Harbour: A Blog about Chesapeake Harbour Life, http://chesapeakeharbour.blogspot .com/ (accessed August 17, 2010).
3. John Moses, interview by Andrew Kahrl, December 12, 2009, Highland Beach, MD, notes in possession of the author.
4. The Ewings of Annapolis, Long and Foster Real Estate, "The Villages of Chesapeake Harbour," http://www.theewingsofannapolis.com/community-info .asp (accessed August 17, 2010).
5. In 2003, Coldwell Banker estimated the average selling price of waterfront homes in the Annapolis area at over $1 million. See "Changing Tides for Residences along Shoreline," *BaS*, October 13, 2003, p. A1.
6. George Phelps, interview by Andrew Kahrl, December 10, 2009, Annapolis, MD, audiotape in possession of the author.
7. Juanita Doris Franklin, interview by Andrew Kahrl, January 14, 2010, Fox-worth, MS, audiotape in possession of the author.
8. Pat Harvey, interview by Andrew Kahrl, January 8, 2010, Waveland, MS, audiotape in possession of the author. On memory of Jim Crow and the civil rights movement in popular culture and urban political economies, see Renee C. Romano and Leigh Raiford, eds., *The Civil Rights Movement in American Memory* (Athens: University of Georgia Press, 2006); and Michele R. Boyd, *Jim Crow Nostalgia: Reconstructing Race in Bronzeville* (Minneapolis: University of Minnesota Press, 2008).
9. Ray Langston, interview by Andrew Kahrl, December 12, 2009, Highland Beach, MD, audiotape in possession of the author.
10. Bill Carson interview by Zeal Harris, http://www.youtube.com/user/ zealousflow#p/u/15/oOhM8CNCRwI (accessed January 21, 2011).
11. Vernie Singleton, "We Are an Endangered Species: An Interview with Emory Campbell," *Southern Exposure* 10 (May–June 1982): 37–39.

12. Coastal zones, as distinct from coastlines, are defined as all lands that are influenced by marine conditions, a geographical category that can encompass lands as far as 70 miles inland from the coast. For an introduction to the geology and morphology of beaches and coasts, see Richard A. Davis Jr. and Duncan M. Fitzgerald, *Beaches and Coasts* (Malden, MA: Blackwell, 2004).

13. On the Sea Islands of South Carolina and Georgia, for example, the hydraulic landscape that planters and enslaved laborers constructed in the antebellum era to service rice plantations had, by the late 1800s, collapsed as a result of the intertwined problems of labor in the post-emancipation South and the vagaries of nature—in the form of a series of devastating hurricanes in the 1890s. These factors, Mart A. Stewart argues, led to a wholesale retreat of white landowners from the coast and the emergence of self-sustaining, subsistence-oriented black landowning communities that "occupied a peripheral position to the larger American economy" but "were on the whole able to remain more independent of white supervision and domination . . . than freedmen and women in other plantation areas in the South." See Mart A. Stewart, "Rice, Water, and Power: Landscapes of Domination and Resistance in the Lowcountry, 1790–1880," *Environmental History Review* 15 (Autumn 1991): 47–64, esp. 59–60.

On the "burden" of coastal landownership in eighteenth- and nineteenth-century America, see Wallace Kaufman and Orrin H. Pilkey Jr., *The Beaches Are Moving: The Drowning of America's Shoreline* (Durham, NC: Duke University Press, 1983). On black watermen and coastal communities in the nineteenth-century South, see also David S. Cecelski, *The Waterman's Song: Slavery and Freedom in Maritime North Carolina* (Chapel Hill: University of North Carolina Press, 2001).

On freedpeople's frustrated struggle to acquire land and become independent of the plantation economy in the postemancipation South, and the short- and long-term consequences of the federal government's failure to enact comprehensive land reforms following the war, see W. E. B. Du Bois, *Black Reconstruction in America, 1860–1880* (New York: Touchstone, 1935), esp. 580–636; Eric Foner, *Reconstruction: America's Unfinished Revolution, 1863–1877* (New York: Harper & Row, 1988); Willie Lee Rose, *Rehearsal for Reconstruction: The Port Royal Experiment* (New York: Bobbs-Merrill, 1964); Claude F. Oubre, *Forty Acres and a Mule: The Freedmen's Bureau and Black Land Ownership* (Baton Rouge: Louisiana State University Press, 1978); and Leon F. Litwack, *Been in the Storm So Long: The Aftermath of Slavery* (New York: Vintage, 1980).

14. Manning Marable, "The Land Question in Historical Perspective: The Economics of Poverty in the Blackbelt South, 1865–1920," in *The Black Rural Landowner—Endangered Species: Social, Political, and Economic Implications*, ed. Leo McGee and Robert Boone (Westport, CT: Greenwood Press, 1979), 12.

15. McGee and Boone, *Black Rural Landowner—Endangered Species*, xvii. On the relatively high proportion of black landowners in the early twentieth-century coastal South, see also J. William Harris, *Deep Souths: Delta, Piedmont, and Sea Island Society in the Age of Segregation* (Baltimore: Johns Hopkins University Press, 2001), 148–51; and Mark Schultz, *The Rural Face of White Supremacy: Beyond Jim Crow* (Urbana: University of Illinois Press, 2005), 46.

16. Bruce Cotten to Sallie Cotten, correspondence, June 19, 1921, SSC/SHC. Between 1883 and 1892, Harris found, the Atlantic coast reported only three lynchings of black men (as compared with forty-nine in the Mississippi Delta), a figure he attributes to the area's higher rates of black landownership and independent farming, which limited economic competition and contact with whites and gave rise to "strong tradition[s] of black community activism." See Harris, *Deep Souths*, 78, and charts 7 and 8 (appendix), 343.

17. Evelyn Williams, *Inadmissible Evidence: The Story of the African-American Trial Lawyer Who Defended the Black Liberation Army* (Brooklyn, NY: Lawrence Hill, 1993), 18.

18. Kaufman and Pilkey, *Beaches Are Moving*, 15–20.

19. This concept of "racial capitalism," which describes the entwined evolution of race and capitalism and underscores the primacy of economic practices in the making of categories of race, was first developed by Cedric Robinson in *Black Marxism: The Making of the Black Radical Tradition* (London: Zed Press, 1983).

20. Quoted in Linda Rocawich et al., "South Coast Follies: Coastal Profiles of Nine Southern States," *Southern Exposure* 10, no. 2 (1983): 101.

21. In the early 1900s the coastal geographer Douglas W. Johnson, through a series of influential studies, including the 1919 publication *Shore Processes and Shoreline Development*, popularized the notion that coastal zones are or could be made stable. See Klaus J. Meyer-Arendt, "Historical Coastal Environmental Changes: Human Responses to Shoreline Erosion," in *The American Environment: Interpretations of Past Geographies*, ed. Lary M. Dilsaver and Craig E. Colten (Savage, MD: Rowman & Littlefield, 1992), 222. "The sudden success of [the internal combustion engine and the automobile]," Kaufman and Pilkey note, "meant that no environment could forbid people entry or resist their inventive efforts at domestication." Kaufman and Pilkey, *Beaches Are Moving*, 173. In 1920, the only Americans with paid vacation time off from their jobs were salaried professionals. By 1937, 40 percent of wage earners in manufacturing, laundries, and extractive industries enjoyed paid vacations. By 1979, nearly 100 percent of employees in "medium to large establishments" had paid vacations. See Thomas Weiss, "Tourism in America before World War II,"

Journal of Economic History 64, no. 2 (June 2004): 289–327, esp. 318. Richard D. Starnes notes that the automobile "began the process of democratizing southern travel." See Starnes, ed., *Southern Journeys: Tourism, History, and Culture in the Modern South* (Tuscaloosa: University of Alabama Press, 2003), 5. See also Howard L. Preston, *Dirt Roads to Dixie: Accessibility and Modernization in the South, 1885–1935* (Knoxville: University of Tennessee Press, 1991). On the history of travel and vacationing and the evolution of travel and leisure-based industries in early twentieth-century America, see also Warren James Belasco, *Americans on the Road: From Autocamp to Motel, 1910–1945* (Cambridge, MA: MIT Press, 1979); Hal Rothman, *Devil's Bargain: Tourism in the Twentieth-Century American West* (Lawrence: University Press of Kansas, 2000); and Susan Sessions Rugh, *Are We There Yet? The Golden Age of American Family Vacations* (Lawrence: University Press of Kansas, 2008).

22. By 1934, one economist surmised, over 90 percent of the money invested in real estate speculation over the previous decade had been irrevocably lost. Quoted in George Brown Tindal, *The Emergence of the New South, 1913–1945* (Baton Rouge: Louisiana State University Press, 1967), 359.

23. Quoted in Carter G. Woodson, *The Rural Negro* (Washington, DC: Association for the Study of Negro Life and History, 1930), 138–39.

24. Quoted in Ted Steinberg, *Acts of God: The Unnatural History of Natural Disaster in America* (New York: Oxford University Press, 2000), 51. On the Florida real estate boom and bust in the 1920s, see pp. 47–68.

25. Henry S. Villard, "Florida Aftermath," *The Nation* (June 6, 1928), 635–36.

26. Cited in Orrin H. Pilkey and Katherine L. Dixon, *The Corps and the Shore* (Washington, DC: Island Press, 1996), 6–8. For an official history of the BEB, see Mary-Louise Quinn, *The History of the Beach Erosion Board, U.S. Army, Corps of Engineers, 1930–63* (Fort Belvoir, VA: Coastal Engineering Research Center, U.S. Army, Corps of Engineers, 1977). See also Meyer-Arendt, "Historical Coastal Environmental Changes," 226.

27. The term "vacationlands" comes from Peter T. Siskind, "Growth and Its Discontents: Localism, Protest, and the Politics of Development on the Postwar Northeast Corridor" (Ph.D. diss., University of Pennsylvania, 2002).

28. R. E. Dorer, "Princess Anne County Leads in Mosquito Control," *Virginia and the Virginia County* (June 1950): 17–19. On the CCC's work in mosquito control and recreational development of coastal zones, see Neil M. Maher, *Nature's New Deal: The Civilian Conservation Corps and the Roots of the American Environmental Movement* (New York: Oxford University Press, 2008), esp. 165–71.

29. National Park Service, Department of Interior, "A Report on Our Vanishing Shoreline" (1955), 9, 12.

30. Lee Owens Jr., interview by William Henderson, April 26, 2000, interview F341.5 .M57 vol. 747, transcript, MOHP/USM. See also "Negroes Had Beach Area Three Years Ago but Lost It Due Number of Reasons," *Biloxi Daily Herald,* May 1960. Figures from Arthur C. Trembanis and Orrin H. Pilkey, "Summary of Beach Nourishment along the U.S. Gulf of Mexico Shoreline," *Journal of Coastal Research* 14 (Spring 1998): 407–17, esp. 413. Public beaches and parks, Kevin Kruse argues, came to be understood by white users as their "racial birthright," paid for with "their" tax dollars and for their exclusive enjoyment. See Kruse, *White Flight: Atlanta and the Making of Modern Conservatism* (Princeton, NJ: Princeton University Press, 2005).

31. Eva Gates, interview by Pic Firmin, November 30, 1999, interview F341.5 .M57 vol. 749, transcript, MOHP/USM.

32. Mamie Garvin Fields, with Karen Fields, *Lemon Swamp and Other Places: A Carolina Memoir* (New York: Free Press, 1983), 191–92. By July 31, 1961, for example, twelve black youths had been reported drowned in Charleston. See "One Drowned, One Missing in River," *CPC,* July 26, 1961; and "Boy, 8, Drowns in River," ibid., July 31, 1961.

33. For a primer on the evolution and contestation in American jurisprudence of the Public Trust Doctrine, which broadly vests coastal lands to the state for public use, see Jack H. Archer, *The Public Trust Doctrine and the Management of America's Coasts* (Amherst: University of Massachusetts Press, 1994). See also Sara Warner, *Down to the Waterline: Boundaries, Nature, and the Law in Florida* (Athens: University of Georgia Press, 2005).

34. On the influence of Progressive-era social reform in the making of urban waterfronts, see Matthew Klingle, "Fair Play: Outdoor Recreation and Environmental Inequality in Twentieth-Century Seattle," in *The Nature of Cities,* ed. Andrew Isenberg (Rochester, NY: University of Rochester Press, 2006), 122–56; Robin F. Bachin, *Building the South Side: Urban Space and Civic Culture in Chicago, 1890–1919* (Chicago: University of Chicago Press, 2004), 169–201. On African Americans' exclusion from and criminalization under Progressive-era social programs and civic reforms, see Khalil Gibran Muhammad, *The Condemnation of Blackness: Race, Crime, and the Making of Modern Urban America* (Cambridge, MA: Harvard University Press, 2010). On the displacement of the poor in the interest of urban environmental beautification and improvement, see Klingle, "Fair Play"; and Roy Rosenzweig and Elizabeth Blackmar, *The Park and the People: A History of Central Park* (Ithaca, NY: Cornell University Press, 1992), 59–91.

35. W. E. B. Du Bois, "The Color Problem of Summer," *Crisis,* July 1929, 235, 250.

36. On the creative ways African American landowners sought to utilize real property for subsistence and entrepreneurship, see Andrew Wiese, *Places of*

Their Own: African American Suburbanization in the Twentieth Century
(Chicago: University of Chicago Press, 2004), 77, 90.

37. St. Clair Drake and Horace R. Cayton, *Black Metropolis: A Study of Negro Life in a Northern City* (Chicago: University of Chicago Press, 1993 [1945]), 387.

38. Juanita Doris Franklin interview. Pat Harvey interview.

39. Thomas J. Sugrue, *The Origins of the Urban Crisis: Race and Inequality in Postwar Detroit* (Princeton, N.J.: Princeton University Press, 1996), 8.

40. W. E. B. Du Bois, *Dusk of Dawn: An Essay toward an Autobiography of a Race Concept* (New York: Schocken Books, 1940), 153. Cited in Barbara J. Fields, "Origins of the New South and the Negro Question," *Journal of Southern History* 67 (November 2001): 817.

41. On the increased judicial application of free-market principles in the adjudication of land disputes, and its impact on African American land tenure, over the course of the twentieth century, see Thomas W. Mitchell, "From Reconstruction to Deconstruction: Undermining Black Landowner-ship, Political Independence, and Community through Partition Sales of Tenancies in Common," *Northwestern University Law Review* 95 (Winter 2001): 505–80.

42. For a powerful work on the practice of contract selling, one of the many forms of race-based exploitation in twentieth-century America, see Beryl Satter, *Family Properties: Race, Estate, and the Exploitation of Black Urban America* (New York: Metropolitan Books, 2009). Satter's insights into the dynamics of housing and real estate in postwar Chicago and, more broadly, the production of racial inequality through exploitative practices deeply inform my ap-proach to the subject of this book.

43. See Arnold R. Hirsch, *Making the Second Ghetto: Race and Housing in Chicago, 1940–1960* (Cambridge: Cambridge University Press, 1983); Kenneth T. Jackson, *Crabgrass Frontier: The Suburbanization of the United States* (New York: Oxford University Press, 1985); Sugrue, *The Origins of the Urban Crisis;* Robert O. Self, *American Babylon: Race and the Struggle for Postwar Oakland* (Princeton, NJ: Princeton University Press, 2003); David M. P. Freund, *Colored Property: State Policy and White Racial Politics in Suburban America* (Chicago: University of Chicago Press, 2007). See also the collection of essays in Kevin M. Kruse and Thomas J. Sugrue, eds., *The New Suburban History* (Chicago: University of Chicago Press, 2006).

44. On the changing face of segregation in places of leisure and commerce from a Jim Crow to a "color-blind," privatized nation, see Bryant Simon, *Boardwalk of Dreams: Atlantic City and the Fate of Urban America* (New York: Oxford University Press, 2004); Jeff Wiltse, *Contested Waters: A Social History of Swimming Pools in America* (Chapel Hill: University of North Carolina Press,

2007); Lizabeth Cohen, *A Consumers' Republic: The Politics of Mass Consumption in Postwar America* (New York: Vintage, 2003), esp. 193–290; and Regina Austin, "'Not Just for the Fun of It!': Governmental Restraints on Black Leisure, Social Inequality, and the Privatization of Public Space," *Southern California Law Review* 71 (1998): 667–714.

45. The argument that the Sunbelt was less a geographically defined region and more an ethos was forcefully articulated by Matthew D. Lassiter and Joseph Crespino in the introduction to their edited collection, *The Myth of Southern Exceptionalism* (New York: Oxford University Press, 2010), 3–22. On the Sunbelt as a "stage of capitalism," see N. D. B. Connolly, *A World More Concrete: Real Estate and the Remaking of Jim Crow South Florida* (Chicago: University of Chicago Press, forthcoming).

46. On the economic and political ascendancy of the Sunbelt, see Bruce Schulman, *From Cotton Belt to Sunbelt: Federal Policy, Economic Development, and the Transformation of the South, 1938–1980* (New York: Oxford University Press, 1991); James C. Cobb, *The Selling of the South: The Southern Crusade for Industrial Development, 1936–1980* (Baton Rouge: Louisiana State University Press, 1982); Matthew D. Lassiter, *The Silent Majority: Suburban Politics in the Sunbelt South* (Princeton, NJ: Princeton University Press, 2006); Carl Abbott, *The New Urban America: Growth and Politics in Sunbelt Cities* (Chapel Hill: University of North Carolina Press, 1981); and the essays in Michelle Nickerson and Darren Dochuk, eds., *Sunbelt Rising: The Politics of Place, Space, and Region* (Philadelphia: University of Pennsylvania Press, 2011). For works that examine the impact of vacation and tourism industries and leisure-based real estate development on the modern South, see Michael N. Danielson, *Profits and Politics in Paradise* (Columbia: University of South Carolina Press, 1995); Russ Rymer, *American Beach: A Saga of Race, Wealth, and Memory* (New York: HarperCollins, 1998); and J. Mark Souther, *New Orleans on Parade: Tourism and the Transformation of the Crescent City* (Baton Rouge: Louisiana State University Press, 2006). See also the collection of essays in Anthony J. Stanonis, ed., *Dixie Emporium: Tourism, Foodways, and Consumer Culture in the American South* (Athens: University of Georgia Press, 2008); and Starnes, *Southern Journeys.*

47. The role of land in shaping categories of race, ethnicity, and power has been richly explored by historians of the American Southwest. See David A. Chang, *The Color of the Land: Race, Nation, and the Politics of Landownership in Oklahoma, 1832–1929* (Chapel Hill: University of North Carolina Press, 2010); Neil Foley, *The White Scourge: Mexicans, Blacks, and Poor Whites in Texas Cotton Culture* (Berkeley and Los Angeles: University of California Press,

1997); and Maria E. Montoya, *Translating Property: The Maxwell Land Grant and the Conflict over Land in the American Southwest, 1840–1900* (Lawrence: University Press of Kansas, 2005).

48. Quote comes from William Cronon's landmark work, *Changes in the Land: Indians, Colonists, and the Ecology of New England* (New York: Hill & Wang, 2003 [1983]). For an excellent study on the interplay of labor, leisure, and land use in a coastal area over the course of the twentieth century, see Connie Y. Chiang, *Shaping the Shoreline: Fisheries and Tourism on the Monterey Coast* (Seattle: University of Washington Press, 2008).

49. Jacquelyn Dowd Hall, "The Long Civil Rights Movement and the Political Uses of the Past," *Journal of American History* 91 (March 2005): 1233–63. For works that locate struggles for environmental rights within a long civil rights tradition, see Robert D. Bullard, *Dumping in Dixie: Race, Class, and Environmental Quality* (Boulder, CO: Westview, 1990); Colin Fisher, "African Americans, Outdoor Recreation, and the 1919 Chicago Race Riot," in *"To Love the Wind and the Rain": African Americans and Environmental History*, ed. Diane D. Glave and Mark Stoll (Pittsburgh: University of Pittsburgh Press, 2006), 63–76; Dolores Greenberg, "Reconstructing Race and Protest: Environmental Justice in New York," *Environmental History* 5 (2000): 223–50; Andrew Hurley, *Environmental Inequalities: Class, Race, and Industrial Pollution in Gary, Indiana, 1945–1980* (Chapel Hill: University of North Carolina Press, 1995); Eileen McGurty, *Transforming Environmentalism: Warren County, PCBs, and the Origins of Environmental Justice* (New Brunswick, NJ: Rutgers University Press, 2007); and Julie Sze, *Noxious New York: The Racial Politics of Urban Health and Environmental Justice* (Cambridge, MA: MIT Press, 2007).

50. The idea that a spirit of congregation among African Americans emerged in the wake of segregation comes from the pathbreaking work of Earl Lewis on African Americans in Jim Crow–era Norfolk, in which he describes a general shift among blacks toward development of the home sphere following bitter setbacks in the workplace and public life in the early twentieth century. Since then, the notion that "segregation became congregation" has come to characterize a general interpretive approach to black life under Jim Crow. Lewis, *In Their Own Interests: Race, Class, and Power in Twentieth-Century Norfolk* (Berkeley and Los Angeles: University of California Press, 1991).

51. George Lipsitz, *How Racism Takes Place* (Philadelphia: Temple University Press, 2011), 60, 61, 20.

52. My thoughts on this subject are strongly influenced by the writing and research of Nathan D. B. Connolly, in particular, "We Are Exactly What We

Seem: Notes on Interpreting a Black Property Rights Movement," a talk given at University of Michigan in November 2010. For video of the talk, see http://inst-tech.engin.umich.edu/leccap/view/carma-rec-u0fxs7awg/10661 (accessed June 13, 2011); Nathan D. B. Connolly, "By Eminent Domain: Race and Capital in the Building of an American South Florida" (Ph.D. diss., University of Michigan, 2008); and Nathan D. B. Connolly, "Sunbelt Civil Rights: Urban Renewal and the Follies of Desegregation in Greater Miami," in Nickerson and Dochuk, *Sunbelt Rising*, 164–87.

1. Corporate Ventures

1. Edward Cooper, "A Prominent Business Man," *BAA*, April 4, 1908; "Jane Moseley," *WB*, July 21, 1906; "The New Boat," *WB*, December 30, 1911; Paul Laurence Dunbar, "Negro Life in Washington" in *Harper's Weekly*, January 13, 1900, in Paul Laurence Dunbar, *The Sport of the Gods, and Other Essential Writings*, ed. Shelley Fisher Fishkin and David Bradley (New York: Modern Library, 2005), 274. For a critical assessment of Dunbar's writings on urban black life and racial uplift, see Kevin K. Gaines, *Uplifting the Race: Black Leadership, Politics, and Culture in the Twentieth Century* (Chapel Hill: University of North Carolina Press, 1996), 179–208.

2. Abram L. Harris, *The Negro as Capitalist: A Study of Banking and Business among American Negroes* (College Park, MD: McGrath Publishing, 1936), 49. In *Black Bourgeoisie*, Harris's colleague, E. Franklin Frazier, concurred. Describing the economic roots of the turn-of-the-twentieth-century black middle class, he wrote, "Except for the insurance companies, the only outlets for the credit resources of Negro banks were in real estate, small and inconsequential retail stores, and the amusement and personal service enterprises conducted by Negroes." E. Franklin Frazier, *Black Bourgeoisie* (Glencoe, IL: Free Press, 1957), 41. On Harris and Frazier's critique of race, class, and political economy, see Jonathan Scott Holloway, *Confronting the Veil: Abram Harris Jr., E. Franklin Frazier, and Ralph Bunche, 1919–1941* (Chapel Hill: University of North Carolina Press, 2002).

3. Booker T. Washington, *The Negro in Business* (Boston: Hertel, Jenkins & Co., 1907), 54.

4. Cited in Brian E. Allnutt, "'The Negro Excursions': Recreational Outings among Philadelphia African Americans, 1876–1926," *Pennsylvania Magazine of History and Biography* 129 (January 2005): 80.

5. Between 1860 and 1870 the city's black population tripled. See Katherine Masur, "Reconstructing the Nation's Capital: The Politics of Race and Citizenship in the District of Columbia, 1862–1878" (Ph.D. diss., University of Michigan, 2001), 13. On Washington's black aristocracy, see Willard B. Gatewood,

Aristocrats of Color: The Black Elite, 1880–1920 (Bloomington: Indiana University Press, 1990), 38–68.

6. Howard N. Rabinowitz called steamboats the South's "most segregated form of travel." See Rabinowitz, *Race Relations in the Urban South, 1865–1890* (New York: Oxford University Press, 1978), 191. "On some river steamboats," the black minister and writer James Corrothers commented, "coloured passengers are not permitted to rent a state-room unless it is directly under the booming whistle, or beside the noisy paddlebox, or the hot, smelling pantry, where it is almost impossible to sleep." James D. Corrothers, *In Spite of the Handicap: An Autobiography* (New York: George H. Doran Co., 1916), 119.

7. See William Howland Kenney, *Jazz on the River* (Chicago: University of Chicago Press, 2005), 17–18.

8. As early as 1854, free black churches in Washington chartered private excursions down the Potomac to raise funds. See Frederick Tilp, *This Was Potomac River* (Bladensburg, MD: Tilp, 1978), 161.

9. Editorial, WP, June 27, 1880; "Sunday at Notley Hall," CA, May 21, 1898.

10. "Can Gamble on the River," WP, August 27, 1911.

11. Editorial, "Battle on River Boat," CA, June 18, 1904; Tilp, *This Was Potomac River*, 305–7; "Gambling on the River," WP, August 6, 1888; "Fresh Planked Shad," WP, April 4, 1892; Minnie Kendall-Lowther, *Marshall Hall and Other Potomac Points in Story and Picture* (Baltimore: Read-Taylor, 1925), 22. At turn-of-the-twentieth-century places of public amusement, the historian David Nasaw argues, "A decent person was someone who looked and acted decent. The well-dressed dandy or sport who made too much noise, spit on the floor, or appeared drunken in public was, no matter his social background or education, not decent." See Nasaw, *Going Out: The Rise and Fall of Public Amusements* (New York: Basic Books, 1993), 32.

12. "Marshall Hall Amusement Park" brochure, ca. 1920s, DCCA/DCPL. See also Kendall-Lowther, *Marshall Hall*. Similarly, in Atlanta, city officials transformed picnic grounds such as Ponce de Leon Park and Piedmont Park into amusement parks that, they hoped, "would encourage democratic ideals" (albeit for whites only). "These parks," Tera W. Hunter notes, "provided ways of reaffirming whiteness through ritual play and reinforcing racial unity against a perceived black threat." See Tera W. Hunter, *To 'Joy My Freedom: Southern Black Women's Lives and Labors after the Civil War* (Cambridge, MA: Harvard University Press, 1997), 146, 147.

13. Letter to editor, "Can't Go on Water," WB, June 6, 1891.

14. "The Junior Excelsiors," WB, July 23, 1887; "Opposition to the Excelsiors," WB, August 25, 1888; advertisement, Collingwood Beach, WB, June 30, 1888;

"About People You Know," *WP*, June 14, 1891; "A New River Resort," *WP*, August 30, 1890; "Rumored River Disaster," *WP*, July 30, 1894.

15. In his 1899 study of black Philadelphians, W. E. B. Du Bois found that most live-in domestic servants received "one afternoon each week and the evening and the evening or the afternoon and evening on alternate Sundays" off from work. See W. E. B. Du Bois, *The Philadelphia Negro: A Social Study* (Philadelphia: University of Pennsylvania, 1899), 468. That a similar pattern existed in Washington is corroborated by excursion announcements in the city's black newspapers. On "freedom bags," see Elizabeth Clark-Lewis, " 'This Work Had a End': African-American Domestic Workers in Washington, D.C., 1910–1940," in *"To Toil the Livelong Day": America's Women at Work, 1780–1980*, ed. Carol Groneman and Mary Beth Norton, 196–212 (Ithaca, NY: Cornell University Press, 1987), 207.

16. For a trip aboard the *River Queen* on September 6, 1901, a "clean-shaven, bearheaded" eighteen-year-old Jas. Banks wore a blue serge coat with silk lapels over a heavy white sweater and light, striped pants. See Instructions to the Force ("Look-out book") September 1, 1901–December 31, 1903, RG 351, MPDDC/NA.

17. "Why the Police at No. 4 'Get Busy' When They Hear the Whistle of the 'Razor Beach' Boat," *WP*, August 23, 1908, p. SM5; "The Man-on-the-Corner," *CA*, August 2, 1902, p. 2. In *The Philadelphia Negro*, Du Bois characterized the class of persons found on a Negro excursion as ranging from the "lowest class of criminals, prostitutes and loafers" (the so-called submerged tenth) to the working poor, comprising "persons not earning enough to keep them at all times above want; honest, although not always energetic or thrifty, and with no touch of gross immorality or crime." Du Bois, *Philadelphia Negro*, 311, 320.

18. "Why the Police at No. 4 'Get Busy' When They Hear the Whistle of the 'Razor Beach' Boat"; Tilp, *This Was Potomac River*, 68; "Negro Excursion Steamers," *WT*, July 26, 1904; editorial, "Collingwood Beach," *WB*, July 21, 1888.

19. In June 1901 a group of African American lawyers accused the Prince George's County sheriff's department of discriminatory treatment of black patrons at Notley Hall, noting that "patrons of Notley Hall are arrested on trivial charges" such as "singing and loud talking," which had been the offense cited in roughly fifty arrests made at Notley Hall already that season. See "Notley Hall," *WB*, June 8, 1901; "Arrests at Notley Hall," *WP*, June 17, 1901.

20. Editorial, "Collingwood Beach," *WB*, July 21, 1888; *Richmond Planet*, quoted in *WB*, April 23, 1898; *CA*, June 14, 1902; "We Would Like to Know," *CA*, July 26, 1902; "We Are Not Alone," *BAA*, August 20, 1898; column, "Little

Colored Americans," *CA*, June 21, 1902; column, "Little Colored Americans," *CA*, August 23, 1902. On Edward E. Cooper, see Willard B. Gatewood Jr., "Edward E. Cooper, Black Journalist," *Journalism Quarterly* 55, no. 2 (1978): 269–75.

21. "Battle on the River Boat," *WB*, June 18, 1904; "Everything Open at Shadyside," *BAA*, July 20, 1912; "Slaves of Shadyside," *BAA*, August 17, 1912; "Notley Hall," *WB*, June 8, 1901.

22. *CA*, December 13, 1902, p. 4; "Patterson in Custody," *WT*, May 21, 1895.

23. "The Investigation of the Steam Boat Company," *WB*, August 18, 1894; "South Washington," *BAA*, August 5, 1899.

24. Carl R. Osthaus attributed black Washingtonians' disillusionment with frugality and savings as a means of social improvement to the collapse of the Freedman's Savings Bank. As a result of rampant corruption and risky investments by its board of directors exposed by the Panic of 1873, countless numbers of freedmen—and women—lost their life savings, and an institution founded to encourage sound spending habits had the opposite effect. It was not until 1888 that another bank for African American investors was established in Washington, and well into the twentieth century, blacks across the country often referred to the Freedman's collapse in explaining why they avoided placing their earnings in savings accounts. Du Bois noted the disastrous psychological consequences of its failure for poor and working-class investors: "All the faith in saving went . . . and much of the faith in men. . . . Not even ten additional years of slavery could have done so much to throttle the thrift of the freedmen as the mismanagement and bankruptcy of the series of savings banks chartered by the Nation for their especial aid." W. E. B. Du Bois, *The Souls of Black Folk* (1903), quoted in Carl R. Osthaus, *Freedmen, Philanthropy, and Fraud: A History of the Freedman's Savings Bank* (Urbana: University of Illinois Press, 1976), 224.

25. "The Investigation of the Steam Boat Company," *WB*, August 18, 1894.

26. Advertisement, Norfolk and Washington Steamboat Company, *WP*, September 22, 1894; "A Transportation Company Incorporated," *WP*, May 5, 1894; "Investigating Their President," *WP*, September 4, 1894; "Still Trying to Oust Patterson," *WP*, September 23, 1894; "They Declared Fraud," *WB*, December 1, 1894; "Set Fire to the Lake," *WP*, May 21, 1895.

27. "Recalls a Mystery Steamship Line," *BAA*, October 17, 1924; "False Leaders," *BAA*, August 26, 1905. In Chicago, St. Clair Drake and Horace R. Cayton cited examples of white merchants vandalizing black competitors, and colluding with landlords to raise the rents on black-owned businesses and with policymakers and inspectors to deny or revoke business licenses and rezone commercial property. See Drake and Cayton, *Black Metropolis: A Study of Negro Life in a Northern City*, vol. 2 (New York: Harper & Row, 1962), 447–49.

28. "Mascot of the River Queen," CA, July 12, 1902. In 1904 the Mount Vernon Ladies' Association, managers of the home of George Washington, took steps to prevent the landing of any boats "used for *negro excursions,* and to guard against the possible use of such boats in the Mt Vernon traffic" (emphasis in original) by insisting on "a special clause" in its contract with the Mount Vernon and Marshall Hall Steamboat Company that prevented the latter from landing at the Mount Vernon wharf any boats other than the white excursion steamer the *Charles Macalester.* Harrison Howell Dodge to Justine Van Rensselaer Townsend, December 17, 2004, Superintendent's Letterbooks, Mount Vernon Archives, Mount Vernon Ladies' Association, Mount Vernon, VA. On African Americans' protest against the Mount Vernon Ladies' Association and their threats of litigation, see Minutes of Council, 1905, Mount Vernon Ladies' Association of the Union, Superintendent's Annual Report to the MVLA, May 1905, Mount Vernon Archives, Mount Vernon Ladies Association; and "No Negro Boat to Land: Remarkable Action of the Mt. Vernon Association—Hon. Frank Hume the Negro's Friend," WB, December 10, 1904. See also Scott E. Casper, *Sarah Johnson's Mount Vernon: The Forgotten History of an American Shrine* (New York: Hill & Wang, 2008), 208 (thanks to Scott E. Casper for graciously sharing this material with me).
29. "The Cat Fight," WB, August 18, 1894.
30. "Still Trying to Oust Patterson," WP, September 23, 1894; "The Investigation of the Steam Boat Company," WB, August 18, 1894; "Pushing the Prosecution," WP, October 9, 1894; "Lady of the Lake Burned," WP, February 15, 1895; "Jury Sets Them Free," WP, July 5, 1895; "Excitement Ran High," WP, September 11, 1894; "A Disgusted Investigator," WP, September 1, 1894.
31. "National Steamboat Company," WP, July 3, 1895; "Steamer George Leary Changes Hands," WP, April 11, 1895; advertisement, WB, August 24, 1895, 6; "A Colored Saratoga," WB, July 27, 1895.
32. "People's Transportation Line," WP, May 9, 1895; "Complimentary Excursion," WT, May 18, 1895; "The Steamboat Failure," BAA, July 8, 1899.
33. "River Front Riot Call," WT, May 31, 1895; "Will Take Soundings," WT, June 3, 1895.
34. "River Front Riot Call," WT, May 31, 1895; "Its President Arrested," WP, June 10, 1897; "The 'George Leary' to Float," CA, August 6, 1898; "A Famous Steamboat Founders at Sea," *Alexandria Gazette,* December 27, 1901; advertisement, CA, January 16, 1904.
35. "The Steamboat Failure," BAA, July 8, 1899; "The Rubber Necks Are Giving It Out," CA, July 28, 1900; "A Prominent Business Man," BAA, April 4, 1908.
36. Harris, *Negro as Capitalist,* 175.

37. In his scathing essay on "Washington's Colored Society," journalist John E. Bruce condemned the treatment elite blacks accorded Jefferson and other "contrabands" in the decades following the war, and celebrated their achievements. "The poor and despised Jew, was never more abused and berated, scorned and ridiculed than were the 'contrabands' of war." In the face of hostility, Jefferson and others, as Bruce put it, "'put money in their purses and to themselves were true,' with them all labor was honorable—they toiled incessantly, acquired property, real and personal, organized benevolent institutions and churches, educated their children, meanwhile the upper class stood looking on with wonder and amazement . . . in a state of supreme disgust and envy." John Edward Bruce, "Washington's Colored Society," 1877, pp. 6–7, BERC/NYPL.
38. Union League Directory, ca. 1901, DCCA/DCPL.
39. On the comparatively high rates of black property ownership in Washington during this period, see Loren Schweninger, "Black Economic Reconstruction in the South," in *The Facts of Reconstruction: Essays in Honor of John Hope Franklin*, ed. Eric Anderson and Alfred A. Moss Jr. (Baton Rouge: Louisiana State University Press, 1991), 167–88.
40. "Lewis Jefferson Obituary," *WP*, August 28, 1946; "An Obituary of Lewis Jefferson," unpublished paper in Moral W. Trent's personal collection, n.d. (photocopy in possession of the author). There is some dispute over Lewis Jefferson's birthplace and early childhood. Jefferson's grandson and the designated heir of his estate, Moral W. Trent, claims that Jefferson was born in South Carolina to a freedwoman who was killed by whites during an assault on an emancipated black community when Jefferson was an infant. According to Trent, during the assault, Jefferson's grandmother escaped to Virginia with the infant in tow. The *Washington Post* obituary for Jefferson, however, lists Orange, Virginia, as his birthplace, as do all U.S. Census population schedules on which his name appears. Moral W. Trent to Andrew W. Kahrl, July 22, 2007, audiotape in possession of the author; Lewis Jefferson, District of Columbia, Schedule No. 1—Population, 12th Census of the United States, 1900, available at *HeritageQuest Online*, http://persi.heritagequestonline.com/ (accessed July 29, 2010). A biography in the 1901 Union League directory indicates that Jefferson owned a blacksmith shop, sold "Pure Bone Meal by the ton," worked as a general contractor, and bought and sold real estate. See Andrew Hilyer, ed., *The Twentieth Century Urban League Directory: Colored Washington, Efforts for Social Betterment* (Washington, DC: Urban League, 1901), 110. The neighborhoods of Southwest D.C. became, as Carole Abrams Kolker put it, a "staging ground for newcomers to the city." Carole Abrams Kolker, "Migrants and Memories: Family, Work, and Community among Blacks, Eastern European Jews, and Native-Born Whites in an Early Twentieth

Century Washington, D.C. Neighborhood" (Ph.D. diss., George Washington University, 1997), 28.

41. "The Colored Steamboat Company," *CA*, November 14, 1903.

42. Advertisement, *CA*, April 11, 1903; "The Jane Moseley," *CA*, March 14, 1903; "Inspecting Somerset Beach," *CA*, August 23, 1902; "A Prominent Business Man," *BAA*, April 4, 1908.

43. *CA*, July 18, 1903; August 1, 1903, p. 5; City Paragraphs Section, *CA*, August 6, 1904.

44. "Mr. Lewis Jefferson," *WB*, May 8, 1909, p. 5; "We Would Like to Know," *CA*, June 28, 1902.

45. See, for example, Locals Section, *CA*, June 20, 1903, p. 3. Following an overhaul and inspection of the *Jane Moseley* in June 1903, Jefferson ran a blurb in the *Colored American* announcing its fitness for travel, and mentioned, "All rumor and talk should now be at an end. Come down and see for yourself." Locals Section, *CA*, June 20, 1903, 16.

46. "The Jane Moseley's Boon," *CA*, August 29, 1903; "The Jane Moseley," *CA*, July 21, 1906.

47. "Petition for Receiver," *CA*, September 19, 1903; *Washington Law Reporter* 32 (1904): 60.

48. "The Colored Steamboat Company," *CA*, April 23, 1904.

49. On citizens associations in Washington, DC, see Howard Gillette Jr., *Between Justice and Beauty: Race, Planning, and the Failure of Urban Policy in Washington, D.C.* (Baltimore: Johns Hopkins University Press, 1995), 81–82.

50. "Will Operate the Jane Moseley," *WP*, June 12, 1904; "False Leaders," *BAA*, August 26, 1905.

51. Advertisement, Excursion Season for 1909, *WB*, May 8, 1909; "Why the Police at No. 4 'Get Busy' When They Hear the Whistle of the 'Razor Beach' Boat"; advertisement, Season of 1910, *WB*, February 19, 1910; Lewis Jefferson, "Important Facts (Concluded)," *WB*, May 29, 1909; Norma A. Baumgartner-Wagner, "Preliminary Report on the Archeological Investigations of the Notley Hall Amusement Park: Phase I Reconnaissance Survey," 1986, pp. 5–6, Notley Hall Folder, PGCHS; "Washington Park," *WB*, May 15, 1909.

52. See Kenneth Marvin Hamilton, *Black Towns and Profit: Promotion and Development in the Trans-Appalachian West, 1877–1915* (Urbana: University of Illinois Press, 1991), 152, 120.

53. Mary Church Terrell Diary, June 27, 1908 (microfilm: frame 416, reel 1), MCTP/LOC; "At Washington Park," *WB*, August 29, 1908; "Testimonial Excursion," *WB*, May 29, 1909; William Henry Jones, *Recreation and Amuse-*

ment among Negroes in Washington, DC: A Sociological Analysis of the Negro in an Urban Environment (1927; repr., Westport, CT: Negro Universities Press, 1970), 49–50; WB, August 8, 1908; "Aim to Better Conditions," WP, May 21, 1905; "Colored Babies' Outing," WP, June 11, 1905; "An Obituary of Lewis Jefferson," unpublished paper in Moral W. Trent's personal collection, n.d. (photocopy in possession of the author); Moral W. Trent, interview by Andrew Kahrl, November 12, 2005, audiotape in possession of the author.

54. Lewis Jefferson, "Important Facts," WB, May 22, 1909.
55. "Bouts on Steamer," WP, October 14, 1908.
56. "Washington Park," WB, May 15, 1909; "Helping the Enemy," WB, August 28, 1909; "Mr. Jefferson's Boats," WB, July 17, 1909; "Eating Crow," WB, August 20, 1910; "The Excursion Season," WB, September 24, 1910.
57. "The River Queen: Col. Lewis Jefferson Now in Charge—The Colored People Have Purchased the Entire Interest of Mr. Bensinger," WB, June 13, 1911; "The Steamer 'River Queen': Col. Lewis Jefferson and His Work," WB, May 13, 1911; "Historic River Queen Soon to Be Memory," *Washington Star*, March 5, 1912, n.p., vertical file, Potomac River Boats, 1900–1939, DCCA/DCPL; "The Angler," WB, May 4, 1912; *Lewis Jefferson, Plaintiff in Error v. District of Columbia*, in *Washington Law Reporter* 41 (1913): 355; "Washington Park Burns," WP, February 3, 1913.
58. "Swimming Pool Wrecked by Blast," *Roanoke Times*, May 27, 1926; Meeting Minutes, May 17, 1926, Roanoke County Board of Supervisors (Roanoke County Courthouse, Roanoke, VA); "Bathing Beach Is Wrecked by an Explosion," NJG, June 5, 1926; "Pine Crest Inn, Negro Amusement Center, Destroyed by Explosion," *Roanoke Times*, September 27, 1926, p. 1. See also Norwood C. Middleton, *Salem: A Virginia Chronicle* (Salem, VA: Salem Historical Society, 1986), 290.
59. "$100,000 Race Beach Resort Faces Foreclosure," *Topeka Plain Dealer*, October 29, 1926; "Pacific Beach Club," *California Eagle*, March 6, 1925; "Pacific Coast Resort Gutted by Fire; Whites Who Made Threats are Blamed," CD, January 30, 1926.
60. "Inquiry Begun in Club Blaze," *Los Angeles Times*, January 22, 1926.
61. "$100,000 Race Beach Resort Faces Foreclosure," *Topeka Plain Dealer*, October 29, 1926; "Beach Lost to Race for $35,000 to House $1,000,000 White Club House: Colored Attorney Fails in Effort to Save Valuable Ocean Frontage for Colored Beach," *Topeka Plain Dealer*, April 1, 1927. See also "Pacific Beach Club Meet Breaks Up in Disorder," CD, December 4, 1926.
62. "Elks Had Better Watch Their Step," BAA, August 27, 1938; "Foxes among Vines," BAA, July 30, 1938.

2. A Sanctuary by the Sea

1. "Gulfside Association," *Foundation*, November 1925, pp. 10–11; "The Waveland Enterprise," *Foundation*, March–April 1924, p. 11; H. J. Mason, "The Gulfside Idea," *Southern Workman* 58 (July 1929): 317; "The Meaning of Gulfside," SWCA, October 17, 1929; J. B. F. Shaw to Bishop R. E. Jones, March 21, 1927, Sc MG 202, box 1, GAS/NYPL; "The Value of Gulfside as an Educational Centre," *Gulfside News*, May–June 1927, Sc MG 202, box 1, GAS/NYPL; "By the Loud Resounding Sea," SWCA, May 3, 1923, p. 3.

2. Quoted in Dan Ellis, "First People of the Pass: Black Heritage," July 2001, p. 14, http://passchristian.tripod.com/HTMLobj-21/BlackHeritage1.pdf (accessed July 27, 2010).

3. Dan Ellis, "Charlot Tract," *City of Pass Christian*, http://city.passchristian.net/charlot_tract.htm (accessed February 9, 2011); Russell Guerin, "Book B—Analysis," http://www.russellguerin.com/history/hancock-county/book-b-analysis/ (accessed May 2, 2011). Guerin also found that the value of land with beach frontage increased dramatically in the 1850s. In contrast to plantation economies where beach frontage offered a means of transporting goods to market, most of the beachfront parcels sold during these years were, he added, for use as residences and small businesses. See Russell Guerin, "Book B—Analysis," http://www.russellguerin.com/history/hancock-county/book-b-analysis/ (accessed May 2, 2011).

4. Dan Ellis, "First People of the Pass: Black Heritage," July 2001, p. 14, http://passchristian.tripod.com/HTMLobj-21/BlackHeritage1.pdf (accessed July 27, 2010).

5. "Bernard Benoit Jr. v. John Brill," in *Reports of Cases Argued and Determined for the State of Mississippi*, vol. 7, ed. W. C. Smedes and R. A. Marshall (Boston: Charles C. Little and James Brown, 1847), 22–38.

6. Herman Melvin Cappie and Ruth Irene Cappie, interview by Michele Mitchell, June 22 and 29, 1996, New Orleans, BTV/RBMSC/DU.

7. "Avon Hotel," *The Historian of Hancock County*, September 2004; Federal Writers' Project, *Mississippi: A Guide to the Magnolia State* (New York: Viking Press, 1938), 173.

8. Thomas R. Savage to George P. Brandt, May 5, 1889, folder 46, WSP/SHC.

9. Morris L. Davis, *The Methodist Unification: Christianity and the Politics of Race in the Jim Crow Era* (New York: New York University Press, 2008), 100. One interviewee recalled that, in his later years, Jones said, "If I don't get to heaven, it's because I couldn't stand the white man," to which she responded, "You must [not] look in the mirror." See Juanita Doris Franklin, interview by Andrew Kahrl, January 14, 2010, audiotape in possession of the author.

10. See Harry V. Richardson, *Dark Salvation: The Story of Methodism as It Developed among Blacks in America* (Garden City, NY: Anchor Press, 1976).

11. James B. Bennett, *Religion and the Rise of Jim Crow in New Orleans* (Princeton, NJ: Princeton University Press, 2005), 8, 105.

12. In his 1937 study of Indianola, Mississippi, the sociologist John Dollard commented, "No better record exists [than the *Southwestern Christian Advocate*] for understanding the hopes and fears of black M.E. church members as their denomination struggled with questions of racial identity and the limits of inclusion." See John Dollard, *Caste and Class in a Southern Town* (New Haven, CT: Yale University Press, 1937), 50.

13. Arnold R. Hirsch, "Simply a Matter of Black and White: The Transformation of Race and Politics in Twentieth-Century New Orleans," in *Creole New Orleans: Race and Americanization,* ed. Arnold R. Hirsch and Joseph Logsdon (Baton Rouge: Louisiana State University Press, 1992), 266.

14. *Crisis,* February 1916, 169. On the Bureau of Negro Work's calls for progressive reform, see *Annual Report: The Board of Home Missions and Church Extension of the Methodist Episcopal Church, for the Year Ending October 31, 1924* (Philadelphia, 1924), 83.

15. Wilma Dykeman and James Stokely, *Seeds of Southern Change: The Life of Will Alexander* (Chicago: University of Chicago Press, 1962), 71. Jacquelyn Dowd Hall notes that, through fostering "close institutional and personal ties with Northern philanthropists," the CIC became "a major conduit for the flow of financial resources into black uplift and protest efforts." Hall, *Revolt against Chivalry: Jessie Daniel Ames and the Women's Campaign against Lynching* (New York: Columbia University Press, 1979), 62.

16. Bishop R. E. Jones Obituary, n.d., box 1, folder 13, REJ/ARC.

17. Cindy S. Aron, *Working at Play: A History of Vacations in the United States* (New York: Oxford University Press, 1999), 111–26. See also Foster Rhea Dulles, *America Learns to Play: A History of Popular Recreation, 1607–1940* (New York: D. Appleton-Century Co., 1940), 259–60.

18. Henry J. Mason, "A Black Chautauqua," *Opportunity: Journal of Negro Life,* August 1929, pp. 241–42.

19. "Waveland's Gulfside Assembly," March 15, 1957, box 1, folder 8, Ray M. Thompson Papers, McCain Library and Archives Collection, University of Southern Mississippi, Hattiesburg; Raymond R. Breaux, "Gulfside: Seventy Years of Service," *New World Outlook* (March–April 1993), 16–18; Mason, "Gulfside Idea," 315; "Gulfside Assembly: The Fulfillment of a Dream," *A Publication of Black Methodists for Church Renewal,* March 1980.

20. "Gulfside Association," *Foundation,* November 1925, pp. 10–11. There are several other reasons for taking out short-term notes to finance the purchase of property. It is an aggressive investment strategy that offers lower interest rates but requires a quick repayment schedule. It also allows a buyer to consummate the deal before he has secured a sufficient number of investors. The short-term

notes also allowed Jones to pay his sellers immediately but provided him a short window to round up investors. This third explanation suggests that Jones first needed to secure title to the land and begin work on its development before he could expect to secure additional investors who might otherwise be skeptical of its feasibility.

21. Mason, "Gulfside Idea," 319; H. J. Mason to George R. Arthur, February 5, 1929, box 208, folder 5, JRFA/FU; "The Value of Gulfside as an Educational Centre," *Gulfside News*, May–June 1927, Sc MG 202, box 1, GAS/NYPL; "Uncle Gulfside's View," *Gulfside News*, May–June 1927, ibid.

22. The early twentieth century witnessed the embrace of seawalls as the panacea for the vulnerability of coastal towns and the volatility of coastal real estate markets. Following a hurricane that leveled the town in 1900, Galveston, Texas, began work on a massive seawall that was completed in 1904. Cornelia Dean, *Against the Tide: The Battle for America's Beaches* (New York: Columbia University Press, 1999), 1–14, 53.

23. "How to Best Exploit the Gulf Coast Country of Mississippi," *SCE*, June 9, 1923; "Waveland's Future Is Promising," *SCE*, April 5, 1924; "Beautification of Our Beach Front," *SCE*, June 1, 1928.

24. Klaus J. Meyer-Arendt, "Historical Coastal Environmental Changes: Human Responses to Shoreline Erosion," in *The American Environment: Interpretations of Past Geographies*, ed. Lary M. Dilsaver and Craig E. Colten (Savage, MD: Rowman & Littlefield, 1992), 225.

25. "Beautiful Shell Beach-on-Bay," *SCE*, May 31, 1924; "National Playg'nd on Miss. Gulf Coast Says Mr. Markham," *SCE*, July 18, 1925; "Planning to Beautify the Gulf Coast," *SCE*, May 1, 1926; "Miss. Gulf Coast Growing into Real Riviera," *SCE*, January 30, 1926; "Colored People Circulating Petition," *SCE*, June 15, 1928.

26. "Mississippi Gulf Coast Growing into Real Riviera," *SCE*, January 30, 1926; "Mississippi Has a Resort Land Boom," *WSJ*, December 4, 1925; "City Beautiful Comes into Its Own: Realty Values," *SCE*, May 2, 1925; advertisement, "Mississippi Coast Club," *SCE*, January 16, 1926; "Golfers Looking Southward," *Chicago Daily Journal*, January 9, 1926, quoted in "Mississippi Gulf Coast Attracts Attention," *SCE*, January 30, 1926; "Millions of Chicago Cash to Gulf Coast," *CT*, n.d., reprinted in *SCE*, February 19, 1927.

27. *SCE*, December 22, 1933, p. 4; Charles L. Sullivan and Murella Herbert Powell, *The Mississippi Gulf Coast: Portrait of a People; An Illustrated History* (Northridge, CA: Windsor, 1985), 142.

28. George N. Coad, "Mississippi Loses Fear of Capital," *NYT*, May 13, 1928.

29. "N.O. Realty Man Says Gulf Coast Peer of Florida," *NOTP*, n.d., reprinted in *SCE*, May 9, 1925.

30. "Our Laws to Blame for This Condition," *SCE*, June 27, 1925; Helen Bullitt Lowry, "New Orleans Booms Quite Decorously," *NYT*, April 18, 1926; "Mississippi Shares in Gains of South," *WSJ*, August 28, 1926.

31. "Mississippi Loses Fear of Capital," *NYT*, May 13, 1928.

32. "Mr. Jos. Labat, of Bay St. Louis, Awarded Contract for New Dormitory at Gulfside," *Gulfside News*, May–June 1927, Sc MG 202, box 1, GAS/NYPL; "Waveland's Gulfside Assembly," March 15, 1957, box 1, folder 8, Ray M. Thompson Papers, McCain Library and Archives Collection, University of Southern Mississippi, Hattiesburg; "The Waveland Enterprise," *Foundation*, March–April 1924, p. 11; Rev. J. T. Jeffrey, Rector to the Rt. Rev. R. E. Jones, May 6, 1927, Sc MG 202, box 1, GAS/NYPL; "Gulfside Association," *Foundation*, November 1925, pp. 10–11.

33. Dedication, State of Mississippi, County of Hancock, book D-5, reel 9489, p. 238, Hancock County Deed Records, LDR/MDAH; "Superintendent's Notes," *Gulfside Visitor*, September–October 1948; Gulfside Association Annual Report, 1943, Financial Statement, Bishop Robert E. Jones, Gulfside, Records of the General Board of Higher Education and Ministry, UMCA/GCAH; "Bumper Cabbage Crop at Gulfside," *Gulfside News*, May–June 1927, p. 1, Sc MG 202, box 1, GAS/NYPL; "Roy L. Smith Service Unit," *Gulfside Visitor*, December 1949; Breaux, "Gulfside: Seventy Years of Service," 17; "Camp Waveland" and "Camp Moorland," pp. 20–22, in "Gulfside Association Hand Book of Information and Calendar of Events for the Summer of 1927," Sc MG 202, box 1, GAS/NYPL.

34. See Michele Mitchell, *Righteous Propagation: African Americans and the Politics of Racial Destiny after Reconstruction* (Chapel Hill: University of North Carolina Press, 2004).

35. School of Practical Methods for Town and Rural Pastors, pamphlet, June 9–19, 1931, box 208, folder 6, JRFA/FU; "School of Missions at Gulfside," *SWCA*, October 17, 1929; J. B. Randolph, president, Claflin College, "Testimonies," in "Just What I Have Been Looking for an Ideal Summer Resort at the Gulf Side Chautauqua and Camp Meeting Ground," pamphlet, n.d., Sc MG 202, box 1, GAS/NYPL.

36. My discussion of space in the ontology of Jim Crow is influenced by the work of Michel-Rolph Trouillot, *Silencing the Past: Power and the Production of History* (Boston: Beacon Press, 1995), 70–107.

37. Pat Harvey, interview by Andrew Kahrl, January 8, 2010, Waveland, MS, audiotape in possession of the author; Juanita Doris Franklin interview.

38. J. Leonard Farmer, "Gulfside and the Summer School for Undergraduate Preachers," *Christian Advocate* (Central Edition), December 11, 1941, p. 797; "School of Missions at Gulfside," *SWCA*, October 17, 1929; Daniel Lyman

Ridout, "The Soul of Gulfside," n.d., box 2, folder 3, quote p. 5, REJ/ARC; Juanita Doris Franklin interview.

39. "Gulfside Clubs: Constitution and By-Laws," n.d., Sc MG 202, box 1, GAS/ NYPL; "Report: Area Council Budget," *Journal of the Eighth Annual Meeting of the New Orleans Area Council, Methodist Episcopal Church* (August 31–September 4, 1927), pp. 43–45, Sc MG 202, box 1, GAS/NYPL.

40. See, for example, Robert E. Jones to P. J. Mavetty, May 5, 1926, Bishop Robert E. Jones, Gulfside, Records of the General Board of Higher Education and Ministry, UMCA/GCAH; and Jones to George Arthur, December 23, 1933, box 208, folder 8, JRFA/FU.

41. Gulfside Assembly Meeting Notes, n.d., box 208, folder 6, JRFA/FU; Advertisement, "The Gulfside Association," *SCE*, April 4, 1925; "Uncle Gulfside's View," *Gulfside News*, May–June 1927, Sc MG 202, box 1, GAS/ NYPL; George R. Rea, "To Whom It May Concern," in Bishop R. E. Jones, "To Touch the Active and Present Day Leadership of the Negro Race in the South Is the Aim of the Gulfside Association," pamphlet, n.d., ibid.

42. Advertisement, "The Gulfside Association," *SCE*, April 4, 1925, 5; "Hancock County Extension Department," *SCE*, June 13, 1925; "Gulfside Haven for All Negroes," *New Orleans Daily States*, January 23, 1927, Sc MG 202, box 1, GAS/ NYPL.

43. "Mississippians Invite Illinois to Visit State," *CT*, September 5, 1926; "Bay St. Louis and Waveland Building Boom Continues," *SCE*, August 5, 1927; "Project for Colored at Gulfside," *SCE*, May 21, 1927.

44. "Gulfside Dedication," *SWCA*, October 13, 1927; "Dedication of Gulfside and Area Council," *SWCA*, November 17, 1927; Harry C. Tartt, interview by William Henderson, November 1, 1999, interview F341.5 .M57 vol. 747, transcript, MOHP/USM.

45. Song Fest resembled the events black colleges hosted for white donors, in which, as Adam Fairclough described, "politicians and trustees were treated to mouth-watering feasts, elaborate entertainments, and fawning attention." Adam Fairclough, " 'Being in the Field of Education and Also Being a Negro . . . Seems . . . Tragic': Black Teachers in the Jim Crow South," *Journal of American History* 87 (June 2000): 76. The program for one Song Fest implored visitors to understand and appreciate "the handicaps under which Negroes have been laboring in their struggle for a fuller and freer development as worthy citizens." Second Annual Song Festival, program, August 28, 1932, Bishop Robert E. Jones, Gulfside, Records of the General Board of Higher Education and Ministry, UMCA/ GCAH.

46. Gulfside Association Report, October 9, 1933, Bishop Robert E. Jones, Gulfside, Records of the General Board of Higher Education and Ministry,

UMCA/GCAH; "Real Spirituals," *SWCA*, September 17, 1931; Gulfside Association Annual Superintendent's Report, May 24, 1934, box 208, folder 8, JRFA/FU; "It Should Be Fostered," *New Orleans Item*, September 1, 1932, Bishop Robert E. Jones, Gulfside, Records of the General Board of Higher Education and Ministry, UMCA/GCAH; Annual Report to the Board of Trustees of Gulfside Association, June 5, 1934, box 208, folder 8, JRFA/FU.

47. "Gulfside Receives Gift of $35,000," *PC*, June 30, 1928; Thomas B. Appleget to Robert E. Jones, May 18, 1928, box 208, folder 5, JRFA/FU. On the history of the Rosenwald Fund, see Peter M. Ascoli, *Julius Rosenwald: The Man Who Built Sears, Roebuck and Advanced the Cause of Black Education in the American South* (Bloomington: Indiana University Press, 2006); and Edwin R. Embree and Julia Waxman, *Investment in People: The Story of the Julius Rosenwald Fund* (New York: Harper, 1949).

48. Summary of the New York Informal Conference on Gulfside Assembly, p. 2, January 6, 1931, box 208, folder 7, JRFA/FU; "A Challenge to Racial Vision," *Gulfside News*, April 1929, p. 2, Bishop Robert E. Jones, Gulfside, Records of the General Board of Higher Education and Ministry, UMCA/GCAH.

49. On the influence of white sponsors on black charities and reform groups, see Deborah G. White, *Too Heavy a Load: Black Women in Defense of Themselves, 1894–1994* (New York: Norton, 1999); and Khalil Gibran Muhammad, *The Condemnation of Blackness: Race, Crime, and the Making of Modern Urban America* (Cambridge, MA: Harvard University Press, 2010), 131–32.

50. Minutes of meeting, New York, January 6, 1931, box 208, folder 6, JRFA/FU; Questions and Answers on Gulfside, March 21, 1931, ibid.; Daniel Lyman Ridout, "The Soul of Gulfside," n.d., box 2, folder 3, quote p. 5, REJ/ARC; Edwin R. Embree to Robert E. Jones, March 21, 1929, box 208, folder 5, JRFA/FU.

51. R. E. Jones to Dr. M. J. Holmes, October 6, 1938, Bishop Robert E. Jones, Gulfside, Records of the General Board of Higher Education and Ministry, UMCA/GCAH; Annual report from July 1, 1928, through July 31, 1929, May 12, 1930, box 208, folder 6, JRFA/FU.

52. Report of GRA's interview with Bishop Jones, September 22–23, 1930, box 208, folder 6, JRFA/FU; Edwin R. Embree to Bishop Jones, September 15, 1930, ibid.

53. "Two High-Class Tourist Hotels on Gulf Coast Sold to Bondholders," *SCE*, August 8, 1930; "Delinquent Tax Sale," *SCE*, February 7, 1930; "'Spanish Acres' Name of Handsome Subdivision to Be Open on the Beach," *SCE*, July 5, 1929; "Mississippi Gulf Coast Potentially Outstanding in Link with New O," *SCE*, February 8, 1929.

54. Gulfside Association Report, October 9, 1933, Bishop Robert E. Jones, Gulfside, Records of the General Board of Higher Education and Ministry, UMCA/GCAH; R. E. Jones to Dr. Edwin R. Embree, November 23, 1929, box 208, folder 5, JRFA/FU; and R. E. Jones to Dr. Edwin R. Embree, May 24, 1934, box 208, folder 7, ibid.; Receipts and Disbursements, 1929–1933, box 208, folder 8, ibid.; Report on Building and Equipment Fund, February 1–December 31, 1930, box 208, folder 6, ibid.; Receipts and Disbursements, 1929–1933, box 208, folder 8, ibid.; R. E. Jones to Dr. Edwin R. Embree, September 22, 1932, box 208, folder 7, ibid.; R. E. Jones to Dr. Edwin R. Embree, June 21, 1932, ibid.

55. Gulfside Association Financial Statement, October 9, 1933, box 208, folder 8, JRFA/FU; Gulfside Association Annual Superintendent's Report, May 24, 1934, ibid.

56. Jackson House pamphlet, 1928, subject file—Gulfside Association, Mississippi Department of Archives and History, Jackson.

57. Timothy B. Echols, "Gulfside to Rebuild," SWCA, February 13, 1936.

58. R. E. Jones to Dr. M. J. Holmes, August 18, 1936, Bishop Robert E. Jones, Gulfside, Records of the General Board of Higher Education and Ministry, UMCA/GCAH; Henry J. Mason, "Shame on America, 'Sweet Land of Liberty,'" SWCA, May 12, 1938.

59. See Davis, Methodist Unification.

60. Crisis, March 1918, 215.

61. Quoted in Henry Nathaniel Oakes, "The Struggle for Racial Equality in the Methodist Episcopal Church: The Career of Robert E. Jones, 1904–1944" (Ph.D. diss., University of Iowa, 1973), 423.

62. Nathaniel F. Forsyth, "The Future of Gulfside: A Twenty-Five Year Plan," n.d., Bishop Robert E. Jones, Gulfside, Records of the General Board of Higher Education and Ministry, UMCA/GCAH.

63. See US v. Harrison County, 399 F.2d 485; 1968.

64. Ibid.

65. See "The Veteran Pastor's Fund," Gulfside Visitor, December 1949.

66. M. S. Davage, Treasurer to Gulfside Association Board of Trustees, Mount Zion Methodist Church, New Orleans, October 23, 1958, box 2, folder 3, p. 2, REJ/ARC; Gulfside Association Board of Trustees, Mount Zion Methodist Church, New Orleans, meeting minutes, October 23, 1958, box 2, folder 3, n.p., ibid.; Daniel Lyman Ridout, "The Soul of Gulfside," n.d., box 2, folder 3, pp. 3, 5, ibid.

67. Linda Green, "Gulfside Center Bridges Segregation Era, 21st Century," February 16, 2005, United Methodist Church, http://archives.umc.org/interior .asp?ptid=2&mid=6714 (accessed July 26, 2005).

68. Quoted in Natasha Trethaway, Beyond Katrina: A Meditation on the Mississippi Gulf Coast (Athens: University of Georgia Press, 2010), 43, 47.

69. Lodie Marie Robinson-Cyrille, interview by Worth Long, August 24, 1999, transcript, MOHP/USM; Ed Moultrie, interview by Andrew Kahrl, January 8, 2010, Waveland, MS, audiotape in possession of the author.

70. Genevieve Gordon, interview by Andrew Kahrl, January 8, 2010, Waveland, MS, audiotape in possession of the author; Raymond Breaux, interview by Andrew Kahrl, January 12, 2010, New Orleans, audiotape in possession of the author; Kelly Ward and Stephen Tyler, producers, *Gulf Coast Memories: Great Memories from the '50s and '60s* (Greater New Orleans Educational Television Foundation, 2002).

3. Building Black Privatopias

1. Gwen Ifill, "Highland Beach Still Haven for Weary City Dwellers," WP, July 11, 1985; Ray Langston, interview by Andrew Kahrl, December 12, 2009, Highland Beach, MD, audiotape in possession of the author; Nurith C. Aizenman, "A Haven for Blacks and History," WP, August 20, 2002; John Moses, interview by Andrew Kahrl, December 12, 2009, Highland Beach, MD, audiotape in possession of the author.

2. Evan McKenzie, *Privatopia: Homeowner Associations and the Rise of Residential Private Government* (New Haven, CT: Yale University Press, 1996).

3. Paul Laurence Dunbar, "Negro Society in Washington," *Saturday Evening Post*, December 14, 1901, in Dunbar, *The Sport of the Gods: And Other Essential Writings*, ed. Shelly Fisher Fishkin and David Bradley (New York: Modern Library, 2005), 286.

4. "Cedar Haven News," WTr, August 12, 1927; Kelly Miller, "Watchtower," AN, June 30, 1934. On black town development, see also Kenneth Marvin Hamilton, *Black Towns and Profit: Promotion and Development in the Trans-Appalachian West, 1877–1915* (Urbana: University of Illinois Press, 1991).

5. See Andrew W. Kahrl, "The Political Work of Leisure: Class, Recreation, and African American Commemoration at Harpers Ferry, West Virginia, 1881–1931," *Journal of Social History* 42 (Fall 2008): 57–77; Mark S. Foster, "In the Face of 'Jim Crow': Prosperous Blacks and Vacations, Travel and Outdoor Leisure, 1890–1945," *Journal of Negro History* 84 (Spring 1999): 130–49; and Willard B. Gatewood, *Aristocrats of Color: The Black Elite, 1880–1920* (Bloomington: Indiana University Press, 1990), 200–202.

6. A. K. Sandoval-Strausz, *Hotel: An American History* (New Haven, CT: Yale University Press, 2007), 299.

7. WB, August 31, 1895. Concerned that it might jeopardize his employment with the federal government, Charles Douglass had his son Joseph listed on the title

to the property acquired from the Brashearses. Following his retirement in 1898, Charles Douglass had all property in Highland Beach that had not already been sold transferred into his name.

8. Quoted in Jack E. Nelson, Raymond L. Langston, and Margo Dean Pinson, *Highland Beach on the Chesapeake Bay: Maryland's First African American Incorporated Town* (Virginia Beach, VA: Highland Beach Historical Association / Donning Co. Publishers, 2008), 14.

9. By the turn of the century, Washington, D.C., had become, historian Jonathan Scott Holloway notes, "black America's intellectual center" and home to the nation's largest and most established black upper class. "No other city," Willard B. Gatewood adds, "possessed such a concentration of 'old families,' . . . whose emphasis on family background, good breeding, occupation, respectability, and color bound them into an exclusive, self-consciously elitest group." See Jonathan Scott Holloway, *Confronting the Veil: Abram Harris Jr., E. Franklin Frazier, and Ralph Bunche, 1919–1941* (Chapel Hill: University of North Carolina Press, 2002), 36; Gatewood, *Aristocrats of Color*, 39. See also Constance McLaughlin Green, *The Secret City: A History of Race Relations in the Nation's Capital* (Princeton, NJ: Princeton University Press, 1967), 129–31.

10. W. E. B. Du Bois, "About Vacations," *PC*, September 18, 1937.

11. Frederick Douglass, quoted in Adele Logan Alexander, *Homelands and Waterways: The American Journey of the Bond Family, 1846–1926* (New York: Vintage, 1999), 446. "The Silvery Waves," *CA*, August 17, 1901.

12. Ray Langston interview. See also Mary Church Terrell, *A Colored Woman in a White World* (Washington, DC: Ransdell, 1940).

13. Paul Laurence Dunbar, "Negro Society in Washington," in *Saturday Evening Post*, December 14, 1901, in Dunbar, *Sport of the Gods*, 288.

14. Figures generated from analysis of Anne Arundel County Circuit Court (Land Records), 1893–1920. Accessed at MDLandRec.Net.

15. Anne Arundel County Circuit Court (Land Records), 1920, Book WNW 28, p. 261, MSA CE 59-239; 1920, WNW 28, p. 262, MSA CE 59-239; and 1920, WNW 35, p. 83, MSA CE 59-246.

16. Anne Arundel County Circuit Court (Land Records, Grantor Index), 1909–1929, f. 0046a, MSA CE 74-75.

17. See Lewis Walker and Benjamin C. Wilson, *Black Eden: The Idlewild Community* (East Lansing: Michigan State University Press, 2002).

18. Quoted in John Fraser Hart, "A Rural Retreat for Northern Negroes," *Geographical Review* 50 (April 1960): 158, 163.

19. Claudia Polley, "Fox Lake: A Resort Like Many Others," *Cultural Resource Management* 20 (May 1997): 55.

20. Quoted in "Cedar Haven News," *WTr*, August 12, 1927, p. 4.

21. Along with Eagle Harbor, Hine was credited with the development of Herald Harbor, Epping Forest, Gunston Manor, Shoreham Beach, Avalon Shores, and Bonniewood, all located outside Washington, D.C., and founded in the 1920s and 1930s. See "Last Rites Held for E. S. Hine, 64, Real Estate Man," WP, December 13, 1939.

22. "Crack Realty Salesman Held 20 Jobs Learning 1," BAA, May 1, 1937.

23. The black press played an important role in promoting black vacation resort ventures. The Washington Tribune began running, in 1927, a summer vacation section, with columns containing news and gossip from various resorts, advertisements for tire retailers, and a list of hotels, cottages, and resorts, from Massachusetts's Berkshire Hills to Virginia's Atlantic coast. The Tribune's vacation section offered African Americans of means a guide to finding places where they could "enjoy a good bed to sleep in and palatable meals with congenial and healthful surroundings," "long . . . the bugbear of the [black] vacationist." It helped them to navigate the treacherous terrain of unfamiliar environments and encouraged the hesitant to venture outside their neighborhoods and communities for pleasure, amusement, and a "change of scenery." See, for example, "Advertisement," WTr, July 1, 1927, p. 2.

24. The Woothrolites, composed of employees of the Woodward and Lothrop department stores, pooled their resources and built their own clubhouse in Cedar Haven. Elizabeth Calvit, "Eagle Harbor, Prince George's County," 1993, unpublished paper, Prince George's County Historical Society. A group of District of Columbia teachers founded a colony at Cedar Haven and constructed a cluster of cottages. Restaurant owners opened seasonal villa-inns that catered to the summer crowds. "Cedar Haven News," WTr, July 22, 1927.

25. "Cedar Haven News," WTr, July 22, 1927, p. 2.

26. Passed by the U.S. Congress in 1937, the Tax Anti-Injunction Statute severely restricted the ability of federal courts to intervene in disputes over property assessments and erected a host of obstacles that had the effect of discouraging victims from pressing their case in court. Under the law, complainants were required to submit their appeal to a county review board, often composed of the same assessors named in the complaint. In court, plaintiffs seeking a reduction in taxation were required to prove "intentional discrimination," often impossible given the haphazard, subjective, and seemingly arbitrary nature of assessments.

27. "Ku Klux Annoy Newark Couple in Many Ways," BAA, July 16, 1927.

28. "Protest Tax Raise in Prince Georges," BAA, February 11, 1928.

29. "Son of Frederick Douglass Dead," BAA, December 3, 1920.

30. "Formation of Two New Towns Asked," WP, March 13, 1929.

31. See Nelson, Langston, and Pinson, Highland Beach on the Chesapeake Bay, 35.

32. Eula G. Brown [pseud.], "Highland Beach: A Paradoxical Community, Article 3," *WTr*, August 16, 1929.

33. This was a familiar tactic used by enterprising developers looking to capitalize on the name and reputation of an existing resort. Less than a decade after word of Idlewild spread throughout Chicago and other northern black metropolises, a rival white real estate firm purchased a large block of land north of Baldwin, the county seat of Lake County, where Idlewild was located, and advertised cheaper lots under the Idlewild name. See Hart, "Rural Retreat for Northern Negroes," 159.

34. "Fashionable Set Revels at Bay Resort," *CD*, August 13, 1927.

35. See *Richard King v. The North Chesapeake Beach Land and Improvement Company*, 143 Md. 693; 123 A. 445 (1923).

36. "$10 Fine for Unauthorized Highland Beach Bathers," *BAA*, August 14, 1926.

37. "Two Candidates for Mayor at Highland Beach," *BAA*, July 30, 1932.

38. Eula G. Brown [pseud.], "Highland Beach: A Paradoxical Community, Article 3," *WTr*, August 16, 1929; "Henderson Tells Why Old Beach Commissioners Quit," *BAA*, August 25, 1928; "Only Colored Md. Town Names Commissioners," *BAA*, August 7, 1926; "Highland Beach Election Arouses Interest," *WTr*, July 23, 1926; "Frederick Douglass Would Turn Over in His Grave If He Could See Highland Beach, the Town He Founded," letter to the editor signed "A. H.," *BAA*, December 12, 1931; Eula G. Brown [pseud.], "Highland Beach: A Paradoxical Community, Article 4," *WTr*, August 23, 1929.

39. "Highland Beach Election Settles Political Issues," *BAA*, August 18, 1928; Louis R. Lautier, "Highland Beach Citizens Making Valiant Fight to Keep Sea Shore Exclusive for 'Socially Prominent,'" *WTr*, August 12, 1927; "Frederick Douglass Would Turn Over in His Grave," *BAA*, December 12, 1931; "Highland Beach Is Summer Resort," *BAA*, October 17, 1925.

40. "Rival Beaches on Chesapeake in Barbed Wire Controversy," *BAA*, July 20, 1929; M. Grant Lucas to the Members of Highland Beach Summer Colony, July 24, 1928, MCTP/LOC; "Warfare at Fashionable Highland Beach; Ex-Mayor Erects Barb Wire 'Spite' Fence," *PC*, July 20, 1929; Eula G. Brown [pseud.], "Highland Beach: A Paradoxical Community, Part 3" *WTr*, August 2, 1929.

41. Florence Murray, "Trouble Starts at Highland Beach When Group Attempts to Keep It Exclusive," n.d., MCTP/LOC; "Fight Is Still on at Highland Beach," *BAA*, July 12, 1930; "Douglass Scion Heads Town of Highland Beach, Md.," *BAA*, August 11, 1928; "Venice Beach Colony Protests County Road," *BAA*, June 7, 1930; "Highland Beach Goes to the Polls on July 25," *BAA*, July 25, 1931.

42. John R. Francis and J. E. Washington, quoted in "Highland Beach, Md., Sick and Tired of Abuses, Wars on Unjust Criticisms," *BAA*, September 24, 1932.

43. Eula G. Brown [pseud.], "Highland Beach: A Paradoxical Community, Article 5," *WTr*, August 30, 1929.

44. Eula G. Brown [pseud.], "Highland Beach: A Paradoxical Community, Article 3," *WTr*, August 16, 1929.

45. "Crowds at Highland Beach Sunday for a Dip in Bay," *BAA*, August 11, 1928; "Society Split over Beach Row," *CD*, July 19, 1930. On "The Stroll," see Davarian L. Baldwin, *Chicago's New Negroes: Modernity, the Great Migration, and Black Urban Life* (Chapel Hill: University of North Carolina Press, 2007), 21–52.

46. Eula G. Brown [pseud.], "Highland Beach: A Paradoxical Community, Part 3," *WTr*, August 9, 1929.

47. M. Grant Lucas to Members of the Highland Beach Summer Community, July 24, 1928, MCTP/LOC; "Highland Beach Hotel Ware Is Raided," *BAA*, July 27, 1929; Eula G. Brown [pseud.], "Highland Beach: A Paradoxical Community, Part 3," *WTr*, August 9, 1929; Eula G. Brown [pseud.], "Highland Beach: A Paradoxical Community, Article 4," *WTr*, August 23, 1929; Eula G. Brown [pseud.], "Highland Beach: A Paradoxical Community, Part 3," *WTr*, August 9, 1929; "Maryland Cops Raid Fashionable Resort," *CD*, August 3, 1929; and Ordinances of Highland Beach, MD, n.d., MCTP/LOC.

48. "Fire Ravages Highland Beach, Md.," *BAA*, January 25, 1930; Louis R. Lautier, "The Capital Spotlight," *BAA*, September 3, 1952.

49. See James W. Loewen, *Sundown Towns: A Hidden Dimension of American Racism* (New York: New Press, 2005).

50. Louis R. Lautier, "Highland Beach Citizens Are Divided over Exclusion," *WTr*, August 19, 1927; "Frederick Douglass Would Turn Over in His Grave," *BAA*, December 12, 1931.

51. "Mayor Henderson Explains Highland Beach Regulations," *BAA*, August 3, 1929; "Frederick Douglass Would Turn Over in His Grave," *BAA*, December 12, 1931; Ralph Matthews, "Finds Baltimore Offers Little for Vacation Time," *BAA*, July 31, 1926; Ralph Matthews, "Heard and Seen in Baltimore," *BAA*, August 21, 1926; Professor Fudge, "Around Baltimore," *BAA*, August 10, 1929; John R. Rudisell, letter to editor, *WTr*, August 26, 1927; W. R. Tillman, "Let Him without Sin," letter to the editor, *WTr*, August 26, 1927; John E. Harris, "A Study in Black & White," *WTr*, September 2, 1927; "High Tides at Highland Beach," *BAA*, August 3, 1929; "Three Very Open Missives from Ralph Matthews to Three Other People," *BAA*, August 27, 1927; W. R. Tillman, "Let Him without Sin," *WTr*, August 26, 1927.

52. Eula G. Brown [pseud.], "Highland Beach: A Paradoxical Community, Part One," *WTr*, July 26, 1929.

53. Helen Monchow, *The Use of Deed Restrictions in Subdivision Development* (Chicago: Institute for Research in Land Economics and Public Utilities, 1928), cited in McKenzie, *Privatopia*, 43–45.

54. M. A. Francis, E. B. Henderson, B. J. Walker, and N. L. Guy to the Townspeople of Highland Beach, July 23, 1928, MCTP/LOC.

55. *Laws of the State of Maryland*, Chapter 119 (April 21, 1933); "Highland Beach, Md., Has Its Own Father Divine Case," BAA, April 29, 1933.

56. See C. Fraser Smith, *Here Lies Jim Crow: Civil Rights in Maryland* (Baltimore: Johns Hopkins University Press, 2008), 142–43.

57. Overall black incomes tripled in the 1940s and increased by another 50 percent in the 1950s. See Andrew Wiese, *Places of Their Own: African American Suburbanization in the Twentieth Century* (Chicago: University of Chicago Press, 2004), 124.

58. Earl Kelly, "Educator Fought for Equal Pay for Black Teachers," AC, October 13, 2009, http://www.hometownannapolis.com/news/can/2009/10/13-44/Educator-fought-for-equal-pay-for-black-teachers.html (accessed July 6, 2010).

59. Anne Arundel County Circuit Court (Land Records), 1939–1940, Book JHH 209, p. 354, MSA CE 59-553; Anne Arundel County Circuit Court (Land Records, Grantor Index), Co–Cz, 1940–1953, pp. 113–21, MSA CE 74-60.

60. Anne Arundel County Circuit Court (Land Records), 1949, Book 517, p. 176, MSA CE 59-861; Anne Arundel County Circuit Court (Land Records), 1949, Book 550, p. 198, MSA CE 59-894.

61. Edwin B. Henderson, "Sports Comment," ADW, April 15, 1950.

62. Anne Arundel County Circuit Court (Land Records, Grantor Index), N–O, 1940–1953, pp. 141–42, MSA CE 74-72; Anne Arundel County Circuit Court (Land Records, Corporation Grantor Index), N–Q, 1953–1967, pp. 25–26, MSA CE 70-9.

63. See Property Owners Association of Arundel-on-the-Bay Inc., Constitutions and Bylaws, Rules and Regulations, Policies, arundelonthebay.org/pdf/constitution&rules.pdf (accessed January 20, 2011).

64. Anne Arundel County Circuit Court (Land Records), 1949, Book 546, p. 29, MSA CE 59-890.

65. Anne Arundel County Circuit Court (Land Records), 1949, Book 548, p. 186, MSA CE 59-892.

66. See, for example, real estate advertisement, WP, July 23, 1950.

67. "Live on the Beach All Year!" BAA, August 22, 1953; "Little Town on the Bay Grows Up," WP, June 11, 1988; Edwin Henderson, "Spread of Colored Summer Homes Seen Sign of Culture," NJG, September 20, 1952.

68. Courtney Mabeus, "No Outsiders Please—Private Beach Communities Taking Steps to Keep Non-Resident Swimmers Away," AC, June 15, 2001.

69. "Live on the Beach All Year!" BAA, August 22, 1953.

70. Sharon Merrick, interview by Andrew Kahrl, April 10, 2010, audiotape in possession of the author.

71. Nelson, Langston, and Pinson, *Highland Beach on the Chesapeake Bay*, 80; Ray Langston interview; John Moses interview; Sharon Merrick interview.

4. Surviving the Summer

1. Peter Badie, interview by Andrew Kahrl, January 11, 2010, audiotape in possession of the author.
2. "2 Boys Drown in Canal," *LW*, June 10, 1939; Kingsley House Extension Program: Development of Program for Negro Children, Summer 1947, box 18, folder 15, KHP/TU; Clarence J. Jackson to Base Commander, June 29, 1942, box 5, folder 7, HNL/TU; Keith Butler, interview by Andrew Kahrl, December 16, 2008, notes in possession of the author.
3. "Give Us a Place on the Lake," *LW*, July 7, 1928; "The Lake and the Season," *LW*, July 14, 1928; Oliver Evans, *New Orleans* (New York: Macmillan, 1959), 132. On Lake Pontchartrain and the origins of jazz music, see Karl Koenig, *The History of Jazz Music on the North and South Shores of Lake Pontchartrain: West End, Spanish Fort, and Milneburg; Covington, Mandeville, Abita Springs; Madisonville, Bogalusa, Hammond, Pontchatoula* (Abita Springs, LA: Basin Street Press, 1996); and Bruce Boyd Raeburn, "'They're Tryin' to Wash Us Away': New Orleans Musicians Surviving Katrina," *Journal of American History* 94 (December 2007): 812–13.
4. See W. H. Bell, "Plan of Property Improvements for the Lake Shore of the City of New Orleans" (1873), in Robert W. Hastings, *The Lakes of Pontchartrain: Their History and Environments* (Jackson: University Press of Mississippi, 2009), 75–76. See also Richard Campanella, *Time and Place in New Orleans: Past Geographies in the Present Day* (Gretna, LA: Pelican Publishers, 2002), 57.
5. On the role of the city's commercial interests in the formation of the levee board, see Ari Kelman, *A River and Its City: The Nature of Landscape in New Orleans* (Berkeley and Los Angeles: University of California Press, 2003), 165. On the formation of nonelected boards in turn-of-the-twentieth-century New Orleans, see Joy J. Jackson, *New Orleans in the Gilded Age: Politics and Urban Progress, 1880–1896*, 2nd ed. (Baton Rouge: Louisiana Historical Association in cooperation with the Center for Louisiana Studies of the University of Southwestern Louisiana, 1997). On the power wielded by these boards over governance in twentieth-century New Orleans, see Arnold R. Hirsch, "Race and Politics in Modern New Orleans: The Mayoralty of Dutch Morial," *Amerikastudien* 35 (April 1990): 469–70. In Plaquemines Parish, royalties from the minerals extracted from levee board lands made it the richest rural parish in the state. See Glen Jeansonne, *Leander Perez: Boss of the Delta* (Baton Rouge: Louisiana State University Press, 1977), 69.

6. The decision's significance, Ari Kelman notes, "was staggering . . . making levees even cheaper and more enticing than ever before" and leading to "a building binge" along the waterfront. See Kelman, *River and Its City*, 167–68.

7. Judy Ann Filipich and Lee Taylor, *Lakefront New Orleans: Planning and Development, 1926–1971* (New Orleans: Urban Studies Institute, Louisiana State University, New Orleans, 1971), 1; Orleans Levee District, "Statement of Purpose," http://www.orleanslevee.com/ (accessed August 5, 2010).

8. "Delegation for Beach Cajoled," *ADW*, July 22, 1932; Hastings, *Lakes of Pontchartrain*, 82. A rich source of material on engineering decisions and labor management during the Lakefront Reclamation Project is the diary of Robert J. Drueding, an Orleans Parish Levee Board civil engineer during the 1930s and 1940s. See Diary, Box 203-4, RJD/UNO.

9. Filipich and Taylor, *Lakefront New Orleans*, 5, 19–21, 38.

10. See Richard Campanella, *Geographies of New Orleans: Urban Fabrics before the Storm* (Lafayette, LA: Center for Louisiana Studies, 2006).

11. Daphne Spain, "Race Relations and Residential Segregation in New Orleans: Two Centuries of Paradox," *Annals of the American Academy of Political and Social Science* 441 (January 1979): 89.

12. "For the Survival of Pontchartrain Beach," January 7, 1966, PBVF/NOPL.

13. Michael Bednar, *L'Enfant's Legacy: Public Open Spaces in Washington, D.C.* (Baltimore: Johns Hopkins University Press, 2006), 47.

14. The Improvement of the Park System of the District of Columbia, 57th Cong., 1st sess., 1902, S. Rep. 166, 125; Shameful History of the Tidal Basin Beach, 69th Cong., 1st sess., Congressional Record 67 (February 8, 1926), 3550; Clarence O. Sherrill, *Improvement and Care of Public Buildings and Grounds, Care and Maintenance of the Washington Monument and of the Highway Bridge across the Potomac River, District of Columbia, and Erection of Monuments, Memorials, etc., Washington, District of Columbia* (Washington, DC: Government Printing Office, 1923), 2196; "Elizabeth Roach Wins Beach Prize," WP, July 18, 1920; Frederick Gutheim, *Worthy of the Nation: The History of Planning for the National Capital* (Washington, DC: Smithsonian Institution Press, 1977), 143. Architectural historian Michael Bednar calls the creation of the parkland along the Potomac "the beginning of the modern city of Washington." See Bednar, *L'Enfant's Legacy*, 47.

15. Julie Sze characterizes public officials' views of public beaches and parks as being "lungs for the city," the means through which health problems could be effaced and social harmony cultivated. See Sze, *Noxious New York: The Racial Politics of Urban Health and Environmental Justice* (Cambridge, MA: MIT Press, 2007), 34.

16. "Colonel Sherrill's Policy," WTr, June 13, 1925; "To Boycott Col. Sherrill's Bathing Beach," WTr, July 1, 1922; "Little Progress Made on the Bathing Beach," WTr,

July 29, 1922; *WP*, March 14, 1954; *WP*, September 10, 1924, September 2, 1938, March 14, 1954; Charles Moore, *Washington, Past and Present* (New York: Century Co., 1929), 292; "The Polluted Potomac," *WP*, September 5, 1925; W. M. Kiplinger, *Washington Is Like That* (New York: Harper, 1942), 102; *WP*, March 14, 1954.

17. "Citizens Aroused over Beach," *WTr*, June 18, 1925; "To Boycott Col. Sherrill's Bathing Beach," *WTr*, July 1, 1922.

18. "Citizens Aroused over Beach," *WTr*, June 18, 1925.

19. "Beach for Colored People Protested: Officials Reply That Congress Alone Has Power to Changes Its Location," *Washington Evening Star*, December 23, 1924; "Second Bathing Beach Is Planned," *Washington Evening Star*, December 19, 1924; "Senate Cuts Off Appropriation for Bathing Beaches," *WP*, February 19, 1925; 69th Cong., 1st sess., *Congressional Record* 67 (February 8, 1926), 3551. For a representative example of opposition to the "colored" bathing beach, see the remarks of Congressman Joseph Byrnes, Tennessee, quoted in 68th Cong., 2nd sess., *Congressional Record* 66 (February 7, 1925), 3233.

20. Thomas to Seligman, May 7, 1926, *Papers of the NAACP, Part 12: Selected Branch Files, 1913–1939, Series A: The South*, microform, reel 6, frame 327; "Youth Is Drown'd in River," *WTr*, June, 29, 1928; "No Place to Swim," *WP*, August 18, 1936; Card WDC 92, note cards, folder 10, box 131-74, EFF/MSRC. On the absence of swimming pools for black Washingtonians, see also Jeff Wiltse, *Contested Waters: A Social History of Swimming Pools in America* (Chapel Hill: University of North Carolina Press, 2007), 142–45.

21. A 1920 article by Ernest T. Attwell, field director of the Colored Bureau of Community Service, in the flagship publication of the Park Institute of America, carried a picture of two black children splashing around in a downtown city fountain with a caption, "They have found a way—the waters of the public fountain serve when no bathing pools are provided for the colored." See Attwell, "Playgrounds for Colored America," *Park International* 1 (November 1920): 224.

22. Minutes of Conference Held between the Committee of Management of the Civic Bureau and the Lake Front Development Committee of the Civic Bureau, February 15, 1929, minutes, 1929, vol. 1, NOAC/UNO.

23. Ibid.

24. Ibid.

25. Anthony J. Stanonis, "White Sites, Black Protests: Urban Tourism and the Origins of the Civil Rights Struggle in New Orleans, 1925–1945," conference paper, Louisiana Historical Association, Alexandria, LA, March 22, 2007, 8–9; Harold Lee to Robert E. Fullilove, August 14, 1943, box 5, folder 15, HNL/TU; Peter Badie interview.

26. "New Orleans Notes," *CD*, July 6, 1935; Herman Melvin Cappie and Ruth Irene Cappie, interview by Michele Mitchell, June 22 and 29, 1996, New Orleans, BTV/RBMSC/DU; William Garibaldi, interview by Andrew Kahrl, January 8, 2008, notes in possession of the author; Peter Badie interview.

27. "New Orleans Whites Push Plans for Lily-White Beach," *CD*, October 1, 1932.

28. Clarence J. Jackson to Base Commander, June 29, 1942, box 5, folder 7, HNL/TU.

29. Peter Badie interview.

30. "Here and There in New Orleans," *CD*, July 25, 1936; "Four Swimmers Drown in River in New Orleans," *CD*, August 3, 1940.

31. "Little Bay Beach Had Successful Season," *NJG*, October 21, 1916; "Little Bay Beach to Have New Mgr., and Many Improvements," *NJG*, April 9, 1921; "Cool Breezes Blow at Little Bay Beach," *NJG*, June 25, 1921; "Little Bay Beach, Local Resort, Swept by Flames," *NJG*, February 16, 1929.

32. "Little Bay Beach Offered to City for Public Recreation Center," *NJG*, January 14, 1928; "Little Bay Beach, Local Resort, Swept by Flames," *NJG*, February 16, 1929; "Little Bay Beach Is Now Under Construction," *NJG*, April 26, 1930; "Colored Norfolkians Left without a Beach Resort by Decision of Zoning Board," *NJG*, June 7, 1930. See also "A Beach Resort That Is Badly Needed," *NJG*, October 1, 1927; "Colored People's Resort," *NLD*, September 24, 1927; and "Opposition to Bathing Beach Here Renewed," *NJG*, July 12, 1930. On Young, see Henry Lewis Suggs, *P. B. Young, Newspaperman: Race, Politics, and Journalism in the New South* (Charlottesville: University Press of Virginia, 1988).

33. Advertisement, Norfolk Beach Resort Corporation, *NJG*, October 9, 1926; "Norfolk Beach," *NJG*, July 31, 1926; "City Hall Still Mum on Parks in Colored Area," *NJG*, May 15, 1926. On the extensive ties between Norfolk's city council and land development companies during these years, see William Edward Spriggs, "Afro-American Wealth Accumulation, 1900–1914" (Ph.D. diss., University of Wisconsin-Madison, 1984), 78–81.

34. Earl Lewis, *In Their Own Interests: Race, Class, and Power in Twentieth-Century Norfolk, Virginia* (Berkeley and Los Angeles: University of California Press, 1991), 84; Thomas C. Parramore, *Norfolk: The First Four Centuries* (Charlottesville: University Press of Virginia, 1994), 313, 327; "26 Persons Drowned during Summer in Local Waters," *NJG*, October 15, 1932.

35. J. Douglas Smith, *Managing White Supremacy: Race, Politics, and Citizenship in Jim Crow Virginia* (Chapel Hill: University of North Carolina Press, 2002), 235–36; "A Bathing Beach for Negroes," *NLD*, January 3, 1930; "City to Begin Work on Park in Near Future," *NJG*, March 3, 1928; John J. Pitt, letter to

editor, *NVP*, July 21, 1923; "Beach Sponsors Are Confident of Victory," *NJG*, October 4, 1930.

36. "Beach Sponsors Are Confident of Victory," *NJG*, October 4, 1930. See also Smith, *Managing White Supremacy*, 138; and Lewis, *In Their Own Interests*, 30.

37. Towns and cities reliant on a deep pool of cheap black labor searched for solutions that, as James R. Grossman points out, "involved only modification of conditions." Grossman, *Land of Hope: Chicago, Black Southerners, and the Great Migration* (Chicago: University of Chicago Press, 1989), 50.

38. "Capt. Wood Will Address Negro Citizens Sunday," *NJG*, February 8, 1930.

39. Thomas Jefferson Wertenbaker, *Norfolk: Historic Southern Port* (Durham, NC: Duke University Press, 1931), 295; Amy Waters Yarsinske, *Norfolk, Virginia: The Sunrise by the Sea; A Tribute to Photographer Carroll H. Walker Sr.* (Virginia Beach, VA: Donning, 1994), 92; Smith, *Managing White Supremacy*, 236–37; "Hearing on Colored Beach Expected to Attract Crowd," *NLD*, January 13, 1930; "Negro Beach Referendum Is Now Suggested," *NLD*, January 15, 1930.

40. "Beach Sponsors Are Confident of Victory," *NJG*, October 4, 1930; "Only 1 Member of Council Was Opposed to It," *NJG*, January 18, 1930; "Negro Beach Referendum Is Now Suggested," *NLD*, January 15, 1930.

41. Among the more influential works on this subject are Arnold R. Hirsch, *Making the Second Ghetto: Race and Housing in Chicago, 1940–1960* (Cambridge: Cambridge University Press, 1983); Thomas J. Sugrue, *The Origins of the Urban Crisis: Race and Inequality in Postwar Detroit* (Princeton, NJ: Princeton University Press, 1996); Kevin M. Kruse, *White Flight: Atlanta and the Making of Modern Conservatism* (Princeton, NJ: Princeton University Press, 2005); David M. P. Freund, *Colored Property: State Policy and White Racial Politics in Suburban America* (Chicago: University of Chicago Press, 2007); and Andrew Wiese, *Places of Their Own: African American Suburbanization in the Twentieth Century* (Chicago: University of Chicago Press, 2004).

42. "Seabrook Beach 'Restricted' Area, Says CO of NOPE," *Sepia Socialite*, June 30, 1945, box 2, folder: Race Relations, NOPD/NOPL.

43. Commanding Officer Fifth Precinct to Superintendent of Police, Police Report, June 25, 1941, box 4, folder 8, HNL/TU. On the NOPD's treatment of black citizens in the 1930s, see William V. Moore, "Civil Liberties in Louisiana: The Louisiana League for the Preservation of Constitutional Rights," *Louisiana History* 31 (Winter 1990): 50–69. On police-community relations in general, see Leonard N. Moore, *Black Rage in New Orleans: Police Brutality and African American Activism from World War II to Hurricane Katrina* (Baton Rouge: Louisiana State University Press, 2010).

44. Louise Marion Bouise, interview by Kate Ellis, June 20, 1994, New Orleans, BTV/RBMSC/DU.

45. "White Ministers Urge Bathing Facilities for Negroes," *Wichita Negro Star*, June 21, 1940; "N. Orleans Beach Ban Assailed," *CD*, July 17, 1943; Robert E. Fullilove, letter to the Editor, *New Orleans Item*, August 5, 1943; Robert E. Fullilove to Harold Newton Lee, August 16, 1943, box 5, folder 15, HNL/TU.

46. "Seabrook Beach 'Restricted' Area, Says CO of NOPE," *Sepia Socialite*, June 30, 1945, box 2, folder: Race Relations, NOPD/NOPL; "Girl Beaten in Fray on Orleans Bus," *CD*, July 24, 1943. For a comparable example of a bus driver servicing the needs of white supremacy through capricious acts of brutality on an unsuspecting black passenger, see Kruse, *White Flight*, 110–111.

47. John Magill, "Rushing into the East," *Louisiana Cultural Vistas*, Spring 2008, 44; R. D. Casey, letter to the editor, *New Orleans Item*, August 30, 1938, quoted in *Black History of New Orleans*, chap. 41, p. 3, box 10, MCC/UNO; A. E. Laneuville, quoted in *Black History of New Orleans*, chap. 41, p. 4, box 10, MCC/UNO; editorial, *LW*, reprinted in *Crisis*, March 1941; Samuel Zemurray to City of New Orleans, April 21, 1938, notarized land deed, in carton 6, Lincoln Beach folder, PSR/NOPL; "18-Year-Old Boy Fatally Stabbed," *LW*, July 15, 1939; *LW*, July 29, 1939, p. 1.

48. "Work on Modern Negro Beach Well Underway," *LW*, May 27, 1939; "No Life Guards for Seabrook Bathers," *LW*, August 12, 1939; "Purposes and Program of the New Orleans Urban League," December 1938, YWCA Papers, Tulane University, cited in Stanonis, "White Sites, Black Protests"; Clarence A. Laws to Mayor Robert Maestri, May 6, 1941, box 4, folder 8, HNL/TU; Peter Badie interview.

49. Clarence A. Laws to John M. Whitney, May 7, 1941, box 4, folder 8, HNL/TU.

50. Whitney's findings and Musser's recommendation are cited in Robert B. Delahoussaye to Office of the Director, City Board of Health, April 27, 1949, folder: January–April 1949, box 28-67, Mss 28, NAACP/UNO.

51. When the black applicant initially placed the highest bid, the levee board tossed out the applications on a technicality, before restarting the bidding process without informing the black applicants. Unsigned to Fontaine Martin, May 23, 1941, box 4, folder 8, HNL/TU.

52. Augustus Ladson, "Negro Amusement Centers: Riverside Beach," Project #1885, Charleston County, United States Work Projects Administration, Federal Writers' Project, South Carolina, 1940(?), South Caroliniana Library (University of South Carolina, Columbia); "Hits Migration, Relief, Frolicking and Traitor in Tuesday Address," *ADW*, September 9, 1940.

53. *NJG*, July 31, 1936, p. 2; "Cottages Add to Enjoyment of Ocean Breeze," *NJG*, May 23, 1936; "Ocean Breeze, New Venture, in Historic Spot," *NJG*, May 27, 1933, in Edna Hawkins-Hendrix, *Our Heritage: Black History: Princess Anne County, Virginia Beach, Virginia: A Pictorial History* (Virginia Beach: Edna

Hawkins-Hendrix, 1998), 144–145; "Local Beaches Complete Preparations for Opening," *NJG*, May 27, 1933.

54. John C. Davis to T. McCall Frazier, state motor vehicle commissioner, reprinted in *NJG*, July 8, 1933.

55. "County Trial Shows Patrons of Ocean Breeze Beach Still Subject to Petty Persecution," *NJG*, August 12, 1933.

56. Ibid.

57. "Drowning Victim," *NJG*, August 12, 1933; "Pulmotor Squad to Answer Beach Calls," *NJG*, August 18, 1934; "Drowning Toll in Tidewater Boosted to 11," *NJG*, July 13, 1935; Flossie Branchcomb, interview by Mary Hebert, August 8, 1995, Norfolk, VA, BTV/RBMSC/DU; E. L. Cook, "Protection Sought," letter to editor, *NJG*, June 30, 1934. During the summer of 1946, childhood sweethearts Geneva Rawls and Louis Stallings both drowned within fifteen minutes after arriving at Ocean Breeze, the latter in an attempt to save his dying companion. Again, reports indicated that, at the time, no lifeguard was in sight. "Childhood Sweethearts Drown While Swimming at Local Beach," *NJG*, July 27, 1946.

58. "Claims Norfolk Negroes Would Rather Pay for Use of Beach Than Use Site Purchased by City," *NJG*, February 17, 1934.

59. "Large Audience Attends Lively Mass Meeting," *NJG*, February 20, 1932; "Negro Beach Referendum Is Now Suggested," *NLD*, January 15, 1930; "The Inquiring Reporter," *NJG*, August 17, 1935; "A Plea for Fair Play," *NJG*, August 4, 1923.

60. "Development of Municipal Bathing Beach Assured," *NJG*, March 9, 1935.

61. For an account of the proceedings, see "Development of Municipal Bathing Beach Assured," *NJG*, March 9, 1935.

62. "5,000 at City Beach Sunday; Race Lifeguards and Officers on Duty," *NJG*, July 25, 1938; "Labor's Love Lost," *NJG*, July 14, 1956; "The Parking Problem at City Beach," letters to editor, *NJG*, August 5, 1961.

63. "Pulmotor Squad to Answer Beach Calls," *NJG*, August 18, 1934; "Youth Saves 2, But One Drowns at City Beach," *NJG*, July 27, 1957.

64. "Three Children Drown While Bathing in Arkansas River," *ADW*, August 10, 1949; "Report on Anson County and Monroe Race Situation," June 28, 1961, box 111, folder: Segregation, General, GTS/NCSA; "Board of Recreation Ends Segregation at Rosedale," *BAA*, October 25, 1952. On Williams and the Monroe, North Carolina, swimming pool case, see Timothy B. Tyson, *Radio Free Dixie: Robert F. Williams and the Roots of Black Power* (Chapel Hill: University of North Carolina Press, 1999), esp. 82–85, 251–60.

65. "Lack of Bathing Beach for Negroes Is Bared to Commission Council," *LW*, July 15, 1944; "Urges Use of Lincoln Beach, Nine Miles from the City with No Transportation Facilities," *LW*, July 7, 1945; "Who 'Represents' Us?" *LW*, July 15, 1939.

66. On the selection of the undeveloped site near Seabrook for the development of the African American residential and recreational subdivision, see Gerald O. Pratt to Mr. Brooke H. Duncan, October 17, 1947, Negro Park folder, Subject Files, Carton S56-25, DMC/NOPL.

67. Kingsley House Extension Program, Development of Program for Negro Children, Summer 1947, box 18, folder 15, KHP/TU; "Who 'Represents' Us?" *LW*, July 15, 1939; Clarence A. Laws to Mayor Robert Maestri, May 6, 1941, box 4, folder 8, HNL/TU.

68. On economic growth and infrastructure improvements under Morrison's administration, see Kent B. Germany, *New Orleans after the Promises: Poverty, Citizenship, and the Search for the Great Society* (Athens: University of Georgia Press, 2007), 23–24; and Edward F. Haas, *DeLesseps S. Morrison and the Image of Reform: New Orleans Politics, 1946–1961* (Baton Rouge, Louisiana State University Press, 1974), 42–65.

69. "Plan Larger Beach," *CD*, April 28, 1951; Burk and Associates Inc., *Lincoln Beach Redevelopment: An Analysis and Design Scheme* (New Orleans: Burk and Associates, 1979), 3.

70. Kevin Weldon Medley, "1954: A Year in the Life of Lincoln Beach," *New Orleans Observer*, 1985, Writers Net, http://www.writers.net/writers/books/24627 (accessed August 5, 2010); Burk and Associates, *Lincoln Beach Redevelopment*, 3. Adam Fairclough argues that the Lincoln Beach revitalization project "enable[ed] the city to clamp down on unofficial bathing by blacks along the city's built-up lakefront, long a source of irritation to whites in that increasingly affluent part of the city." See Fairclough, *Race and Democracy: The Civil Rights Struggle in Louisiana, 1915–1972* (Athens: University of Georgia Press, 1995), 152.

71. Marion E. Jackson, "Sports of the World," *ADW*, October 19, 1958. On the opening of Pontchartrain Park and its early years of growth, see Arnold R. Hirsch, "Race and Renewal in the Cold War South: New Orleans, 1947–1968," in *The American Planning Tradition: Culture and Policy*, ed. Robert Fishman (Baltimore: Johns Hopkins University Press, 2000), 219–39. On the opposition of white residents and businesses in Gentilly-Woods to the location of Pontchartrain Park, see "Reasons for, Against Negro Park Are Aired," *Gentilly Herald*, February 10, 1950, in Negro Park folder, Subject Files, Carton S56-25, DMC/NOPL; Norman E. Anseman to Mayor Morrison, April 27, 1950, ibid.; Hibernia National Bank to Mayor Morrison, May 24, 1950, ibid.; Kiwanis Club of Greater Gentilly to Commissioner Lionel G. Ott, May 31, 1950, ibid.; and Inter-office Memorandum from Robert E. Wall to Mayor Morrison, May 11, 1953, ibid. On "Negro expansion areas" in other southern cities, see Wiese, *Places of Their Own*, esp. 164–208.

72. "Pontchartrain Park Rezoning Bid Fails," *LW*, March 30, 1963.

73. Warren Brown, "New Orleans Memories: Dreams from the Seat of a '57 Chevy," WP, September 4, 2005; John Harold Boucree, interview by Kate Ellis, July 5, 1994, New Orleans, BTV/RBMSC/DU.

74. Germany, *New Orleans after the Promises*, 69.

75. See *Ghetto of Desire*, 1966, box 21, folder 1, FST/ARC.

5. Family Ties

1. James Sprunt, *Tales and Traditions of the Lower Cape Fear, 1661–1896* (Wilmington, NC: Le Gwin Brothers, 1896), 50–51; "Freemans Part of Seabreeze History for 135 years," WSN, July 5, 1981. On the role of families and kinship networks in securing abandoned or confiscated lands and defending property rights in the post-emancipation South, see Steven Hahn, *A Nation under Our Feet: Black Political Struggles in the Rural South from Slavery to the Great Migration* (Cambridge, MA: Belknap, 2003), 166–70. See also Dylan C. Penningroth, *The Claims of Kinfolk: African American Property and Community in the Nineteenth-Century South* (Chapel Hill: University of North Carolina Press, 2003).

2. See David S. Cecelski, *The Waterman's Song: Slavery and Freedom in Maritime North Carolina* (Chapel Hill: University of North Carolina Press, 2001), 207.

3. In his 1936 study of rural Georgia, Arthur Raper found that black landowners emerged as institutional leaders within black communities and mediators between black tenant farmers and local white power structures. See Raper, *Preface to Peasantry: A Tale of Two Black Belt Counties* (1936; repr., Columbia: University of South Carolina Press, 2005), 139.

4. Jennifer J. Edwards, "A Color Line in the Sand: African American Seaside Leisure in New Hanover County, North Carolina" (master's thesis, University of North Carolina, Wilmington, 2003), 11. One biography reports that, by the late nineteenth century, Robert Bruce Freeman owned between five thousand and six thousand acres in New Hanover County. See William M. Reaves, *"Strength through Struggle": The Chronological and Historical Record of the African-American Community in Wilmington, North Carolina, 1865–1960*, ed. Beverly Tetterton (Wilmington, NC: New Hanover County Public Library, 1998), 393.

5. Cecelski, *Waterman's Song*, 211. On the Wilmington Race Riot, see David S. Cecelski and Timothy B. Tyson, eds., *Democracy Betrayed: The Wilmington Race Riot of 1898 and Its Legacy* (Chapel Hill: University of North Carolina Press, 1998).

6. On the formation of communities of black landowners in the late nineteenth and early twentieth century, see Hahn, *Nation under Our Feet*, 459–61.

7. See Evelyn A. Williams, *Inadmissible Evidence: The Story of the African-American Trial Lawyer Who Defended the Black Liberation Army* (Chicago:

Lawrence Hill Books, 1993), 19. On the harvesting of timber along the Atlantic seaboard by black landowners, see J. William Harris, *Deep Souths: Delta, Piedmont, and Sea Island Society in the Age of Segregation* (Baltimore: Johns Hopkins University Press, 2001), 141.

8. Lewis Philip Hall, *Land of the Golden River: Historical Events and Stories of Southeastern North Carolina and the Lower Cape Fear* (Wilmington, NC: Hall, 1975), 190; Edwards, "Color Line in the Sand," 21.

9. Margaret Rogers, interview by Kara Miles, n.d., Wilmington, NC, tape 1, side A, BTV/RBMSC/DU.

10. Edwards, "Color Line in the Sand," 18; Hall, *Land of the Golden River*, 116.

11. *Wilmington News*, May 26, 1923, quoted in Ray McAllister, *Wrightsville Beach: The Luminous Island* (Winston-Salem, NC: John F. Blair, 2007), 69.

12. "Wilmington, N.C.," *PC*, September 20, 1924; McAllister, *Wrightsville Beach*, 72.

13. "Pajamas and Overalls Get Stares in North Carolina," *BAA*, August 31, 1929; Edwards, "Color Line in the Sand," 24; "Serves as an Inspiration to His Profession," *NJG*, May 9, 1936; Reaves, "*Strength through Struggle*," 70.

14. Phyliss Craig-Taylor, "Through a Colored Looking Glass: A View of Judicial Partition, Family Land Loss, and Rule Setting," *Washington University Law Quarterly* 78 (Fall 2000): 737–88.

15. Wilbur Cross, *Gullah Culture in America* (Westport, CT: Praeger, 2008), 78; Emergency Land Fund, *The Impact of Heir Property on Black Rural Land Tenure in the Southeastern Region of the United States* (Washington: Farmers Home Administration, 1980), 124; Janice F. Dyer and Conner Bailey, "A Place to Call Home: Cultural Understandings of Heir Property among Rural African Americans," *Rural Sociology* 73 (September 2008): 318.

16. Williams, *Inadmissible Evidence*, 53–54. *Freeman Beach LLC v. Freeman Heirs*, New Hanover County File No. 08 SP 1038, Southern Coalition for Social Justice, Durham, NC (additional copy in the possession of the author). See also Anna Stolley Persky, "In the Cross Heirs," *ABA Journal*, May 2009, http://www.abajournal.com/magazine/in_the_cross_heirs.

17. Aubrey Parkman, *History of the Waterways of the Atlantic Coast of the United States*, National Waterways Study, U.S. Army Engineer Water Resources Support Center, Institute for Water Resources, NWS-15 (January 1983), 75. The idea of a waterway connecting ports along the eastern seaboard dates back to the early republic. Amid a growing outcry over the fees canal owners charged, and a chorus of calls for a federal takeover of the private, for-profit canal industry, Congress enacted a series of measures designed to create a free and open waterway along the Atlantic coast from Maine to Georgia. Throughout the nineteenth century, coastal cities competed to connect their ports to the intracoastal waterway in order to

facilitate their ties to global markets. During and immediately following World War II, coastal cities rushed to widen, deepen, and connect waterways to the ICW in order to attract military contracts. Seeking to retain the city of Wilmington's wartime shipbuilding industries, in 1945 the state of North Carolina created the North Carolina Ports Authority, whose first order of business was to ensure that the ports of Wilmington and Morehead City conformed to federal ocean-carrying vessel standards. Upon completion, Wilmington's civic leaders celebrated the new artery connecting Wilmington to the ICW via the Myrtle Grove Sound as a "great value to commerce" and predicted that it would reduce shipping rates on produce and manufactured products by an average of three dollars a ton. See Ann Marea Simons, "An Analysis of the Atlantic Intracoastal Waterway and Selected Ports" (master's thesis, Florida Atlantic University, 1999), 19; and Edwards, "Color Line in the Sand," 27.

18. Edwards, "Color Line in the Sand," 28.

19. Williams, *Inadmissible Evidence*, 21.

20. Clyde Vernon Kiser, *Sea Island to City: A Study of St. Helena Islanders in Harlem and other Urban Centers* (1932; repr., New York: Atheneum, 1969), 82.

21. Ibid., 65–66.

22. Harry L. Moseby to Walter White, August 9, 1937, Roy Wilkins to J. L. LeFlore, March 13, 1937, and Carol King to Wilkins, March 16, 1937, Part 12, Series A, Reel 3, Mobile Branch, Papers of the NAACP.

23. "Lights and Shadows," *CD*, May 17, 1930.

24. *Harry L. Moseby et al. v. Frank Roche et al.*, Appeal Filed in Alabama Supreme Court, October 1936 (1 Div. 940), copy in Mobile Branch, NAACP Papers.

25. Moseby to White, August 9, 1937, Roy Wilkins to J. L. LeFlore, March 13, 1937, and Carol King to Wilkins, March 16, 1937, Mobile Branch, NAACP Papers.

26. Williams, *Inadmissible Evidence*, 51–52.

27. See ibid., 51–63.

28. Assata Shakur, *Assata: An Autobiography* (Westport, CT: Lawrence Hill Co., 1987), 25.

29. David Wade and Mamie Wade, interview by Kara Miles, July 15, 1993, Wilmington, NC, tape 1, side A, BTV/RBMSC/DU; Shakur, *Autobiography*, 25.

30. David Wade and Mamie Wade, interview by Kara Miles; Billy Freeman, interview by Dick Gordon, "Remembering Bop City," *The Story*, American Public Media, July 25, 2009.

31. Margaret Fredlaw, interview by Chris Stewart, July 21, 1993, Wilmington, NC, tape 1, side B, BTV/RBMSC/DU; Save Freeman Beach Video Library, "William and Jimmy Freeman Oral History Interview," http://www.savefreemanbeach.com/video-library.html (accessed July 13, 2010); Edwards, "Color Line in the

Sand," 29; "50 Arrested for Beach 'Trespass,'" *BAA*, September 6, 1947; Billy
Freeman, interview by Dick Gordon, "Remembering Bop City."

32. Shakur, *Autobiography*, 26–27; David Wade, interview by Kara Miles.

33. Williams, *Inadmissible Evidence*, 56.

34. Ibid., 57.

35. Owen J. Furuseth and Sallie M. Ives, "Individual Attitudes toward Coastal
Erosion Policies: Carolina Beach, North Carolina," in *Cities on the Beach:
Management Issues of Developed Coastal Barriers*, ed. Rutherford H. Platt,
Sheila G. Pelczarski, and Barbara K. R. Burbank (Chicago: University of
Chicago, Department of Geography, Research Paper No. 224, 1987), 186;
Edwards, "Color Line in the Sand," 42; Evelyn A. Williams to Col. Adolph A.
Hight, district engineer, Corps of Engineers, Wilmington District, May 21,
1979, photocopy in *Freeman Beach LLC v. Freeman Heirs*, New Hanover
County File No. 08 SP 1038, Southern Coalition for Social Justice, Durham,
NC (additional copy in the possession of the author).

36. C. Scott Graber, "Heirs Property: The Problems and Possible Solutions,"
Clearinghouse Review 12 (September 1978): 278–79.

37. See Orrin H. Pilkey and Katharine L. Dixon, *The Corps and the Shore*
(Washington: Island Press, 1996), 78, 88–89.

38. Quoted in Edwards, "Color Line in the Sand," 45.

39. David Wade, interview by Kara Miles.

6. Spinning Sand into Gold

1. Bruce Pegg, *Brown-Eyed Handsome Man: The Life and Hard Times of Chuck
Berry* (New York: Routledge, 2002), 63.

2. Zastrow Simms, telephone conversation with Andrew Kahrl, November 23,
2010, notes in the possession of the author.

3. Anne Arundel County Circuit Court (Land Records), 1905, Book GW 41,
p. 376, MSA CE 59-109.

4. A photo in a 1954 newspaper article shows a group of children picnicking at
Carr's Farm in 1909. See *BAA*, August 14, 1954. "Annapolis Happenings," *BAA*,
July 29, 1916.

5. Anne Arundel County Circuit Court (Land Records), 1917–1918, Book GW 139,
p. 97, MSA CE 59-207.

6. "Mosquito Beach, 1953–Present," 1990, MBCC/ARC.

7. Quoted in "Negro Business Enterprises," *Southern Workman*, September 1899,
p. 357. For accounts of groups visiting from out of state, see "Beach Rendezvous for Vacationers," *NJG*, August 3, 1929.

8. "Heart Attack Fatal to Bay Shore Hotel Founder," *NJG*, September 6,
1930; "Bay Shore Hotel Has $35,000 in Reserve Fund," *NJG*, November 1,
1930.

9. Anne Arundel County Circuit Court (Land Records), 1921–1922, Book WNW 47, p. 266, MSA CE 59-258; Anne Arundel County Circuit Court (Land Records), 1929, Book FSR 56, p. 284, MSA CE 59-400; Anne Arundel County Circuit Court (Land Records), 1932–1933, Book FSR 106, p. 491, MSA CE 59-450; Anne Arundel County Circuit Court (Land Records), 1933, Book FSR 111, p. 380, MSA CE 59-455; Anne Arundel County Circuit Court (Land Records), 1936, Book FAM 148, p. 334, MSA CE 59-492; Anne Arundel County Circuit Court (Land Records), 1936, Book FAM 151, p. 569, MSA CE 59-495; Anne Arundel County Circuit Court (Land Records), 1932–1933, Book FSR 104, p. 138, MSA CE 59-448.

10. Advertisement for Carr's Farm, *BAA*, July 4, 1931; advertisement for Sparrow's Beach, *BAA*, August 31, 1935; advertisement for Sparrow's Beach Beauty Contest, *BAA*, August, 22, 1936; advertisement for Sparrow's Beach Inter-City Amateur Contest, *BAA*, September 3, 1938; advertisement for Sparrow's Beach "Bigger and Better Than Ever," *BAA*, May 1, 1937; advertisement for the Holy Redeemer Church's Annual Bus Ride, *BAA*, August 22, 1936; Joan Slade Gray, quoted in Deanwood History Committee, *Washington, D.C.'s Deanwood* (Charleston, SC: Arcadia, 2008), 112.

11. Charles H. Williams, "To Members of the New Bay Shore Corporation Board of Directors," April 10, 1972, CHW/HU; Charles H. Williams to Shareholders, January 22, 1940, CHW/HU; Purchases, Sales, and Gross Profits, 1940–1953, CHW/HU; Charles H. Williams to Mr. Harris, February 20, 1947, CHW/HU.

12. "E. Hines Sock Draw in Philly and D.C.," *Billboard*, April 4, 1942, 25.

13. Cited in Ken Vail, *Count Basie: Swingin' the Blues, 1935–1950* (Lanham, MD: Scarecrow, 2003), 39.

14. In Harlem, the numbers king Casper Holstein employed thousands of blacks and became a leading philanthropist and lending institution for African Americans shunned by white-owned banks. In Chicago, Davarian L. Baldwin found policy barons supported jazz clubs, athletic teams, and other leisure enterprises as a way to, as Baldwin put it, " 'launder' respectability (and their money) while providing economic stability to capital-intensive sporting industries that black entrepreneurs were excluded from because of limited finances." Baldwin, *Chicago's New Negroes: Modernity, the Great Migration, and Black Urban Life* (Chapel Hill: University of North Carolina Press, 2007), 49.

15. Juliet E. K. Walker, quoted in Shane White et al., *Playing the Numbers: Gambling in Harlem between the Wars* (Cambridge, MA: Harvard University Press, 2010), 216.

16. Dan Burley, "Talking About," *Jet*, June 30, 1955, 47. On Adams, see also Antero Pietila, *Not in My Neighborhood: How Bigotry Shaped a Great American City* (Chicago: Ivan R. Dee, 2010), 105–28.

17. Louis Lautier, "Capital Spotlight," *BAA*, September 2, 1944.

18. See "Willie Adams," *Baltimore Magazine*, January 1979, 58–59; Frederick N. Rasmussen, "Former Numbers Runner Became Venture Capitalist," *BaS*, June 29, 2011; Rasmussen, "'Little Willie' Had His Hand in Many Business Ventures," *BaS*, July 3, 2011; C. Fraser Smith, *Here Lies Jim Crow: Civil Rights in Maryland* (Baltimore: Johns Hopkins University Press, 2008), 113–20; and Pietella, *Not in My Neighborhood*, 115–27.

19. Quoted in Pietila, *Not in My Neighborhood*, 118.

20. Information compiled from an examination of Anne Arundel County Land Records through MDLandRec.net.

21. "Thrown from 'Caterpillar,'" *BAA*, July 8, 1950; "The New Carr's: Playground of the East," *BAA*, June 9, 1951.

22. On Blum, see "Morris Blum Signs Off Half-Century after Starting WANN-AM," *BaS*, January 22, 1998; and "Morris H. Blum, 95, a Pioneer in Racial Relations in Radio," *BaS*, March 22, 2005. On the rise of black-oriented radio, see William Barlow, *Voice Over: The Making of Black Radio* (Philadelphia: Temple University Press, 1999); Mark Newman, *Entrepreneurs of Profit and Pride: From Black-Appeal to Radio Soul* (New York: Praeger, 1988); Louis Cantor, *Wheelin' on Beale: How WDIA-Memphis Became the Nation's First All-Black Radio Station and Created the Sound That Changed America* (New York: Pharos, 1992); and Brian Ward, *Radio and the Struggle for Civil Rights in the South* (Gainesville: University Press of Florida, 2004).

23. Preston Lauterbach, *The Chitlin' Circuit and the Road to Rock 'n' Roll* (New York: Norton, 2011), 147. On the role of black deejays as "trendsetters" in 1950s and 1960s urban black America, see Nelson George, *The Death of Rhythm and Blues* (New York: Pantheon, 1988), 43, 51.

24. Anne Arundel County Circuit Court (Land Records), 1948, Book 505, p. 105, MSA CE 59-849.

25. Directors of New Bay Shore Corporation to Mr. Lockwood, September 14, 1953, CHW/HU.

26. "Vacationers Offered Variety of Activities at Bay Shore," *NJG*, June 22, 1946.

27. See, for example, *Richmond Times-Dispatch* to Charles H. Williams, May 11, 1960, CHW/HU; Martha B. Brayton to Charles H. Williams, May 29, 1956, ibid.

28. Charles H. Williams to Mr. J. C. Wellsted, December 26, 1956, CHW/HU; Purchases, Sales, and Gross Profits, 1940–1953, ibid.; Expenses, 1940–1953, CHW/HU; Census of Business, 1954, ibid.; Charles H. Williams to Unemployment Compensation Commission of Virginia, January 30, 1961, ibid.; and Janie M. Haskins to Charles H. Williams, February 27, 1956, ibid.

29. Irvin G. Abeloff to Charles H. Williams, April 23, 1954, CHW/HU; Schedules of Taxes and Insurance, 1961, ibid.

30. See, for example, Coming to Bay Shore, June 5 and 12, 1955, CHW/HU.

31. "$100,000 Beach Resort to Open Here on May 30," *NJG*, May 19, 1945.

32. "A Fine Day at the Beach," *Life*, August 18, 1947, 121; Donald E. Morgan, interview by Blair L. Murphy, July 19, 1995, Norfolk, VA, BTV/RBMSC/DU.

33. See "Cocktail Chit Chat," *Jet*, August 18, 1955, 45.

34. Dudley Cooper to Globe Poster Co., January 13, 1947, folder 1, box 2, DCOVAP/ODU.

35. See Charles H. Williams to Mr. Harris, February 20, 1947, CHW/HU.

36. Advertisement, *LW*, August 17, 1963; Roy L. Washington, interview by Andrew Kahrl, January 12, 2010, New Orleans, audiotape in possession of the author; Willie Williams, interview by Andrew Kahrl, January 5, 2010, New Orleans, audiotape in possession of the author.

37. See LBVF/NOPL; *Employers Liability Assurance Co. v. Butler*, 318 F.2d 67, United States Court of Appeals Fifth Circuit, http://bulk.resource.org/courts .gov/c/F2/318/318.F2d.67.19599_1.html (accessed August 5, 2010); New Orleans Radio Shrine, "E-mail Memories," http://www.walkerpub.com/radio _memories_email31.html (accessed August 5, 2010); "What's Happening in New Orleans," *CD*, July 14, 1951; "You've Got a Lot of Nerve," August 2, 2008, the Gentle Bear, http://gentlebear.wordpress.com/2008/08/02/youve-got-a-lot-of -nerve/ (accessed August 5, 2010); Kevin Weldon Medley, "1954: A Year in the Life of Lincoln Beach," *New Orleans Observer*, 1985, Writers Net, http://www .writers.net/writers/books/24627 (accessed August 5, 2010); Theresa Gonzalez (née Brossett), interview by Andrew Kahrl, September 9, 2008, notes in possession of the author.

38. Medley, "1954: A Year in the Life of Lincoln Beach"; "Closes Season," *PC*, September 8, 1956; William Garibaldi, interview by Andrew W. Kahrl, January 15, 2008, notes in possession of the author; "Memories of East Look Like Its Future," *NOTP*, July 12, 2007.

39. "Police Officer Will Be Sought for Charleston," *NJG*, March 13, 1948; Jason Annan and Pamela Gabriel, *The Great Cooper River Bridge* (Columbia: University of South Carolina Press, 2002), 91; "River Baptism at Charleston Beach Site," *ADW*, September 13, 1946.

40. See, for example, Joe Igo, Steve Lasker, Ken Steiner, et al., "The Duke Ellington Itinerary, 1930–1940," http://home.swipnet.se/dooji/1930–1940.pdf (accessed August 5, 2010). Herb Frazier, "Riverside Became a Refuge amid Segregation," *CPC*, August 12, 2001.

41. "Hidden Heritage," *CCP*, July 2, 2008.

42. Cora Reid, interview by Zeal Harris, http://www.youtube.com/user/zealousflow #p/u/3/MEQI_qF1jWs (accessed January 21, 2011); Bill Carson, interview by Zeal Harris, http://www.youtube.com/user/zealousflow#p/u/14/zwIakC27SEM (accessed January 21, 2011).

43. On "black dancers" at Carolina Beach, see Jennifer J. Edwards, "A Color Line in the Sand: African American Seaside Leisure in New Hanover County, North Carolina" (master's thesis, University of North Carolina, Wilmington, 2003), 31–35. On music and youth race relations in the postwar South, see Pete Daniel, *Lost Revolutions: The South in the 1950s* (Chapel Hill: University of North Carolina Press, 2000), esp. 121–47; Peter Guralnick, *Sweet Soul Music: Rhythm and Blues and the Southern Dream of Freedom* (New York: HarperCollins, 1986); Charles Joyner, "A Region in Harmony: Southern Music and the Soundtrack of Freedom," *Journal of Southern History* 72 (February 2006): 3–38; and Brian Ward, *Just My Soul Responding: Rhythm and Blues, Black Consciousness, and Race Relations* (Berkeley and Los Angeles: University of California Press, 1998).

44. Bill Carson interview.

45. Frazier, "Riverside Became a Refuge amid Segregation," CPC, August 12, 2001.

46. "'Lady Day' Set to Start Tour of Dixie One-Niters," AN, June 24, 1950; David Hume, "Maryland's Jolly Jackpot," *The Nation*, February 13, 1960, pp. 140–42.

47. "Supreme Court Reverses Numbers Verdict," BAA, March 20, 1954.

48. Lorraine Ahearn, "Forgotten Force," n.d., photocopied from George Phelps's personal collection, article in possession of the author; E. B. Rea, "Pennsylvania Avenue," BAA, March 10, 1951; George Phelps, interview by Andrew Kahrl, April 7, 2010, Annapolis, MD, audiotape in possession of the author; Lorraine Ahearn, "Forgotten Force," n.d., photocopied from George Phelps's personal collection, article in possession of the author.

49. See, for example, Allison Davis, Burleigh B. Gardner, and Mary P. Gardner, *Deep South: A Social Anthropological Study of Caste and Class* (Chicago: University of Chicago Press, 1941), 499.

50. See Khalil Gibran Muhammad, *The Condemnation of Blackness: Race, Crime, and the Making of Modern Urban America* (Cambridge, MA: Harvard University Press, 2010), esp. 195–96; and Kevin J. Mumford, *Interzones: Black/White Sex Districts in Chicago and New York in the Early Twentieth Century* (New York: Columbia University Press, 1997).

51. David E. Barlow, "Minorities Policing Minorities as a Strategy of Social Control: A Historical Analysis of Tribal Police in the United States," *Criminal Justice History* 15 (1994), 154.

52. Muhammad, *Condemnation of Blackness*, 259.

53. Editorial, BAA, August 3, 1912.

54. "White Officer Admits Story Is Frame-Up," NJG, August 14, 1937; "Probe Beach Discrimination," NJG, September 13, 1930.

55. On efforts among urban black populations to organize forms of community policing to both meet immediate needs and generate policy reform, see Muhammad, *Condemnation of Blackness*, 185–89.

56. "The Fabulous Captain George Brown," *BAA*, March 12, 1960; "Former Park Manager Recalls Old Shore Resort," *BAA*, June 27, 1925.

57. Handwritten notes, Bay Shore Meeting, March 10, 1948, CHW/HU.

58. George Phelps, interviews by Andrew Kahrl, December 10, 2009, and April 7, 2010, Annapolis, MD, audiotapes in possession of the author.

59. Larry Griffin interview in "Carr's Beach Historic Music Festival," *AC*, June 28, 2010, http://www.hometownannapolis.com/video/1277734096CarrsBeachHistoricMusicFestival (accessed November 5, 2011).

60. "Liquor Peddling Stopped," *WP*, August 16, 1950; George Phelps, interview by Andrew Kahrl, December 10, 2009; *Pip and Zastrow: An American Friendship*, DVD, directed by Victoria Bruce and Karin Hayes (New York: Urcunina Films, 2008); Larry Griffin telephone conversation with Andrew Kahrl, November 30, 2010, notes in possession of the author; "The New Carrs Beach: Playground of the East,'" *BAA*, June 9, 1951; "Carrs Beach Enjoys Best Season in 2-Year History," *BAA*, October 13, 1951.

61. Zastrow Simms telephone conversation; "For All We Know: Elizabeth M. Oliver," *BAA*, July 30, 1083.

7. The Price We Pay for Progress

1. Charles H. Williams to Vincent J. P. Connolly, April 10, 1973, CHW/HU; Harry L. Batt to Victor Schiro, January 14, 1966, carton S66-21, Pontchartrain Beach—1966 folder, VHS/NOPL; Charles H. Williams to Shareholders, May 7, 1973, CHW/HU.

2. Edna Cole, interview by Berkeley Hudson, October 24, 1999 (K-0783), Chatham Voices, in SOHP/SHC; Whitney and Barbara Irwin, interview by Anna Mitchell, October 7, 1999 (K-0794), in SOHP/SHC. Thanks to Bruce E. Baker for alerting me to the contents of these oral history interviews. See also Spencie Love, "Chatham County, Community at the Crossroads: A Southern/African American Oral History Seminar," *Journal of American History* 87 (September 2000): 614–21.

3. Quoted in Samuel B. Hays, *Beauty, Health, and Permanence: Environmental Politics in the United States, 1955–1985* (New York: Cambridge University Press, 1987), 164.

4. Linda Rocawich et al., "South Coast Follies: Coastal Profiles of Nine Southern States," *Southern Exposure* 10, no. 2 (1983): 94; Robert G. Healy and James L. Short, "Changing Markets for Rural Lands: Patterns and Issues," in *Beyond the Urban Fringe: Land Use Issues of Nonmetropolitan America*, ed. Rutherford H. Platt and George Macinko (Minneapolis: University of Minnesota Press, 1983), 117, 124–25, 132. Coastal zones, Dolores Hayden notes, experienced some of the more pronounced effects of fringe development. See Hayden, *Building Suburbia: Green Fields and Urban Growth, 1820–2000* (New York: Vintage,

2003), 181–200. In his ethnographic study of a southern black community in the South Carolina / Georgia low country conducted in the 1980s and 1990s, William W. Falk documented African Americans' succumbing to—or, as many at the time saw it, cashing in on—the growing thirst for land by water that accompanied the rise of the Sunbelt. The community, he noted, had little history of sharecropping, and a comparatively large number of black landowners living on what had historically been unproductive and unpredictable land, and many were not aware of the market value of their property, a fact that developers (through purchasing land at far below market values or through tax liens) were quick to exploit. See William W. Falk, *Rooted in Place: Family and Belonging in a Southern Black Community* (New Brunswick, NJ: Rutgers University Press, 2004), 127–33. On rural African Americans' struggle to hold on to land in the modern South, see also Carol Stack, *Call to Home: African Americans Reclaim the Rural South* (New York: Basic Books, 1996) and the series of articles published by the Associated Press in 2001 titled "Torn from the Land," http://www.commondreams.org/headlines01/1202-03.htm (accessed February 19, 2011). On the need to incorporate rural areas located outside the physical boundaries of metropolitan areas into our framework of analysis, see Andrew Needham and Allen Dietrich-Ward, "Beyond the Metropolis: Metropolitan Growth and Regional Transformation in Postwar America," *Journal of Urban History* 35, no. 7 (2009): 943–69.

5. Bostwick H. Ketchum, ed., *The Water's Edge: Critical Problems of the Coastal Zone* (Cambridge, MA: MIT Press, 1972), 10, 12; Dennis W. Ducsik, *Shoreline for the Public: A Handbook of Social, Economic, and Legal Considerations Regarding Public Recreational Use of the Nation's Coastal Shoreline* (Cambridge, MA: MIT Press, 1974), 53–54.

6. Rutherford H. Platt, "Congress and the Coast," *Environment* 27 (July–August 1985): 14. By 2025, according to one estimate, the percentage of Americans living within eighty miles of a coast is expected to balloon to 75 percent. See "Buying Back Beaches," *CSM*, September 8, 1998. The coastal zones of post–World War II Western Europe similarly moved from the periphery to the center of regional economies as vacationing and tourism spread along with the rise of the modern liberal nation state. See Tom Selwyn, "Privatising the Mediterranean Coastline," in *Contesting the Foreshore: Tourism, Society, and Politics on the Coast*, ed. Jeremy Boissevain and Tom Selwyn (Amsterdam: Amsterdam University Press, 2004), 35–60.

7. On the National Flood Insurance Program, see Rutherford H. Platt, *Disasters and Democracy: The Politics of Extreme Natural Events* (Washington, DC: Island Press, 1999), 9–46; Ted Steinberg, *Acts of God: The Unnatural History of Natural Disaster in America* (New York: Oxford University Press, 2000), 103–21; and Erwann O. Michel-Kerjan, "Catastrophe Economics: The National Flood

Insurance Program," *Journal of Economic Perspectives* 24 (Fall 2010): 165–86. On the Army Corps of Engineers, see Cornelia Dean, *Against the Tide: The Battle for America's Beaches* (New York: Columbia University Press, 1999). The most accessible account of the nature of beach ecologies and the environmental consequences of beach development and replenishment in twentieth-century America remains Wallace Kaufman and Orrin H. Pilkey Jr.'s *The Beaches Are Moving: The Drowning of America's Shoreline* (Durham, NC: Duke University Press, 1983).

8. H. Crane Miller, "The Barrier Islands: A Gamble with Time and Nature," *Environment* 23 (November 1981): 7.

9. On how the Sunbelt economy gave rise to a "politics of moderation" built on "the twin pillars of rapid economic development and enforced racial harmony . . . through spatial policies of suburban sprawl and urban containment," see Matthew D. Lassiter, *The Silent Majority: Suburban Politics in the Suburban South* (Princeton, NJ: Princeton University Press, 2006), esp. 11. See also Nancy MacLean, "From the Benighted South to the Sunbelt: The South in the Twentieth Century," in *Perspectives in Modern American: Making Sense of the Twentieth Century,* ed. Harvard Sitkoff (New York: Oxford University Press, 2001), 202–26.

10. James W. Silver, *Mississippi: The Closed Society* (London: Victor Gollancz, 1964). In 1961, NASA announced plans to construct a 13,500-acre test facility in Hancock County. At the time, it was the largest construction project in the history of the state of Mississippi and the second largest in the nation. Ernest Zebrowski and Judith A. Howard, *Category 5: The Story of Camille; Lessons Unlearned from America's Most Violent Hurricane* (Ann Arbor: University of Michigan Press, 2005), 76.

11. Kaufman and Pilkey, *Beaches Are Moving,* 139; Zebrowski and Howard, *Category 5,* 72–84; Gilbert R. Mason and James Patterson Smith, *Beaches, Blood, and Ballots: A Black Doctor's Civil Rights Struggle* (Jackson: University Press of Mississippi, 2000), 150. On the collapse of massive resistance and rise of "strategic accommodation" in Mississippi, see Joseph Crespino, *In Search of Another Country: Mississippi and the Conservative Counterrevolution* (Princeton, NJ: Princeton University Press, 2007). On the role of military contracts and federal defense spending in the Sunbelt economy, see Ann R. Markusen, *The Rise of the Gunbelt: The Military Remapping of Industrial America* (New York: Oxford University Press, 1991).

12. Report of Activities for Month of August 1961, Florida: General Case Material, 1961–1962, *The Papers of the NAACP,* Part 23, *Legal Department Case Files, 1956–1965, Series A: The South* (Bethesda, MD: University Publications of America, 1997), microform, reel 10, frame 60. On the wade-ins that took place on Florida beaches in the 1960s, Gary R. Mormino commented, "Business-

men and politicians realized the only thing more unsettling than blacks and whites swimming together on public beaches were newsflashes of empty . . . coasts, the result of costly boycotts and protests." See Gary R. Mormino, *Land of Sunshine, State of Dreams: A Social History of Modern Florida* (Gainesville: University Press of Florida, 2005), 311–12.

13. Cannon to Sanford, n.d. (1961?), Segregation-General folder, box 111, General Correspondence 1961, GTS/NCSA.

14. *US v. Harrison County*, 399 F.2d 485l, 1968.

15. Robert C. Thomas to Director, State Sovereignty Commission, June 27, 1960, Mississippi State Sovereignty Commission, SCR ID no. 2-57-0-24-1-1-1, MDAH.

16. Raymond Breaux, interview by Andrew Kahrl, January 12, 2010, New Orleans, audiotape in possession of the author; Mary King, *Freedom's Song: A Personal Story of the 1960s Civil Rights Movement* (New York: Morrow, 1987), 449; Jerry Ruth Williams, "57. MissionCast—Rebuild Gulfside Assembly," YouTube, http://www.youtube.com/watch?v=rT8AfRf7z44 (accessed July 26, 2010). On the Waveland meetings, see also James Forman, *The Making of Black Revolutionaries: A Personal Account* (Washington, DC: Open Hand Publishing, 1985 [1972]), 411–32.

For all the ink spilled on Freedom Summer and the work of SNCC in Mississippi, no historian bothered to question how the Gulf Coast, and Gulfside in particular, became one of the few places in the state where blacks and whites could meet and organize without fear of assault. The most telling example of the failure of civil rights scholars to consider issues of space and place in the making of the movement comes from the book *Many Minds, One Heart: SNCC's Dream for a New America*, by Wesley C. Hogan, in which the role of Gulfside as a place of organization for movement activists, and the site of a pivotal meeting of SNCC members in the fall of 1964, is mentioned only in passing. See Hogan, *Many Minds, One Heart: SNCC's Dream for a New America* (Chapel Hill: University of North Carolina Press, 2007), 202. Citing the work of Lester Salmon, Charles M. Payne mentions that owning land correlated to higher rates of activism and organization, especially as the degree of danger a certain activity posed increased. See Payne, *I've Got the Light of Freedom: The Organizing Tradition and the Mississippi Freedom Struggle* (Berkeley and Los Angeles: University of California Press, 1995), 281–82. Carol Stack also mentions, "Landholding black farmers achieved a degree of economic independence from the local white establishment that propelled them into important, sometimes heroic, roles during the civil rights movement." See Stack, *Call to Home: African Americans Reclaim the Rural South* (New York: Basic Books, 1996), 42. On the pivotal role of black landowners in housing and organizing civil rights workers in the rural South, see Richard A. Couto, *Ain't Gonna Let Nobody Turn Me*

Around: The Pursuit of Racial Justice in the Rural South (Philadelphia: Temple University Press, 1991), 298.

17. R. E. Jones, Superintendent to Gulfside Association Board of Trustees, Mount Zion Methodist Church, New Orleans, October 23, 1958, box 2, folder 3, p. 6, REJ/ARC; Gulfside Association Board of Trustees, Mount Zion Methodist Church, New Orleans, February 24, 1959, minutes of the meeting of the executive committee, box 1, folder 8, p. 3, ibid.

18. See Peter C. Murray, *Methodists and the Crucible of Race, 1930–1975* (Columbia: University of Missouri Press, 2004), 133.

19. William Talbot Handy, "Additional Service—Post-Retirement," n.d., box 8, folder 1, p. 32, REJ/ARC.

20. Pat Harvey, interview by Andrew Kahrl, January 8, 2010, Waveland, MS, audiotape in possession of the author; Robert Leroy Wilson, *The Gulfside Assembly* (Philadelphia: Board of Missions, Methodist Church, 1968), 1.

21. Charles H. Williams to National Newspapers Publishers Association, January 28, 1955, CHW/HU. In South Florida, Nathan D. B. Connolly documents efforts by white hoteliers to woo African American vacationers in the post–World War II years. See Connolly, "By Eminent Domain: Race and Capital in the Building of an American South Florida" (Ph.D. diss., University of Michigan, 2008), 260–66.

22. Application for Loan, February 13, 1964, Charles H. Williams to National Newspapers Publishers Association, January 28, 1955, CHW/HU. On the origins of the Small Business Administration, see Jonathan J. Bean, *Beyond the Broker State: Federal Policies toward Small Business, 1936–1961* (Chapel Hill: University of North Carolina Press, 1996).

23. Charles H. Williams to Douglas Chamberlin, January 16, 1976, CHW/HU; New Bay Shore Corporation, Income and Expenses for the Year Ended December 31, 1962, ibid.; Unaudited Income and Expenses, New Bay Shore Corporation, Year Ended December 31, 1966, ibid.; Unaudited Statement of Income and Retained Earnings, New Bay Shore Corporation, December 31, 1969, ibid.; Bay Shore Properties Inc., Balance Sheet, December 31, 1973, ibid.; Administrative Research Associates, Hampton, VA, "Hampton, Virginia: Waterfront Economic Study," prepared for Hampton City Planning Commission, September 1967, pp. 30, 50–51.

24. Bill from City of Hampton to New Bayshore Corp., November 21, 1971, CHW/HU; William L. Eure Jr. to Charles H. Williams, November 14, 1961, ibid.; Robert T. Powers to Charles H. Williams, April 12, 1974, ibid.; Charles H. Williams to Dr. Jerome Holland, January 30, 1968, ibid.; Charles H. Williams to John D. Chamberlin Sr., December 9, 1970, ibid.

25. On the City of Hampton's acquisition of the property in 1978, consult the City of Hampton Property Database, Real Estate Information, Search by Address

(Thimble Shoals Court), http://www.hampton.gov/sol/propertysearch/ (accessed February 23, 2011). Real estate listings for Chesapeake Landing advertise private beach access. For the website of a local real estate agent, see http://www.roseandwomble.com/ (accessed February 23, 2011).

26. Larry Griffin, telephone conversation with Andrew Kahrl, November 30, 2010, notes in the possession of the author; comments by unnamed white male posted on http://www.oprah.com/community/message/533983; Caryl Rivers, *Aphrodite at Mid-Century: Growing Up Catholic and Female in Post-War America* (New York: Doubleday, 1973), 69.

27. Larry Griffin, telephone conversation.

28. "120-Acre Bay Tract Sold," *Norfolk Ledger Star*, November 2, 1965; Edna Hawkins-Hendrix, *Our Heritage: Black History: Princess Anne County, Virginia Beach, Virginia: A Pictorial History* (Virginia Beach, VA: Edna Hawkins-Hendrix, 1998), 147; Obie McCollum, "Looking On in Norfolk," *NJG*, November 6, 1965.

29. Peter A. Low to Victor H. Schiro, August 5, 1964, folder: Lincoln Beach—1964, VHS/NOPL; "Poor Kids to Face 'Swim-less' Summer," *LW*, May 16, 1964; "2 More Youths Drown as City Pools Stay Closed," *LW*, July 18, 1964.

30. In her study of the 1956 Crystal Beach race riot, Victoria W. Wolcott shows that whites "invoked the right to safety and security, particularly from African American youth," to defend segregated leisure spaces and, as black youth asserted their right to enjoy places of public amusement in greater numbers, developed strategies similar to those witnessed at Pontchartrain Beach to "limit the number of low-income urban patrons and ensure a middle-class customer base." See Wolcott, "Recreation and Race in the Postwar City: Buffalo's 1956 Crystal Beach Riot," *Journal of American History* 93 (June 2006): 88–89. On the emergence of new ticketing strategies aimed at limiting the influx of poor and minority visitors, see also David Nasaw, *Going Out: The Rise and Fall of Public Amusements* (New York: Basic Books, 1993), 254–55; and Judith A. Adams, *The American Amusement Park Industry: A History of Technology and Thrills* (Boston: Twayne, 1991), 107, 146. On other uses of "legal control and supervision of [black] public leisure activities," see Regina Austin, "Not Just for the Fun of It! Governmental Restraints on Black Leisure, Social Inequality, and the Privatization of Public Space," *Southern California Law Review* 71 (May 1998): 667–714, esp. 670.

31. Ken McGruder, interview by Andrew Kahrl, January 5, 2010, audiotape in possession of the author; Ethel Ellis, interview by Andrew Kahrl, January 12, 2010, New Orleans, audiotape in possession of the author. On June 3, 1967, a mob of fifty-plus white teenagers viciously assaulted, with bottles, rocks, and metal pipes, sixteen African Americans ranging in age from fifteen to thirty-

four, who were throwing a going-away party for two black males set to deploy to Vietnam. See Folder: Brutality, Box 28-54, Mss 28, NAACP/UNO.

32. In Gary, Indiana, Andrew Hurley similarly found that, years after the desegregation of beaches and parks, blacks tended to visit beaches in the evening hours so as to minimize the possibility of conflict, and congregated in large groups. See Hurley, *Environmental Inequalities: Class, Race, and Industrial Pollution in Gary, Indiana, 1945–1980* (Chapel Hill: University of North Carolina Press, 1995), 122.

33. Harry L. Batt to Victor Schiro, January 14, 1966, carton S66-21, Pontchartrain Beach—1966 folder, VHS/NOPL; Denise Trowbridge, "Pontchartrain Beach Amusement Park: Pontchartrain Beach Is Still Part of Locals' Lives 20 Years after Closing Its Doors," *Liquid Weekly*, September, 2001, posted on Denise Trowbridge website, December 2, 2008, http://www.denisetrowbridge.com /2008/12/pontchartrain-b.html (accessed August 9, 2010). See also "For the Survival of Pontchartrain Beach," carton S66-21, Pontchartrain Beach—1966 folder, VHS/NOPL. On water leisure spaces and racial violence in the civil rights era, see Jeff Wiltse, *Contested Waters: A Social History of Swimming Pools in America* (Chapel Hill: University of North Carolina Press, 2007), 154–80. Kevin Kruse describes working-class whites' resentment at the integration of places of public amusement by wealthy white politicians and their allies in the business community who themselves often belonged to private country clubs. Integration of public golf courses, beaches, and swimming pools, he argues, led to working-class white abandonment of these places and embrace of individualism and privatism. See Kruse, *White Flight: Atlanta and the Making of Modern Conservatism* (Princeton, NJ: Princeton University Press, 2005), 106–30; and Kruse, "The Politics of Race and Public Space: Desegregation, Privatization, and the Tax Revolt in Atlanta," *Journal of Urban History* 31 (July 2005): 610–33. On racial violence in desegregated public amusement parks, see Wolcott, "Recreation and Race," 88–89. See also Nasaw, *Going Out*, 253–55.

34. Kruse, *White Flight*.

35. L. J. Holstein to Dudley Cooper, January 14, 1970, folder 16, box 2, DCOVAP/ODU.

36. Willie Williams, interview by Andrew Kahrl, January 5, 2010, New Orleans, audiotape in possession of the author; Ken McGruder interview.

37. Les Landon, "Look What They've Done to My Lake, Ma," *New Orleans Magazine*, July 1979, pp. 39–43. "Lake Pontchartrain on Verge of Once Again Becoming Hot Swimming Spot," *City Business North Shore Report*, August 1, 2004.

38. William Garibaldi, interview by Andrew Kahrl, January 8, 2008, notes in possession of the author; Simon, *Boardwalk of Dreams*, 99.

39. Philip A. Smith, "Mt. Vernon View Accord Near," *WP*, July 20, 1967; Sterling Seagrave, "Piscataway Bay Park Development Plans Set," *WP*, November 13, 1963; "Interior Suit Filed on Park," *WP*, November 29, 1970; "U.S. Agrees on Payment to Goldstein," *WP*, May 2, 1972; "11 Injured at Marshall Hall," *WP*, August 5, 1973; Paul Hodge, "Marshall Hall Roller Coaster Blown Down; Park May Close," *WP*, August 18, 1977; "Wilson Line Gets Week to Settle Its Debts," *WP*, April 13, 1978; "Wilson Boat Line Sold for $1.5 Million but $2 Million in Liabilities Remain," *WP*, September 8, 1978; "Marshall Hall Park Closing Attractions after 91 Years," *WP*, May 24, 1979.

40. John Harold Boucree, interview by Kate Ellis, July 5, 1994, New Orleans, BTV/ RBMSC/DU.

41. Ducsik, *Shoreline for the Public*, 46–47. See also Brett Williams, "Gentrifying Water and Selling Jim Crow," *Urban Anthropology* 31, no. 1 (2002): 93–120.

42. On rising levels of pollution in Lake Pontchartrain, see, for example, Margaret Olmsted, "Lake Pontchartrain as a Special Management Area," December 1983, in MM/NOPL, box J-24, folder: Environmental Series: Lake Pontchartrain—Special Management Area, Louisiana Division, City Archives and Special Collections, New Orleans Public Library. See also Reginald Stuart, "Louisiana Awakening to the Need to Deal with the Pollution of Its Paradise," *NYT*, November 28, 1982.

43. Burk and Associates Inc., *Lincoln Beach Redevelopment: An Analysis and Design Scheme* (New Orleans: Burk and Associates, 1979), 9, 22; Mary Croom Fontenot, interview by Andrew Kahrl, January 7, 2010, audiotape in possession of the author; "Lincoln Beach Neighbors Want It Cleaned Up," *NOTP*, February 17, 1998; "Eastern N.O. Residents Want Old Beach, Houses Cleaned Up," *NOTP*, September 2, 1994.

44. Anonymous, Speedguide On-Line Discussion, January 22, 2005, http://forums .speedguide.net/showthread.php?t=166870 (accessed August 9, 2010); Burk and Associates, *Lincoln Beach Redevelopment*, 1.

45. Laura O. Taylor and V. Kerry Smith, "Environmental Amenities as a Source of Market Power," *Land Economics* 76 (November 2000): 553; Marge Lennon, "Sharing the Vacation Home," *Saturday Evening Post*, November 1980, 40–41; "Two Groups Propose Time-Share Legislation," *ABA Journal* (May 1980): 543–44; "What Vacation Time-Sharing Can Mean to You," *Ebony*, June 2000, p. 18.

46. Curtis J. Berger, "Timesharing in the United States," *American Journal of Comparative Law* 38 (1990): 131–51; Jane Bryant Quinn, "The Trap in Time Shares," *Newsweek*, July 12, 1993, p. 48; "Two Groups Propose Time-Share Legislation," *ABA Journal* (May 1980): 543–44; "Investing Timeshares," *Black Enterprise*, February 1999, p. 208. By 2000 a reported 1.8 million households

owned time-shares. See "What Vacation Time-Sharing Can Mean to You," *Ebony*, June 2000, p. 18.

47. Edwin Henderson, "Spread of Colored Summer Homes Seen Sign of Culture," *NJG*, September 20, 1952.

48. "Pressures on Coastal Environments: Population: Distribution, Density, and Growth" (February 1998), p. 13, available at http://oceanservice.noaa.gov/websites/retiredsites/supp_sotc_retired.html; John R. Wennersten, *The Chesapeake: An Environmental Biography* (Baltimore: Maryland Historical Society, 2000), 211; Eugene L. Meyer, "It's the Bay, Not the Beltway, That Defines Washington," *WP*, August 11, 1991.

49. Tom Horton, cited in Wennersten, *Chesapeake*, 209. On the state of the Chesapeake in the early 1980s, see ibid., 211.

50. Tom Vesey, "Some in Anne Arundel See Salvation in Sewers, Others See Overdevelopment," *WP*, September 30, 1986.

51. John Moses, interview by Andrew Kahrl, December 12, 2009, Highland Beach, MD, audiotape in possession of the author; Robert Barnes, "Little Town on the Bay Grows Up," *WP*, June 11, 1988; Mary Ann French, "A Resort in Retreat? Black Beach Community Fights to Survive," *WP*, September 3, 1991; Vince Leggett, interview by Andrew Kahrl, December 11, 2009, Annapolis, MD, notes in possession of the author.

52. "Arundel Neighbors Run into Stop Sign: Change in Road Called Economic Bias," *WP*, March 28, 1990.

53. Sharon Merrick, interview by Andrew Kahrl, April 10, 2010, audiotape in possession of the author.

54. Anne Arundel County Circuit Court (Land Records), 1971, Book 2392, p. 624, MSA CE 59-2736; Anne Arundel County Circuit Court (Land Records), 1973, Book 2633, p. 778, MSA CE 59-2977.

55. AACS, February 4, 1992, 1; George Phelps, interview by Andrew Kahrl, December 10, 2009, Annapolis, MD, audiotape in possession of the author.

56. *Harbour Views*, pamphlet, vol. 4, Summer 1986, Chesapeake Harbour North, file no. P19890004, Anne Arundel County, Office of Planning and Zoning, Annapolis, MD.

57. Ibid.; "Pressures on Coastal Environments: Population: Distribution, Density, and Growth" (February 1998), 13, available at http://oceanservice.noaa.gov/websites/retiredsites/supp_sotc_retired.html; Chesapeake Harbour North, Subdivision Number 89-006, Project Number 89-004, Planning and Zoning Report, March 9, 1989, Chesapeake Harbour North, file no. P19890004, Anne Arundel County, Office of Planning and Zoning, Annapolis, MD.

58. Chesapeake Harbour North Petition, n.d., ibid.; Robert and Anne Harbrant to Frank Ward, Office of Planning and Zoning, March 14, 1989, ibid., Margaret L. DeAnbough to Frank Ward, March 19, 1989, ibid.

Lassiter and Kruse attribute the resurgence of the Democratic Party in suburbs of Virginia and North Carolina in recent years to a desire to preserve a quality of life that many see as under assault by overdevelopment and sprawl. Though they don't push this topic further, this latest political realignment (foreshadowed in the quote cited herein) points to a further class stratification of environmental amenities and hazards, as middle-class suburbanites expect—indeed, demand—of their elected officials preservation of an unsustainable "quality of life" and implicitly endorse "NIMBY" policies that further shift onto the poor the burden of exposure to environmental hazards and other attributes of modern society that diminish the quality of life. See Matthew D. Lassiter and Kevin M. Kruse, "The Bulldozer Revolution: Suburbs and Southern History since World War II," *Journal of Southern History* 75 (August 2009): 706.

59. Evelyn A. Williams to Col. Adolph A. Hight, District Engineer, Corps of Engineers, Wilmington District, May 21, 1979, photocopy in *Freeman Beach LLC vs. Freeman Heirs*, New Hanover County File No. 08 SP 1038, Southern Coalition for Social Justice, Durham, NC (additional copy in the possession of the author). See also Jennifer J. Edwards, "A Color Line in the Sand: African American Seaside Leisure in New Hanover County, North Carolina" (master's thesis, University of North Carolina, Wilmington, 2003), 46.

60. *Freeman v. Spinnaker Point Ltd.*, 317 N.C. 333, 346 S.E.2d 140, 1986; Mamie and David Wade, interview by Kara Miles, July 15, 1993, Wilmington, NC, tape 1, side A, BTV/RBMSC/DU.

61. See Thomas W. Mitchell, "From Reconstruction to Deconstruction: Undermining Black Landownership, Political Independence, and Community through Partition Sales of Tenancies in Common," *Northwestern University Law Review* 95 (Winter 2001): 505–80.

62. Jesse Morris and Robert S. Browne, Frogmore Conference on Heir Property Report, folder 10, box 34, BERC/NYPL. In one case from coastal South Carolina cited by the legal scholars Faith R. Rivers and Jennie Stephens, a judge ordered a partition sale of seventeen acres following the filing of a petition by one of the co-tenants. The land was subsequently acquired by an outside interest for $900,000, who immediately resold the property for $3 million. After the lawyers extracted their cut, each of the twenty-five heirs who had previously lived on the land received a check for $27,000—"just enough to purchase a mobile home." See Rivers and Stephens, "Preserving Heirs' Property in Coastal South Carolina (Charleston, South Carolina)," in *Breakthrough Communities: Sustainability and Justice in the Next American Metropolis*, ed. M. Paloma Pavel (Cambridge, MA: MIT Press, 2009), 188.

63. C. Scott Graber, "Heirs Property: The Problems and Possible Solutions," *Clearinghouse Review* 12 (September 1978), 277; Patricia Jones-Jackson, *When*

Roots Die: Endangered Traditions on the Sea Islands (Athens: University of
Georgia Press, 1987), 166–67.

64. In Alabama, for instance, attorneys were entitled to receive 10 percent of the
value of the total land sold. See Graber, "Heirs Property," 273–84. In one
example, the ELF found that a probate judge in Alabama who entered office
in the early 1970s owning an insignificant amount of land left the bench years
later owning over fifteen thousand acres in a county with an 80 percent black
population. Emergency Land Fund, *The Impact of Heir Property on Black
Rural Land Tenure in the Southeastern Region of the United States* (1980),
44–45, 291–92.

65. On Hurricane Camille, see Charles L. Sullivan, "Camille: The Mississippi
Gulf Coast in the Coils of the Snake," *Gulf Coast Historical Review* 2, no. 2
(1987): 49–78; and Fabian B. Husley, "Clio and Camille: A Report on the
Damage to Historical Landmarks on the Mississippi Gulf Coast," *Louisiana
Studies* 10, no. 1 (1971): 7–14.

66. "Severe Damage to Church Property," *Mississippi Methodist Advocate*, August
30, 1969.

67. Zebrowski and Howard, *Category 5*, 240.

68. Cited in Rocawich et al., "South Coast Follies," 112–13. On the influence of
federal subsidization of flood insurance on the development of barrier islands,
see H. Crane Miller, "Castles in the Sand: Building on Barrier Islands,"
Southern Exposure 10 (1982): 44–48.

69. Robert Goodman, *The Luck Business: The Devastating Consequences and
Broken Promises of America's Gambling Explosion* (New York: Free Press, 1995),
4; Michael Nelson and John Lyman Mason, "The Politics of Gambling in the
South," *Political Science Quarterly* 118 (Winter 2003/2004): 645–69; Matt
Taibbi, "How to Steal a Coastline," *Rolling Stone*, April 20, 2006, pp. 32–36;
Ken Belson and Gary Rivlin, "The Perils of Casinos That Float," *NYT*,
September 7, 2005. See also Reilly Morse, *Environmental Justice through the Eye
of Hurricane Katrina*, report prepared for the Joint Center for Political and
Economic Studies Health Policy Institute, Washington, DC, 2008, p. 8.

Mississippi's seemingly incongruous embrace of gambling and social
conservatism underscores Kevin Kruse and Matthew Lassiter's argument that
the ascendancy of corporate power and the Republican Party in the modern
South was not simply due to a white southern backlash against civil rights, but
also the product of changes in the demographic composition and political
economy of the region in the decades following World War II. It also high-
lights a broader phenomenon, suggested in Bethany Moreton's study of
Walmart, of social conservatives infusing corporate capitalism with religious
meaning as a means of resolving its inherent contradictions. See Lassiter and
Kruse, "Bulldozer Revolution," 698–99; and Bethany Moreton, *To Serve God*

and Wal-Mart: The Making of Christian Free Enterprise (Cambridge, MA: Harvard University Press, 2009).

70. Pat Harvey interview; Ed Moultrie, interview by Andrew Kahrl, January 8, 2010, Waveland, MS, audiotape in possession of the author. On the Gulfside capital campaign, see Ciona Rouse, " 'We Have to Rebuild Gulfside,' United Methodists Say," United Methodist Church News Archives, September 19, 2005, http://archives.umc.org/interior.asp?mid=9882 (accessed May 17, 2011).

71. Roy L. Washington, interview by Andrew Kahrl, January 12, 2010, New Orleans, audiotape in possession of the author; "Lincoln Beach Public Access Evaluation: Master Plan and Environmental Site Assessment," NOBC/NOPL, 2000–, RFP: LBVF/NOPL; "Lincoln Beach & Haynes Blvd. Camps," *New Orleans Magazine,* March 1999, found at New Orleans History—Lake Pontchartrain, http://www.stphilipneri.org/teacher/pontchartrain/section.php?id=159 (accessed August 10, 2010); Mary Croom Fontenot interview. In 1995 the property's owners, the Houston, Texas–based Carmac Holdings Inc., who had acquired the land in a complex land swap with the levee board in 1985, donated it to the levee board in exchange for a $2.5 million tax write-off. See "Revitalized Beach Project May Be Dead in the Water," NOTP, September 11, 1995.

72. Linda S. Reed, letter to editor, "Faults Board on Lincoln Beach," NOTP, July 28, 1998.

73. Michele R. Boyd, *Jim Crow Nostalgia: Reconstructing Race in Bronzeville* (Minneapolis: University of Minnesota Press, 2008), xiv.

74. See Darwin BondGraham, "The New Orleans That Race Built: Racism, Disaster, and Urban Spatial Relationships," *Souls* 9, no. 1 (2007): 4–18; J. Mark Souther, "Suburban Swamp: The Rise and Fall of Planned New-Town Communities in New Orleans East," *Planning Perspectives* 23 (April 2008): 197–219; and Diane E. Austin, "Coastal Exploitation, Land Loss, and Hurricanes: A Recipe for Disaster," *American Anthropologist* 108 (December 2006): 682.

75. "Going Back to Lincoln Beach," NOTP, February 20, 1998; "New Orleans Agrees to More Than $200 Million Settlement to Prevent Sewage from Flowing into Nearby Waters," Department of Justice Press Release, April 8, 1998, http://www.justice.gov/opa/pr/1998/April/168.htm.html (accessed August 9, 2010); "Levee Board Sees Way Out of Deal on Lincoln Beach," NOTP, June 16, 1998; "Activists Ask Foster to Help Lincoln Beach," NOTP, August 8, 1998; Reed, "Faults Board on Lincoln Beach"; "Levee Board a Target Again," NOTP, July 1, 1998.

76. Taibbi, "How to Steal a Coastline," 32–36; Mary Croom Fontenot interview; Naomi Klein, *The Shock Doctrine: The Rise of Disaster Capitalism* (New York: Picador, 2007), esp. 513–534. Along with the suspension of the Davis-Bacon

Act, which sets limits on minimum-wage standards for federally funded construction projects, other neoliberal policies enacted in the immediate aftermath of the storm included the expansion of school vouchers, lifting environmental restrictions, and waiving the estate tax for storm-related deaths. See Peter McLaren and Nathalia E. Jaramillo, "Katrina and the Banshee's Wail: The Racialization of Class Exploitation," *Cultural Studies / Critical Methodologies* 7 (May 2007): 215.

The most open expression of a sentiment shared by many came from Louisiana Republican congressman Richard Baker, who said, "We finally cleaned up public housing in New Orleans. We couldn't do it, but God did." Quoted in "Some GOP Legislators Hit Jarring Notes in Addressing Katrina," *WP*, September 10, 2005. Days later, Baker introduced before Congress HR 4100, a bill that proposed the creation of the Louisiana Recovery Development Corporation. Critics charged that the plan amounted to a wholesale privatization of public institutions and services in the city. See also Ari Kelman, "Even Paranoids Have Enemies: Rumors of Levee Sabotage in New Orleans's Lower 9th Ward," *Journal of Urban History* 35 (July 2009): 627–39.

77. Deon Roberts, "N.O. City Councilwoman Cynthia Willard-Lewis Left Outside on $300M Lincoln Beach Project," *RedOrbit*, April 2, 2007, http://www.redorbit.com/news/politics/888623/no_city_councilwoman_cynthia_willardlewis_left_outside_on_300m_lincoln/index.html (accessed November 5, 2011).

78. See Rouse, " 'We Have to Rebuild Gulfside,' United Methodists Say."

79. Taibbi, "How to Steal a Coastline," 32–36. As one coastal real estate economist found, over the long term, hurricanes have, if anything, a positive effect on coastal real estate values. See Sarah Max, "Gulf Coast Revival," *Money Magazine*, April 2006, p. 60.

80. Annalyn Swan, "Out of the Rubble . . . Condos and Slots?" *Newsweek*, October 3, 2005, p. 24; "Mississippi Senate Clears Bill to Permit Casinos on Dry Land," *WSJ*, October 4, 2005. See also E. Michael Powers, "Relaxed Casino Siting Rules Prime Gulf Building Boom," *ENR: Engineering News-Record*, December 5, 2005, p. 13; Roger Yu, "Casinos Flush with Cash in Mississippi," *USA Today*, May 15, 2006; Peter Sanders, "Casinos Emerge as Winners in Wake of Hurricane Katrina," *WSJ*, August 3, 2006; "Cashing In," *WSJ*, August 3, 2006; Robert S. Young and Orrin H. Pilkey, "Castles in the Sand," *NYT*, December 13, 2006.

81. Suzanne Goldenberg, "Scientists Dispute White House Claim that Spilled BP Oil Has Vanished," *Guardian* (UK), August 18, 2010, found at *Guardian* website, http://www.guardian.co.uk/environment/2010/aug/18/bp-oil-spill-vanished (accessed August 19, 2010).

Epilogue

1. See June Manning Thomas, "Blacks on the South Carolina Sea Islands: Planning for Tourist and Land Development" (Ph.D. diss., University of Michigan, 1977); Patricia Jones-Jackson, *When Roots Die: Endangered Traditions on the Sea Islands* (Athens: University of Georgia Press, 2004); William W. Falk, *Rooted in Place: Family and Belongings in a Southern Black Community* (New Brunswick, NJ: Rutgers University Press, 2004); Faith R. Rivers, "The Public Trust Debate: Implications for Heirs' Property along the Gullah Coast," *Southeastern Environmental Law Journal* (2007); Faith R. Rivers, "Inequity in Equity: The Tragedy of Tenancy in Common for Heirs' Property Owners Facing Partition in Equity," *Temple Political and Civil Rights Law Review* 17 (Fall 2007): 1–81.

2. See Michael N. Danielson, *Profits and Politics in Paradise: The Development of Hilton Head Island* (Columbia: University of South Carolina Press, 1995); and Margaret A. Shannon and Stephen W. Taylor, "Astride the Plantation Gates: Tourism, Racial Politics, and the Development of Hilton Head Island," in *Southern Journeys: Tourism, History, and Culture in the Modern South*, ed. Richard D. Starnes (Tuscaloosa: University of Alabama Press, 2003), 177–95.

3. Writing about the reconstruction of kinship and community ties in the post-emancipation South, Dylan C. Penningroth comments, "Land, which embodied both economic hope and ancestral identity, could divide black people as well as unite them." See Penningroth, *The Claims of Kinfolk: African American Property and Community in the Nineteenth-Century South* (Chapel Hill: University of North Carolina Press, 2003), 172. This proved no less true nearly a century and a half later. For a telling example of a dispute among heirs property holders leading to a forced partition sale that resulted in the displacement of landholding families and a windfall for the successful bidder see Tony Bartelme, "Heirs Property Tangle Leads to Loss of Land," *CPC*, December 24, 2000; "Families Evicted from Heirs' Property," *CPC*, September 28, 2001; and "Heirs Land at Risk: Cainhoy Case Draws Attention to Loophole in Legal System," *CPC*, June 23, 2002.

4. See Susan E. Webb, "The Bus from Hell-Hole Swamp: Black Women in the Hospitality Industry," in *Communities of Work: Rural Restructuring in Local and Global Contexts*, ed. William W. Falk, Michael D. Schulman, and Ann R. Tickamyer, 267–90 (Athens: Ohio University Press, 2002).

5. Groups include the Center for Heirs Property Preservation and Heirs Property Law Center, both in Charleston, SC; the Penn Center on St. Helena Island, SC; and the Heirs Property Retention Coalition, a national organization of lawyers, advocates, and academics. In 2006 the American Bar Association

formed an heirs property task force, led by the legal scholar Thomas W. Mitchell. In 2011 the National Conference of Commissioners on Uniform State Laws approved the Uniform Partition of Heirs Property Act, drafted by Mitchell, which addressed some of the worst abuses of the partition sale process.

6. See Dahleen Glanton, "Heirs to Ex-Slaves Struggle to Keep Property in Family," *CT*, July 17, 2006; and Bruce Smith, "Slave Descendents Can Reap Millions from $225 Land," *Jacksonville Florida Times-Union*, October 15, 2006.

7. Terry Yasuko Ogawa, "Wando-Huger: A Study of the Impacts of Development on the Cultural Role of Land in Black Communities of the South Carolina Lowcountry" (MS thesis, University of Michigan, 2008), 2–4.

8. See "Social Swirl," *ADW*, July 17, 1960, August 5, 1962; "Bradley Beach Motel," advertisement, *ADW*, May 19, 1963.

9. *South Carolina's Treasured Coast: Singleton Beach Place Community Tour* (Digital Video Listing Service, 2006), http://www.dvls.tv/content_distribution/products/singleplayer.php?uid=resortquest&token=rk1d56gxP9&contentid=41& filetype=.flv (accessed August 16, 2011).

10. Colin Moore and Robert Washington, "'The Island Colonies': A Profile of Rural Poverty" (1971?), pp. 3–4, in Johns Island folder, BERC/NYPL. One study of the Sea Islands found that majority black municipalities were more pro-development and skeptical to slow-growth initiatives than wealthier, predominantly white municipalities. See Cassandra Y. Johnson and Myron F. Floyd, "A Tale of Two Towns: Black and White Municipalities Respond to Urban Growth in the South Carolina Lowcountry," *Research in Human Ecology* 13, no. 1 (2006): 23–38.

11. Quoted in Thomas, "Blacks on the South Carolina Sea Islands," 66. On the deceptive tactics used by the Land Title Clearance Program on heirs property owners see Jesse Morris and Robert S. Browne, Frogmore Conference on Heir Property Report, folder 10, box 34, BERC/NYPL.

12. See Randall Peterson, "For Sale by Owners," *Mother Jones*, March–April 2007, pp. 28–31.

13. Smith, "Slave Descendents Can Reap Millions from $225 Land." Articles from the "Torn from the Land" series can be accessed at http://www.theauthenticvoice .org/Torn_From_The_Land_Intro.html (accessed May 25, 2011).

14. On March 18, 1975, Charleston, SC, attorney George Payton was shot and killed in his office. The murder remained unsolved, but investigators stated that it was likely related to a dispute over Payton's role in clearing titles to black-owned heirs properties on Hilton Head Island. See "Threats Reported but Motive Lacked," *BAA*, May 29, 1975; "Clue Told for Payton Slaying," *BAA*, July 12, 1975; and Thomas, "Blacks on the South Carolina Sea Islands," 68.

15. See Ogawa, "Wando-Huger," 4–9.

16. Thelma Byas, telephone conversation with Andrew Kahrl, June 1, 2011, notes in the possession of the author.

17. See Jaime Dailey, "Dispute over Heirs Property on Hilton Head Island," WTOC-11, http://www.wtoc.com/Global/story.asp?S=14425613, April 11, 2011; "Controversy Continues over Sale of Heirs Property," WTOC-11, http://www .wtoc.com/Global/story.asp?S=14450362, April 14, 2011; "Hilton Head Families Forced to Move off Heirs Property," WTOC-11, http://www.wtoc.com/Global /story.asp?S=14636543, May 12, 2011 (all accessed May 25, 2011); Tom Barton, "Hilton Head's Purchase of Heirs Land Fuels Emotions; Councilman Cites 'Mistake' in Proposing Sale," *Hilton Head Island Packet*, April 13, 2011.

PRIMARY SOURCES

Manuscript Collections

Artificial Collection of Rare Items for District of Columbia History, ca. 1791–1990. DC Community Archives, Washingtoniana Division. District of Columbia Public Library, Washington, DC.

Behind the Veil Collection. Rare Book, Manuscript, and Special Collection Library. Duke University, Durham, NC.

Black Economic Research Center. Records. Schomburg Center for Research in Black Culture, Manuscripts and Archives. New York Public Library.

Chief Administrative Office. Correspondence. Louisiana Division, City Archives and Special Collections. New Orleans Public Library.

Christian, Marcus. Collection. Louisiana and Special Collections. Earl K. Long Library. University of New Orleans.

Cooper, Dudley, and Ocean View Amusement Park. Papers. Special Collections. Perry Library. Old Dominion University. Norfolk, VA.

Cotten, Sallie S. Papers. Southern Historical Collection. Wilson Library. University of North Carolina. Chapel Hill, North Carolina

Drueding, Robert J., Collection. Louisiana and Special Collections. Earl K. Long Library. University of New Orleans.

Frazier, E. Franklin. Papers. Moorland-Spingarn Research Center. Howard University, Washington, DC.

Free Southern Theater. Papers. Amistad Research Center. Tulane University, New Orleans.

Gulfside Association Scrapbook. Schomburg Center for Research in Black Culture, Manuscripts and Archives. New York Public Library.

Jones, Robert Elijah. Papers, 1872–1965. Amistad Research Center. Tulane University, New Orleans.

Kingsley House. Papers. Special Collections. Jones Hall Library. Tulane University, New Orleans.

Land Deed Records. Mississippi Department of Archives and History. Jackson, MS.

Lee, Howard Newton. Papers. Howard-Tilton Library. Tulane University, New Orleans.

Lincoln Beach Vertical File. Louisiana Division, City Archives and Special Collections. New Orleans Public Library.

Mayor Marc Morial. Records. Louisiana Division, City Archives and Special Collections. New Orleans Public Library.

Metropolitan Police Department of the District of Columbia. Records. National Archives, Washington, DC.

Mississippi Oral History Project. Center for Oral History and Cultural Heritage. University of Southern Mississippi, Hattiesburg.

Morrison, De Lesseps S. Collection. Louisiana Division, City Archives and Special Collections. New Orleans Public Library.

Mosquito Beach Community Collection, 1953–1990. Archives, Avery Research Center for African American History and Culture. College of Charleston, Charleston, SC.

NAACP–New Orleans Branch. Louisiana and Special Collections. Earl K. Long Library. University of New Orleans.

New Orleans Association of Commerce. Records. Louisiana and Special Collections. Earl K. Long Library. University of New Orleans.

New Orleans Building Corporation. Records, 2000–. Louisiana Division, City Archives and Special Collections. New Orleans Public Library.

New Orleans Police Department. Clippings, 1944–1946. Louisiana Division, City Archives and Special Collections. New Orleans Public Library.

Rosenwald, Julius, Fund Archives. Special Collections and Archives. Franklin Library. Fisk University, Nashville, TN.

Sanford, Terry. Governor's Papers, 1959–1965. North Carolina State Archives. Raleigh.

Savage, William R. Papers. Southern Historical Collection. Wilson Library. University of North Carolina, Chapel Hill.

Schiro, Victor Hugo. Collection. Louisiana Division, City Archives and Special Collections. New Orleans Public Library.

Sens, Paul. Records. Louisiana Division, City Archives and Special Collections. New Orleans Public Library.

Southern Oral History Program. Southern Historical Collection. Wilson Library, University of North Carolina, Chapel Hill.

Terrell, Mary Church. Papers. Manuscripts Division. Library of Congress.

United Methodist Church Archives. General Commission on Archives and History, Madison, NJ.

Williams, Charles H. Papers (unprocessed). University Archives. Hampton University Museum. Hampton University, Hampton, VA.

Interviews by Author

Peter Badie, January 11, 2010

Raymond Breaux, January 12, 2010

Ethel Ellis, January 12, 2010
Mary Croom Fontenot, January 7 and 9, 2010
Juanita Doris Franklin, January 14, 2010
William Garibaldi, January 15, 2008
Theresa Brossett Gonzalez, September 9, 2008
Genevieve Gordon, January 8, 2010
Pat Harvey, January 8, 2010
Ray Langston, December 12, 2009
Vincent Leggett, December 11, 2009
Kenneth McGruder, January 5, 2010
Sharon Merrick, April 10, 2010
John Moses, December 12, 2009
Ed and Paula Moultrie, January 8, 2010
Sheila Murdoch, April 10, 2010
George Phelps, December 10, 2009, April 7, 2010
Edith Smith, January 6, 2010
Moral W. Trent, November 12, 2005
Roy L. Washington, January 12, 2010
Willie Williams, January 5, 2010

ACKNOWLEDGMENTS

My fascination with the beach, and my interest in it as a subject of historical inquiry, did not come through a transcendental moment by the sea, but through less romantic, but for most Americans, far more typical experiences. I was born in a small town in central Ohio, over five hundred miles from the Atlantic coast. Trips to the beach took us to a cleared patch of land, blanketed with trucked-in sand, on a man-made lake where my parents owned a summer cabin. Despite the modest accommodations, all members of our property owners' association (and their approved guests) were sure to wear beach tags on their bathing suits, lest they be stopped and questioned by the security guards charged with keeping out persons from the county who could not afford a summer home there. I still vividly recall the annual ritual of handing out beach tags to family members and close family friends, and the smug sense of superiority I felt by virtue of having affixed to my swim trunks a small piece of plastic that was unavailable to others, and that announced my status as someone who enjoyed exclusive access to a private beach. Looking back, it's easy to note the absurdity of my thoughts, as well as the actions of those charged with keeping non–property owners off the beach. These were, after all, man-made beaches less than the length of a football field that consisted of equal parts sand and dirt. But as I discovered over the course of writing, my childhood attempts to define myself through the places I could go for fun and amusement (and that others could not, except upon invitation) were also quite revealing of the larger issues and problems this book attempted to tackle, ones which, in our daily lives, often have little direct relation to the issue of race in contemporary society but which are inseparable from the history of race.

My path to becoming a historian of the American experience began at Kenyon College, where I learned to love the craft of history from Peter Rutkoff and Will Scott. The model of teacher and scholar, Peter and Will have had an indelible impact on the lives of generations of students. I am lucky to count them as mentors and friends. At Indiana University, I was fortunate to study under an accomplished and dedicated group of scholars. I thank, in particular, Claude Clegg, Steven Stowe, Khalil Gibran Muhammad, Matthew Pratt Guterl, and John Bodnar for bringing my research interests into focus and getting this project off the ground. At Marquette University, I have benefited immeasurably from the support of Jim Marten, who as chair of the history department has created an ideal working environment and has gone to great lengths to provide me with the time and resources needed to complete this book.

Despite rumors to the contrary, I conducted much of the research for this book not on the beach wearing sunblock and flip-flops, but rather in archives clad in white gloves and handling fragile documents, or online downloading piles of articles from databases and requesting obscure documents through interlibrary loan. All of this work would not have been possible were it not for the generous assistance of the staffs of the following libraries and archives: Indiana University's Herman B. Wells Library; Harvard University's Widener Library; Marquette University's Raynor Library; the Southern Historical Collection at the University of North Carolina at Chapel Hill; the Rare Book, Manuscript, and Special Collections Library at Duke University; the Amistad Research Center at Tulane University; the City Archives and Special Collections at the New Orleans Public Library; the Louisiana and Special Collections at the University of New Orleans's Earl K. Long Library; the Moorland-Spingarn Research Center at Howard University; the Special Collections and Archives at Fisk University; the Special Collections and Washingtoniana divisions at the District of Columbia's Martin Luther King Jr. Memorial Library; the University Archives at Hampton University; the Manuscript, Archives, and Rare Books Division of the New York Public Library's Schomburg Center for Research in Black Culture; the Mississippi Department of Archives and History; the North Carolina State Archives; the Maryland State Archives; the United Methodist Archives Center at Drew University; and the Avery Research Center at the College of Charleston.

I feel truly fortunate to have enjoyed a great deal of support in the form of research fellowships and grants from the following institutions: the Andrew W. Mellon Foundation and the American Council of Learned Societies; the W. E. B. Du Bois Institute for African and African American Research at Harvard University; the Louisiana Endowment for the Humanities through its Louisiana Publishing Initiative Grants Program; Indiana University's History Department; Marquette University's College of Arts and Sciences; Duke University's John Hope Franklin Research Center for African and African American History and Culture; the University of North Carolina at Chapel Hill's Southern Historical Collection; the University of South Carolina's Institute for Southern Studies; and the North Caroliniana Society.

Along with institutions, I relied on the knowledge, wisdom, and advice of fellow scholars, artists, activists, and local people who generously shared their time and thoughts with me and took an interest in my work. I can safely say this book would not have been possible without them. For reading portions of the book in its various stages and providing critical feedback, I thank Davarian Baldwin, Al Brophy, Michael Carriere, Scott Casper, Nathan Connolly, Alison Clark Efford, Tom Guglielmo, Evelyn Brooks Higginbotham, Brian McCammack, Todd Michney, Kali Murray, Eric Sandweiss, Bryant Simon, Rob Smith, Anthony Stanonis, William Julius Wilson, and Victoria Wolcott. Nathan Connolly, in particular, had an incredible influence on this project during its latter stages, carefully reading chapters, offering timely and thoughtful comments and suggestions, and regularly challenging my thoughts and assumptions. Through the works of visual artist Juan Logan and his engagement with my work, I came to see the shore—as both place and idea—in new and refreshing ways. For their assistance in my fieldwork in Maryland, Virginia, North Carolina, and the Gulf South, I would like to thank the following persons and institutions: Chris Brook of the Southern Coalition for Social Justice, Mary Croom Fontenot of All Congregations Together–New Orleans, Juanita Doris Franklin, Francesca "Zeal" Harris, Pat Harvey, Janice Hayes-Williams, the Reverend Douglas Haywood, Raymond Langston, Vincent Leggett, Riley Morse of the Mississippi Center for Justice, Jack Nelson, George Phelps Jr., and Vernie Singleton. Gordon Thompson patiently worked with me to produce the original maps included in this book. The following students provided critical research assistance: Miraf Bistegne, Christopher Luedke, Jeffrey Ramsey, Alison Brown, and Leah Davis. Kathleen McDermott of Harvard University Press took an early interest in this project, helped shepherd it to publication, and has been a wonderful editor throughout the process.

I came to Harvard University's Du Bois Institute in 2008 as part of a fabulous group of Fellows. For providing me with an incomparable setting to work, write, and learn, I especially thank Henry Louis "Skip" Gates Jr., Evelyn Brooks Higginbotham, and the DBI staff, in particular Vera Grant and Donald Yacavone. For sharing their thoughts and offering insights into my research at public forums and conversations during that year, I thank Jennifer Nash, Joanna Lipper, Chris Vogner, Kevin Mumford, Paul Kaplan, Hope Lewis, Faith Smith, Zöe Burkholder, Chris Matthews, Scott Kurashige, Erin Royston Battat, and Rachel Devlin.

I acquired a personalized education on corporate and property law from a close group of friends who all happened to be in law school at the time. For always being there to field random questions on various aspects of the law, I thank Gabe Acinapura, Jake Armstrong, Elizabeth Dyer, Christina Knopf, Erica Lubans, William C. Means Jr., and Selah Wyche. For great food, great conversations, and wonderful hospitality during my many research trips, I especially thank John and Penelope Rahming, Christopher Harter and Elizabeth McMahon, Norman and Farideh Goldin, Paul and Rosalie Acinapura, Mark Simundson and Loretta Sevier, and Ted and Cindy Sevier.

Finally, I must thank my family for their love, support, and patience. From an early age, my parents, Timothy and Susan Kahrl, encouraged my interest in history and supported my pursuit of it as a career. My wife, Aileen, laughed when she came across an acknowledgment written by another historian to his wife thanking her for learning to appreciate the inordinate amount of time it takes to write a single book. No doubt, had this project been in her capable hands, it would have been on the shelves years ago. Aileen read every single page of this book (sometimes, several times) and was its most thorough and perceptive critic. Her brilliance, talents, and generosity continue to amaze me. Her love and affection sustain me.

As we put this baby to bed, we welcomed the arrival of our daughters, Elodie and Muriel. Their beautiful, smiling faces light up our lives and make them whole. May they someday read these words and capture a glimpse of their daddy as a young man, filled with wonder at the journey that lies ahead.

INDEX

A&R Development (Baltimore, Md.), 233

Act for the Protection and Improvement of Beaches along the Shores of the United States (1936), 10

Adams, Charles "Hoppy," 191–192. *See also* Carr's and Sparrow's Beaches (Annapolis, Md.); WANN-AM (Annapolis, Md.)

Adams, William L. "Little Willie": youth and early adulthood, 188; business holdings, 188–190, 200; real estate investment and development, 188–190, 200, 233–235; lending policies, 189; Victorine Adams (wife), 189; Oak Grove Beach Company, 189–190; Carr's Beach Amusement Company, 190; Elktonia Beach, 190; Kefauver committee testimony, 200; A&R Development, 233; political activities, 233. *See also* Carr's and Sparrow's Beaches (Annapolis, Md.); Numbers (illegal lottery)

Albermarle Sound (N.C.), 7

Alexander, Will, 77

All Congregations Together (ACT) (New Orleans, La.), 246, 247

Alton, Joseph Jr., 200–201, 234

American Shore and Beach Preservation Association, 9–10

Amusement parks, desegregation of, 223–225. *See also* Marshall Hall Amusement Park (Washington, D.C.); Ocean View Amusement Park (Norfolk, Va.); Pontchartrain Beach (New Orleans, La.)

Anacostia River (Washington, D.C.), 125, 128

Angler (steamboat), 47

Annapolis, Md., African American population, 102, 110, 179–180, 183, 185, 192

Anne Arundel County, Md.: sheriff's department, 200–202, 205–208; zoning board, 232, 235–237

Apperson, J. W., 66, 78

Army Corps of Engineers: Beach Erosion Board, 10; role in development of coastal South of, 10–11; beach restoration and replenishment, 83, 176–177, 213–214, 237–238; and African American land loss, 165–166, 177, 211–213, 237–238; Intracoastal Waterway (Wilmington, N.C.), 165–166; Carolina Beach inlet, 175, 177; Jordan Lake (N.C.), 211–212; lawsuits against, 237–238; seawall construction, 248. *See also* Engineering, shoreline

Aron, Cindy, 60

Arson: *Lady of the Lake* (steamboat), 32–33; Washington Park (Md.), 47; Kessler's Mill (Roanoke, Va.), 47–48; Pine Crest Inn (Roanoke, Va.), 48; Pacific Beach Club (Huntington Beach, Calif.), 49; Ware's Hotel (Highland Beach, Md.), 105–106; Little Bay Beach (Norfolk, Va.), 133; Shell Island (Wrightsville Beach, N.C.), 159

Arundel-on-the-Bay, Md.: sales of homes to African Americans in, 111–112; "white flight" from, 111–112; appreciation of property values in, 232

Ashley River (Charleston, S.C.), 12

Asmard, Charles and Madelon, 55–56

Associated Charities (Washington, D.C.), 45

Atlantic City, N.J., 203

Automobile, influence of, on coastal and vacation home real estate development, 8, 9, 92–94, 104–105

Badie, Peter "Chuck," 115, 130–131,141
Bailey, George, 204
Baltimore, Md.: informal economy of, 188, 200; Pennsylvania Avenue, 189; African American beach resorts in, 204
Baltimore Afro-American, 27, 38, 107, 112–113, 203, 208
Banks, Frank D., 181
Barbour, Haley, 248
Barlow, David E., 202
Barrier islands, development of, 58, 78, 214, 242
Basie, Count, 186
Batt, Harry, 121–122, 210, 223, 227. *See also* Pontchartrain Beach (New Orleans, La.)
Bay Highlands, Md., 97–99
Bay Ridge (Md.), 88–89, 91
Bay Shore Beach and Hotel (Hampton, Va.): acquisition and commercial development, 181–182; finances, 182, 185–186, 195, 219–221; 1933 storm, 185; attractions, 186, 193; music performances, 186, 195; expansion and improvements, 193; food and drink stands, 193; nightclubs, 193; transportation to, 193; conferences and conventions at, 193–195; advertising and promotion, 195; workforce, 195; white youth at, 198–199; policing and security, 205; effects of desegregation on, 210, 219–221
Bay St. Louis, Miss., 57, 62, 65–66, 78, 243
Bell, W. H., 118
Bensinger, Samuel, 43–44, 45, 46–47
Berry, Chuck, 172, 178
Bilbo, Theodore, 68
Biloxi, Miss.: segregation of beaches in, 11, 84–85; wade-ins and riots, 215, 216; industry, 241–242; casinos, 243; post-Katrina recovery, 248
Black Economic Research Center, 239. *See also* Heirs' property
Black elite: attempts to develop pleasure resorts for, 33–34, 48–50; patronage of places of public amusement, 44–46; impact of Jim Crow on, 88–90; vacation destinations of, 88–89; in Washington, D.C., 89–90; social world of, 90; exclusionary mechanisms of, 97–99, 100–102, 104–105, 108–109; attitudes

toward black poor, 99–100; criticisms of, 106–108; children of, 113–114; desegregation and, 230–233. *See also* Class (black Americans); Highland Beach, Md.
Black Metropolis (Drake and Cayton), 14
Bland, Bobby Blue, 172
Blum, Morris H., 191–192. *See also* WANN-AM (Annapolis, Md.)
Bop City. *See* Freeman Beach (N.C.)
Borgne, Lake (New Orleans, La.), 118, 129–130
Bowen, George T., 91
Boyd, Michelle, 245
Bradley Beach (Hilton Head Island, S.C.), 253
Brandt, George, 57
Brashears, William, 89
Bright, Lem, 132–134
British Petroleum (BP), 249
Brooks, Robert N., 71, 72, 83
Brown, Adolph "A. D.," 250–252, 254–257
Brown, Eula G. (pseud.), 103
Brown, George, 204
Brown, James, 1, 172, 198, 208
Brown, Lindsey, 159
Browne, Robert E., 239
Brown's Grove (Baltimore, Md.), 204
Brown v. Board of Education (1954), 110, 225
Bruce, Blanche K., 90
Bruce, Roscoe Conkling, 45
Buckroe Beach Amusement Park (Hampton, Va.), 182, 198
Burke, French, 182
Burke Beach (Hilton Head Island, S.C.), 253
Buzzard Point (Washington, D.C.), 125–126
Byrnes, Joseph, 127
Byron, JoAnne (Assata Shakur), 171–172, 174

Calloway, Cab, 199
Campanella, Richard, 121
Campbell, Emory, 256
Cannon, Hugh, 216
Cape Fear River, N.C., 165, 176. *See also* Carolina Beach Inlet, environmental impact of; Intracoastal Waterway (ICW)
Cape May, N.J., 88
Cappie, Herman Melvin and Ruth Irene, 56, 130–131

Carolina Beach, N.C.: founding and development of, 157, 159, 165; annexation of beachfront property, 165; beach segregation, 173, 216; harassment of African Americans in, 173–174; beach replenishment, 176–177, 237–238; beachfront building permits, 177; Freedom Riders in, 216

Carolina Beach Inlet, environmental impact of, 175–177, 237–238. *See also* Freeman Beach (N.C.)

Carr family: landholdings, 179–180; Frederick Carr, 179–180, 182; land partition and distribution, 182–183; land sales, 182, 233–235; commercial real estate development by, 183, 193; Elizabeth Carr, 183, 190; Florence Sparrow, 183, 234; Frederick and Grace Smith, 190

Carr's and Sparrow's Beaches (Annapolis, Md.): establishment and early development, 183–184; advertising and promotion, 183–185, 186, 190–191, 208; attractions and accommodations, 183, 185, 190; business models, 183–185, 190, 193, 207–208, 222; regional customer base, 183, 185, 190, 199; bathing beauty contests, 184–185; workforce, 185; music performances at, 186, 190, 191, 208–209, 221, 222; William L. "Little Willie" Adams's investment in, 190; expansion and improvements, 190; influence of urban life and culture on, 190–191; slot machines at, 190, 199–200; management, 190–191, 208; nightclub, 190, 208–209; Charles "Hoppy" Adams, 192; *Bandstand on the Beach*, 192–193; juke joints, 193; relations with white neighbors, 200, 205; policing and security, 200–202, 205–208; illegal activities at, 205–208; white impressions of, 221–222; closing and redevelopment, 222, 233–237

Carr's Beach Amusement Company, 190, 205, 222, 234

Cecelski, David, 157

Cedar Haven (Md.), 94–95

Ceruti, E. Burton, 48, 50

Charles, Ray, 206

Charles Macalester (steamboat), 24

Charleston, S.C., 11–12, 143, 181, 198–199, 252–253, 254

Charlot tract (Pass Christian, Miss.), 55–56

Chase, W. Calvin, 31–32. *See also Washington Bee*

Chatham County, N.C., 211–212

Chautauquas, 60, 69. *See also* Gulfside Assembly (Waveland, Miss.); Methodist Episcopal (ME) Church

Chavis, Joe, 181

Chesapeake Bay: environmental degradation of, 231, 235–237; Critical Areas Act (1984), 235–237. *See also* Maryland Western Shore

Chesapeake Harbour, Villages of (Annapolis, Md.), 1–2, 235–237. *See also* Duck's Run Partnership (Annapolis, Md.)

Chicago, Ill.: vacationers and investors on Mississippi Gulf Coast from, 52, 57, 64–66; rural retreats for African Americans from, 92–93

Chicago Defender, 168

Children and childhood: summer camps and, 14, 70–72; summer vacation resorts and, 113–114; consumerism and, 197. *See also* Drowning deaths (black Americans); Gulfside Assembly (Waveland, Miss.); Highland Beach, Md.

"Chitlin Circuit": emergence of, 186–187; Apollo Theater (Harlem), 187; Howard Theater (Washington, D.C.), 187, 191; Royal Theater (Baltimore, Md.), 191; radio and rise of, 192–193; demise of, 209. *See also* Bay Shore Beach and Hotel (Hampton, Va.); Carr's and Sparrow's Beaches (Annapolis, Md.); Freeman Beach (N.C.)

Churches: excursions, 22, 36, 46, 169, 180, 183, 185; efforts to combat recreational inequality by, 140; baptisms, 173, 198. *See also specific churches and denominations*

City Beach (Norfolk, Va.): acquisition of property for, 137–138, 148; African American protests over, 146–147; management and staffing of, 148–149; deterioration of, 148–149; threats to health and safety of bathers at, 149

City Beautiful movement, 123

Civilian Conservation Corps (CCC), 10. *See also* New Deal

Civil Rights Act (1964), 222–223

Civil rights movement: environmental justice and, 12–13, 150–152; and right to leisure and recreation space, 17, 127–128, 140–141, 146–147, 149–150, 151–152, 227; Freedom Riders, 216; importance of African American-owned land in, 216–217; public accommodations, 219; neighborhood investment and economic justice, 244–247

Civil rights protests: over funding for black beaches and recreational facilities, 146–147; over drowning deaths, 149–150, 154; over leasing and management of black beaches, 199

Civil rights strategies: threat of integration, 147; wade-ins, 151–152, 215–216; specter of disease and epidemics, 152

Clark, H. A., 51

Clark, Hal H., 48–50

Class (black Americans): land ownership and, 8, 15–16; leisure spaces and, 14, 33–34, 44–46, 86–88, 99, 171–173, 196, 209; middle class attitudes toward poor, 27–28, 53, 70–71, 209; conflicts, 46, 97, 103–104, 106–108, 150–151; vacationing and, 88–90, 93, 113–114, 161, 228–230; and Great Migration, 99; skin tone and, 106–107, 172; childhood, 113–114; hair and, 172; desegregation, 220, 227–229. *See also* Black elite; Racial uplift

Class (white Americans): segregated public spaces and, 121–122; and response to civil rights movement, 215–216; public spaces desegregation and, 223–224; vacationing and, 229–230

Coastal capitalism, 4: and rise of Sunbelt South, 9, 10–11, 16–17; and racial segregation, 12

Coastal engineering. *See* Engineering, shoreline

Cobb, James, 68

Cobb Island, Md., 33–34

Cole, Edna, 211–212

Cole, Nat King, 172, 198

Coleman, R. W., 140

Collingwood Beach (Va.), 26–27, 34

Colombia Beach (Md.), 110

Colonial Beach (Va.), 33

Colored American, 27, 42

"Colored" public beaches: inferiority of, 125, 130, 141–143, 148–149; remote location of, 125–126, 129–130, 137, 141; health and safety concerns, 125, 130–132, 141–143, 152; naming of, 126–127, 141; staffing and emergency preparedness, 130–131, 143, 145–146, 148–149; and maintenance of Jim Crow, 135, 140; closing and abandonment of, 223, 227–228. *See also specific beaches*

Committee on Interracial Cooperation (CIC), 60

Congress, U.S.: Tidal Basin bathing beach appropriations, 122–127; Hurricane Katrina disaster relief, 248

Consumerism: beaches as sites of, 183–185, 189, 195–198, 209; and urban informal economy, 188–189; racial segmentation of, 196–197; children and, 197; and civil rights movement, 219

Cooke, Sam, 208

Cooper, Dudley, 196, 224. *See also* Ocean View Amusement Park (Norfolk, Va.); Seaview Beach and Hotel (Norfolk, Va.)

Cooper, Edward E., 38

Corcoran, William Wilson, 39

Cotten, Bruce, 7

DeAnbough, Margaret, 237

Deepwater Horizon well explosion (2010), 249

De la Brosse, Julia, 55

Dent, Thomas C., 154

Desegregation, effects of, on black-owned businesses, 210, 219–221

Diggs, J. Eugene, 147

Dismond, Geraldyne, 161

Domino, Fats, 172, 198, 227

Douglass, Charles, 88–91, 95

Douglass, Frederick, 91

Douglass, Haley, 95: governance of Highland Beach, 96–97, 100, 101–102, 103, 105, 108–109; real estate interests of, 97–103, 105. *See also* Highland Beach, Md.

Douglass, Joseph, 95–96, 97, 98, 99

Drowning deaths (black Americans): Charleston, S.C., 12; New Orleans, 115, 130–132, 150, 154, 223; Washington, D.C., 127–128, 150; Norfolk, Va., 134–135, 145–146, 149; Little Rock, Ark., 149–150; Monroe, N.C., 150

Du Bois, W. E. B.: on "color problem of summer," 13, 90; on race as legal construct, 15; on Central Jurisdiction, 82

Duck's Run Partnership (Annapolis, Md.): acquisition of former Carr's and Sparrow's Beaches site, 234–235; development and marketing of Villages of Chesapeake Harbour, 235–237

Dunbar, Paul Laurence, 20, 86, 91

DuPree, Reese, 186

Durrette, Clairice, 167–168

Duvall, Howard, 89

Dyson, Frederick, 37

Eagle Harbor, Md.: founding and development, 93–94; property taxes, 95; incorporation of, 96

Eastport, Md., 207

Echols, Timothy B., 80

Eldridge v. Trezevant (1896), 119

Elktonia Beach (Md.), 190. *See also* Adams, William L. "Little Willie"

Emancipation, and rise of black landownership, 7, 155–156

Embree, Edwin R., 77, 78, 79

Emergency Land Fund, 241

Engineering, shoreline: economic effects of, 10, 64–66, 220–221; environmental effects of, 10, 176, 238; racial segregation and, 11–12, 65, 84–85; beach replenishment, 83, 176–177, 213–214, 237; drowning deaths and, 130, 176; erosion as a result of, 165–166, 175–176, 237. *See also* Army Corps of Engineers; Public Law 727 (1946); Seawalls

Environmental Protection Agency (EPA), 245

Environmental racism: leisure and recreation and, 12–13; real estate development and, 116; shoreline engineering and, 165–166, 176–177

Families, effects of landownership on, 155, 161, 166–167, 211–212, 250–252. *See also* Heirs' property; *specific families*

Farmer, J. Leonard, 72

Farmers and farming (black Americans): on Maryland's Western Shore, 89, 178, 179–180; in coastal North Carolina, 155–157; on South Carolina Sea Islands, 180–181; in Chatham

County, N.C., 211–212; and land loss, 211–212; 238–241. *See also* Heirs' property

Farmers Home Administration (FmHA), 211; and heirs' property, 176

Farm laborers, leisure activities of, 171–172, 180–181

Fats Wallace and His Rhythm Aces, 143

Fearrington Village (Chatham County, N.C.), 212

Federal government: coastal protection and development, 9–10, 82–83, 213–214; flood control and insurance, 10, 211, 213–214; beach desegregation, 216

Ferguson, Bill, 256

Fields, Mamie Garvin, 11–12

Fishing, commercial and sport: North Carolina, 157, 175; South Carolina Sea Islands, 180–181

Fishing Creek Farm (Md.), 232

Flood Control Act (1936), 10

Flood insurance. *See* National Flood Insurance Act (1968)

Florida: 1920s real estate boom, 9; tax code, 66–67

Fort Lauderdale, Fla., beach desegregation, 215–216

Fortune, T. Thomas, 22

Fox Lake, Ind., 93

Francis, John R., 91, 103

Franklin, Juanita Doris, 3, 14, 72

Fraser, Charles S., 250

Freedman's Transportation, Land, and Improvement Company (Washington, D.C.): incorporation, 39; advertising and promotion, 40; stock offering, 40; finances, 41; shareholders, 41–42; dissolution, 43. *See also* Jefferson, Lewis

Freeman Beach (N.C.): disputed ownership claims to, 170–171, 174–175, 177; construction and financing of, 171, 173–174; crowds at, 171–172; music performed at, 172; business model, 173–174; erosion of, 175–176, 177, 237–238; Hurricane Hazel (1954), 176

Freeman family: Alexander and Charity Freeman, 155–156; Robert Bruce Freeman, 155–156, 162, 166, 171, 174; landholdings, 155–156, 157, 162, 164–165; land loss, 157,

Freeman family (continued)
164–165, 175–177, 237–238; residential and
commercial real estate development by,
161–162, 171–174; heirs' property, 162, 164–165,
237–238; Ellis Freeman, 164; beachfront
property, 164–165, 170–171, 174–177, 237–238

Galbraith, John Kenneth, 9
Galpin, Charles J., 9
Gambling industry, 242; in Maryland, 199–200;
in Mississippi, 242–243, 248. See also
Numbers (illegal lottery)
Gamby, Littleton, 190
Gateway Development LLC (Hilton Head
Island, S.C.), 255. See also Brown, Adolph
"A. D."
Gatewood, Askew, 189
Gentilly Woods (New Orleans, La.), 153
George Leary (steamboat), 33, 37–38, 51
Georgia Sea Islands, 8, 163
Gex, E. J., 74
Ghetto of Desire (play), 154
Glymont, Md., 30, 33
Goldstein, Joseph, 225–227. See also Marshall
Hall Amusement Park (Washington, D.C.)
Great Migration: response of southern
industries to, 136; land ownership and,
166–167; heirs' property and, 167
Gulf and Ship Island Railroad, 57
Gulfport, Miss., 57, 75, 248
Gulfside Assembly (Waveland, Miss.):
"Gulfside Idea," 53; acquisition of property,
61–62; Jackson House, 61, 69, 70, 76–77,
80; construction and development, 62–63,
68–70, 73–75, 83–85; finances, 62, 68–69, 73,
76–81, 84, 217–219; fund-raising, 62, 72–74,
80–81, 83–84; Sixteenth Section land, 62,
218–219; mortgages, 68–69; lot sales
campaign, 69, 77–78; boys' school, 69–70,
74, 76, 80; youth camps, 70–72; farm, 70;
racial uplift and, 70–71; School for Practical
Methods for Town and Rural Pastors, 71;
spiritual dimensions of, 72, 80, 85, 243;
Gulfside Clubs, 73; relations with local
whites, 73–76, 79, 244; dedication ceremony,
75; interracial events at, 75–76; Song Fest,
75–76; philanthropic support of, 76–79, 84;

landscaping and maintenance, 77; property
taxes, 77–78, 79, 217, 243; land sales, 78, 217,
218–219; effects of Great Depression on,
78–79; health conferences, 79–80; Summer
Normal School, 79–80; insurance policy,
80; Central Jurisdiction, 82–84; Mississippi
State Sovereignty Commission investigation
of, 216–217; civil rights activities at, 217;
integration of Methodist church and,
217–219; Hurricane Camille, 241; "Moving
Forward" capital campaign, 243–244; Ernest
T. Dixon Retirement Village, 244; Norris
Hall, 244; Hurricane Katrina, 244, 247–248.
See also Jones, Robert E.; Methodist
Episcopal (ME) Church; Mississippi Gulf
Coast

Hall, Jacquelyn Dowd, 17
Hampton, Va., 220–221
Hampton Institute, 181. See also Bay Shore
Beach and Hotel (Hampton, Va.)
Hancock County, Miss.: business community
of, 73–75; health board, 80; sixteenth section
land, 218–219
Handy, William Talbot, 218
Harbrant, Robert and Anne, 237
Harlem, N.Y., 167
Harpers Ferry, W.V., 88
Harris, Abram, 21, 38
Harrison County, Miss., 64, 83: U.S. Justice
Department lawsuit against, 216
Harvey, Pat, 3, 14, 72
Healy, Robert G., 213
Hearly, George, 74
Heath, Jack, 23
Heirs' property: definition and legal status of,
162–163; causes of, 163–164; geographical
distribution of, 163, 250; problems with,
164, 170–171; shareholders of, 167, 239–241,
251–252; exploitation of owners of, 174–175,
237–241, 251–256; exclusion from federal
lending programs, 176; forced partition sales
of, 237, 238–241, 250–251, 254; efforts to
preserve, 239, 251. See also Freeman family;
Hilton Head Island, S.C.
Henderson, Edwin B., 112
Henderson, John, 56

Heritage Foundation, 247

Highland Beach, Md.: founding and early development, 89–91; lot sales, 90–92, 95–96, 101; Twin Oaks cottage, 91; relations with neighboring villages, 92, 97–98, 100–102, 112–114; incorporation of, 96–97, 102–103; tensions and divisions among property owners, 97, 100–101, 103–106; non–property owners' criticisms of, 97, 103, 105–108; property disputes, 97, 105; privatization of public space in, 99–105; policing and security, 100–101; town charter, 102–103, 108–109; property assessments, 103; commercialization of, 104–106; Ware's Hotel, 104–106, 109; elections, 105; children and childhood, 113–114; decline of (1970s), 230–231. See also Arundel-on-the-Bay, Md.; Bay Highlands, Md.; Oyster Harbor, Md.; Venice Beach (Md.)

Hill, Frank and Lulu: migration to New York City, 166; return to North Carolina, 170; encounters with Jim Crow legal system, 170, 174–175, 177; savings and investments, 171. See also Freeman Beach (N.C.); Freeman family

Hill, John Bright, 174–175

Hilton Head Island, S.C., 250–257; African American land loss on, 250–254, 255–256; African American beaches on, 253; forced removal of black landowners from, 255–256

Hilyer, Andrew, 39

Hine, E. S., 93, 95

Homeowners' associations. See Property owners' associations

Home Real Estate Realty Company (Carolina Beach, N.C.), 164, 170–171, 174–175

Home Realty Company (Wilmington Beach, N.C.), 158

Hoover, Herbert, 53

Housing Act (1949), 176

Hughes, David, 56

Huntington Beach, Calif., 48–49

Hurricanes, 9; 1915 Gulf of Mexico storm, 58; 1916 Gulf of Mexico storm, 64; 1947 Gulf of Mexico storm, 83; Hazel, 176; 1933 Atlantic storm, 185; Camille, 241–242; Katrina, 244, 246–248

Hynson, Carroll, 112

Idlewild, Mich., founding and promotion, 92–93

Illinois Central Railroad (I.C.), 65–66. See also Mississippi Gulf Coast

Independent Steamboat and Barge Company (Washington, D.C.), 43–47

Informal economy, 14; jitneys, 131, 139, 145; suppression of, 145, 205–208; boarding houses and hotels, 180, 181, 193, 198; food and drink stands, 181, 185, 186, 193; do-drop inns, 181, 198; beaches as sites of, 181, 198, 205–208; ghettoization and rise of, 187; and urban black life and culture, 187; and support of black-owned businesses, 187–189

Interior, U.S. Department of, Potomac waterfront conservation, 226

Intracoastal Waterway (ICW), 165–166, 175. See also Army Corps of Engineers; Carolina Beach, N.C.; Myrtle Grove Sound (N.C.)

Jackson County, Miss., 215

Jaffe, Louis, 135–136

Jamar, William and Margaret, 111–112

James Island, S.C., 180

Jane Moseley (steamboat), 34, 36–37, 39, 40–43, 45

Jefferson, Lewis: entrepreneurial activities, 39; real estate holdings, 39; youth and early adulthood, 39; lawsuits against, 42; charitable work, 42–43, 45; business partnerships, 43–44, 46–47. See also Freedman's Transportation, Land, and Improvement Company (Washington, D.C.)

John D. Rockefeller Fund, 76

Johns Island, S.C., 240, 253

Johnson, Edward Bradford, 97

Jones, Horace, 252

Jones, Robert E.: racial identity, 58; education, 59; editor, Southwestern Christian Advocate, 59; appointment as bishop, 59–60; Committee on Interracial Cooperation, 60; purchase of Gulfside property, 61–62; support of Central Jurisdiction, 81–82. See also Gulfside Assembly (Waveland, Miss.); Methodist Episcopal (ME) Church

Jordan Lake (N.C.), 211–212

Julius Rosenwald Fund, 76–79

Justice Department, U.S., Harrison County (Miss.) beach desegregation lawsuit, 216

Kapelow, Stephen, 227

Kay Realty Company (Annapolis, Md.), 112

Kefauver Committee (Special Committee to Investigate Organized Crime in Interstate Commerce), 200

Kennon, Robert, 152

Kessler's Mill (Roanoke, Va.), 47–48

Kiser, C. V., 167

Klein, Naomi, 247

Lady of the Lake (steamboat), 30, 32, 34, 51

Lakefront Reclamation Project (Lake Pontchartrain): origins of, 118–119; completion of, 119–120; environmental effects of, 119, 130; real estate development following completion of, 120–121. *See also* New Orleans, La.; Orleans Levee Board; Pontchartrain, Lake (New Orleans, La.)

Langston, John Mercer, 91

Langston, Ray, 3, 86, 113

Lautier, Louis R., 106

Laws, Clarence A., 152

LeFlore, John T., 170

Legare, Solomon, 180

Limited liability companies (LLC), 252, 254–256

Lincoln Beach (New Orleans, La.): acquisition of property, 141; water pollution at, 141–142, 152; facilities, 143; lease, 143, 152; protests against, 150–152; endorsements by black leaders, 150–151, 152–153; expansion and refurbishment, 152–153, 154, 196; advertising and promotion, 197; company picnics, 197; corporate partnerships, 197; talent shows at, 197; music performances, 197–198; bathing beauty contests, 197–198; closing of, 223; abandonment and decay of, 227–228; nostalgia for, 244–245; redevelopment proposals, 244–246, 247. *See also* Orleans Levee Board

Lipsitz, George, 18

Little Bay Beach (Norfolk, Va.), 132–134

Little Rock, Ark., 150

Louisiana: levee boards, 118–119; legislature, 119; petrochemical industry, 244–245

Louisiana Weekly, 116, 117, 150–151, 152, 223

Louisville & Nashville Railroad (L&N), 65

Madden, Martin, 127

Maestri, Robert S., 121

Mandel, Marvin, 233

Mandeville, La., 117

Marable, Manning, 7

Marshall, Thurgood, 110, 170, 217

Marshall Hall Amusement Park (Washington, D.C.), 24–25, 31, 34, 43; desegregation of, 225–226; opposition to redevelopment of, 226–227; deterioration and closing, 226–227

Maryland: state supreme court of, 99; legislature, 102–103; gambling industry, 199–200; politics, 233

Maryland Western Shore: population growth and development (1920s), 92, 102, 182; post–World War II, 109–110; spread of African American summer villages on (post–World War II), 109–114; environmental degradation of, 110–111, 231–232, 235–237; real estate development (1960s–1980s), 231–233, 234–237

Mary Washington (steamboat), 24

Mason, Gilbert, 215–216

Mason, Henry J., 81

Matthew and Teena Jones LLC, 252, 254–257

Mayo Beach, Md., 222

McKenzie, Evan, 86

Memory (African American collective): land loss and, 2–3, 56, 212, 233, 246–247; segregation nostalgia, 221, 244–245

Merchants Bank and Trust Company (Bay St. Louis, Miss.), 62, 68–69, 74, 79

Methodist Episcopal (ME) Church: slavery issue, 58; Colored Methodist Episcopal (CME) Church and, 58; African Methodist Episcopal (AME) Church and, 58–59; in post-emancipation South, 58–59; Bureau of Negro Work, 59; racial segregation of, 59–60; Southwestern District, 59, 62, 73; and Chautauqua movement, 60–61; Central Jurisdiction, 81–83; integration of, 217–218

Miller, Kelly, 87

Mills v. Lowndes et al. (1939), 110

Mississippi: sixteenth Section land, 62; seawall commission, 64; Municipal Zoning Act (1925), 65; 1890 constitution, 66; tax code, 66–67; corporate regulations, 66–68; Office of Revenue Collection, 67, 96; New Corporation Act (1928), 68; Department of Education, 79; civil rights movement in, 215–217; Gaming Control Act (1990), 242; gambling industry deregulation (post-Katrina), 248

Mississippi Gulf Coast: beach segregation and desegregation, 11, 65, 84–85, 215–216; exploration and settlement, 54, 55–58; environmental conditions, 54, 57–58; free black population, 54–55; extension of railroads to, 57, 64–65; road construction, 57, 64–65, 83; residential segregation, 57, 84–85; 1915 storm, 58; 1920s real estate boom, 63–68; 1916 storm, 64; seawalls (funding and construction), 64, 248; boosterism, 65–67, 215; Chicago capitalists' investment in, 65–66; Prohibition, 66; casinos, 66, 242–243, 248; development of barrier islands (Dog's Key, Deer Island, Petit Bois Island), 66, 78, 242; business community of, 73–75; service workforce, 74; effects of Great Depression on, 78; post–World War II growth and development, 82–85; 1947 storm, 83; beach construction and replenishment, 83–85; privatization of public space along, 85; Hurricane Camille, 241–242; post-Camille economic recovery, 241–242; Gulf Islands National Seashore, 242; Hurricane Katrina, 247–248; *Deepwater Horizon* well explosion, 249

Mississippi State Sovereignty Commission, 216–217

Mitchell, Rufus, 190–191, 208

Mobile, Ala., 167–169

Mon Louis Island, Ala.: "colored" Creole landowners on, 167–168; white summer home construction on, 167–168; African American beach resorts on, 168–170; white terrorism of African American beach resort operators on, 168–170

Moreau, Charles G., 74

Morrison, Delesseps S. "Chep," mayoral administration: Pontchartrain Park, 151, 153; "colored" recreational facility construction, 152; Lincoln Beach expansion and refurbishment, 152–153

Morton, Jelly Roll, 118

Moseby, Harry, 167–170

Moses, John, 3, 86, 112, 113, 232

Mosquito Beach (James Island, S.C.), 180–181

Mosquito control, 10

Motley, Constance Baker, 217

Moul, G. Edward, 110

Mount Vernon, Va., 24

Mount Vernon and Marshall Hall Steamboat Company, 31, 43

Mount Vernon Ladies' Association (MVLA), 226

Muhammad, Khalil Gibran, 203

Myrtle Grove Sound (N.C.), 155–156, 161–162; ecological effects of Intracoastal Waterway (ICW) on, 165–166, 173. *See also* Freeman family

NAACP (National Association for the Advancement of Colored People): New Orleans branch, 139; Mobile, Ala., branch, 169–170; Biloxi, Miss., branch, 215; Hilton Head, S.C., branch, 254

National Flood Insurance Act (1968), 213–214

National Housing Act (1934), 138–139

National Park Service, 226–227, 242

National Steamboat Company (Washington, D.C.), 33, 37–38

Neal, John, 189–190

Negro as Capitalist, The (Harris), 21

Neville Brothers, 198

Newcombe Realty Company (Annapolis, Md.), 112

New Deal: and economic development of the coastal South, 10–11; African Americans' exclusion from public-works projects, 128. *See also specific legislation and agencies*

New Hanover County, N.C.: African American landownership in, 155–157; coastal development in, 157; Superior Court of, 164–165; probate court, 170–171, 174–175. *See also* Carolina Beach, N.C.

New Orleans, La.: residential segregation, 115, 121–122; segregation of recreational facilities in, 115–116, 121–122; Audubon Park, 115; canals, 116, 118, 129, 131, 132, 141, 142, 150, 154, 228; "colored" recreational facilities in, 116, 132, 152; drainage, 118–121; Ordinance 16542, 140; police brutality in, 140–141; Little Woods, 141–142, 150–151; Seventh Ward, 151; Lower Ninth Ward, 154, 246–247; Desire housing project, 154; desegregation of, 223–224; "white flight" from, 225, 227; New Orleans East, 244–245; tourism economy of, 244–247; Hurricane Katrina, 246–247

New York Times, 67, 68

Nixon, Walter L., 242

Nolatown Development Group (New Orleans, La.), 247. *See also* Lincoln Beach (New Orleans, La.)

Norfolk, Va.: segregation of recreational facilities in, 132; population growth during World War I, 132; zoning, 133; suppression of black beach resort development in, 133–134; city council, 133, 135–138, 146–148; residential segregation, 134–135; living conditions of black population in, 134–136; white moderates, 135–137; labor and industry, 136; recreation bureau, 148–149

Norfolk Beach Resort Corporation, 133–134

Norfolk Journal and Guide, 47, 133, 135, 144, 146, 149

Norfolk Ledger-Dispatch, 135

North Carolina: cultural differences between coast and interior of, 7–8; civil rights movement in, 150, 216; Sunbelt-style growth in, 211–212, 213; state court of appeals, 238

North State Realty and Investment Company (Carolina Beach, N.C.), 161. *See also* Freeman family; Seabreeze, N.C.

Notley Hall (Md.), 25, 27, 43. *See also* Washington Park (Md.)

Numbers (illegal lottery): bankers, 187–188; support of black-owned businesses, 187–189. *See also* Adams, William L. "Little Willie"; Baltimore, Md.; Informal economy

Obama, Barack, 249

Ocean Breeze Beach (Norfolk, Va.): white ownership of, 143, 146; music performances at, 143–144; contract with Norfolk Southern Bus Company, 144; threats to health and safety of bathers at, 145–146

Ocean View Amusement Park (Norfolk, Va.), 137, 196; desegregation of, 224

Ocean View neighborhood (Norfolk, Va.): commercial and residential development of, 137; white homeowners' protests against "colored" bathing beach at, 137–138, 146–148

Orleans Levee Board: establishment of, 118–119; expropriation powers, 119; Seabrook, 129–130, 138–139; Lincoln Beach, 141–143, 245–246; lakefront redevelopment (1980s), 227. *See also* Lakefront Reclamation Project (Lake Pontchartrain); Lincoln Beach (New Orleans, La.); New Orleans, La.

Oyster Harbor, Md.: founding and development of, 110–111; new versus longtime property owners in, 232–233

Pacific Beach Club (Huntington Beach, Ca.): stock offering, 48; advertising and promotion, 48–49; construction of, 48–49; white opposition to, 49–50

Parks, Jerome, 234–237. *See also* Chesapeake Harbour, Villages of (Annapolis, Md.)

Parmele, C. B., 158

Pass Christian, Miss., 54–57

Patterson, John W., 28–38

Patuxent River (Md.), 93, 95

Paul, Malcolm, 175

People's Transportation Company (Washington, D.C.), 29–38; stock offering, 29; shareholders, 30–32

Phelps, George, Jr., 1–2, 200–202, 205–208, 234–235; Phelps Protection Systems Inc., 234; Investment Dynamics, 234. *See also* Anne Arundel County, Md.: sheriffs' department; Carr's and Sparrow's Beaches (Annapolis, Md.)

Pilkey, Orrin H., 8, 248

Pilot Boy (steamboat), 25

Pinchback, P. B. S., 45, 91

Pine Crest Inn (Roanoke, Va.), 48

Pittsburgh Courier, 82

Police and policing: of African American beaches and resorts, 27, 139–140, 200, 202,

203, 205–208; African American private security forces, 43, 201–202, 203–208; brutality, 140–141, 202–203, 206–207; harassment, 144–145; corruption, 145, 149, 202–203, 207; African American police officers, 200–201; of black-on-black crime, 202; Progressive era "professionalization" of, 202–203; urban segregation and, 202–203; of African American property, 202, 204; African American informers, 203; "Negro affairs" units, 203

Pontchartrain, Lake (New Orleans, La.): social and environmental conditions (nineteenth and early twentieth centuries), 117–118; Milneburg, 117–118, 121, 152; Spanish Fort, 117, 126; West End, 117–118, 152, 246; Lake Vista, 120; economic development of, 120–121, 138–143, 244–246; racial segregation of, 121–122; African Americans' forced removal from, 139–140; fishing camps, 141–142, 225; environmental degradation of, 142, 152, 225, 245–246; desegregation of, 223–234. *See also* Lincoln Beach (New Orleans, La.); Pontchartrain Beach (New Orleans, La.); Pontchartrain Park (New Orleans, La.); Seabrook (New Orleans, La.)

Pontchartrain Beach (New Orleans, La.): opening of, 121–122; environmental effects of, 130; desegregation of, 210, 223–224; closing of, 225, 227

Pontchartrain Park (New Orleans, La.): and middle- and upper-class blacks' desire for lakefront housing, 150–152; white home-owner opposition to, 153; design and layout of, 153; homeowner politics in, 153–154

Potomac River: common property on, 22–23; travel and transportation on, 22–23; riverboat gambling on, 22–23; jurisdiction of, 23; prostitution on, 23; shoreline development, 23–24; policing of, 23, 27, 36; Analostan Island, 125; Columbia Island, 125; ecology, 125; Francis Scott Key Bridge, 125; Great Falls, 125; pollution of, 125–126; shoreline conservation, 226; Piscataway Bay, 226

Prince George's County (Md.) tax assessor's office, 95

Princess Anne County (Va.) sheriff's department, 144, 149

Prohibition, 66

Property owners' associations: origins of, 108; use of deed restrictions by, 108–109, 111; African Americans' formation and embrace of, 110–112; as defense mechanism against racial integration, 111; mobilization against location of African American beaches by, 131, 137–138

Property rights, African Americans' defense of, 97, 100, 105, 133, 204

Property taxes: discriminatory assessments, 94–95; delinquency, 167–168

Property values, coastal zones: post–World War II appreciation of, 11; perceived effects of African American beaches on, 129, 131, 133, 136–138, 147–148; shoreline engineering and, 220–221; public wastewater treatment and, 232

Protestant Ministers Union (New Orleans, La.), 140

Public beaches, African American. *See* "Colored" public beaches

Public health: beaches and, 123, 135–136; racial segregation and, 123–125, 134–135; water pollution and, 125–126, 142, 152; summer season and, 134–135

Public Law 727 (1946), 82–83

Public Trust Doctrine, 99

Public Works Administration, 185

Pugh, Lillian, 80

Racial uplift: entrepreneurship and, 21, 38, 50–51; working-class leisure activities and, 27–28; summer camps and, 45, 70–71; gender and, 70–71; personal health and hygiene and, 70–71; land improvement and beautification and, 76–77; recreation and, 81

Radio, black-oriented, 191–193: events sponsored by, 197, 198. *See also specific radio stations*

Rea, George R., 62, 74, 79

Reagan, Ronald, presidential administration, 241

Real estate industry (Jim Crow): attempts to expropriate black-owned land by, 102, 182–183; black vacation homes as arm of,

Real estate industry (Jim Crow) *(continued)*
109–113; and efforts to limit location of black
leisure space and limit black spatial mobility,
129–131, 132, 136–138, 146, 150–154; New Deal
and, 138–139; white resort town development,
157–159; legal chicanery, 170–171, 174–175

Real estate industry (Sunbelt): African
American land loss, 16–17, 233–235, 237–241,
250–251, 253–254, 255–256; African Americans' participation in, 17–18, 233–235,
244–245, 251–256; waterfront property,
212–213, 220–221, 222, 226, 231–232; retirees
and, 212, 231; coastal counties, 213; federal
assistance to, 213, 214; barrier island development, 214, 242; beach stabilization and,
220–221; and privatization of leisure space,
221, 224, 235, 253; impact on black summer
communities of, 231–233; exploitative tactics
of, 237–241, 250–251, 253–257

Real estate law, trends in judicial interpretations of, 214, 238–239, 240–241. *See also*
Heirs' property

Research Triangle Park (N.C.), 212

Richard, Little, 172

Riley, Bob, 249

River Queen (steamboat), 24, 31, 40, 43, 45, 47

Rivers and Harbors Act (1930), 10

Riverside Beach (Charleston, S.C.), 143,
198, 199

River View (Va.), 24, 46

Roanoke, Va., 47–48

Rogers, Theo, 233

Roosevelt, Franklin D., 10

Sandoval-Strauz, A. K., 89

Sanford, Terry, 216

Saratoga, N.Y., 88

Sasscer, Lansdale, 93, 96

Savage, Thomas, 57

Savannah, Ga., 253

Scanlonville, S.C., 198

Schiro, Victor, 223

Schlusemeyer, William, 110–111

Screw pump, 118, 121

Seabreeze, N.C.: founding and development,
161–162; shoreline erosion, 165–166, 173, 176;
white youth at, 198. *See also* Freeman family

Seabrook (New Orleans, La.): African
Americans' informal use of, 129; white
opposition to designation as "colored"
beach, 129–131; threats to health and safety
of bathers at, 130–132; African Americans'
forced removal from, 139–140, 150; location
of black residential subdivision at, 151–152;
wade-ins at, 151–152. *See also* Orleans Levee
Board; Pontchartrain Park (New Orleans,
La.)

Sea Coast Echo (Bay St. Louis, Miss.), 65,
73–74, 74, 74–75

Sea Pines Plantation (Hilton Head Island,
S.C.), 250; Land Title Clearance Program,
254

Seaview Beach and Hotel (Norfolk, Va.):
investment and development, 195–196;
finances, 196; advertising, 196; hiring
practices, 196; closing and redevelopment,
222–223

Seawalls: funding and construction of, 64, 119,
213; effects on coastal economies of, 64–65,
220–221, 248; effects on coastal ecologies of,
64, 248; inadequacies of, 83

Septic tanks, 214, 231–232

Shadyside (Baltimore, Md.), 204

"Shag" (dance), 199

Shakur, Assata. *See* Byron, JoAnne (Assata
Shakur)

Shelley v. Kraemer (1948), 111

Shell Island (N.C.): financing, 158; construction and promotion, 158–159; white
opposition to, 159; arson attacks on, 159

Sherman, William Tecumseh, 6

Sherrill, Clarence O., 123, 125–127

Simms, Zastrow, 206, 209

Singleton Beach (Hilton Head Island, S.C.), 253

Slavery, coastal south, 6–7

Sledge, Percy, 222

Small Business Administration (SBA), 219–221.
See also Bay Shore Beach and Hotel
(Hampton, Va.)

Snowden, Carl O., 192

Snow's Cut, 165–166, 173. *See also* Intracoastal
Waterway (ICW); Myrtle Grove Sound
(N.C.)

Somerset Beach, Va., 40

South Carolina Sea Islands: emancipation on, 6–7; migrants from, 167. *See also* Heirs' property; Hilton Head Island, S.C.

Southern Realty and Development Company (Carolina Beach, N.C.), 157

Southwestern Christian Advocate, 59, 81

Spain, Daphne, 121

Spinnaker Point LLC (Carolina Beach, N.C.), 177, 237–238. *See also* Freeman Beach (N.C.)

Steamboats and steamboat companies (Potomac River): as risky investment, 21–22, 38, 41; excursions on, 22; segregation policies of, 22, 24–25, 40; gambling and boxing matches aboard, 23, 26, 45; riverside resorts owned by, 24; entertainment aboard, 25–26, 36; white-owned "Negro excursion" boats and resorts, 25–28, 30–31, 38, 40, 43, 45; exploitative practices, 26–28, 34–38; African American investors, 29–32, 38, 40; African American owners, 29–47; competitive practices, 30–31, 34, 40, 45; shareholder meetings, 32; contract sales of, 34–37. *See also* Potomac River; *specific steamboats and steamboat companies*

Stewart, John, 93

Stocks, John, 242

Student Nonviolent Coordinating Committee (SNCC), 217. *See also* Gulfside Assembly (Waveland, Miss.)

Summer resort towns and villages, African American: emergence of (1920s), 92–93, 95–96; promotional strategies, 92–94, 133–134; white developers of, 93, 97–98, 110–111, 158; municipal incorporation of, 96–97; policing and security, 100; proliferation of (post–World War II), 110–111; sabotage of, 134; racial integration of, 231–233. *See also specific towns and villages*

Taibbi, Matt, 243

Taylor, O. T., 92

Terrell, Mary Church, 44, 91

Terrell, Robert, 44

Thomas, Irma, 198, 227

Thomas, Robert C., 216

Thomas, William H., 32, 33. *See also* People's Transportation Company (Washington, D.C.)

Tibbert, Isaac M., 34–37, 39

Tidal Basin (Washington, D.C.) bathing beach: planning and construction, 122–123; African American protests against, 127; dismantling of, 127

Timeshare resorts, 229–230. *See also* Vacationing and tourism industry (Sunbelt south)

Tourism. *See* Vacationing and tourism industry (Sunbelt south)

Tyler, S. Heth, 136–137

United States v. 717.42 Acres of Land (1980), 242

Urban League, New Orleans branch, 152

U.S. Forest Service, 213

Vacationing and tourism industry (Sunbelt south): and African American history and heritage, 1–2, 244–246; response to civil rights movement by, 215–216; decline of black landownership and rise of, 217–219, 222–223, 237–238, 250–251, 252; marketing to African American consumers by, 228–230; regulation of, 230; African American efforts to capitalize on rise of, 253. *See also* Timeshare resorts

Vardamann, James K., 66

Venice Beach (Md.), 92, 100–102, 106

Villard, Henry S., 9

Violence: at black beaches and resorts, 26–27, 205–207, 209; and stereotypes of black leisure, 27, 99, 221–222. *See also* Arson; Police and policing

Virginia Beach, Va., 10, 147–148

Vogel, Mark, 232

Walke, Ada, 135

Walker, Juliet E. K., 187

Walker, Madame C. J., 92

Wall Street Journal, 67

Wando River, S.C., 143

WANN-AM (Annapolis, Md.): adoption of black-oriented format, 191; *Bandstand on the Beach*, 192–193

Ware, Richard, 91, 104–106

Washington, Booker T., 21, 44, 166

Washington, D.C.: African American migration to, 22, 39; Excise Board, 47; elite black community, 89–90; Potomac Flats,

Washington, D.C. *(continued)*
122; McMillan Plan, 122; Potomac Parks
(East and West), 122–123; Lincoln Memorial,
128; segregation of recreational facilities, 123;
Rosedale neighborhood, 150
Washington Bee, 27–28, 31–32, 33–34, 46
Washington Park (Md.): policing and security,
43; founding and promotion, 43–44; African
American civic and political events at,
44–45. *See also* Jefferson, Lewis
Washington Tribune, 97, 103
Water Conservation Fund, 213
Watts, Irving M., 195, 223
Waveland, Miss.: seawall funding and construc-
tion, 64; business community of, 74; black
spatial mobility in, 85; Hurricane Katrina, 247
Weller, Charles, 45
Wells, Otto, 137
Wetlands: draining of, 10, 69, 77, 118–199, 122,
231, 235–237; restoration of, 245–246
White, Walter, 169, 203
Wilder, Andrew Jackson "Apple," 181
Wilkins, Roy, 170
Williams, Charles H., 186, 197, 210, 212, 219–221.
See also Bay Shore Beach and Hotel
(Hampton, Va.)
Williams, Evelyn, 8, 237–238
Williams, Robert F., 150
Wilmington, N.C.: African American
community, 8, 161, 166; race riot (1898),

156–157; connection of port to Intracoastal
Waterway (ICW), 165; Camp Lejeune,
198
Wilson, Jackie, 208
Wilson, Woodrow, 57
Wilson steamboat line, 225, 227. *See also*
Goldstein, Joseph; Marshall Hall Amuse-
ment Park (Washington, D.C.)
WLEE-AM (Richmond, Va.), 195
WMRY-AM (New Orleans, La.), 197
Wood, A. Baldwin, 118
Wood, J. D., 137, 147
Woolen, L. T., 25
Works Projects Administration (WPA), 128
World War II: race relations in the South
during, 198–199; African American
returning veterans, 200, 202
Wormley, James, 91
Wright, Ernest, 152–153
Wright, Thomas H., 158
Wrightsville Beach, N.C.: founding and
development of, 157–158, 159; "pass system"
in, 158
Wynn, Chandler, 189

Young, P. B., 133
Young, Robert S., 248

Zemurray, Sam, 141
Zihlman, Frederick, 127